AF352483

THE HISTORICAL IMAGINARY

Quebec National Cinema in the Twenty-First Century

The Historical Imaginary

Quebec National Cinema in the Twenty-First Century

AMY J. RANSOM

UNIVERSITY OF TORONTO PRESS
Toronto Buffalo London

ISBN 978-1-4875-6096-6 (cloth)   ISBN 978-1-4875-6099-7 (EPUB)
                                   ISBN 978-1-4875-6097-3 (PDF)

Library and Archives Canada Cataloguing in Publication

Title: The historical imaginary : Quebec national cinema in the twenty-first century /
    Amy J. Ransom.
Names: Ransom, Amy J., 1964–, author
Description: Includes bibliographical references and index.
Identifiers: Canadiana (print) 20250325829 | Canadiana (ebook) 20250325845 |
    ISBN 9781487560966 (cloth) | ISBN 9781487560997 (EPUB) |
    ISBN 9781487560973 (PDF)
Subjects: LCSH: Motion pictures – Québec (Province) – History – 21st century. |
    LCSH: Motion picture industry – Québec (Province) – History – 21st century. |
    LCSH: Motion picture producers and directors – Québec (Province) – History –
    21st century.
Classification: LCC PN1993.5.C3 R36 2026 | DDC 791.4309714 – dc23

Cover design: Rafael Chimicatti
Cover image: *Le 15 février, 1839* (dir. Pierre Falardeau, 2001) used by permission.

The manufacturer's authorized representative in the European Union for product
safety is Mare Nostrum Group B.V., Mauritskade 21D, 1091 GC Amsterdam,
The Netherlands. Email: gpsr@mare-nostrum.co.uk.

This book has been published with the help of a grant from the Federation for the
Humanities and Social Sciences, through the Awards to Scholarly Publications Program,
using funds provided by the Social Sciences and Humanities Research Council of Canada.

University of Toronto Press acknowledges the financial support of the Government of
Canada, the Canada Council for the Arts, and the Ontario Arts Council, an agency of
the Government of Ontario, for its publishing activities.

For my son, Richard, who grew up with this project — and the music of Karkwa — in the background.

Contents

Illustrations

Acknowledgments

This project has been over a decade in the making, and its roots can be traced back to the very turn of the millennium that I will refer to as a hinge moment in Quebec national cinema throughout this book. In the late 1990s, I moved to Massachusetts, which allowed me to travel regularly to Montreal, and I was mesmerized by the handful of films I saw each visit. I'm not sure exactly what resonated with me, but I was stunned by the depth and quality, as well as the unique quirkiness of Louis Bélanger's *Post Mortem* (1999), Rodrigue Jean's *Full Blast* (1999), Denis Villeneuve's *Maelström* (2000), André Turpin's *Un Crabe dans la tête* (2001), and Catherine Martin's *Mariages* (2001), among many other auteur films. But I was equally impressed by the quality of commercial films that drew on Hollywood genres, adapting their conventions for local audiences, such as the sport biopic *Maurice Richard* (Charles Binamé, 2005), or the action comedy *Bon Cop, Bad Cop* (Éric Canuel, 2006). It wasn't until after 2010, however, that I started thinking and writing academically about the many films I had seen, first through the lenses of horror, science fiction, and sports studies. But in 2013, I published an article on three turn-of-the-millennium films that held particular significance for me, and my first "thank you" goes out to my friend and colleague Miléna Santoro, who co-edited the special issue of the *American Review of Canadian Studies* on Quebec cinema with Denis Bachand, Vincent Desroches, and André Loiselle (vol. 43, no. 2) in which that essay appeared. The encouragement I received influenced my decision to dedicate my fall 2013 sabbatical to developing a book proposal on twenty-first-century Quebec film. My next "thank you" is for Sophie Beaulé, another dear friend and colleague, for offering me a room in Montreal for nearly a month of research at the Cinémathèque québécoise.

As time passed and a second sabbatical was approved to "complete" this project in spring 2020, I now had two decades and an ever-growing corpus of films to discuss. As the manuscript reached exorbitant proportions, I realized that I had the fuel for not just one, but several books, and that what had begun as the first chapter or two of my initial project was actually a book on its own. I am extremely grateful to Central Michigan University's College of Liberal Arts and Social Sciences for funding several conference presentations and two sabbaticals, and to my University of Toronto Press editor, Mark Thompson, for his patience as I put off submission from year to year until I finally found the necessary focus to complete the present study. I would like to express additional thanks to the anonymous external evaluators for UTP; their perceptive and sometimes detailed comments helped tighten this project further. Thank you, also, to copy editor Ryan Perks for his additional helpful suggestions. I would also like to acknowledge the support of CMU's Office of Research and Graduate Studies for funding additional conference travel and the purchase of DVDs.

Above all, I would like to thank my friends and colleagues in the American Council for Québec Studies; since I became involved with this group at its 2010 conference in Burlington, Vermont, I have found a supportive academic community that has encouraged and fostered my intellectual and personal growth. Conference interactions, both in paper sessions and at dinners afterwards, have given me valuable feedback, introduced me to alternative perspectives, and just plain helped make what we do as academics seem worthwhile in a world (or at least a nation) that doesn't seem to appreciate intellectual inquiry very much. Thank you, Jane Moss, Leslie Choquette, Sam Fisher, Kevin Christiano, Charles Batson, Amy Reid, Olivia Choplin, Mercédès Baillargeon, Yulia Bosworth, Mark Richard, Alexandre Turgeon, Julie Rogers, Elizabeth Robinson, Luc Bellemare, and so many others for the time spent with you conversing about Quebec at our biennial conferences and executive committee meetings. I would also like to acknowledge the generosity of Bernadette Payeur, Manon Leriche, and Jules Falardeau for permission and assistance obtaining the image from Pierre Falardeau's *Le 15 février, 1839* on the cover of this volume, an image that, to my mind, sums up the mediated nature of historical film: a blurry image seen indirectly through a distorted mirror. Finally, I am grateful for the support of my family and my partner, who, even though they don't understand my strange and foreign obsessions, give me the time and space to pursue them.

THE HISTORICAL IMAGINARY

Introduction: Quebec National Cinema in the New Millennium: Between Hollywood and the World

Although the majority of twenty-first-century Québécois look towards the future, engraved upon every automobile licence plate since 1978 is the motto *Je me souviens* (I remember). The Canadian province's unique history informs Quebec's vibrant francophone cultural production: literature, music, the visual arts, theatre, television, and film. Stock footage from its historical memory includes colonization by France, conquest by Great Britain, emphasis on survival for a historically Catholic, French-language culture, and its eventual modernization and secularization, including aspirations for national sovereignty, for some. Occasionally, it also acknowledges the primacy of the Indigenous presence on the territory now known as Quebec and recognizes the contribution from multiple cultural communities beyond the French. Critics have repeatedly viewed Quebec's fictional narratives, including film, through the lens of Benedict Anderson's "imagined community," positing that such narratives contribute to the construction of a collective national identity.[1] One of the best-known and most comprehensive studies of Quebec film in English, Bill Marshall's *Quebec National Cinema* (2001), outlines how the French-speaking Canadian province's film production through the year 2000 justifies its qualification not as a regional cinema, but as a national one. Picking up where Marshall left off, I first undertook this study as a comprehensive survey of Quebec's film production in the twenty-first century. As the size of the corpus grew, however, over the course of two decades, it became clear that no single volume could do it justice, but that history and memory continue to play – sometimes despite assertions to the contrary – a significant role in Quebec national cinema.

Like Marshall's, this book examines twenty-first-century film in Quebec through the lens of national cinema, but it chooses a specific corpus of films: those set in a past time frame. Its analyses tease out how these "historical" films contribute to the contemporary (re)construction of a collective past, memorializing long-accepted icons, revisiting historical clichés, and creating new "sites of memory"[2] to rally a specifically national consciousness. As Quebec's filmmakers increasingly engaged with (or rejected) Hollywood's genre system in the twenty-first century, however, the notion of the historical film became increasingly complicated, as a variety of film genres – all related through their being set in a past era – developed unique iterations in Canada's majority French-speaking province. The present study, then, draws primarily upon genre theory, but also invokes other theoretical frameworks from film and cultural criticism, including adaptation theory and discussions of "national" and "art" cinemas. Central to my overarching argument lies the assertion that the new millennium marks a significant, and not a random, turning point for Quebec national cinema.[3]

By all accounts, Quebec cinema in the twenty-first century has reached an unparalleled level of maturity, dynamism, creativity, and productivity that position it strangely in relation to both to Hollywood and its others, the various categories film scholars have coined to mark an opposition to film's dominant paradigm. As a North American nation founded by European settlers, Quebec is rarely included in discussions of global or world cinema. Furthermore, its deployment of French, still a dominant world language in the postcolonial era,[4] situates it differently in relation both to the cinemas of "small nations," like Denmark or Hungary, and to other "non-nation-state" cinemas of the former British Empire, like those of Scotland and Wales. Instead, its proximity to the United States and its geopolitical reality as part of Canada have, for better or for worse, resulted in a unique complicity with Hollywood and its genres. Not only has its institutional maturity begun to position Quebec film as an artistic rival for French national cinema, but the willingness to embrace its "Americanicity"[5] through the exploitation of popular genres has also allowed a number of box office hits to rival Hollywood fare on the province's big screens.

Quebec film and filmmakers have risen to their current prominence through an array of circumstances, including a long, albeit interrupted, cinematic history. In other arenas, the term "the Quebec Model" is used to tout the province's accomplishments as a pluralistic society that recognizes and accommodates minorities or its development of natural resources in a purportedly ethical and sustainable manner that recognizes Indigenous rights.[6] We might similarly identify a Quebec Model for the development of a successful national cinema. First and foremost, Quebec's filmmakers benefit from funding subsidies and tax credits available at both the provincial (Quebec) and federal (Canada) levels, including SODEC (Société de développement des entreprises culturelles), and Telefilm Canada. Increased profitability of popular films has also led to the creation of private film production companies, such as Melenny Films and Go Films, among others, while the spirit of collaboration and mutual aid among independent filmmakers has resulted in production collectives like ACPAV (Association coopérative de productions audio-visuelles), and Les Films de l'Autre. International collaborations with other francophone nations like France and Switzerland also facilitate the development of film in Quebec and its cultivation of an international audience.

Quebec cinema's dynamic synergy with its flourishing television industry has also contributed to its success. Anticipating future television airings has encouraged Radio-Canada, TVA, and other television interests to invest in feature film production, but above all the cultivation of a star system remains key to success with a loyal local audience. As a cinema of recognition, Quebec film offers viewers images through which they recognize themselves via the local language, geography, and culture, but also through familiar and beloved stars like Céline Bonnier, France Castel, Suzanne Clément, Michel Côté, Roy Dupuis, and Claude Legault. At the same time, Montreal has become a frequent shooting location for non-Québécois films, and the province's film industry has taken increasing advantage of the "Hollywood North" phenomenon,[7] honing its professionals' skills and supplementing their incomes by producing episodes for television series and films to be shown in the United States.[8] Finally, Quebec's synergetic relationship with Hollywood has led to the development of a hybrid aesthetic. Thus, one of the keys to its success has been its "glocal" blending of internationally popular film genre conventions borrowed from Hollywood with local cultural specifics that foster the sense of recognition and build audience loyalty.

In addition to the infrastructure for film production, a healthy art and industry also needs a wider array of institutions, including a critical establishment, programs for the study of film, and a series of awards and prizes to recognize accomplishment in the medium. These, too, have developed in Quebec with film studies programs at the Inis (Institut national de l'image et du son), the Université de Montréal, Concordia University, the Université du Québec à Montréal, Bishop's University, and even at the CÉGEP (Collège d'enseignement général et professionnel) level, such as the Collège Ahuntsic. In addition to regular rubrics for film criticism in the province's dailies like *La Presse* and *Le Devoir*, specialized magazines devoted to the film industry include *Séquences*, *24 images*, and *Ciné-Bulles*, as well as online academic journals like *Nouvelles Vues : revue sur les pratiques, les theories et l'histoire du cinéma au Québec* and *CiNéMAS : revue d'études cinématographiques*. The Cinémathèque québécoise in Montreal houses an important research collection and hosts retrospectives, and members of the industry participate not only in the annual Canadian film award system, the Genie Awards, but also celebrate film accomplishment in Quebec at an annual gala to award the Prix Iris.[9]

Film is perceived in Quebec as having contributed significantly to the national cultural awakening most frequently identified with the 1960s, and a number of directors who began their careers with Canada's National Film Board / Office national du film, like Michel Brault and Denys Arcand, remained active in the very late 1990s and early 2000s. Discussing their work is unavoidable, but this study focuses largely on two younger generations of directors born since 1960, another factor that ties Quebec national cinema to its historical development and adds significance to the year 2000 as a hinge date. The fact is that filmmakers coming into their prime in the new millennium represent the first generations of Québécois to be born and raised in the post–Quiet Revolution context of franco-nationalist activism and the secularization of social services, including the educational system.[10] Unlike earlier generations who were told that they were *né pour un petit pain* (born for a small piece of bread), believing themselves instead to be truly *Maîtres chez nous* (masters in their own house), this new generation of filmmakers – including Denis Villeneuve, Jean-Marc Vallée, Philippe Falardeau, Manon Briand, and Louise Archambault – appears mentally and emotionally empowered to revisit collective memory, to explore new territory, and to reconceptualize national identity by offering the Québécois an evolving image of themselves and their role in the Canadian confederation, the North American continent, and the world beyond. By 2010, yet another generation of even younger directors, including Anne Émond, Sébastien Pilote, Simon Lavoie, Sophie Deraspe, and Mathieu Denis, contributes to what critics identify as the "renouveau du cinéma québécois."[11]

This introduction lays out the theoretical underpinnings for key terms used throughout the book, outlining both Quebec cinema's position between Hollywood and the world, as well as the institutional debates internal to it. After defining "Québécois" film and identifying the corpus to be analysed, it engages the notion of the "national cinema" and addresses the tensions between popular demand for Hollywood-style genre films, industrial and state requirements for profitability, and the auteurist desire to view film as the seventh art. To provide context for the book's subsequent chapters, each of which analyses films in a genre related to the visual representation of the past, the introduction offers a brief historical overview of the development of film in Quebec, as well as a summary of twenty-first-century trends. Although each individual chapter will address the theory behind the specific genre in question, the introduction concludes with a discussion of the two principles undergirding this study's analyses: the historical imaginary and *lieux de mémoire*.

"Quebec national cinema" and Defining "Québécois film"

One of the first requirements of any study is to define its object or corpus. Because of Montreal's significance as a major film-producing city in Canada and North America, defining "Québécois film" has certain pitfalls. In its widest acceptation, we might view any film made in the province of Quebec as such, but such a definition would then include English-language studio-for-hire films like *The Good Lie* (2012), not to be confused with Philippe Falardeau's film of the same title, released in 2014 and starring Reese Witherspoon. This low-budget thriller, directed by Shawn Linden, with an anglophone cast, featured Québécois leading lady Julie Le Breton in a secondary role, but even dubbed in French as *Histoire à faire peur* (literally, "a scary story"), the film could hardly be discussed within the framework of "Quebec national cinema," despite being shot in Montreal. Similarly, several cable television series like the Syfy channel's North American adaptation of the BBC's *Being Human* (2011–14) was filmed in Montreal (standing in for Boston) with episodes directed by leading Québécois directors Érik Canuel and Charles Binamé. Such activity is only marginally pertinent to the present discussion. The Quebec film industry's deployment of such strategies – providing facilities and offering the services of talented francophone crew members to English-language film producers and directors – both muddies the definitional waters *and* represents a significant factor in its recent success. Further complications occur when dealing with co-productions with France, such as the horror film *Martyrs* (2008); filmed largely in Montreal, its Catholic subtext might resonate as Québécois, but care is taken so that the locations are not recognizably North American. Furthermore, French director Pascal Laugier casts the requisite French Canadian actors (Xavier Dolan, Juliette Gosselin, and Catherine Bégin) in minor roles, and all actors speak in Standard International French.[12] Similarly, Montreal's anglophone filmmakers prove problematic for this category; for example, Jacob Tierney's films like *The Trotsky* (2009) and *Good Neighbours* (2010) are deeply rooted in the realities and fantasies of the bilingual metropolis, but do not necessarily fit the definition of "Quebec national cinema." Conversely, the films of internationally acclaimed Québécois director François Girard, such as *Thirty Two Short Films About Glenn Gould* (1993)[13] and *The Red Violin* (1998),[14] reached only tangentially into his native soil. Girard seemed uninterested in contributing to the national genre until his recent work, *Hochelaga, terre des âmes* (2017; discussed in chapter 1), which directly engages Quebec history.

The expression "Quebec national cinema" thus becomes more useful than the more generic "Quebec film." Following Anthony Smith, this study views national cinema as "the visual representation of national identity";[15] Quebec's national identity is historically rooted in the French Canadian community, with the French language and Catholic religion as foundational elements, but with an ever-evolving, more contemporary conception of civic nationalism, including the official desire to accommodate cultural difference within the secular welfare state.[16] For the purposes of this study, and for most critics and scholars active in Quebec's film and academic institutions, then, "Quebec national cinema" is defined here as the body of French-language films having a significant majority of French Canadian writers, directors, cast, and crew on their production teams, featuring action largely rooted in the province of Quebec. Furthermore, following Bill Marshall's assertion that "fictional feature films … represent the main cinematic site in which the imagined (but no less 'real') community of the nation is constructed and constituted,"[17] the focus here is on feature-length fiction films. That said, because of the various synergies at work in the province's visual media institutions, as well as the changing technologies of cinematography (from celluloid to digital), television series and telefilms, documentary films, and video productions may be mentioned.

Given its official political status as a province of the sovereign nation of Canada coupled with a large proportion of its population's aspiration for sovereignty, referring to a "national" cinema in relation to Quebec may raise additional questions. Indeed, Bill Marshall describes a publisher's initial rejection of the manuscript for his now landmark *Quebec National Cinema* "on the grounds that Quebec 'is not a nation,' whereas 'Canada is.'"[18] Since then, however, while on the one hand former Canadian Prime Minister Stephen Harper ostensibly resolved such debates with his 2006 declaration that the Québécois people form a distinct nation "within a united Canada,"[19] on the other hand the national waters have been muddied anew with the advent of the so-called post-national era.[20] Having ostensibly abandoned the campaign for sovereignty and/or seeing itself as an integral part of a global community, some argue that Quebec has entered a post-nationalist or even post-national era, but the return to power of the nationalist, autonomist Coalition Avenir Québec in 2018 and 2022 suggests the contrary. The present study embraces the "nation" as a category that holds continued validity in the political, cultural, and economic spheres, as well as in the construction of personal identities,[21] underscoring the role of visual media in the ongoing processes of constructing the nation and the self. Even such recent studies as Michael Gott and Thibaut Schilt's *Quebec Cinema in the 21st Century: Transcending the National* (2024), which expressly focus on the increasingly transnational nature of film from Quebec, acknowledges its ongoing dialogue with the national.[22]

Drawing on Andrew Higson's seminal article "The Concept of National Cinema,"[23] but building more directly on the theoretical principles and historical groundwork performed by Bill Marshall in *Quebec National Cinema*, the present study takes as a given the existence of Quebec national cinema. The notion of a "national cinema," and national cinemas themselves, appear to be constructions developed largely in opposition to the internationally hegemonic "Hollywood film."[24] Such a concept partially hinges upon the usefulness of the political nation-state as an organizing category for a body of film production. In its most basic conception, for example, "French national cinema" involves the body of films produced in France, so adeptly studied by Susan Hayward in *French National Cinema* (1993).[25] But in his 1989 article, Higson calls for a deeper conception of national cinema to include not just the mechanics of geography and production, but also "how actual audiences construct their cultural identity in relation to the various products of the national and international film and television industries."[26]

The potential role in nation building that film and other mass media might play has long been recognized in Canada and elsewhere. Created by an act of Parliament in 1939, the mandate of the National Film Board / Office national du film, as outlined in the *National Film Act* of 1950, was "to promote the production and distribution of films designed to interpret Canada to Canadians and to other nations."[27] Government subsidies are perceived as an investment in fostering a sense of community and establishing a common cultural identity for the nation's citizens. In a paradox typical to the Quebec condition, Quebec national cinema grew out of this Canadian federal institution, and it continues to benefit financially from its ambiguous status, since the majority of fiction features it produces receive funding or tax credits from both federal and provincial bodies. But also because of the continued ambiguities of the industry's national status, Bill Marshall's observation that "Quebec film texts tend to be vehicles for competing (as opposed to totalizing) discourses of the nation"[28] prevails in the twenty-first century. Above all, it is important to note here that in the Quebec context nationalism does not necessarily equate to sovereigntism; many franco-nationalists in Quebec believe that their nation can best thrive within the political framework of the Canadian confederation.

Despite the differing images of the nation that individual films might propose, national cinemas generally foster "a feeling of belonging" among citizens;[29] films that actively seek to do so have been described as a "cinema of recognition." Simplistically viewed, such a cinema presents a national audience with recognizable characters, portrayed by well-known actors, speaking in regional accents, and appearing in local settings, all elements through which they might recognize themselves on-screen. In Quebec that sense of recognition is clearly indicated with the catch phrase *de chez nous*. But Gilles Deleuze has further theorized the concept as applied to film studies; effectively paraphrased by Felicity J. Colman, he argues that "recognition occurs through complex processes, and is not just a matter of viewing an image on a screen. Rather, that image must contain the processes of thought within it to be affective, actionary, perceivable."[30] The analyses of historical films and related genres are particularly pertinent because in addition to the elements of the cinema of recognition listed above, they also deploy emotionally charged references to a collective past. Because many of these references may only be perceivable to local audiences, a good bit of the analytical work in this study lies in revealing those shared references to its targeted external readership. Finally, many of the films in this corpus may claim, in one way or another, that they are also "actionary," a neologism that I take to mean that they propose images that elicit action, even the relatively passive action of *remembering* the national past.

Given Quebec's ambiguous status as a nation, its small-scale presence on the stage of global powers, and its relatively limited market share (a population of just over eight and a half million),[31] the term "small nation" may perhaps be applicable here. In *Small Cinemas in Global Markets: Genres, Identities, Narratives* (2015), Janina Falkowska and Lenuta Giukin define this relatively new rubric in film studies as follows: "Usually a small cinema is ... one which is new, appears for the first time on the world stage, and is an emerging star. It offers a new look into the affairs of the country it comes from, is innovative and uncompromising."[32] In some ways, twenty-first-century Quebec film fits squarely within this category, although it also occasionally exceeds its defining traits. Whereas its current level of maturity is new, it has a long history, and this is not the first time Québécois films and directors have appeared on the world stage. In the 1970s and 1980s, Claude Jutra and Denys Arcand garnered international attention for the artistic quality of their films, with Arcand's Academy Award nominations for Best Foreign Language Film[33] for *Le déclin de l'empire américain* (1986) and *Jésus de Montréal* (1989). These were also Canada's first entries to make the shortlist of Oscar nominees since the category's inception in 1956. Significantly, Arcand did not win the Oscar until *after* the year 2000, with *Les invasions barbares* (2002). Including Arcand's win and Deepa Mehta's *Water* in 2006, five of Canada's entries for Best Foreign Language Film made the shortlist as Oscar nominations between 2000 and 2020. The other three are works by significant contemporary Québécois directors: Denis Villeneuve's *Incendies* (2010), Philippe Falardeau's *Monsieur Lazhar* (2011), and Kim Nguyen's *War Witch* (2012). In addition to the prestige of these Oscar nominations, several French Canadian directors have made successful feature-length films in Hollywood. Jean-Marc Vallée's *Dallas Buyers Club* (2013) received massive critical acclaim, winning some eighty film awards, including an Oscar, a Golden Globe, and a Screen Actors Guild Award for Matthew McConaughey's performance. After successes like *Prisoners* (2013), *Sicario* (2015), and *Arrival* (2016), Denis Villeneuve was assigned the prestigious, enormously budgeted *Blade Runner 2049* (2017) and *Dune* (2021 and 2023). In addition to this acknowledgment of quality by Hollywood, Quebec's younger auteur directors have been increasingly recognized on the international film festival circuit, including Namur, Karlovy Vary, Busan, and many others. At the most prestigious of these, Cannes, Xavier Dolan has become a controversial darling,[34] Denis Côté won best director at Locarno for both *Curling* (2010) and *Boris sans Béatrice* (2016),[35] François Delisle presented *Chorus* (2015) and the experimental film *Le météore* (2013) at Sundance and Berlin, and Philippe Lesage's *Genèse* (2018) won best film at both Valladolid and Los Cabos. Thus, since the year 2000, Québécois cinema and its filmmakers have clearly appeared as rising stars on international screens. Furthermore, this study argues that Quebec cinema in the twenty-first century also "offers a new look into the affairs of the country it comes from" and "is innovative and uncompromising."[36]

Pioneered by Mette Hjort in *Small Nation, Global Cinema: The New Danish Cinema* (2005), the term "small nation cinema" appears even more applicable to Quebec's situation in the manner adopted by David Martin-Jones for his study *Scotland: Global Cinema – Genres, Modes and Identities* (2009).[37] Although Denmark is a sovereign state, Scotland – like Quebec – is not, although some constituents aspire towards its becoming one. As their titles indicate, however, both Hjort and Martin-Jones situate the national corpuses that they analyse in relation to "global cinema." They argue that the cinemas of small nations invoke national points of reference while at the same time acknowledging trends towards globalization that both threaten national identities and offer opportunities to disseminate those identities beyond national borders. As Hjort asserts with co-editor Duncan Petrie in *The Cinema of Small Nations* (2007), "small nations or states, it is widely recognized in the specialised literature, are necessarily a relational phenomenon."[38] This is particularly true for Quebec, with its several poles of political, cultural, and geographic relationality, which include the rest of Canada, the United States, and its former colonial metropoles France and England. This relationality appears clearly in its referentiality to Hollywood films and genres, its strategic positioning of Montreal within the Hollywood North phenomenon, but also the French film canon's influence on Québécois directors and its exploitation of co-productions with francophone European nations like France, Belgium, and Switzerland.

Between Art and Industry

In addition to the questions that might arise as to whether or not French-language film from Quebec constitutes a national cinema, even if we agree that it represents a "small nation cinema," the problem of the nature of film itself arises. A perennial question in film studies remains: Is cinema an art or an industry? This study problematizes the dichotomous manner in which these two categories have been approached, while at the same time acknowledging differences between what David Bordwell refers to as "art cinema"[39] and the box office hits that Quebec's film critics refer to as "le cinéma grand public" – that is, mass-audience film. Whereas the art film has been associated with both formalistic and narrative experimentation, auteur film theory, and cinema's aspirations to be an elite culture industry with little concern for accessibility or profitability, popular genre film has been associated with formulaic plots, studio production apparatuses, and the desire to reach the greatest common denominator to maximize audience (and thus profit) shares. In the case of Quebec, this division has become a source of further contention because national subsidizing bodies, such as SODEC and Telefilm Canada, have shown concern for the profitability of the films they fund.[40] Furthermore, as with the paradigmatic case of Alfred Hitchcock, in Quebec some auteur directors aspire both to place their individual stamp upon a film while at the same time reaching a wide audience by exploiting popular genre tropes, achieving a profitability that also helps secure funding for their next project.

Despite many films' aspirations towards "universality," to the extent that cinema is an aesthetic endeavour that also reflects the culture that produces it, film may readily be viewed as a national art form. But, while this study spends more time analysing films that have artistic merit, it also problematizes how notions of "national cinema" have been preoccupied with canon formation at the expense of the cultural contribution of popular genre films to the construction of national identity. In their introduction to *Global Art Cinema* (2010), for example, Rosalind Galt and Karl Schoonover posit that "in common usage, 'art cinema' describes feature-length narrative films at the margins of mainstream cinema, located somewhere between fully experimental films and overtly commercial products."[41] This definition proves relatively useful in the Quebec context, in which the full range of cinematic production, from "mainstream," commercially motivated popular genre romantic comedies, thrillers, and action adventure films have begun to flourish, pushing more experimental films to the margins without completely dislodging them. Furthermore, over the generations Quebec consistently produces directors distinctly designated as auteurs, including not only the internationally recognized Claude Jutra and Denys Arcand, but also Jean Pierre Lefebvre, Gilles Carle, and Gilles Groulx. Among filmmakers still active today, Bill Marshall includes André Forcier and Robert Morin,[42] and this study introduces two new generations of Québécois auteurs, as well as a few masters of popular genre films from Quebec.

All too frequently the notion of a national cinema remains limited to art film, excluding the popular. For example, Christopher Gittings states his goal clearly at the beginning of *Canadian National Cinema*: "I take the canon of Canadian film here to be the sometimes narrowly prescribed lists of films that critics and institutions have overdetermined as the films that matter, the key texts of a Canadian national cinema."[43] This is not the place to rehearse ongoing debates about the validity of canon formation, including its exclusions and the privileged elite who decide which are "the films that matter," but two key points that are central to the aims of this book must be made here. The first is that canon formation tends to discourage originality in the scholarly realm; indeed, one of the reasons I undertook this study was because I was tired of reading analyses of the same handful of French Canadian and Québécois films, Gittings's so-called "films that matter." The second is a position theorized by Tim Edensor in *National Identity, Popular Culture and Everyday Life* (2002) that subtends not just this study but my entire career as a scholar: acknowledging the role of popular culture in nation building, coupled with the admission of the increasing irrelevance of "higher" forms of artistic culture in relation to national identity. Edensor argues not only that "the national [is] constituted and reproduced, contested and reaffirmed in everyday life," but that, more than ever, national identity today is "shaped through shared points of commonality in popular culture."[44] In the Quebec context, the films and directors most praised by institutional critics (stakeholders in the creation of a national canon of film) are frequently those that are viewed by the fewest number of Québécois. Conversely, as Bill Marshall asserts, "popular cinema provides some of the clearest visual and aural recognition of 'Quebec.'"[45] Although it is an unfortunate reality, the present author, resident of a small town in central Michigan, can possibly claim to have seen *more* Québécois films produced since the year 2000 than many citizens of Quebec due to the limited release of independent films. That said, canon formation in Quebec has been going on for some time,[46] and the province's contemporary filmmakers have been schooled in programs that privilege the study of a certain corpus of films. For that reason, then, some background on the history of film in Quebec appears necessary to lay the groundwork for the analyses that follow, particularly since referencing that canon offers young filmmakers yet another means of territorializing their work.

A Very Brief History of Film in Quebec

Although virtually ignored by the larger discipline of film studies, Quebec film has a long but interrupted history of quality, including often unacknowledged technical contributions to the cinematic art. French Canadian film certainly existed prior to 1960, but we can only properly speak of "Québécois" film after that date due to two nearly coincidental developments. Not only does the term "Québécois" begin to replace "French Canadian" at that time, but Canada's National Film Board / Office national du film created a specific section for the production of French-language films in 1956. The efforts of filmmakers like Pierre Perrault, Gilles Groulx, and Michel Brault to use film for franco-nationalist purposes under the aegis of the ONF coincides with the series of pro-francophone and pro-provincial rights reforms commonly referred to as the Quiet Revolution. As eminent critic and historian Gilles Marsolais asserts:

> Even though the most remote origins of Quebec cinema go back to the beginning of cinematographic activity in Canada, the existence of a distinct Québécois cinema, one that clearly announces its difference, occurs at the end of the 1960s. No authorized critic today would dare cast doubt about the existence of a Québécois cinema with its own personality.[47]

And, twenty-first-century Quebec national cinema remains largely in dialogue with its origins in the 1960s, as younger directors have both sought to break with or pay homage to its pioneers. The brief history presented here gives only a broad strokes picture of its origins and development. Those interested in a more complete account prior to the year 2000 should consult Bill Marshall's touchstone *Quebec National Cinema* (2001), Janis L. Pallister's *The Cinema of Quebec: Masters in Their Own House* (1995), or Scott MacKenzie's *Screening Québec:*

Québécois Moving Images, National Identity, and the Public Sphere (2004). And for an overview that spans into the twenty-first century, Germain Lacasse's article "Quebec Cinema: Telling Pictures" is an excellent resource.[48]

As early as 1906, French Canadian entrepreneur Léo-Ernest Ouimet opened the Ouimetoscope in Montreal, one of the first projection movie houses in North America.[49] Unfortunately, in spite of this promising early start, through the first decades of the twentieth century two forces – American competition in the film industry and the Catholic Church's desire to preserve traditional French Canadian culture from the forces of modernity – raised obstacles to the flourishing of a local film industry in Quebec.[50] Somewhat ironically, however, the pioneers of French Canadian film were priests, Maurice Proulx and Albert Tessier, whose respective documentaries, *En pays neufs* (1937)[51] and *Hommage à notre paysannerie* (1938), recorded the province's traditional agricultural lifestyles for posterity. It was not until the 1940s and 1950s that a fiction film industry developed with notable contributions like Fyodor Otsep's *Le Père Chopin* (1945), Paul Gury's *Un homme et son péché* (1949) and *Séraphin* (1950),[52] and Jean-Yves Bigras's *La petite Aurore, l'enfant martyre* (1955).[53] With the exception of Otsep's urban thriller *La Forteresse / Whispering City* (1947),[54] these films, too, tended to depict a timeless image of rural French Canadian life.

After World War II a new social and political climate fostered film's development in what was then known as *la belle province*. First, the Canadian federal government, which saw film's potential for the construction of the nation, creating the National Film Commission in 1939 to produce filmed propaganda for the war effort, moved the renamed National Film Board / Office national du film (which I henceforth refer to by its French abbreviation, ONF) from Ottawa to Montreal in 1956. Furthermore, the predominantly anglophone institution recognized the *fait français* within Canada through the creation of the French Unit, which, given an increasing level of autonomy, also became increasingly problematic, as its members fell under the sway of the second major trend contributing to the development of a distinct French-language film in Quebec:[55] the rise of modern franco-nationalism and the so-called Quiet Revolution. Moving from the documentary form in the 1950s into the fiction features of the 1960s through the 1980s, pioneering filmmakers like Pierre Perrault (1927–99),[56] Michel Brault (1928–2013),[57] Claude Jutra (1930–85),[58] Gilles Groulx (1931–94),[59] Jacques Godbout (b. 1933),[60] Gilles Carle (1938–2009),[61] Jean Pierre Lefebvre (b. 1941),[62] and Denys Arcand (b. 1941)[63] laid the groundwork for contemporary Québécois cinema.

During that burgeoning period of the late 1950s through the 1960s, French Canadian innovation influenced film around the world, although this is frequently unacknowledged or misattributed. The international trend towards a self-conscious, highly realistic, documentary, and often anti-Hollywood style of filmmaking frequently referred to as "cinéma-vérité" developed in Quebec largely under the aegis of the ONF's French Unit into what was known there as *le cinéma direct*,[64] which "refers first and foremost to a technique of simultaneous sound and image recording."[65] Key to this minimalist, documentary style's international development was the contribution of Québécois filmmaker Michel Brault, who brought the handheld camera to France, where he worked with Jean Rouch on the foundational film *Chronique d'un été* (1961). As André Loiselle argues, "perhaps for the first time in the history of cinema, a French Canadian was actually *teaching* something to his French counterparts."[66] During the ONF period it was also very easy to identify what we will call a "Quebec national cinema," since "through *Cinéma direct* spontaneous events and real people's lives became the basis for filmic production."[67] Paraphrasing Michel Euvrard and Pierre Véronneau, Christopher Gittings asserts that "French-speaking directors in Quebec saw the direct method as a means of constructing community by representing the Québécois to themselves."[68]

At the same time, the province was undergoing a period of radical change. The rise of secular franco-nationalism as a cultural phenomenon facilitated the development of an audience for films that showed images of Quebec to the Québécois people. In addition to such documentary films as *Les raquetteurs* (Michel Brault and Gilles Groulx, 1958) and *Pour la suite du monde* (Michel Brault and Pierre Perrault, 1963),[69] in the 1960s ONF filmmakers began to develop fiction features that borrowed from *cinéma direct*'s techniques. Thus, Claude Jutra's *À tout prendre* (1963),[70] Gilles Groulx's *Le chat dans le sac* (1964),[71] and Gilles Carle's *La vie heureuse de Léopold Z* (1965)[72] represent what Bill Marshall refers to as "foundational fictions."[73] They were also politically and intellectually engaged with the promotion of the French language and culture during this period of modernization and secularization known as the Quiet Revolution.[74] Having cut their teeth within the framework of the state-sponsored institution of the ONF, these same filmmakers formed independent production companies to produce films in the 1970s and 1980s that have become touchstones in the province's film history. Jutra garnered international recognition with *Mon oncle Antoine* (1971) and *Kamouraska* (1973),[75] while Carle built on the success of these period pieces with his adaptations of literary classics, including *Les Plouffe* (1981)[76] and *Maria Chapdelaine* (1983).[77] This cohort was joined by Francis Mankiewicz, whose *Les bons débarras* (1980) is "one of the most lauded films in the Canadian pantheon."[78] In addition, brothers Claude and Denis Héroux, whose entrepreneurial skills allowed them to develop a film and television production mini-empire, exploited the era's newfound sexual freedom in erotic films like *Valérie* (1968).[79]

Because of its origins in ONF documentary, Quebec national cinema has been rooted in the cinéma-vérité tradition, with the stated aim of showing Québécois life in a "realistic" fashion to its audience, generally the people of Quebec. But, through the 1980s, filmmakers in Quebec began move away from the documentary realism of the 1960s and 1970s, drawing on the synergies of state and private funding to produce bigger-budget films with production values closer to those of Hollywood or France. Such films also tended to fare better at the box office, allowing for commercial and popular success heretofore unknown in the province. Although the documentary tradition can still be seen in the work of many young filmmakers, twenty-first-century filmmaking in Quebec has been reshaped by the work of Gilles Carle, Denys Arcand, and Jean-Claude Lauzon, who paved the way for the stylistic and generic breakthroughs that would influence the development of the next generations.

First, Gilles Carle developed a new type of film, accessible to the general public but also based on literary classics. In his early filmmaking career at the ONF, Carle differentiated himself from his colleagues in his goals, as suggested not just by his pioneering docufiction *La vie heureuse de Léopold Z* (1965), but also by comments in a series of interviews with Michel Coulombe in 1994. Lamenting a tradition of "the sad, miserabilist Quebec documentary,"[80] Carle sought to celebrate life in Quebec while at the same time remaining true to his own reality and that of those around him.[81] Although set in the difficult time and place of World War II–era working-class Montreal, *Les Plouffe* (1981) serves up a rather joyous and colourful image of French Canadian family life. Coulombe's reaction to seeing the film in theatres illustrates clearly how Carle's film produced the effect of recognition to rally a sense of national community. For the younger Coulombe, although *Les Plouffe* was "a film dedicated to a period that I didn't know …, I greeted this film and its characters … as if I had always known them, as if they belonged to me personally."[82] Carle's film adaptation of a national classic, followed up by his adaptation of another foundational literary work, *Maria Chapdelaine* (1983), thus allowed the viewer to appropriate as his own a past reality about the imagined community of the nation and to internalize it, revealing on-screen a universe that is "unique and profoundly Québécois."[83] Carle's willingness to adopt a more seamless, Hollywood-style narrative, his deployment of warm (rather than acerbic or satirical) humour, and his adaptation of literary classics, although not totally unprecedented,[84] influenced the development of a more mainstream *cinéma grand public* in Quebec.

Whereas Carle's films did not export well, Denys Arcand's[85] deeply enracinated yet also "universally" appealing films *Le déclin de l'empire américain* (1986)[86] and *Jésus de Montréal* (1989)[87] brought Quebec national cinema to the attention of international audiences. Although the characters of *Déclin*, revisited in the Oscar-winning *Les invasions barbares* (2003), were clearly recognizable types to Québécois, Arcand's ability to inject acerbic social commentary with a more light-hearted form of humour, coupled with the universal nature of his characters' dilemmas, represented, alongside Carle's work, another break with the oft-commented *misérabilisme* of earlier documentary or art film in Quebec. That

Arcand is a filmmaker's filmmaker also helped his international reputation, as he injects his work with an auteur's stylistic touches.

Perhaps even more influential, stylistically speaking, on twenty-first-century Quebec filmmakers, however, is the work of Jean-Claude Lauzon (1953–97). In his regrettably short career, the visionary Lauzon would provide young directors with a model of stylistic freedom, allowing them to experiment with magical realism and other non-realistic techniques. In part because of his early and dramatic demise in a plane crash during a hunting expedition, Lauzon's two feature-length films – *Un zoo la nuit* (1987) and the autobiographical *Léolo* (1992)[88] – have become iconic reference points for twenty-first-century film-makers, admired for their technical and narrative innovation. In a chapter on "The Canadian Fantastic" in *Film in Canada*, Jim Leach argues that "the boundary between everyday reality and myth becomes even more uncertain in Lauzon's delirious rendering of his own childhood in *Léolo*."[89] Through his film's uncertain chronology, fantasy sequences, and rejection of the plausible, Lauzon opened the door for a subsequent generation of Quebec filmmakers, like Denis Villeneuve and Philippe Falardeau, to experiment with a sort of magical realism just coming into vogue in international art film at the turn of the millennium. Indeed, two members of this *nouvelle génération*, Louis Bélanger and Isabelle Hébert, respectively, directed and wrote the scenario for an homage-documentary, *Lauzon Lauzone* (2001), signalling Lauzon's significance, which far outweighs the size of his extant film corpus.

While many of the former ONF cohort (most born in the 1930s) remained active into the 1990s and beyond, in addition to Arcand and Lauzon, an entire generation of directors born in the 1940s and 1950s – the baby boomers – rose to the fore in the 1990s, including Pierre Falardeau (1946–2009),[90] Robert Morin (b. 1949),[91] Léa Pool (b. 1950),[92] and Robert Lepage (b. 1957).[93] Benefiting from the institutional groundwork laid by their forebears, they, too, experimented with new film techniques and technologies. Indeed, as David Pike argues in his study of 1980s film,

the vexed relationship between popular Quebecois cinema and the art film that developed during the 1960s, hand in hand with the radical politics of the period, led to the self-conscious recourse by later film-makers such as Jean-Claude Lauzon, Robert Lepage, and Léa Pool to non-local genres, music, and other cultural markers as a way of countering what they saw as the suffocating restrictions of Quebecois cinema.[94]

Their work, along with that of others of their generation, laid the foundations for the great diversity of styles and genres in Quebec national cinema in the twenty-first century. Whereas Pierre Falardeau remained one of the "main representatives of a militant, nationalist cinema in Quebec,"[95] his over-the-top satirical portrait of a "colonized" Québécois, *Elvis Gratton* (1981), reveals the significance of comedy in Quebec national cinema. Originating in a series of shorts, the character Elvis Gratton developed into a viable franchise with sequel films and a television series through the 1990s and early 2000s, becoming a veritable culture hero.[96] Furthermore, the popular success of the Elvis Gratton films allowed Falardeau to produce *Le party* (1990) and *Octobre* (1994), both of which engage the 1970 October Crisis, one metaphorically, the other literally.[97] Robert Morin, frequently working under the aegis of the Montreal Video Coop and in a style that harks back to the techniques of *cinéma direct*, has also become known for socially and political engaged films that frequently play with the conventions of popular genre films, like the crime film *Requiem pour un beau sans-coeur* (1992). Like Morin, who has remained active into the twenty-first century, playwright Robert Lepage established himself as a serious, technically rigorous film auteur in the 1990s with now classic works like *Le Confessionnal* (1995)[98] and *Le polygraphe* (1996).[99] A number of other directors, some journeymen and others acknowledged auteurs, began their careers in the 1990s but continued to produce relevant films into the 2000s; these include Jean Beaudin (1939–2019), Charles Binamé (b. 1949), Bernard Émond (b. 1951), André Forcier (b. 1947),[100] and Catherine Martin (b. 1958), among others. Their works, set in a range of historical periods, will be discussed in the chapters to come.

One of the ironies of twenty-first-century Quebec cinema continues to be the paucity of women directors; despite the province's frequent references to the role that women and feminism played in the nationalist movement since the 1970s, Quebec national cinema remains overwhelmingly the domain of men. That said, in the 1970s, in conjunction with Quebec's feminist movement and its engagement with nationalist politics,[101] a women's film movement also developed. The only female filmmaker at the ONF in the 1960s and 1970s, documentarian Anne Claire Poirier (b. 1932), is a signal figure for women's film in Quebec, known especially for her docufiction *De mère en fille* (1968).[102] Poirier also shares credit, with Mireille Dansereau (b. 1943), for *La vie rêvée* (1972), the first fiction feature film made in Quebec by women.[103] In 1971 Poirier helped establish a forum for female filmmakers with the *En tant que femmes* documentary series, which included works by Poirier, Dansereau, Hélène Girard, and Aimée Danis.[104] Poirier's *Mourir à tue-tête / A Scream from Silence* (1979),[105] dealing with rape, is considered a landmark work in feminist film. They set the stage for women directors like Paule Baillargeon (b. 1945), Micheline Lanctôt (b. 1947), and Léa Pool working in the 1980s and 1990s.[106] Both Lanctôt's and Pool's period films from the new millennium will be discussed in subsequent chapters.

Many filmmakers active from the 1970s to the 1990s continued to direct well into the new millennium, so their names recur in the pages that follow, but this study also introduces film scholars and students to a new cohort of directors whose work first appeared in the very late 1990s and who came to prominence in the twenty-first century. In addition to the now well-known names of Generation X directors born in the late 1960s and early 1970s, this study analyses the early work of millennial filmmakers born after 1981, and who are already establishing solid careers in Quebec's film art and industry. The next section, then, surveys the younger auteurs of twenty-first-century Quebec film and outlines some of the debates that preoccupy filmmakers and critics in this period.

The *nouvelle génération* and the *renouveau*: Filmmakers Rising in the New Millennium

Given Quebec film's long history, the turn of the millennium may appear to be a convenient though rather arbitrary choice for the organization of this study, but in fact it also marks a significant turning point in the nation's filmmaking art and industry for several reasons.[107] As we have seen, Quebec national cinema's role in mirroring and constructing a collective memory and identity has been taken as a given by both filmmakers and critics since its development in the late 1950s and early 1960s.[108] Yet it was not until 1999 that the province's film industry instituted the Prix Iris, its own award for excellence in cinema distinct from the Canadian Genie Awards. Also around the turn of the millennium, Quebec's film critics began to discuss the presence of a *nouvelle génération* of young filmmakers who had begun to revitalize both the industry and the art form.[109]

Indeed, my interest in twenty-first-century Quebec film originated with an article published in the *American Review of Canadian Studies* on "Deterritorialization and the Crisis of Recognition in Turn of the Millennium Québec Film."[110] In that essay, I argue that three seminal films, Louis Bélanger's *Post Mortem* (1999), Denis Villeneuve's *Maelström* (2000), and André Turpin's *Un crabe dans la tête* (2001), mark a turning point in Quebec national cinema. In support of my assertions, I cite scholars Yves Lever, Christian Poirier, and Daniel Chartier's identification of a *nouvelle génération*[111] of filmmakers active in Quebec. Already in 1997, Michel Coulombe had argued that Quebec national cinema was at a turning point,[112] but it was precisely around the start of the new millennium that this alternative direction in Quebec national cinema really took off, as evident not just in the work of (then) young filmmakers like Villeneuve (b. 1967), Bélanger (b. 1964), Turpin (b. 1966), and others in their cohort like Louise Archambault (b. 1970), Manon Briand (b. 1964), Philippe Falardeau (b. 1969), Benoît Pilon (b. 1962), and Jean-Marc Vallée (1963–2021). Through their work, informed by Arcand and Lauzon, this new generation of filmmakers has contributed to the development in Quebec of a form of auteur cinema that draws on Hollywood genres and often appeals to a broader public than the more limited art house or international film festival audiences.

Certainly, the dichotomy between independent art film and popular genre film continues to prevail in Quebec, with groups of directors associated with each camp. That said, many individual films and filmmakers blur the boundaries between these two realms, with some recognized auteurs finding popular success in addition to critical acclaim, and some popular genre directors' bodies of work suggesting at times their auteur status, or at least auteurist aspirations. Benefiting from institutions set in place by their predecessors, auteur directors like Villeneuve, Vallée, and Philippe Falardeau contributed to the development of the seventh art in Quebec, bringing new international clout to Quebec as a filmmaking nation. At the same time another group of popular-genre directors produced genuine made-in-Quebec box office hits, fostering the industry's commercial viability at home. Perhaps above all, though, the exponential increase in the sheer number of films and the great diversity in genres and subgenres produced since the year 2000 demonstrates the viability of Quebec national cinema in the twenty-first century.

This second significant group of directors active in Quebec today, although often deprecated by institutional film critics because of the popular nature of their work, has followed in Carle's footsteps. Beginning their careers in the mid- to late 1990s, they cultivated a form of *cinéma grand public* (popular genre cinema for the general public) that draws on successful Hollywood genres while at the same time reflecting uniquely and profoundly Québécois preoccupations. Furthermore, their work occasionally reflects aspects of art or auteur film. These include Luc Dionne (b. 1960), Érik Canuel (b. 1961), Émile Gaudreault (b. 1964), Daniel Grou (a.k.a. Podz; b. 1967), Ken Scott (b. 1970), Ricardo Trogi (b. 1970), and Francis Leclerc (b. 1971), among others. These directors have written and/or directed a number of the major popular successes of the new millennium, including heritage films like *Aurore* (Luc Dionne, 2005), *Le Survenant* (Érik Canuel, 2005), and *Maurice Richard* (Charles Binamé, 2005) (discussed here in chapters 3 and 4), comedies like *Bon Cop, Bad Cop* (Érik Canuel, 2006), *Horloge biologique* (Ricardo Trogi, 2005), and *De père en flic* (Émile Gaudreault, 2009), and thrillers like *Les 7 jours du Talion* (Daniel Grou, 2010). Also contributing to this strain of contemporary Québécois film are significant writers and actors, including Sophie Lorain (b. 1957), Luc Picard (b. 1961), Réal Bossé (b. 1962), Claude Legault (b. 1963), and Patrick Huard (b. 1969), some of whom have also directed highly popular successes. Furthermore, as their films are often identifiable by certain thematic or stylistic markers, several of these popular film directors, like Grou, Canuel, and Trogi, can arguably be described as auteurs as well.

Official chronologies might situate these two groups of directors, all born between 1960 and 1975, astride two different generations, identifying some as baby boomers (1946–64) and others as Gen Xers (1965–81). In the Quebec context, however, I view the hinge date not as 1964, but as 1960, the beginning of the Quiet Revolution. In that sense, these two groups of directors belong to the same generation: the first Québécois born and schooled entirely under the new, secularized educational system, raised in a climate of franco-nationalist self-promotion, including the triumph of the Parti québécois in the 1976 elections. Over the past two decades that "new" generation of filmmakers has now become the status quo having produced a significant corpus ripe for analysis, as demonstrated by a developing body of scholarly studies of their work.

Of equal or greater interest here, perhaps, as an indicator of new trends in Quebec national cinema in the second decade of the twenty-first century is an even younger generation, identified with yet another "renouveau du cinéma québécois."[113] At times re-engaging the nationalist debates of earlier filmmakers since the golden age of the ONF documentaries, but also invoking the paradigms of minority cinemas around the world, this group includes Denis Côté (b. 1973), Sophie Deraspe (b. 1973), Rafaël Ouellet (b. 1974), Stéphane Lafleur (b. 1976), and Maxime Giroux (b. 1976).[114] Other young directors to rise in this period include Sébastien Pilote (b. 1973), Mathieu Denis (b. 1977), Anaïs Barbeau-Lavalette (b. 1979), Simon Lavoie (b. 1979), Charles-Olivier Michaud (b. 1979), Anne Émond (b. 1982), Chloé Robichaud (b. 1988), and Xavier Dolan (b. 1989).[115] Foremost among these is Dolan, the youngest of these rising talents (discussed in chapter 5),[116] who before the age of thirty already had written, directed, and edited seven fiction features; of these, *Juste la fin du monde* was filmed as a French co-production and *The Death and Life of John F. Donovan* (2018, co-written with Jacob Tierney) is an English-language production filmed in New York and London, and starring major Hollywood and British actors. Dolan has also become the *chef de file* of the rising subgenre of queer film, with works like *J'ai tué ma mère* (2009), *Laurence Anyways* (2012), *Tom à la ferme* (2013), and *Matthias et Maxime* (2019), dealing directly with gay and trans identities. Working both independently and together Mathieu Denis and Simon Lavoie have established a corpus of politically engaged films that revisit the Québécois tradition of nationalist cinema, with *Le déserteur* (2008), *Laurentie* (2011), *Corbo* (2014), and *Ceux qui font les révolutions à moitié n'ont fait que se creuser un tombeau* (2016), some of which are discussed in subsequent chapters.

Given its unstated aim of depicting Quebec society as modern and evolving, engaged with global trends, one of the ironies of twenty-first-century Quebec cinema continues to be the paucity of women directors.[117] This is particularly noteworthy given the key role played by women in Quebec literature, the feminist engagement in the sovereigntist movement, and the fact that Quebec has lead the charge in erasing the gender inequities inherent in the French language. In addition to Léa Pool and Micheline Lanctôt, actress Carole Laure (b. 1949) also directed several films in the new millennium, and Catherine Martin, discussed in chapter 3, has a respectable body of work to her name. Among Villeneuve's contemporaries in the *nouvelle génération*, the only women directors mentioned regularly are Louise Archambault and Manon

Briand; however, in the up-and-coming generations, Sophie Deraspe, Anne Émond, and Anaïs Barbeau-Lavalette have made significant contributions to Quebec national film, and a number of younger women, such as Chloé Robichaud, Sophie Dupuis (b. 1986), and Sonia Bonspille Boileau (b. 1979), have made critically acclaimed first films. But all too many women directors have failed to move beyond film-school shorts and documentaries or have managed to finance only a single fiction feature. Thus, whereas the "chick flick" is an under-represented genre in Quebec film, the male melodrama has risen to the fore; overall those genres associated with male viewers continue to dominate the province's screens.[118] That said, more recent initiatives have begun to close the gender gap in Quebec filmmaking, with groups like Réalisatrices équitables working to promote women directors and policy statements from institutions like SODEC's 2017 statement on gender parity.[119] Furthermore, beyond the director's chair, women wield significant positions in Quebec's film industry, helping to shape its direction in the new millennium. In addition to important screenwriters like Nathalie Petrowski and Hélène Beaugrand-Champagne, producers Nicole Robert, casting director Lucie Robitaille, costume designer Francesca Chamberland, and other talented women have had a hand – although often behind the scenes – in shaping the direction of Quebec film in the twenty-first century.

Two developing trends in Quebec cinema in the new millennium must be mentioned, although their contributions are barely touched on in this volume: immigrant cinema[120] and Indigenous cinema. Mainstream nationalist groups in Quebec since the 1980s have expressed the need to develop an inclusive identity for a pluralistic society that recognizes the contribution of what the province terms its "cultural communities" and, more recently, the Indigenous peoples on whose territory all newcomers, including the French, have settled. An overview of twenty-first-century Quebec cinema certainly reflects this pluralistic image, and a growing body of criticism has begun to define and analyse films by and about communities in Quebec – Italian, Jewish, Haitian, Lebanese, and others – who arrived more recently than the so-called *Québécois de souche* (old-stock Quebeckers).[121] In addition to critically acclaimed films about the migrant experience in Quebec by Franco-Québécois directors – most notably Denis Chouinard's *Ange de goudron / Tar Angel* (2001), Villeneuve's *Incendies* (2010), and Falardeau's *Monsieur Lazhar* (2011) – a number of filmmakers of diverse origins have increasingly contributed to Quebec's film scene. Writers Dany Laferrière (b. 1953) and Wajdi Mouawad (b. 1968) have both directed films based on their works, *Correct film titles as follows: Comment conquérir l'Amérique en une nuit / How to Conquer America in One Night* (2004) and *Littoral* (2004), respectively; Maryanne Zéhil has written and directed four features, and Ky Nam Le Duc has directed two features, most notably *Le meilleur pays du monde / Canada* (2019). Among second-generation immigrants, Ivan Grbovic (b. 1979) has earned critical acclaim for his

Roméo 11 (2011) and *Les oiseaux ivres* (2021). Perhaps most notably Kim Nguyen (b. 1974) has carved out an international, bilingual career addressing an array of topics, from the pseudo-medieval European setting of *Le marais* (2002), to the very Québécois, idiosyncratic science-fictional *Truffe* (2008), to the French colonial presence in North Africa in *La Cité / The City of Shadows* (2010), and child soldiers in Africa with *Rebelle / War Witch* (2012). Since immigrant films tend to present contemporary realities, their general absence from this study of historical films makes sense. That said, readers will not fail to note – as have critics of Quebec national cinema – that Quebec's nostalgic historical films tend to project a homogeneous image of the nation as white, French, and Catholic, a criticism I will address in the chapters that follow.

Indigenous cinema is also developing rapidly in Quebec, as attested by a growing number of academic studies.[122] The Wakiponi Mobile film project, sponsoring young Indigenous filmmakers, along with dramaturge Yves Sioui Durand's *Mesnak* (2011), helped create the conditions for several fiction filmmakers to emerge in the last decade, translating contemporary Indigenous realities to Quebec's small and big screens. Sonia Bonspille Boileau's *Le Dep* (2015) and Chloé Leriche's *Avant les rues* (2016) have garnered significant attention from critics, as have other recent films by and about twenty-first-century life on the reserve or for so-called "urban Indians" in Montreal or Quebec City, like settler director Myriam Verreault's *Kuessipan* (2019). But to what extent do such films belong to the category "Quebec national cinema"? While on the one hand, excluding the Indigenous presence from depictions of life in Quebec represents a dangerous elision, on the other, including Indigenous films in a study of settler films might be considered a colonizing gesture in and of itself. Although several clearly historical Indigenous films with links to Quebec have been made, I have decided not to address these here for several reasons. Zacharias Kunuk's *Atanarjuat* (2001) offers a well-known example of Indigenous film from Canada; two subsequent, less well-known films by his Igloolik Isuma production company, forming what has been called the "Fast Runner Trilogy," have a Quebec connection. Both *The Journals of Knud Rasmussen* (Norman Cohn and Zacharias Kunuk, 2006) and *Before Tomorrow* (2008) received tax credits and other support from the Province of Quebec, and the latter was co-directed by Madeline Ivalu and Québec-born Hélène Cousineau. Although a portion of Inuit homeland remains within the borders of Quebec (i.e., Nunavik), since the creation of Nunavut and the location of Kunuk's production company there, it did not make sense to me to include a discussion of those films here. It was a more difficult decision – one ultimately made for reasons of time and space – to omit analysis of two films that revisit the 1990 Oka Crisis, Sonia Bonspille Boileau's *Rustic Oracle* (2019) and Tracey Deer's *Beans* (2020).[123] What cannot be omitted in a study of historical films from twenty-first-century Quebec, however, is how Franco-Québécois directors engage with and represent the Indigenous peoples that their ancestors displaced, as seen in the discussion of *Hochelaga, terre des âmes* in chapter 1 and *Maïna* in chapter 2.

Between the "historical imaginary" and *lieux de mémoire*

Working along a gamut (instead of a dichotomy) that runs between independent art film and *cinéma grand public*, Quebec's directors explore a vast range of film genres in the new millennium, from the "stupid" comedy[124] to the action adventure, the horror film and thriller to the intelligent satire, the "romcom" and the "biopic." Given the veritable explosion of films produced in Quebec since 2000 (well over five hundred), even after limiting the corpus to films set in the past, important choices had to be made about how to organize the discussion of these films. Genre, then, serves as a meaningful guide for this book's organization, but it is approached as a sort of "fuzzy set," as Brian Attebery has applied the linguistic term to literary genres,[125] since Quebec filmmakers delight in blurring generic categories and seem to have crafted some new subgenres of their own.

Furthermore, two key theoretical notions inform this analysis: Thomas Elsaesser's "historical imaginary" and Pierre Nora's *lieux de mémoire* (sites of memory).[126] Theorizing European cinema's obsession with the past, Elsaesser proposes the notion of the "historical imaginary," which "stands in dialogue with the idea of the nation in the political and historical realm," and which, through "an appeal to memory and identification," fosters "a feeling of belonging."[127] Broadly conceived, the historical imaginary acknowledges the subjective, even imaginative nature of history, as it includes not just historical "fact" – since, of course, what is fact and what is fiction has become increasingly blurred in the post-postmodern twenty-first century – but also received ideas and myths about history or historical figures. The historical imaginary provides an umbrella term under which all the various genres set in the past – the historical film per se, the biopic, the period piece, the literary adaptation, and so on – could be gathered. Furthermore, Elsaesser argues that the imagined aspects of collective memory contribute just as much (probably more) to national identity than do any objective idea of historical fact. Quebec's cinema clearly draws on and contributes to the construction of its historical imaginary, engaging historical narrative to foster a distinct national identity within the larger geographical contexts of Canada and North America, dialoguing as well with France and the francophone world.

Invoking Eric Hobsbawm's notion of the "invented tradition,"[128] Pierre Nora introduced the now oft-invoked concept of *lieux de mémoire*, or sites of memory, in a monumental history of France.[129] Described as a location where "memory crystallizes and secretes itself,"[130] a *lieu de mémoire* refers not just to a physical site or location, but also to people, things, even literary or artistic works, and even concepts and ideas. Of all the numerous events, people, ideas, and so on that happen over the history of the nation, these chosen "sites for anchoring [a nation's] memory" become invested with a particular national meaning.[131] As the films discussed here all contribute actively to the construction of Quebec's collectively imagined historical past, they also either invoke established *lieux de mémoire* or work towards the construction of new ones.

Throughout this volume, then, I invoke Elsaesser's "historical imaginary" in reference to an array of film genres that directly engage the past, each in a different manner. Most obviously, the historical film per se (chapter 1) proposes an accurate, "authentic" version of the past events it depicts; similarly, the biopic (chapter 4) purports to reveal a certain truth about an individual who has contributed significantly to national culture. More open about their relationship to fiction, film adaptations of literary works written and/or set in past times (chapter 3), and "period films" based on original scenarios but with a historical setting (chapter 5), also contribute to the historical imaginary. Auteur directors also engage with the national past, albeit in a more personalized, fantastical manner (chapter 2). Just as these various genres sound an entire gamut of relationships to historical accuracy, they also reflect an array of ideological positions and invoke a spectrum of affects, ranging from nostalgia for an idealized past to the rejection of a past perceived as backward, at the root of present-day societal dysfunctions. The chapters that follow treat a group of films that generally reflect a type of manner or a lens through which the past can be viewed, and which frame that vision of the past in a specific way that contributes to the construction of Quebec as a nation.

The chapters of this book, then, are organized around an established (and in one case newly proposed) film genre that deploys the historical imaginary. Because the presentation of Quebec history in these films and what it means for audiences in Quebec today is the focus of my analysis, within each chapter films are discussed (for the most part) chronologically according to the time in which they are set, rather than when they were produced (as is the case with most film studies). Each chapter then closes with a more extended analysis of a signal or representative film from the last five years of the period covered here, 1999 through 2021. I seek to provide only enough historical background to allow readers unfamiliar with Quebec's rich and complex history follow the line of argument, but for those seeking a bit more context, I recommend Jacques Lacoursière and Robin Philpot's *A People's History of Quebec*, a highly accessible general history in English.[132] For those interested in a more rigorous and detailed account, Paul-André Linteau, René Durocher, Jean-Claude Robert, and François Ricard's two-volume *Quebec: A History* remains a touchstone work.[133] Above all, however, my interpretation of Quebec's history derives from the work of Jocelyn Létourneau, and two noteworthy studies by this historian inform my analyses, *A History for the Future* (2004) and *La condition québécoise : une histoire dépaysante* (2020).[134]

Chapter 1, "'Faithful' Representations of the Past: Franco-Nationalist Sites of Memory on Film," analyses what I refer to as "historical films per se" – that is, films that primarily seek to depict specific and well-known historical events in the national past and purport to do so with a measure of accuracy. In addition to often stating their documentary sources, these films frequently make claims about their truth value, and all memorialize signal events, recalling them back into the present and sometimes revising received ideas about widely accepted *lieux de mémoire*. Historical events depicted in these films include the Patriots Rebellions of 1837–8, the Front de Libération du Québec (FLQ) and the 1970 October Crisis, and the 1989 shooting at Montreal's École Polytechnique. Chapter 1's corpus includes films by senior statesmen, such as Michel Brault's *Quand je serai parti … vous vivrez encore* (1999) and Pierre Falardeau's *Le 15 février, 1839* (2001), and *nouvelle génération* director Denis Villeneuve's *Polytechnique* (2009). Films dealing with the terrorist activities of the FLQ include *La Maison du pêcheur* (2013), the work of Brault's long-time assistant Alain Chartrand; *Les rois mongols* (2017), by Luc Picard, a popular actor turned director; and *Corbo* (2014), a film by Mathieu Denis, a rising star of the *renouveau*. The first chapter concludes with a reflection on the historical vignettes gathered in François Girard's *Hochelaga, terre des âmes* (2017) as a revised historical narrative for contemporary Quebec.

A significant number of films that might superficially be called "historical" actually depict the past through the lens of another film genre or offer a completely revised historical reality, sometimes in a ludic manner. Chapter 2, "Stretching the Historical Imaginary: Revisiting Sites of Memory in Historical Fantasy," analyses a group of hybrid films that, although they are set in a distinctly identified historical period, actually deploy the conventions of popular film genres, such as the melodrama, the romance, or the horror thriller. These include films by directors of *cinéma grand public*, such as Jean Beaudin's *Nouvelle-France* (2004) and the Indigenous romance-adventure *Maïna* (Michel Poulette, 2013). This chapter also defines a new film genre, the "historical fantasy," to discuss films that largely distort or parody the commonly held historical narrative, as seen in work of auteurs André Forcier and Olivier Asselin, and the film adaptations of works by storyteller Fred Pellerin. Chapter 2 concludes with an analysis of rising director Maxime Giroux's stylized depiction of a period deeply integrated into Quebec's *mythistoire*, *La Grande Noirceur* (2018).

Chapter 3, "Adapting the *Grande Noirceur* to the Screen: The *Roman du Terroir* and the Quebec Heritage Film," revisits and develops the notion of the "Quebec heritage film" recently outlined by Liz Czach.[135] It examines representations of a mythologized period of Quebec's history referred to as *la Grande Noirceur* (the Great Darkness) in literary adaptations of the *roman du terroir* (novel of the land) and in remakes of films and television series set in Quebec's second period of colonization in the late nineteenth and early twentieth centuries. Early in the twenty-first century a series of relative blockbusters, *Séraphin : un homme et son péché* (Charles Binamé, 2002), *Aurore* (Luc Dionne, 2005), and *Le Survenant* (Érik Canuel, 2005), brought this much-maligned period back to life for filmgoers. As a counterpoint, the chapter also discusses a feminist imagining of this period, Catherine Martin's *Mariages* (2001). In contrast with the ambivalent nostalgia of the *cinéma grand public*, Francis Leclerc's adaptation of his father's autobiographical novel, *Pieds nus dans l'aube* (2017), evokes the same period with fondness, marking the beginning of a revisionist attitude towards the *Grande Noirceur*, as well as a break with the overwhelming image of national victimhood that Czach finds in earlier heritage films. And *renouveau* director Sébastien Pilote's adaptation of a French Canadian *lieu de mémoire, Maria Chapdelaine* (2021) even points to a *néo-terroir* movement in the province's noosphere. In addition, chapter 3 addresses several revisionist films that, in one way or another, seek to correct the negative images of the Catholic Church's influence on Quebec society prior to 1960, including Benoît Pilon's *Le Club Vinland* (2020), Micheline Lanctôt's *Pour l'amour de Dieu* (2011), and Léa Pool's feel-good film *La passion d'Augustine* (2015). The chapter closes with a recent film that searingly condemns the *terroir* mentality, Simon Lavoie's adaptation of Gaétan Soucy's postmodern revisitation of this period, *La petite fille qui aimait trop les allumettes* (2017).

"Creating New Sites of Memory: The Rise of the Biopic in Twenty-First-Century Quebec," chapter 4, analyses the development of a relatively new genre in Quebec national cinema. It argues that the choice of subjects for biopics reflects the contemporary desire to identify and memorialize "film-worthy" individuals from Quebec's past to establish new *lieux de mémoire* that avoid the potentially divisive pitfalls of political figures. Largely products of the studio system of *cinéma grand public*, the *biopic québécois* focuses on valiant sports figures, as seen in *Maurice Richard* (Charles Binamé, 2005) and *Louis Cyr, l'homme le plus fort du monde* (Daniel Roby, 2017), revising a national image of losers, proposing positive models of achievement. Similarly, the musical biopic shows twenty-first-century Québécois how entertainers have represented the nation at home and abroad, although many of them met tragic ends, as seen in the career of big band singer Alys Robi, depicted in *Ma vie en cinémascope* (Denise Filiatrault, 2004), or that of piano virtuoso and composer André Mathieu in *L'enfant prodige* (Luc Dionne, 2010). Other musical biopics memorialize rock icons from the more recent past, including Gerry Boulet of the 1970s rock band Offenbach in *Gerry* (Alain Desrochers, 2011) and André "Dédé" Fortin of the 1990s band Les Colocs in *Dédé, à travers les brumes* (Jean-Philippe Duval, 2009). Quebec filmmakers have also turned to notorious criminals for inspiration for new *lieux de mémoire*, as seen in in *Le piège américain* (Charles Binamé, 2008), which features gangster Lucien Rivard, whose criminal activities are linked to conspiracy theories surrounding the John F. Kennedy assassination, and *Monica la Mitraille* (Pierre Houle, 2004), a fictionalized account of bank robber Monica Proietti. This chapter closes with an examination of a controversial literary icon from the very recent past, Nelly Arcan, in Anne Émond's experimental biopic *Nelly* (2016).

Finally, Chapter 5, "'Enthralling Narratives of Bittersweet Reminiscence': Memoirs and Period Pieces," examines not only an entire spate of period films set in the 1960s and largely based on individual memoirs or autobiographical novels, but also analyses films that look with nostalgia on the 1980s and even the early 1990s. Critics could not fail to note the release of a series of nostalgic films that depict the 1960s through the lens of a child's memory, most of which target a *grand public* audience, including Léa Pool's *Maman est chez le coiffeur* (2008), Philippe Falardeau's *C'est pas moi, je le jure* (2008), and Francis Leclerc's *Un été sans point ni coup sûr* (2008). These dramedies (dramas infused with a sense of humour) typically involve a child's loss of a parent, and they document the social changes of the 1960s as a moment to revisit, proposing the child as a metaphor for the nation, losing its innocence as it achieves maturity in modernity. Significantly, younger directors turn to the 1980s for inspiration as they revisit the era of their own childhood or youth, as seen in Louis Bélanger's critical and popular success *Gaz Bar Blues* (2003) and Ricardo Trogi's comedic memoirs in his breakout series *1981* (2009), *1987* (2014), and *1991* (2017). This chapter closes on a significant film by one of the nation's most talented and controversial young directors, wunderkind Xavier Dolan's account of gender identity and transformation at the cusp of the 1990s in *Laurence Anyways* (2012).

This study concludes that Quebec's motto of *Je me souviens* (I remember) remains significant in the twenty-first century as revealed by the analysis of an extensive and varied body of films that set out to depict the national past. Drawing on the historical imaginary – some with far more imagination than others – the films studied here depict Quebec as a nation torn between remembering and forgetting. At the root of this ambivalence lies a troubled colonial past, including a sense of guilt regarding the historical treatment of Indigenous peoples already present on the territory when the French arrived, feelings of defeat and oppression after New France was lost to the English, a desire to memorialize periods of active resistance against English-language colonizers, and the need to come to terms with the present-day reality of Quebec as a pluralistic society. With an ambivalent nostalgia, these films revisit established sites of memory and propose new ones, some looking upon the past with humour and whimsy, many reproducing received notions and historical clichés, but a few participating in the process of questioning and revising dominant historical narratives of French Canadian victimhood, proposing a history on which a healthier national future and identity can be built.

1 "Faithful" Representations of the Past: Franco-Nationalist Sites of Memory on Film

Film creates a vision of history, participates in the construction of its representation.

Pierre Véronneau[1]

Already in the nineteenth century, Ernest Renan famously posited that any conception of the nation must begin with the sense of a common past[2] – a truism whose pertinence to Quebec seems particularly clear given the province's motto of *Je me souviens* (I remember). Preserving the traditions, language, culture, and religion of the French-speaking people who colonized what is now Quebec has been at the forefront of nationalist movements, sovereigntist or not, since France ceded these territories to the British Empire in 1763. Indeed, the provincial motto foregrounds memory's significance for Quebec's "imagined community," as Benedict Anderson theorizes the nation.[3] Constructed by the narratives its people tell, its self-image develops not only through the non-fiction genres of history, memoir, and biography, but also in fiction, including novels and feature films, as venerable film historian Pierre Véronneau, cited in the epigraph above, insists. This chapter, then, teases out how the historical film in twenty-first-century Quebec projects a vision of the national past, developing a collective image of "this is where we came from."

Despite the national motto invoking memory, as recently as 2015 Véronneau nonetheless lamented the paucity of historical films in the Quebec canon, which included "few period reconstructions, few biographical films, few works that articulate history, in the collective and objective sense of the term, with collective memory."[4] Since the year 2000, however, filmmakers have increasingly addressed this lack, suggesting to André Loiselle that "nostalgia and a fixation on ancestral roots ... became the dominant ethos of Quebec in the nineties and early in the new century."[5] Owing in part to developments in the film industry, including bigger budgets and a corps of experienced design professionals, one of the outstanding features of twenty-first-century Quebec national cinema is the preponderance of productions set completely or partially (through significant flashback sequences) in the past. Nonetheless, in regard to historical films per se, those primarily concerned with relating a significant past event remain relatively rare, and those that are, as we shall see in this chapter, tend to revisit moments framed as trauma: the Patriots Rebellions of 1837–8, terrorist activities by the Front de Libération du Québec (FLQ) and the October Crisis of 1970, and the 1989 massacre at the École Polytechnique. Perhaps paradoxically, these largely revisionist films nonetheless follow a French Canadian tradition that paints the fallen victim in terms of a martyred hero.

In his path-breaking essay *The Film in History: Restaging the Past* (1980), Pierre Sorlin addresses the difficulty of defining the historical film per se. The films discussed in this book can all be described as "historical" in that they directly engage the province's "historical capital" as Sorlin describes it:

> The cultural heritage of every country and every community includes dates, events and characters known to all members of that community. This common basis is what we might call the group's "historical capital," and it is enough to select a few details from this for the audience to know that it is watching an historical film and to place it, at least approximately. When the period is less well known, or does not belong to the common heritage, then the film must clearly stress the historical nature of the events.[6]

This chapter focuses on what I term the "historical film per se," defined as a film based on actual past events and whose primary narrative thrust claims to present viewers with an accurate or truthful depiction of those events. Despite its truth claims, however, it is important to stress that any historical narrative offers only a version of the events it presents, a version informed by ideology.

Marcia Landy argues in the introduction to *The Historical Film: History and Memory in Media* (2001) that "versions of history thus play a powerful role in determining how individuals and groups inherit and understand their social and cultural milieu. History and memory have also played a part in destabilizing conceptions of the nation."[7] The very fact that a film is made *about* an event, coupled with the version of events that it depicts, and the "methods by which a film identifies itself as historical and allows the audience to find its bearings,"[8] contributes to the nation's historical capital. But the films analysed here approach the historical capital in various ways, sometimes conservatively and sometimes with an eye towards revision, but most often in a way that suggests ambivalence. While the viewer brings his or her preconceived ideas concerning historical referents, filmmakers use various techniques to control viewer perception for their own ideological aims. More recent theoretical interventions on the adequacy of film for the representation of history call our attention precisely to the constructed nature of the historical film. As Marnie Hughes–Warrington observes in her introduction to *The History on Film Reader* (2009), "All historical films, like written histories, are constructions, and none of them are stylistically or temporally seamless."[9] Eminent historian Natalie Zemon Davis addresses the degrees of authenticity possible for a historical film and how directors may or may not strive for "authenticity" and "accuracy" in their filmic visions of the past.[10] The analyses that follow thus tease out these relationships between historical accuracy and fiction and how films deploy historical capital in order to construct the nation.

Historian Pierre Nora introduced the concept of *lieux de mémoire* (sites of memory) in a voluminous project of French national history that included essays on an array of icons that hold particular meaning for the French Republic, such as the Eiffel Tower, the motto *Liberté, fraternité, égalité*, and the tricolour flag.[11] A significant task undertaken by a handful of filmmakers beginning in the mid-1990s and continuing into the new millennium has been that of reviving and revisiting Quebec's *lieux de mémoire*, particularly those viewed as precursors to the modern franco-nationalist and sovereigntist movements developing in the 1960s. Perhaps unsurprisingly, Quebec's film auteurs largely sidestep moments now considered ideologically problematic: Europeans' first contact with and colonization of the land they came to call New France in the sixteenth, seventeenth, and eighteenth centuries, especially those involving the Catholic Church and Indigenous primacy on the territory. Even the English Conquest of New France is largely sidelined. Instead, late twentieth- and early twenty-first-century *cinéastes* turn to two events of francophone resistance rooted in secular values systems: the 1837–8 Patriots Rebellions in Upper and Lower Canada and the FLQ activities culminating in the 1970 October Crisis. This chapter begins, then, not at the beginning of Quebec as New France, but rather later, looking at cinematic interpretations of these two signal moments for twenty-first-century viewers.

Memorializing the Patriots Rebellions of 1837–8: *Quand je serai parti ... vous vivrez encore* and *Le 15 février, 1839*

Throughout this volume, I argue that the year 2000 represents a watershed date in the development of Quebec film, focusing largely on younger filmmakers' rise to prominence during this period. I begin, however, with two historical films, both aimed at fostering the franco-nationalist sentiments at the heart of Quebec national cinema, by revered elder statesmen. Whereas Michel Brault's *Quand je serai parti ... vous vivrez encore* (1999) marks the end of an era, Pierre Falardeau's *Le 15 février 1839* (2002) inspires a new generation of auteurs who continue to memorialize for contemporary Québécois the oppression and resistance of the past. Both films present rigorously researched but nonetheless fictional accounts of the Patriots Rebellions of 1837–8. Initially, rebellion leaders William Lyon Mackenzie in Upper and Louis-Joseph Papineau in Lower Canada sought reform through the political process; many of their grievances echoed those of the former American colonies, such as the denunciation of taxation without representation, but they also targeted a system that favoured a privileged few among new arrivals from Great Britain. These legitimate pleas going unheard, armed rebellions against the British Crown broke out in both provinces in 1837 and 1838. In Quebec, the uprisings culminated in hundreds of deportations to the Australian penal colony, and the execution by hanging of twelve men between 15 December 1838 and 15 February 1839.[12]

In his study *Cinema as History: Michel Brault and Modern Quebec* (2007), André Loiselle inextricably links the province's history with the oeuvre of one of its most significant filmmakers:

> Over the half-century span of his career, Brault contributed to some two hundred productions and, according to a 2003 list of the best Quebec films ever made, collaborated on three of the five greatest masterpieces of Quebec cinema ...
>
> Brault's cinematic output represents a subtle and complex but uncannily accurate audiovisual historiography of his nation's passage through the second half of the twentieth century.[13]

A pioneer of the documentary-style *cinéma direct*, politically engaged filmmaking frequently viewed as definitive of Quebec national cinema before 2000, Michel Brault (1928–2013) closed his illustrious career with the historical drama *Quand je serai parti ... vous vivrez encore / The Long Winter*, which premiered in March 1999 as the new millennium approached. *Quand je serai parti* frequently reveals its desire to create the illusion of historical accuracy, but at the same time takes dramatic licence with historical facts and characters to offer a coherent aesthetic product that participates in a nationalist, even sovereigntist polemic. Rooted in authentic documents, the film's title quotes from the "Political Testament" of Patriot leader Chevalier de Lorimier[14] and opens with an epigraphical citation from the papers of an eyewitness, British soldier John Fraser. At the film's conclusion, a title screen acknowledges additional documentary sources: the "notes and journals of" real-life Patriots François-Xavier Prieur (1814–91), Azarie Archambault (1811–91), Jean-Joseph Girouard (1794–1855), and Hippolyte Lanctôt (1816–87). The voice-over narration of the film's protagonist, the fictionalized composite François-Xavier Bouchard (Francis Reddy), and sequences depicting him writing a letter and a prison journal underscore the film's concern for written documentation as a source of historical "truth."

Quand je serai parti guides the viewer through its chronological framework via titles and other diegetic and extradiegetic devices. Despite its ostensible concern for historical accuracy, it opens with a fictionalized flashback to some thirty years earlier, establishing decades of British oppression in Lower Canada through the hero's father, Thomas Bouchard. Literalizing the fiery brutality of the Crown's justice, the elder Bouchard is branded, the punishment for an undisclosed crime. The fragmented body of the colonial subject is shot in black and white through prison bars; close-ups feature shackled hands and feet, and the sequence's only colour appears in the red of burning coals. As the father agonizingly cries his submission, "Vive le roé, vive le roé, vive le roé" (Long live the king), the English-speaking prison director lectures him on the power of the British Empire. Although in this prologue, the younger Thomas Bouchard is played by Sébastien Gauthier, Claude Gauthier (b. 1939) portrays him in the rest of the film. This casting decision is significant since the singer-songwriter turned actor had earlier played one of three men arbitrarily arrested and tortured in a Montreal prison in *Les ordres* (1971), Brault's damning statement on the *War Measures Act* during the 1970 October Crisis, another franco-nationalist site of memory discussed in this chapter.

After this prologue, title cards summarize the events of 1837–8, including the first violent conflicts between Patriots and military forces, and the rebels' flight across the border to Vermont. Another title over an exterior shot of a colourful fall forest situates the viewer in the immediate action of the film: "Fall 1838, François-Xavier Bouchard, son of Thomas, returns from exile." Subsequent sequences follow the general course of historical events, including the formation of the Frères Chasseurs, a secret society modelled on the American Sons of Liberty, rallying speeches by Patriot leaders, and a battle sequence, followed by the arrest, imprisonment, and the eventual hangings of 15 February 1839, the focus of Pierre Falardeau's film. But *Quand je serai parti* simplifies and repackages a much more complex sequence of events – an entire series of skirmishes involving dozens of leaders, hundreds of Patriot foot soldiers, combatting local loyalist militiamen in addition to British forces at sites along the Richelieu Valley – through the focalizing perspective of a single central character. Filmic interpretations of history generally lend themselves to the "great man" theory, since known political and historical figures belong to the body of historical capital; instead, Brault invents an "average" French Canadian forced into the role of hero by the circumstances around him. Although his real-life model, François-Xavier Prieur, was a middle-class shopkeeper, Brault's François-Xavier Bouchard is a farmer's son, a man of the people who interprets the events depicted for the popular audience Brault seeks to educate. By focusing on the *petite histoire*, Brault brings history down to the level of his viewers; significantly, he also brings his historical figures down to the social level of his target audience. By transforming the Patriots Rebellions from a conflict led largely by middle-class elites into a working-class uprising, Brault incites his target audience similarly to become involved in nationalist, even separatist politics, following the notion that a cinema of recognition must be "affective, actionary, perceivable."[15]

Brault closes his construction of the Patriots Rebellions as a *lieu de mémoire* by connecting the past depicted on-screen with the present day. In a final sequence, the camera pans slowly over Montreal's Monument of the Patriots, a statue erected on the former site of the Pied-du-Courant jail where they were held and executed, now framed by an overpass, with cars moving along it. This image both aids the viewer in transitioning back into the modern world at the film's conclusion, indicating that the past can be left behind, but it also encourages viewers to remember these events. *Quand je serai parti* thus invokes distancing techniques identified by eminent historian Natalie Zemon Davis with exemplary historical films, *"reminding viewers of the distance between past and present."*[16] Furthermore, Brault's citation of his sources is among the various *"ways of showing where knowledge of the past comes from"* that Davis encourages historically rigorous filmmakers to employ.[17]

In terms of aesthetic choices, without the luxury of length afforded by a television miniseries, for example, Brault has limited time to cover a complex sequence of events. He thus simplifies these by focusing on one composite, fictionalized character, combining a series of rallying speeches into a single, exemplary one, and conflating an entire sequence of discrete skirmishes into one relatively lengthy battle sequence with several phases. Apart from the ideologically motivated decision to elide the anglophone presence among the rebels in Lower Canada, and the transformation of middle-class rebellion leaders into peasant and working-class foot soldiers, Brault gives viewers a big-picture, chronological overview of the actual events of the Patriot uprising and its consequences. For *Le 15 février, 1839 / February 15, 1839* (2002), Pierre Falardeau (1946–2009) employs the opposite strategy. By focusing on a much shorter time frame and limiting the film's action largely to Montreal's Pied-du-Courant jail, Falardeau creates a unified work of art without sacrificing historical accuracy. He also shifts focus from the "little man" to promote the "great man" approach to history,[18] contributing to the (re)construction of a *lieu de mémoire*, Patriot leader Chevalier de Lorimier, as a secular victim-hero for contemporary Quebec.

To serve his populist agenda, Brault relegated de Lorimier to a secondary role in *Quand je serai parti* and cast an up-and-coming actor (David Boutin) to play him; in *Le 15 février, 1839* Falardeau brings de Lorimier to the fore of his dialogue-heavy drama and casts the established fan favourite Luc Picard (b. 1961) in the title role. An outspoken nationalist, Picard's breakout big screen role had been as an FLQ cell leader in Falardeau's *Octobre* (1994); as de Lorimier, his compelling screen presence conveys the force of this Patriot's political convictions and strength of character as he faces death by hanging. Brault's junior by a decade, Pierre Falardeau released his last film in 2004. Like Brault, Falardeau establishes the historical veracity of his filmed account of past events by scrupulously referencing documentation, including direct quotations from de Lorimier's "Political Will" and the prison journals of François-Xavier Prieur, the leader's cellmate during his final days (and the model for Brault's lead character, François-Xavier Bouchard). *Le 15 février, 1839* features many real-life Patriots seen in *Quand je serai parti*, but with few of the historical deformations made by Brault: Prieur (Martin Dubreuil), François Nicolas (Michel Lajoie), Rémi Narbonne (Jean Falardeau), Amable Daunais (Sébastien Ricard), Dr. Henri Brien (Mario Bard), as well as prison artist Jean-Joseph Girouard (Jean-François Blanchard). Falardeau also documents diversity in Patriot partisanship, introducing viewers to Charles Hindelang (Frédéric Gilles), a Parisian of Swiss heritage, and the Irish Canadian Lewis Harkin (Jerry Snell).

Like Brault, Falardeau opens with a prologue establishing English brutality through the motif of fire, as volunteers[19] and redcoats destroy a suspected Patriot farm, butcher livestock, and rape the women in retaliation. Indeed, critics accused *Le 15 février, 1839* of anti-anglophone propaganda.[20] Title cards situate viewers in time, flashing forward to December 1838, depicting the harsh conditions of daily life and the struggle to maintain human dignity in prison. This opening sequence introduces characters as types, but also individualizes them; for example, Hindelang plays the *bon vivant* who hides his fear of death behind the clown's mask, and Brien represents the shivering coward. In its claustrophobic examination of prison life, critics likened this film to Falardeau's contemporary prison drama *Le party* (1990).[21] Despite Falardeau's illustration of the resilience of the human spirit and the courage of most of these political prisoners, death looms over this sombre production, which culminates on the gallows. In contrast with *Quand je serai parti*, which shows the hangings only indirectly (Brault depicts the executions only via a mirror held out a cell window, an image also exploited by Falardeau, as seen in this book's cover illustration), *Le 15 février* is largely about its protagonists' behaviour as they face certain death. For that reason, the film's gallows sequence is particularly significant; Falardeau carefully reconstitutes the reactions of all five men hanged that day, including Narbonne's attempt to survive by grabbing the noose. Above all, his martyr-hero remains unvanquished, as Picard recites the closing lines of de Lorimier's actual "Political Testament" just before the trap door falls: "Vive la liberté! Vive l'indépendance!" (Long live liberty! Long live independence!).

The film's greatest moment of pathos occurs when de Lorimier is granted a conjugal visit with his wife, Henriette (Sylvie Drapeau), on Valentine's Day 1839. The couple's leave-taking reinforces the film's construction as tragedy, but, although de Lorimier is ultimately a victim of British injustice, he remains a heroic model for contemporary Québécois, facing death with dignity reinforced by political conviction. Falardeau's achievement is twofold: Not only does he engage the audience with a retelling of history that spurs recognition through affect, but he also changes *how* the Québécois spectator recognizes him- or herself in the moving images. Instead of reproducing the miserabilist victimhood so despised by Gilles Carle,[22] he inspires a twenty-first-century film movement

Figure 1.1. A priest (Julien Poulin) who supports the Patriots Rebellion comforts the indomitable de Lorimier (Luc Picard) on the gallows, just before his final proclamation, "Vive la liberté! Vive l'indépendance!"

that revises this cinematographic approach to history and begins to search for heroes rather than victims.

In his comparison of these two films, Jerry White notes the generation gap between Brault and Falardeau but refuses the easy reduction "of Brault being the older, wiser artist … a compromised liberal, safely ensconced in the cocoon of the Quebec film community since his days at the" ONF, and "Falardeau being the younger, more passionate and more naïve upstart … a radical, independent, Third-Cinema style political filmmaker."[23] White argues instead that Brault's modernist film aesthetics offer an "always critical and often conflicted [approach] in terms of politics and ideology," whereas Falardeau's purportedly independent approach actually draws on the conventions of "a Hollywood-derived, emotionally manipulative form of classical realism" deployed in the service of a clear political agenda.[24] Although I come to somewhat different conclusions about Brault's neutrality,[25] I agree with White that there is a certain irony to Falardeau's deployment of a Hollywood aesthetic to further his political aims. The generation gap that White underscores, noting that "Falardeau … is *literally* part of the generation of Quebec filmmakers that comes right after Brault,"[26] is highly significant for my argument that the year 2000 is a watershed date. Whereas *Quand je serai parti* marks the end of an era in 1999, Falardeau's work marks a transitional period, an observation borne out by the conservative Telefilm Canada's funding of Brault's project and its initial rejection of Falardeau's, a media kerfuffle that became known as "L'Affaire Falardeau-Téléfilm."[27]

The controversial nature of Falardeau's films – from the grotesque parodies of the Elvis Gratton franchise to the depiction of convicted terrorists as sympathetic human beings in *Octobre* – made him something of an outsider in the Quebec film industry. His insistence on leading viewers towards a *prise de conscience* perturbed the status quo, as Georges Privet describes: "In an era of store-window cinema, in which institutions proudly sent films that were supposed to be daring off to the four corners of the earth, Falardeau presented us with a Quebec that was monstrous, but larger than life."[28] Contemporary critics Pierre Barrette and Marie-Claude Loiselle assert, respectively, that "he is an *auteur* in the fullest and strongest sense of the term" and "one of Quebec's most important filmmakers."[29] Nonetheless, old-guard critics like Yves Lever dismissed him as a minor filmmaker.[30] I see Falardeau's mixed reception at the dawn of the new millennium as symptomatic of a moment of change;[31] a hinge figure, Falardeau maintains the political engagement of Brault's generation but brings to his filmmaking a visual style and narrative flair borrowed from Hollywood. This hybridization of local settings and political engagement, coupled with a universal spin on the narrative element, and the deployment of classical film technique to carry the viewer on an ideological and emotional roller coaster ride will become mainstream practice for Québécois filmmakers rising in the new millennium.

Despite their different approaches, as André Loiselle asserts, "both filmmakers thus seek to generate a *lieu de mémoire* …, a 'space of memory' where the Québécois can face their national trauma through a nostalgic sharing of the monument that at once evokes and masks the events of 1838–1839."[32] Indeed, Brault wanted to make his film about the Patriots Rebellions precisely "because we never talk about it."[33] For their filmmakers, these films are just as much about the present as they are about remembering Quebec's past; as Marco de Blois observes, Falardeau's *15 février* "appeared as a work full of meaning, which brutally recalls that the Quebec question is still not settled."[34] The same may be said about more recent homages paid to another national trauma, the FLQ's kidnapping and murder of Pierre Laporte in October 1970. Although the majority of Québécois condemned the terrorist activities of the Front de Libération du Québec during the 1960s, many credit the extremists' activities in late 1970, coupled with the governmental backlash that followed, with playing a signal role in the rise of the sovereigntist movement. For that reason, twenty-first-century film repeatedly revisits the October Crisis as a *lieu de mémoire*, revising the official historical narrative in such a manner that – if it doesn't quite condone terrorist activity in the interest of nationalism – attempts to render terrorists' actions understandable to contemporary viewers.

"C'est des bons qui font du mauvais": The FLQ and the October Crisis in *La Maison du pêcheur*, *Corbo*, and *Les rois mongols*

Prior to the year 2000, two major films in the Québécois canon by Michel Brault and Pierre Falardeau, respectively, dealt with the dramatic events of the 1970 October crisis, which culminated in the military occupation of Montreal after the Front de Libération du Québec kidnapped two political figures.

Focusing not on the terrorists themselves, whose status as victims remains debatable, Brault's *Les ordres* (1974) fictionalizes the experience of individuals arrested without due process after the declaration of the *War Measures Act*.[35] In contrast, Falardeau's *Octobre* (1994) focuses viewer attention upon more ambiguously sympathetic protagonists: members of the Chénier cell of the FLQ who kidnapped provincial Minister of Labour Pierre Laporte.[36] Starring Luc Picard, this claustrophobic drama attempts to make viewers understand how these and other members of the FLQ could have been brought to the point of violent action in their desire to obtain greater respect for French Canadians / Québécois in North America. Since the year 2000, several films revisit these national traumas, all seeking to engage some form of historical truth.[37] The following analysis outlines how these films commemorate past struggles, reminding baby boomers and their children, raised after the Quiet Revolution and now benefiting from the material comforts of a neoliberal economy, that the privileges and prosperity currently enjoyed by Québécois did not always prevail. Although they favour secular, liberal, and/or socialist political agendas and social visions, these films carry on the mission of ethnic nationalist historians of the past, like François-Xavier Garneau (1809–66) or Lionel Groulx (1878–1967), exhorting compatriots not to forget.

Films in the new millennium problematize official images of FLQ members as terrorists and convicted killers, commemorating their radicalism as an essential step on the path to contemporary francophone cultural, if not political, sovereignty in Quebec. Indeed, *La Maison du pêcheur / Summer Crisis* (2013) prequels Falardeau's *Octobre*, purporting to tell the "true story" of the Chénier cell's radicalization in summer 1969. Its political aims appear clearly in its tag line, "Chaque révolution a ses origines" (Every revolution has its origins), implying that these men are revolutionary heroes rather than terrorists. Not without flaws, especially in its treatment of female characters, the film nonetheless represents a significant historical revisionism, reminding contemporary viewers of the injustices faced by French Canadians, not just prior to the Quiet Revolution, but well after, thus justifying the FLQ's sovereigntist aims. Brault's assistant director on *Les ordres*, writer and director Alain Chartrand (b. 1946), dedicated several years to the development of this project. His final film before retiring, *La Maison du pêcheur* was praised for its convincing "recreation of events."[38] Given its sympathetic treatment of the Rose brothers, those ultimately responsible for the death of Pierre Laporte in October 1970, it is not surprising that the film developed out of an idea by Jacques Bérubé, a longtime friend of Paul Rose, who worked on the scenario with Mario Bolduc for ten years.[39]

Future Chénier cell member Bernard Lortie (Mikhail Ahooja) focalizes the action of *La Maison du pêcheur*, recounting his *prise de conscience* about French Canadian oppression, first in relation to the fishermen of the Gaspé Peninsula, his home territory, and then beyond. It depicts his transformational encounter with three political activists from Montreal who arrive in Gaspé and rent the *boîte à chansons*, a beachside barn-cabaret, of the film's title: Paul Rose (Vincent-Guillaume Otis), his brother Jacques Rose (Benoît Langlais), and Francis Simard (Charles-Alexandre Dubé). They do so not just to entertain the public but also to politicize locals, raising consciousness about the sovereigntist movement. At this point in time, the future *felquistes* (as FLQ members are called), although influenced by the Marxist anti-colonialism of Frantz Fanon and Albert Memmi, affiliate themselves with a legitimate political organization, the Rassemblement pour l'indépendance nationale, precursor to René Lévesque's Parti québécois. In Gaspé, faced with resistance by local small business owners who cater to anglophone tourists, the Rose brothers and Simard are themselves further radicalized.

La Maison du pêcheur presents the future FLQ kidnappers sympathetically, while caricaturing their foils, local Gaspé townsmen. Its revisionist approach builds viewer understanding for their later, more radical activities, including casting fan favourite Vincent-Guillaume Otis[40] and camera-friendly newcomer Mikhail Ahooja, an actor with roots in a cultural community other than the French Canadian, in lead roles. Those well-known activities – the kidnapping and murder of Pierre Laporte in October 1970 – are used to frame the film's main narrative, and by opening with the kidnappers' arrest, Chartrand constructs a parallel to the more clear-cut injustices depicted in Brault's *Les ordres*. Furthermore, *La Maison du pêcheur* deploys explanatory titles to guide viewer reception, opening with black typescript appearing on a white screen suggestive of teletype copy; these roll over the faint image of a flag, that of the Patriots of 1837–8, informing the viewer of the film's historical aspirations, situating its political stance through a dedication, and finally establishing the facts about the 1970 October Crisis in a manner that clearly alludes to Brault's classic:

Ce film a été inspire d'une histoire vécue.
Certains événements ont été modifiés à des fins dramatiques.

À mon père syndicaliste.

Après l'enlèvement du ministre Pierre Laporte par la cellule Chénier du Front
de Libération du Québec (FLQ), le gouvernement du Canada a décrété la loi des
mesures de guerre et dépêché 800 soldats au Québec.
Plus de 4600 perquisitions ont eu lieu et 502 personnes ont été emprisonnés sans
mandat.

This film was inspired by a real-life story.
Certain events have been modified for dramatic emphasis.

To my unionist father.[41]

> After the kidnapping of Minister Pierre Laporte by the Chénier cell of the Front de Libération du Québec (FLQ), the Government of Canada decreed the *War Measures Act* and sent 800 soldiers to Quebec.
> More than 4,600 searches occurred and 502 individuals were imprisoned without warrants.

This reference to warrantless arrests and government oppression frames Chartrand's depiction of the arrest of Bernard Lortie and two women sheltering the *felquistes* through the lens of Brault's innocent arrestees in *Les ordres*. He thus suggests that, although perhaps not entirely innocent, these young men were victims of systemic oppression, and they took heroic – albeit perhaps misguided – action to change it.

Chartrand accomplishes this in various ways, including several passages of dialogue in which Paul Rose, for example, cites statistics to decry the (very real) economic oppression of French Canadians then prevalent in Quebec and Canada. Lortie, son of a Gaspé fisherman whose business has failed due to similar economic injustices, expounds emotionally upon the way large commercial fisheries have invaded local waters, often aided by federal and provincial governments. Above all, unsympathetic portrayals of area businessmen, supported by Mayor Roland Bujold (Raymond Bouchard), local and provincial police, and even the minister of tourism, fuel viewer sympathy for these young idealists and their rejection of the narrow-minded Gaspé capitalists catering to American and Anglo-Canadian tourists, who are also characterized as obnoxious and/or ignorant. Chartrand may have drawn upon Gilles Carle's early ONF film on the region, *Percé on the Rocks* (1964), which he mentions as influential in his youth.[42]

After the opening colour sequence of the arrests, the image dissolves into black and white and a title card, "Gaspésie, été 1969," situating the viewer in time and space with the nostalgic image of a fishing boat at sea. *La Maison du pêcheur* establishes the locals' subaltern status as the Lortie patriarch has sold his fishing boat; young women, like Lortie's girlfriend, Geneviève (Geneviève Boivin-Roussy), work as waitresses serving tourists visiting the national landmark of the Rocher Percé. Gaspé in the late 1960s appears riddled with signage in English, businesses flying the Canadian maple leaf and the US stars and stripes; there is not a blue-and-white *fleurdelisé* in sight. The film introduces worker-capital conflict in terms of individual oppression as hotel owner Albert Anctil (Nicolas Canuel, who frequently plays obnoxious heavies) harasses one of Geneviève's co-workers (Sandrine Bisson) about her cigarette breaks. Central to the conflict between local businessmen and the newcomers at the Maison du pêcheur is André Duguay (caricatured by Luc Picard), proprietor of a campground neighbouring the cabaret, which has begun to give out free drinks and allow itinerant hippies to camp free of charge on its beachside lot. Chartrand portrays these local characters as stereotypically backward-thinking petit bourgeois, stock-in-trade types harkening back to earlier pre–Quiet Revolution political figures, like Maurice Duplessis, complicit with anglophone capitalist interests. The antipathetic trio of Duguay, Anctil, and Mayor Bujold, elites who exploit an unjust system that favours them, attempt to force the young idealists out of town, first denying the Roses a "permit" to do business there. In response, since they can't collect payment without said permit, the nationalist tricksters offer free liquor and camping, attracting noisy crowds of hippies. The mayor then convinces the minister of tourism to buy the activists off with a $15,000 grant to start a youth hostel the next summer. Finally, a pack of goons raids the Maison, lighting fire to tents outside and beating up patrons inside; when the provincial police do nothing, the Rose brothers realize the futility of their efforts in Gaspé. These injustices thus radicalize the young men, who will return to Montreal to become the Chénier cell, eventually perpetrating the kidnaping and murder of Pierre Laporte.

The film's conclusion, also shot in colour, bookends the narrative begun in the opening frame as title cards again inform the viewer of the fate of these men after their arrest. Although it clearly states the men's culpability for actions narrated in Pierre Falardeau's *Octobre* but *not* depicted in Chartrand's film, *La Maison du pêcheur* establishes viewer sympathy for Lortie in particular. By eliding their more controversial, illegal activities, Chartrand manipulates viewer empathy through the closing titles:

Paul Rose, Jacques Rose et Francis Simard seront arrêtés le 28 décembre 1970, deux mois après Bernard Lortie.
Les quatre hommes décideront d'assumer collectivement la responsabilité de la mort du ministre Pierre Laporte.
Ils seront condamnés aux peines suivantes :
   Paul Rose : à perpétuité.
   Francis Simard : à perpétuité.
   Jacques Rose : deux ans de détention préventive, huit ans de pénitencier.
   Bernard Lortie : un an de détention préventive, vingt ans de pénitencier.

Paul Rose, Jacques Rose, and Francis Simard will be arrested on 28 December 1970, two months after Bernard Lortie.
The four men will decide to assume collective responsibility for the death of the Minister Pierre Laporte.
They will be condemned to the following sentences:
   Paul Rose: life.
   Francis Simard: life.
   Jacques Rose: two years of pre-trial detention, eight years in prison.
   Bernard Lortie: one year of pre-trial detention, twenty years in prison.

The use of the future tense has a certain logic as the film's action ends *before* these events, which remain in the future; but it also engages viewers affectively as they contemplate how these young men's lives will be impacted because of their commitment to the cause of sovereignty. Furthermore, each title card is illustrated *not* by the image of the real-life person, but with the pencil-drawn image (mimicking a courtroom drawing) of the actor portraying him, thus blurring the lines between the historical reality of terrorism and its filmed image, associating these historical figures not with real men but with the charismatic actors who portrayed them and for whom, due to Quebec's well-developed star system, viewers have a pre-developed sympathy. Even if viewers condemn these men's ultimate actions, it is difficult not to be moved by their fate, particularly since the film implies that despite their misguided methods, their ends were righteous. Finally, the film fails to remind viewers that, in fact, the most severe of these sentences were not fully served, and these men were allowed to resume their lives: Lortie was paroled in 1977; Paul Rose and Simard were paroled in 1982.

While *La Maison du pêcheur* depicts the Rose brothers financing their operations by using unpaid-for credit cards, justifying this activity by blaming the corrupt, capitalist banking system, it memorializes FLQ members as heroic activists. It otherwise elides the criminal aspects of their activities, depicting these and the government's response as key to the radicalization of a larger segment of the Quebec populace in favour of independence. Mainstream historians in Quebec largely agree that the application of the *War Measures Act* in response to the kidnappings of James Cross and Pierre Laporte was an excessive move, politically motivated by conservatives like Montreal Mayor Jean Drapeau and federalists like Canadian Prime Minister Pierre Trudeau and Quebec Premier Robert Bourassa, that backfired. Whereas widespread support for the FLQ had never existed, the occupation of Montreal and the mass arrests of "suspected sympathizers" – fictionalized in Brault's *Les ordres* – led to a radicalization of nationalist sentiment among Franco-Québécois.[43] Although the vast majority of Québécois rejected the FLQ's terrorist activities, the governmental backlash during the October Crisis of 1970 radicalized some moderate nationalists who experienced the presence of the Canadian Army in Montreal as a state of siege, the idea of sovereignty did not seem so far-fetched after all. The early 1970s then saw the rise of the Parti québécois with René Lévesque's compromise platform of "sovereignty-association."

Quebec film critics received *La Maison du pêcheur* precisely as invoking an important historical moment in the province's history, one that has perhaps been overlooked: "Alain Chartrand brings forth this capital moment in our history, reminding us that great changes are sometimes born of the will of a handful of idealists."[44] Indeed, an announcement of the film's imminent release asserts that it serves to "fill a lapse in collective memory."[45] Not all agreed, however, and the conservative *Le Devoir*'s Odile Tremblay – an institution in Quebec film herself – judged it as biased.[46] Without a doubt, Chartrand memorializes FLQ members, if not excusing them, then at least explaining the reasons behind their later actions. In contrast with the vision offered by Chartrand, a long-term member of Quebec's film establishment, just a year later, a rising star of the *renouveau* generation offered a dramatically different image of the early days of the FLQ.

Corbo (2014), directed by Mathieu Denis (b. 1977), depicts the true story of a teenage boy involved in an earlier phase of FLQ activities: mailbox bombings that began in 1963. The film is set in 1966, and its protagonist, Jean Corbo, is a sixteen-year-old idealist of Italian and French Canadian heritage; his increasing disaffection with his family's bourgeois values and a chance encounter with a youth already implicated in the FLQ, the more hardened François (Antoine L'Écuyer), provide him the opportunity to act on his revolutionary ideals. Casting Anthony Therrien, who had played the younger version of the oppressed son in *Le torrent* (2012), Simon Lavoie's adaptation of Anne Hébert's *anti-terroir* classic (discussed in chapter 3), reinforces *Corbo's* depiction of its title character as a Québécois victim-hero. *Corbo* follows Pierre Falardeau's model for deeply territorialized, politically engaged films that document francophone oppression and resistance, while borrowing sophisticated film and storytelling techniques from Hollywood. More nuanced and dedicated to historical realism than Chartrand's film, it establishes the basis for the sense of injustice felt by radical franco-nationalists, but more clearly portrays Corbo's death as the waste of a potentially valuable life, ultimately condemning the validity of FLQ methods.

By integrating Montreal's cultural communities into the cycle of oppression and resistance, *Corbo's* focus on a character of Italian heritage marks a significant change in direction in films of the new millennium, reflecting attempts to construct a pluralist national identity. Furthermore, its casting of Dino Tavarone (b. 1942), the symbolic godfather of Montreal's Italian community after his roles in cult television series like *Omertà* (1996–7), as patriarch Achille Corbo authenticates *Corbo's* depiction of a successful immigrant family. Admittedly, its assimilation into Québécois society is partly due to intermarriage, as Jean's mother, Mignonne, is a Franco-Québécois, played by respected character actress Marie Brassard. *Corbo's* inclusion of Montreal's cultural communities in the rise of contemporary nationalist consciousness revises the image of separatism lingering after then-Premier Jacques Parizeau of the Parti québécois blamed the "vote ethnique" for the failure of the 1995 referendum on sovereignty.[47]

Like *La Maison du pêcheur*, *Corbo* features an idealistic protagonist who experiences a *prise de conscience*, convinced that violence is necessary to effectuate political change; both films portray these young men as manipulated by older, more radical others, and both leave the viewer saddened by the waste of a young life. *Corbo*, however, more clearly condemns the FLQ's methods in achieving its ends. Both films' images of 1960s youthful idealism offer nostalgic self-reflections for their baby boomer viewers, who can identify with images of their younger selves, almost celebrating the protagonists' sacrifice. In addition, by featuring young men, they appeal to a new generation of filmgoers, inviting them to sympathize with past struggles for francophone self-affirmation, and reminding contemporary youth about historicized injustices to combat the current perception of the province's neoliberal, post-nationalist complacency. These films contribute to the construction of a contemporary Québécois identity that, at minimum, values the idealism of a past, but more heroic and activist, era, perhaps also suggesting the need for continued vigilance, even a renewal of sovereigntist attitudes, today.

Although technically a literary adaptation, like the other films discussed in this chapter the main goal of Luc Picard's *Les rois mongols / Cross My Heart* (2017) remains that of (re)telling a particular story from history, invoking the events of October 1970 as a backdrop and even motivation for its central narrative. Adapted from her youth novel *Salut, mon roi mongol!* (1998) by Nicole Bélanger,[48] and described as "an allegory of the October crisis,"[49] the film depicts four children imitating, in their own manner, the kidnapping of Pierre Laporte. Inspired by unfolding events, Manon (Milya Corbeil-Gauvreau) convinces her cousin Martin (Henri Richer-Picard, the son of the director and actress Isabel Richer) to help kidnap an elderly woman, Rose Robinson (Clare Coulter). With her father dying of cancer and her mother in a state of nervous depression, Manon's actions represent a desperate attempt to avoid foster care and separation from her younger brother Mimi (Anthony Bouchard), but also to simply be *heard*. During Montreal's 1970 occupation, they remove a friend's wheelchair-bound grandmother to a dilapidated hunting camp in Saint-Zénon and discover that she is anglophone: "Une *bloke*. Nous avons enlevé une hostie de bloke!" (A bloke. We've kidnapped a damned Limey!) Sequences during which the children attempt (and eventually succeed in) communicating with Rose comment allegorically on French-English relations in Quebec. Mimi, hoping to gain a grandmother in Rose, reassures her: "Tu sais, c'est pas grave que t'es une anglaise. C'est pas de ta faute" (You know, it's okay that you're English. It's not your fault). Rose obliges Mimi and attempts to read him a story in French, but frustrated by their mutual misunderstanding, she instead recounts in English the familiar tale of the three little pigs. The fairy tale establishes common cultural ground between the two communities, but hints at colonialism's inherent racial injustices, as Rose names her pigs Brownie, Whitey, and Blackie. As Rose teaches the younger children English, and they teach her French, the crux of their mutual misunderstanding appears when they ask her where she learned to speak English:

ROSE: I didn't learn English. I *am* English.
DENIS: Elle dit qu'elle est née de même. [She says she was born that way.]

Les rois mongols thus problematically links English-French tensions not just to linguistic and cultural difference, but in an essential sense to identity. While Rose's assertion that her language defines her identity underscores the deep role that language plays in constructing national identity, it also undermines the very possibility of mutual understanding that the film purportedly holds out.

By focalizing the events of October 1970 through the eyes of children, *Les rois mongols* deploys a pedagogy that specifically functions to help a younger generation understand a particularly conflicted period of the national past, a key goal it shares with the historical film per se.[50] As Manon watches televised coverage of the unfolding drama, she asks her father to explain; like other historical films, *Les rois mongols* enhances its reality effect by using archival news footage, including broadcasts of the FLQ Manifesto being read on Radio-Canada as part of the kidnappers' demands and media reports of Pierre Laporte's death. But it also stages fictional sequences in which the children, typically in moments of tension in their own unfolding drama, witness tanks rolling through the streets of Montreal, encounter military vehicles patrolling at night to enforce curfew, and even interact with individual soldiers. One such incident invokes the film's title, explained earlier in a playful sequence in which Mimi and his cousin Denis (Alexis Guay) play the children's game of the *Rois mongols* (Mongol kings). Denis, exotically costumed in a makeshift cape and crown, commands Mimi to stare him in the eyes and recite the phrase, "Salut, mon roi mongol," as many times as he can; when he bursts out laughing, he loses. Later, Martin laughingly challenges a Canadian soldier barely older than himself by standing in front of him and reciting the same phrase. Since he gets no reaction, he laughs and moves on, defusing the potentially tense situation, but the sequence signals francophone resentment at Montreal's occupation, as if by a barbarian imperial force. The game's name has multiple meanings; literally, it refers to some Eastern despot like Genghis Khan, demanding homage, but *mongol* in French also represents an politically incorrect insult, the equivalent of "retard" in English. The film thus characterizes official forces of order and those who invoked them (Trudeau, Bourassa, Drapeau) as "idiot kings," likening modern Quebec's leaders to the original *roi nègre*, a derogatory term coined by André Laurendeau to refer to Maurice Duplessis because – like an African leader under a colonial system – he allowed the province's resources to be plundered by external capitalists for his own personal gain.

Through its political allegory, *Les rois mongols* touches on multiple aspects of injustice, but addresses the issues it engages with the nuance of fiction and ultimately teaches a lesson of mutual humanity. By creating a parallel structure in which the children's actions mirror those of the FLQ, however, the film implicitly fosters viewer understanding for the terrorists and their demands. It establishes nostalgia through its coming-of-age narrative coupled with a wistful original musical score (by Viviane Audet, Robin-Joël Cool, and Alexis Martin) punctuated with popular songs from the era by nationalist artists like Robert Charlebois ("Te v'là"), Jean-Pierre Ferland ("La route 11"), and Harmonium ("Un musicien parmi tant d'autres"). Above all, Manon communicates the anger and frustration of the oppressed in a very personal way; early in the film, inspired by the FLQ Manifesto, she writes a "Manifeste pour les enfants négligés du monde entier" (Manifesto for the neglected children of the whole world). Later, she expresses the sentiment of her impotence and the disrespect with which children in her patriarchal, Catholic society are treated: "Personne ne nous dit jamais rien. Comme si on n'était pas du vrai monde. Comme si on n'avait pas d'opinion" (No one ever tells us anything. As if we weren't real people. As if we didn't have an opinion). Furthermore, her kidnapping victim's submission and eventual understanding suggest the Stockholm syndrome that Falardeau's *Octobre* portrays Pierre Laporte as experiencing.[51] Like these children, we are interpellated to understand, the members of the FLQ felt anger and frustration at the daily injustices faced by French Canadians, but also a sense of powerlessness and that their voice was not heard, so that they were forced by circumstances to undertake dramatic, albeit misguided action. Manon's father, Pierre (Martin Desgagné), tells his daughter that the kidnapping enables Québécois "Pour exiger des affaires en échange" (To demand things in exchange). But the film also explicitly asks viewers to excuse the FLQ's actions, as her father explains to her that "C'est des bons qui font du mauvais" (These are good guys doing bad things). The film refuses, however, to trivialize the children's (or the FLQ's) action, and they are punished in the end. But, as Manon Dumais suggests, this "charming adaptation" seeks to "tell young people about a tragic historical moment, but also to recall that despite its gains – health insurance, child protection services, Law 101 – today's society is not so different from yesterday's."[52]

The historical film per se, as analysed here, tends to linger on national traumas as rallying moments during which the "imagined community" comes together in response to a tragedy like the execution of the Patriots in *Le 15 février, 1839*. Whether or not viewers agree with the actions of the FLQ as depicted in *La Maison du pêcheur*, they can relate to the traumatizing effects of the *War Measures Act* in October 1970. Indeed, many viewers may remember that period. But Denis Villeneuve memorializes a much more recent trauma in *Polytechnique*, a film that closely resembles the historical film per se.

National Trauma for the New Millennium: Denis Villeneuve's *Polytechnique*

Arguably Quebec's most significant director to emerge in the twenty-first century, Denis Villeneuve (b. 1967) created a historical dramatization of the mass murder of fourteen women[53] at Montreal's École Polytechnique on 6 December 1989 that differs in many ways from the rest of his film corpus. In contrast with his early experimentation with magical realism and a brilliant visual style (partially attributable to Villeneuve's frequent director of photography, André Turpin), along with more recent forays into Hollywood science fiction, *Polytechnique* (2009) is filmed in black and white, in a straightforward, documentary-like style. The film not only commemorates a national trauma on its twentieth anniversary but also pays homage to the national cinematic tradition rooted in the *cinéma direct* techniques and aesthetics of Pierre Perrault, Michel Brault, and other pioneers,[54] a tradition Villeneuve has alternately been praised and castigated for forgetting.[55] With *Polytechnique*, however, as Maude Gauthier argues, Villeneuve works precisely towards the construction of a new site of memory: His film is "a work of collective memory" that seeks to "connect a national wound to popular feminism in Quebec society."[56]

Although Villeneuve has been the focus of feminist critiques for this film and *Blade Runner 2049*,[57] *Polytechnique* nonetheless invokes women's struggles for equality by dramatizing one man's anti-feminist rampage. Despite the care Villeneuve takes to ensure that the film not be a memorial to the assassin, specifically by denying his shooter (Maxim Gaudette) a name, viewers *are* provided an explanation for his behaviour that mirrors that of the real-life Marc Lépine, who perpetrated the shootings and then turned his gun on himself. The latter left a suicide note justifying his attack as purging the male bastion of the engineering school of female interlopers who had usurped his own rightful place. Born Gamil Garbi to an Algerian father and French Canadian mother, but later adopting the latter's surname, Lépine was subsequently described in media accounts as being indoctrinated in extremist Muslim misogyny, which many commentators see as the origin of his anti-feminist sentiments. Whereas Villeneuve's film elides this element and thus eschews fuelling anti-Arab discourses (pertinent in France and Quebec, as in the rest of post-9/11 North America), it underscores the anti-feminist subtext of its shooter's behaviour.[58] Like other historical films discussed here, images of his written words document the motivation behind his violent actions.

Overall, though, *Polytechnique* focuses more closely upon Lépine's victims. Above all, Villeneuve not only depicts the short-term impact of the massacre itself upon those killed and wounded but also stresses its long-term effects upon two fictionalized survivors, Valérie (Karine Vanasse) and an ambivalent hero figure Jean-François (Sébastien Huberdeau). One man and one woman, these characters stand in metonymically for the men and women of Quebec, representing possible reactions to the traumatic experience. Significantly, although Valérie is scarred by what she has witnessed and riddled with survivor's guilt, she manages to rebuild her life, and the film concludes with the revelation that she is pregnant. Excoriated by feminist critics precisely because it overwrites generations of feminist activism in Quebec,[59] relegating Valérie to one of the two roles available to women in a pre–Quiet Revolution Quebec (motherhood or a religious vocation) that she has sought to escape by attending the Polytechnique, Villeneuve's conclusion nonetheless focuses on an act of survival for its female protagonist. In stark contrast, *Polytechnique*'s male protagonist, Jean-François, is unable to move forward. Despite his heroic act of remaining in the building and attempting to help people escape to safety, he ultimately cannot cope with what he has witnessed and, tragically but quietly, kills himself. A manifestation of masculine guilt and the effort to, if not overcome, then at least counterbalance, the hegemonic misogyny of the killer, Jean-François represents a different type of manhood, one capable of both action and caring.[60] He also represents, with his generic name – which contains the French equivalent of John and the Christian name based on the former spelling for French nationality (Français) – a Québécois everyman. Through his suicide, then, the film forecloses the option for this type of masculinity and, by portraying a man as the ultimate victim of mass violence levelled against women, feeds into a contemporary backlash, a perceived crisis in masculinity.[61] Indeed, Maude Gauthier argues that, instead of focusing on Lépine's misogyny, the print media's response to Villeneuve's film framed the massacre as a national trauma: "The killings are presented as a tragedy in the modern history of Quebec, a wound to Québécois society as a whole, including men and women (not just the victims, … their families and their friends …)." But she also admits that "sometimes … making this wound visible, exploring it, is a means of healing it."[62] Given the very *real* nature of an event constructed as national trauma, which has led to specific efforts both to memorialize Lepine's victims and to prevent such catastrophes in the future,[63] we might set aside for the moment valid objections to the film (and media responses to it in Quebec) on feminist grounds. Doing so, we can understand that Villeneuve's respectful and anti-sensationalistic, but also emotionally impactful, film could serve as a means of "working through" the trauma.

There is another collective trauma that has yet to be addressed here, perhaps the deepest and most pervasive of all in the history of Quebec, Canada, and, indeed, all of the Americas, that of the colonial and postcolonial violence perpetrated on the Indigenous peoples present on the territory at the time of contact. And a growing body of film scholarship has begun to acknowledge the significant contribution to our understanding of that history found in the touchstone documentaries of Alannis Obamsawin (b. 1972) and recent fiction features about the 1990 Oka Crisis by Indigenous filmmakers. Similarly, Zacharias Kunuk's *Atanarjuat* (2001) and the other films included in the Fast Runner Trilogy, *The Journals of Kund Rasmussen* (2006) and *Before Tomorrow* (2008), memorialize the past from an Indigenous perspective. A study of Quebec national cinema, however, is not the place to consider films that seek to establish Indigenous visual sovereignty. But how are relationships between Indigenous and settler peoples depicted by the Franco-Québécois directors that we can more clearly associate with "Quebec national cinema"? Historical fiction films that tackle this topic in the new millennium are relatively rare and, as we shall see from the analysis of *Maïna* (in chapter 2), their success at respectful acknowledgment of such violence has been hit or miss. Perhaps the most ambitious of these attempts at a sort of filmic effort towards truth and reconciliation occurs in François Girard's *Hochelaga, terre des âmes*, which engages multiple *lieux de mémoire* and their interpretation in the present by a young Mohawk anthropologist.

A History for the Future: François Girard's *Hochelaga, terre des âmes*[64]

Jocelyn Létourneau's *A History for the Future: Rewriting Memory and Identity in Quebec* (2004) outlines the simplified version of its history prevalent in the nation's collective memory,[65] including the internalization of significant *lieux de mémoire*. But Létourneau also addresses how a shared story linked to French Canadian ethnicity and its oppression by British and Anglo-Canadian institutions must evolve if Quebec is to move forward as a pluralistic nation. As this book shows, Quebec national cinema in the twenty-first century frequently reflects the long-held, Franco-centric ideology of resistance and oppression. Increasingly, however, contemporary filmmakers contribute to Létourneau's project of constructing a history for the future, rewriting memory and identity in such a way that all members of a diverse Québécois society are included in the national project.[66] Most often, however, feature films offer a contradictory mix of conservative and progressive attitudes, resulting in an ambivalence that allows for multiple interpretations of on-screen representations of historical events.

Hochelaga, terre des âmes / *Hochelaga, Land of Souls* (2017) is an ambitious film that revisits several *lieux de mémoire*, weaving them together with a present-day narrative frame that represents contemporary Quebec as having been constructed by exchanges between an array of ethnic groups. In his only explicitly Québécois film, internationally acclaimed director and screenwriter François Girard (b. 1963) depicts twenty-first-century Quebec as a pluralistic society, acknowledging that multiple groups have contributed to its development. Described as a "historical fantasia,"[67] its magical realist elements exclude *Hochelaga, terre des âmes* from categorization as a historical film per se, but its explicit engagement with the related disciplines of history and archaeology, coupled with its desire for detailed historical reconstitution, suggest discussion here, at the end of chapter 1 and transitioning into chapter 2, which deals with what I call "historical fantasy." Girard's film brilliantly intercalates sequences from present-day Montreal with key moments from its past, reprising the structure adopted for his internationally acclaimed breakout film, *The Red Violin* (1998). Engaging the key topoi in national identity of memory and territory, its intrigue hinges upon the discovery of a very precise geographic location: the site believed to be the original

Figure 1.2. The Prophet (Raoul Max Trujillo) connects past to present, comforting Dawit Asigny's Mohawk ancestor (Samian) after a defeat in the pre-contact era.

Iroquoian village of Hochelaga, upon which the francophone metropolis of Montreal was founded.

Hochelaga, terre des âmes acknowledges the territorial primacy of Indigenous peoples on what is now Quebec in two interconnected narrative sequences, one set in present-day Montreal and another in a remote, ancestral dreamtime. Reflecting Natalie Zemon Davis's criteria for historical authenticity on film,[68] they link present and past, establishing a relationship between the film's protagonist, Dawiit Baptiste Asigny, a Mohawk doctoral candidate in archaeology, and the Prophet, an Indigenous shaman who serves as a chorus figure. As Baptiste's archaeological dig unfolds, historical vignettes tell the story behind the artefacts discovered in the layers of soil beneath McGill University's Percival Molson Stadium. These include a pre-contact battle between unnamed Indigenous groups, Jacques Cartier's 1535 meeting with Iroquoian Chief Tennawake, an interracial love story from the 1660s, and an incident from the 1837 Patriots Rebellion. Girard uses the device of the McGill football team and its players to create a pretext for Asigny's dig and to establish a metaphor for contemporary Quebec as a pluralistic society. Although it frequently deploys a form of "plastic shamanism," clichéd appropriations of Indigenous motifs,[69] to a certain extent Girard's complex story, infused with magical realism, achieves its end.

The Prophet weaves together the narrative's various episodes, magically suggesting the coexistence of past and present. Played by multi-ethnic actor Raoul Max Trujillo,[70] the character represents a spiritual and moral Indigenous presence overseeing the territory across time. As a wholly imaginary being, the Prophet's costume melds diverse Indigenous cultures, and his appearance blowing smoke to the four cardinal points, accompanied by utterances like "West wind, repel the fire of hatred,"[71] admittedly deploys the stereotype of Indigenous cultures as more spiritually attuned than Western ones. Despite these elements of plastic shamanism, he plays a unifying structural role in the film, knitting the various vignettes into an aesthetic whole. Above all, the Prophet appears *first* on-screen, thus giving primacy to an Indigenous voice, his Algonquian dialogue subtitled for viewers. In addition to foregrounding the Indigenous presence on the territory of Quebec since time immemorial, the device also underscores the notion of Indigenous survivance,[72] as the Prophet links the present-day Asigny to an ancestor of the same name.

Although he faces hurdles, Asigny's ultimate success shows viewers that Indigenous people survive in the contemporary world. As an archaeologist, Asigny uses the tools of Western science to uncover both the collective roots of Montreal's foundation and his individual identity as a Mohawk. Embodied by Franco-Algonquin rapper Samian, this "urban Indian" character reveals the ongoing battle for Indigenous peoples to overcome the challenges of endemic poverty and prejudice. Baptiste has struggled financially and has partially forgotten his family and his cultural roots on the reserve. The film reinscribes a certain paternalism through his Franco-Québécois mentor, Professor Antoine Morin (Gilles Renaud), whose assistance is vital in identifying the dig site and securing permission to excavate, but Morin also exhibits awareness of the racial dynamics in play, telling Asigny, "tu peux pas laisser cela à un blanc" (you can't leave this to a white person). Girard's sincere attempt to address racial inequities in Quebec for a general audience by underscoring these through dialogue, however, fall flat in the face of sustained readings in Indigenous criticism, which would argue that the film itself represents simply another form of settler appropriation of Indigenous narratives.[73]

Morin obtains permission to dig in an otherwise inaccessible, even symbolically sacrosanct, location after a natural catastrophe strikes during a game hosted by the McGill University football team, the Redmen. As a sinkhole forms in midfield, the significantly named quarterback, Charles Leblanc ("the white"), is engulfed by the earth. As a television news anchor (Caroline Dhavernas) describes, "le sol s'est littéralement dérobé sous ses pieds" (the ground literally fell out from under his feet) – the white man literally lost the ground he stood on, a metaphoric admission of the untenability of the ideological justifications for colonization. This seemingly divine intervention targets the occidental hubris behind the team's name, the Redmen, an appropriation of an outmoded, even derogatory term for Indigenous people by a bastion of the anglophone colonial presence in Montreal.[74] Indeed, we must read the coach's pep talk to the team ironically, questioning his notions of home and territory, as he exhorts players in English: "This field is sacred. This field is ours. This is home. ... Who the hell's going to take away what belongs to us?" Through the device of the sinkhole, *Hochelaga, terre des âmes* symbolically punishes this appropriation, via which these (mostly) white men travesty themselves as "Redmen," in defence of a "home" field that they themselves have taken from its original inhabitants. Although any cause-and-effect link to Girard's 2017 film is unclear, McGill announced in April 2019 that, due to faculty and student protests and the Canadian Truth and Reconciliation Commission's recommendations, it would change the team's name; they are now the Redbirds.[75] In some sense, it might be argued that – even if indirectly – Girard's film achieves the aim of the cinema of recognition to deploy emotionally charged references to the collective past that may even lead not just to passive remembrance, but also to action in the present.

Hochelaga, terre des âmes again gives precedence to an Indigenous voice as Asigny defends his dissertation, presenting each find to an audience, and thus integrating Indigenous presence and participation in the specifically Québécois *lieux de mémoire* that each artefact invokes. As Asigny digs further back in time, searching for evidence of the site where Jacques Cartier first encountered the original village of Hochelaga, historical vignettes illustrate the artefacts he uncovers, teaching about the extended relationships between French, Iroquois, Algonquin, Huron, English, and even peoples of African origin on the territory. Each signal item that Asigny unearths, in addition to opening a window onto a particular historical moment, also contributes to his own journey of self-discovery. Having finally found proof of Hochelaga's original site, the location where French and Indigenous people first met in what would one day be Montreal, he celebrates with a phone call to his mother, identifying himself by his Mohawk name, Dawiit. Her response reveals the significance of this act, signalling the first time he has fully embraced his Indigeneity.

The first of what Asigny terms his "découvertes incidentelles" (incidental discoveries) is an iron oven door from the Chaligny foundry in northern France, dating to the 1660s; Girard transports viewers back in time to witness a tragic love story between a young Algonquian woman, Akwi (Tanaya Beatty, Da'naxda'xw/ Awaetlatla), and Étienne Maltais (Emmanuel Schwartz), a French-born trapper. The relationship is founded in mutual respect, as signalled by the exchange of love tokens, his willingness to learn her language, and her song of return for him. But disease abruptly ends it, as Étienne falls sick from the "fièvre pourpre" (purple fever).[76] Étienne's stay in Montreal's Hôtel-Dieu, its oldest hospital, founded by Jeanne Mance in 1659, introduces a *lieu de mémoire*, but also reveals contemporary, secularized Quebec's ambivalence to the nation's Catholic origins. While one nun (Karelle Tremblay) genuinely cares for Étienne's well-being, the priest (Miro Lacasse) is angry and judgmental, condemning him to hell for having fornicated with a "créature du Malin" (creature of Evil). His encounter with a former companion on the voyage from France to the New World, Alexis Leblanc (David La Haye) – the disappeared football player's ancestor – allows for explicit commentary on national identity. Leblanc, still a Frenchman at heart, decries his fate, whereas Maltais replies, "On n'est plus français" (We're no longer French), thus establishing his embracing the future Quebec as his own. On the one hand, this episode engages contemporary discourses about Québécois culture as a product of *métissage* between French and Indigenous peoples;[77] on the other, it kills off the French settler, reversing the actual trajectory of epidemic. Instead of European diseases decimating Indigenous populations (a trope seen in *Before Tomorrow* and *Ce qu'il faut pour vivre*), in *Hochelaga, terre des âmes* the Frenchman dies, leaving Akwi to survive. In an effective illustration of intercultural exchange, the two lovers haunt each other during an oneiric sequence, in which Akwi ritually paints Maltais's body lying in state in a curtained French bed, preparing him for burial according to her traditions. *Hochelaga, terre des âmes*'s magical realist elements undermine, of course, any pretentions to Western standards of historical rigour, but that may be precisely their goal. Just as the Mohawk Asigny enhances his self-knowledge through science, Girard infuses his historical film with an acknowledgment of spiritual forces that also convey truth. While on the one hand, Girard lends primacy to the surviving Indigenous woman, giving her the right to bury her deceased lover, on the other, the plastic-shamanist depiction of these elements undermines the director's intentions. In the end, one wonders if *Hochelaga, terre des âmes* truly offers a chance at reconciliation, or whether it simply presents self-sufficient Franco-Québécois viewers with a kinder, gentler, more twenty-first-century vision of colonial conquest.

The next historical episode, triggered by Asigny's discovery of a cache of arms, occurs early in the 1837 Patriots Rebellion, just after the confrontation between the Sons of Liberty and members of the pro-empire Doric Club. Girard takes Pierre Falardeau's lesson of acknowledging that the rebellion was *not* just a French Canadian struggle even further by including an Irish and even an English character among the Patriots' supporters. He also uses casting to elicit viewer sympathy, as his Patriot, Léopold Lacroix, is played by Sébastien Ricard (a.k.a. Biz of the nationalist hip hop group Loco Locass). Clad in the red Phrygian bonnet of the Patriots, Lacroix and Timothy O'Neill (Christopher B. McCabe) run through the fields outside Montreal, seeking refuge. Arriving at a gated estate, they are greeted by Aurélien Tennawake (Jacques Newashish, Atikamekw), groundskeeper for Madame Sarah Walker (Siân Phillips); although her late husband had been a staunch supporter of empire, his widow has republican leanings. A good friend of Patriot leader Wolfred Nelson – a figure almost completely elided in Brault's and Falardeau's Patriot films – she permits the refugees to bury guns in her stable; unfortunately, redcoats arrive before they can safely flee. The British officer, Colonel Philip Thomas (Linus Roache), orders his men to chase down the Patriots and shoot them like dogs. He remains to question Madame Walker; not only is he rude to the aging society dame, he is openly racist to her maidservant Rose (Mylène Wagram), who attests to the African Canadian presence in historical Quebec.[78] While the segment establishes the injustices meted out by representatives of the British Empire on the territory of Quebec, it also shows that not all anglophones are bad, insisting particularly on Irish participation in the Patriot movement in Lower Canada. In contrast to accepted wisdom that Quebec's Indigenous peoples are hostile to the French language and Quebec's independence, the Iroquoian Tennawake displays solidarity with the French resistance fighter, cradling the dead Lacroix in his arms, echoing Akwi's song for her lover 150 years earlier.

Tennawake's eponymous ancestor plays a key role in the film's final historical sequence, as the blind but visionary chief who cautiously welcomes Jacques Cartier's 1535 arrival at Hochelaga, unwittingly showing him the site he will claim in the name of François I by planting a cross on Mont Royal. Once again, *Hochelaga, terre des âmes* gives primacy to an Indigenous point of view in its depiction of the European invaders' arrival. On the one hand, Cartier and his group reveal undaunted courage, as they leave their ship and willingly follow an armed group of "savages"; on the other, they are characterized as dirty, smelly, superstitious, and uncivilized by the Iroquoians who meet them. For example, the warrior who escorts the Frenchmen notes that they "puent" (stink). Because Tennawake (Wahiakéron Gilbert, Mohawk) is blind, Cartier's gifts must be described for him, also allowing for commentary; these include the crucifix found by Asigny identified as "un Guerrier malade" (a sick warrior), porcelain plates bearing the image of François I, called "un chaman fou" (a crazy shaman), and a haloed female saint, referred to as "une femme qui brûle" (a burning woman).[79] The French are also superstitious, fearing the ghost of Donnacona, a critical reference to the Iroquoians from Stadacona whom Cartier essentially kidnapped and brought back to France after his first voyage in 1534.[80] These Indigenous people view the French, based on their iconography, as venerating torture; Girard thus reverses conventional historical accounts of the Iroquois as torturers, responsible for the long and painful deaths of missionaries, now collectively known as *les Saints Martyrs canadiens*.[81] Although Tennawake initially holds the signal right of *naming* the territory, as he indicates they are in Hochelaga, Kanata, Cartier appropriates this right, ascending the hill with his Indigenous guides, planting a cross, and naming it Mont Réal. Girard depicts this incident in such a manner that viewer sympathy lies with the Indigenous people, and the French settlers are seen as dirty and arrogant, with a perverse system of beliefs, an image consistent with the twenty-first-century *bien pensant* (right-thinking) values of his liberal, secular viewers.

Despite its many shortcomings if read from the perspective of Indigenous studies, *Hochelaga, terre des âmes* strives to show Quebec audiences that Indigenous peoples inhabited this land long before the French, that they have contributed to its development throughout history, and that they survive today with dignity. It also acknowledges the presence of other groups, for example through quarterback Charles Leblanc's girlfriend, Nasrin (Naiade Aoun), a Lebanese Muslim, who carries his child; she takes a taxi with a Haitian driver speaking French and Kreyol. But above all, the device of the football team, presented in the film's conclusion marching out onto the metaphorical battlefield, introduces an array of cultural communities as the announcer (Paul Doucet) calls their names: Tim Kwan, Adam O'Neill, Mario Lacroix, Kenny Tennawake, Daniel Rose, and Charles Leblanc. It thus also acknowledges the contribution not just of two "founding" peoples, the English and the French, but of a whole variety of groups, to the creation of contemporary Quebec as a multicultural society. Introduced as "Your Redmen," however, the team's name disturbs the film's politically correct agenda, critically suggesting the problematic reappropriation of this territory for individuals who have now become metaphorical *Indigènes*. Despite the film's frequent acknowledgment of Quebec as a multilingual province, including the presence of English as well as Indigenous languages, there is an uncomfortable potential linkage here between Indigenous peoples and French Canadian settlers as *both* being oppressed by the English precisely because of McGill's status as a bastion of anglophone privilege in Montreal.

Conclusion

Although it remains relatively rare on the landscape of the *cinématographie québécoise*, the historical film per se typifies the received idea of "Quebec national cinema" as filmmakers use it explicitly as a tool for nation building. The film representations of the 1837–8 Patriots Rebellions and the October 1970 crisis analysed here remind twenty-first-century viewers of the francophone nation's past struggles. Although they invoke the long-held national narrative of oppression, they nonetheless revise this narrative, proposing that, despite their failure, their protagonists represent heroes of resistance whose actions ultimately succeeded in changing linguistic and cultural power dynamics in Quebec. Whereas the Patriots can be represented as unambiguous heroes, as freedom fighters who become victims of imperial power, the battle for local sovereignty waged by the FLQ remains admittedly problematic even for franco-nationalist filmmakers. Although the extent to which they seek to rehabilitate members of the FLQ varies, these films' common goal is to remind contemporary Québécois that their current situation of relative self-determination should not be taken for granted, as they memorialize events viewed as traumatic, but also necessary. In contrast, Denis Villeneuve's invocation of a much more recent national trauma in *Polytechnique* suggests the senselessness of violence in contemporary Quebec, a just society that offers opportunity to all. Through its fictionalization of the events it portrays, it lies at the margins of the historical film per se, but *Polytechnique*'s sober, almost documentary treatment of the national tragedy aligns this film closely with the genre studied in this chapter.

It is not surprising that Quebec's twenty-first-century historical films commemorate some of the most dramatic, violent moments in the province's history. Such moments lend themselves to spectacular representation on the big screen.

What is, perhaps, surprising is their tendency – in a supposedly post-national era (although the Coalition Avenir Québec seems to have assumed the momentum lost by the Parti québécois) – to memorialize gestures of resistance, even if those gestures fail. Despite the advent of the new millennium, a certain sector of Quebec's film institutions and audiences continues to adhere to a discourse that nourishes old grievances, lingering on loss and martyrdom, representing what Marc Angenot calls the "ideology of resentment."[82] Although many films produced in Quebec in this period focus not on the province's losers, but rather on its cultural and economic winners,[83] the historical film per se reminds viewers in the new millennium of a history of oppression, but also of resistance and survival. Quebec's history includes, of course, not just the colonial oppression of the French by the British Empire (and later by federalist Anglo-Canada and the neo-imperial United States), but also an initial and ongoing oppression of Indigenous peoples by the French and later by Anglo- and French Canadians. Partially in the wake of Canada's *Truth and Reconciliation Act* (2008), a handful of historical films recount an earlier national trauma, one on which Quebec as a nation was founded: the colonial oppression experienced by Indigenous peoples – mainstream Quebec's Others.

Although not without flaws, Girard's *Hochelaga, terre des âmes* works towards the type of recognition called for by Canada's Truth and Reconciliation Commission, organized in 2008 and operating until 2015, as do films by both Franco-Québécois and Indigenous filmmakers. Although it compares unfavourably with clear examples of Indigenous visual sovereignty,[84] such as Tracy Deer's *Beans* or Madeline Ivalu and Hélène Cousineau's *Before Tomorrow*, *Hochelaga, terre des âmes* succeeds much better in its acknowledgment of the Indigenous presence on what has become the settler territory of Quebec than does another representation of Indigenous peoples by a Franco-Québécois director, Michel Poulette's *Maïna*, a nonetheless unique film depicting Indigenous peoples in the pre-contact era. This largely inauthentic and fetishized portrayal of the Indigenous peoples who inhabited the north-eastern portion of present-day Quebec strays so far afield from (pre-)historical verisimilitude that it can no longer be considered a historical film per se. It opens, then, the discussion of a significant number of genre-bending films that I refer to as "historical fantasies," the subject of chapter 2.

2 Stretching the Historical Imaginary: Revisiting Sites of Memory in Historical Fantasy

Memory, insofar as it is affective and magical, only accommodates those facts that suit it … *Lieux de mémoire* are created by a play of memory and history, … are mixed, hybrid, mutant, … only exist because of their capacity for metamorphosis, an endless recycling of their meaning and an unpredictable proliferation of their ramifications.

Pierre Nora[1]

Despite their attempts to establish truth through documentation and documentary techniques like title cards and stock footage, the historical films discussed in chapter 1 necessarily fictionalize their subject matter, offering twenty-first-century viewers a certain image of the collective past. As Julianne Pidduck insists, "cinema can never offer an unmediated window onto the past, and historical fiction and costume drama alike depict the past through the stylistic, critical and generic vocabularies of present cultural production," circulating "memory-images … in the moment of production and consumption."[2] But some film-makers take this mediation of the past much farther than others, dropping the pretence of historical accuracy, stretching the historical imaginary to its limits in their borrowings from Quebec's historical capital as settings for more openly fictional and often quite fantastical narratives. These films reflect more clearly the "affective and magical" aspects of memory observed by Pierre Nora in the epigraph cited above. This chapter analyses films that I identify as "historical fantasy": works that deploy familiar *lieux de mémoire*, set in a recognizable historical period, but which play fast and loose with the truth claims or invocations of historical accuracy found in the historical film per se, sometimes introducing counterfactual, whimsical, or even supernatural elements. Some of these appropriate sites of memory to infuse a popular film genre with local interest, thus territorializing Hollywood genres like the thriller or the horror film. Such is the case with *Le poil de la bête* (Philippe Gagnon, 2010) and *Chasse-galerie* (Jean-Philippe Duval, 2016), which draw, respectively, on Québécois literary traditions of the werewolf and a canoe made to fly through a pact with the devil. Conversely, a handful of Quebec's film auteurs turn to the past for inspiration, constructing historical fantasies that likewise engage the past, but use their unique visions to comment on Quebec society, then and now. This chapter explores how twenty-first-century filmmakers more freely exploit Quebec's sites of memory but nonetheless contribute to the construction of the national historical capital as they adopt and/or deform its received images.

Quebec's relationship with colonialism is complex, viewing itself as a territory doubly colonized, first by the French, and then the British. Franco-nationalist discourses have claimed an affinity with other "subject" peoples, at times controversially appropriating for French Canadians the status of a "native" people after the Conquest of 1763. This may explain the dearth of historical films about Quebec's origins in New France; indeed, Australian director Bruce Beresford's English-language *Black Robe* (1991) arguably remains the most rigorous visual document of that period.[3] Not only does acknowledgment of the Indigenous presence disrupt the discourse of French primacy, it also triggers a sense of liberal guilt about various forms of colonial violence towards the so-called First Nations of Canada. As demonstrated in chapter 1's analysis of *Hochelaga, terre des âmes*, one thrust of twenty-first-century Quebec national cinema is the construction of a national narrative of inclusion and a celebration of cooperation, a literal and cultural *métissage* between French newcomers and Indigenous peoples, often contrasted with the conquest approach associated with the British Empire and the United States. This carefully constructed image of collaboration between French explorers, trappers, traders, settlers, and Indigenous peoples in the early colony,[4] however, is frequently based on a form of selective collective memory, which, as Pierre Nora reminds us, "only accommodates those facts that suit it."[5] As Indigenous cinema developing since 2000 documents, francophone Quebec's relationship with the Indigenous is much more ambivalent and problematic than this image suggests. Nonetheless, the adventure-romance *Maïna* (2013), created by Franco-Québécois writers and filmmakers for a general audience, appropriates the pre-Contact Indigenous experience into a seamless origin story for Quebec.

Further complicating matters, Quebec's history involves two different moments of francophone colonization of the land: the initial colonial period of New France from 1608 to 1763, and a second French Canadian movement dating from roughly 1870 to 1930 to clear and colonize the boreal forests beyond the original St. Lawrence valley settlements. Significantly, the handful of twenty-first-century films set in New France and/or dealing with its demise at the dawn of the British colonial era participate in the development of popular genres and, all of them infused with gothic elements, reflect the nation's ambivalence towards this period, the source of an uncanny haunting.[6] In addition to *Maïna*, this corpus includes the melodrama *Nouvelle-France* (2004), both analysed in this chapter. The frontier mentality and backwoods decor shared between the initial settling and clearing of the St. Lawrence valley recurs in a second wave of colonization farther north and west in the post-Confederation era. The *contes de village* of storyteller Fred Pellerin further transform this period of the *Anciens Canadiens* into a mythical time infused with the magic of memory; their affective appeal for contemporary audiences led to three film adaptations, *Babine* (2008), *Ésimésac* (2011), and *L'arracheuse de temps* / *The Time Thief* (2020), two of which are discussed in this chapter. Also analysed here, the historical fantasies of auteur filmmakers André Forcier and Olivier Asselin deploy and distort national and international historical clichés for both aesthetic and ideological purposes, calling attention to their constructed nature through their very distortion. Finally, the chapter concludes with a study of how a rising director, Maxime Giroux, re-engages Quebec's historical master narratives in the stylized depiction of *La Grande Noirceur* (2018).

Romancing the Origin Story: *Maïna* and *Nouvelle-France*

In contrast with the pretensions to historical veracity evident in the films of auteur directors like Pierre Falardeau's *Le 15 février, 1839*, Mathieu Denis's *Corbo*, and Simon Lavoie's *Le déserteur* (set in World War II), films dealing with Quebec's early origins seem to rely on popular genre conventions and display little concern for accuracy. Interestingly, Québécois producers tasked Swiss-born Pierre Billon to write the scenarios for two films that romanticize the national origin story, *Nouvelle-France* / *Battle of the Brave* (2004) and *Maïna* (2013), directed by Michel Poulette (b. 1950). Based on Dominique Demers's[7] prehistoric novel, set 3,500 years ago and focusing on conflicts between the ancestors of the Indigenous Innu and Inuit peoples who inhabit the region today,[8] the film adaptation shifts the intrigue to the moment immediately prior to contact – almost as if its Franco-Québécois creators could not completely imagine the "New World" without Europeans, *Maïna* concludes on a shot of French vessels nearing shore. Its plot, involving an Innu (called the Montagnais throughout much of the province's post-contact history) chief's daughter and her people's clash with the Inuit to the north, her proto-feminist characterization, and an interracial romance, offers a paradigm of inauthenticity to be avoided. Although historical conflicts between Innu and Inuit are well documented,[9] *Maïna* follows Demers's foreword, staging inter-ethnic conflict and exchange as a cultural universal: "Their encounter was the stage of a great cultural shock that engendered numerous fruitful technological exchanges, but that also sometimes led to racism and violence. In all times, it seems, humans have feared difference and been suspicious of the Other."[10] The implicit parallels drawn between Indigenous peoples and European colonizers thus normalizes violence while emphasizing technological exchange as unproblematically positive. Indeed,

Maïna's representation of Indigenous peoples follows a general trend in Canadian and Québécois film identified by Christopher Gittings as "whiting-out the Indigene," in which producers create "spectacle screen Aboriginals from the materials of white fantasy."[11]

Maïna attempts to reflect Quebec's official ideology of respect for difference and participates in the construction of a postmodern Québécois identity as an accommodating, even hybrid nation. As an example of *cinéma grand public*, it draws on popular genres to market its atypical characters and subject matter, reminiscent less of Zacharias Kunuk's acclaimed *Atanarjuat* (2001) and more of Jacques Dorfmann and Pierre Magny's *Agaguk* (1992), based on an Yves Thériault novel and starring Americans Lou Diamond Phillips and Jennifer Tilly as its Inuit main characters.[12] Evocative of historical film techniques, *Maïna* links its historicized protagonists to modern Quebec by situating them for viewers in time and space through the opening image of a map of present-day Quebec and a title card: "In the far north of America / Before contact with Europeans." Then, images meant to read as "primitive" recode areas of the map as "Inuit" (the Ungava Peninsula) and "Innu" (the territory below), mimicking an ethnographic approach. An epigraphical citation frames this parable about the acceptance of difference – "The oldest and strongest emotion of mankind is fear, and the oldest and strongest kind of fear is the fear of the unknown" – suggesting that conquering one's fears is key to embracing difference. The remark, however, is attributed to horror writer Howard Philipps Lovecraft,[13] certainly a curious choice, but one that reveals *Maïna*'s creators' affinity for the fantastic, the magical aspects of memory invoked by Pierre Nora above.

As the heroine of an adventure romance, the Innu princess Maïna (Roseanne Supernault, Métis) is characterized as an extraordinary individual, at odds with cultural norms as a hunter and, eventually, the foundress of a new, hybrid society with her destined Inuk lover, Natak (Ipellie Ootoova, Inuit).[14] In addition to its anachronistically feminist agenda, the film deploys the usual stereotypes about Indigenous respect for nature and spirituality, as Maïna overcomes fear while hunting her totem animal, the wolf, and singing it into the afterlife, for example. In contrast with its overall plastic shamanism, *Maïna* deals with language, however, in a rather sophisticated manner, reflective of a specifically Québécois sensitivity to the politics of language.[15] This is particularly evident in the "first contact" sequence, triggered by the arrival on Innu territory of Inuit seeking what their shaman, Merkusaq (Pakak Innuksuk, Inuit, of *The Journals of Knud Rasmussen*), calls the "living stone," in which they magically see herds of caribou.[16] Maïnu's father and her clan's chief, Mishta-Napeu (Graham Greene, Oneida), attempts to communicate peacefully, but the language barrier prevents real understanding; indeed, most viewers – meant to identify with the Innu heroine – also fail to understand Merkusaq, since his words are subtitled not in French or English, but in the Inuktitut alphabet. For the moment, the Inuit remain Other for characters and spectators alike; while this might appear laudable, in the Quebec context linking the Franco-Québécois with Indigenous groups can be problematic. Not content with appropriating for themselves an Indigenous status in relationship to the English, there has also been a recent (and much-criticized) movement on the part of some French Canadians to reclaim a purportedly lost Indigenous heritage and identity. Rather than viewed as the expression of a desire for reconciliation, such actions have been interpreted as yet another form of settler appropriation of Indigenous lands, rights, and culture.[17]

Maïna implicitly criticizes the racism that fear of the Other triggers by attributing it to its antagonist, the Innu villain, Saitu (Flint Eagle, Mohawk), who makes fun of the Inuit's "slanted" eyes and says that the "Strangers" eat children. Aggression being the bully's response to fear, he leads an attack on the Inuit, killing their shaman; in retaliation, they kidnap an Innu child, Nipki (Uapshkuss Thernish, Inuit), Maïna's unofficial godson. By projecting intercultural conflict onto two Indigenous groups, the film avoids uncomfortable images of similar conflicts between Europeans and Indigenous peoples, but it also offers the pretext for its heroine's extraordinary journey. As she follows the Inuit into the Far North to rescue her ward, Maïna eventually pairs with Natak and accepts his culture's practices, uniquely adapted to life in the Arctic. Never forgetting her own origins, however, she sews a costume for herself that symbolically operates a form of cultural *métissage*. Rejected by their people and sent into exile, however, the interracial couple founds a new society, bringing together the best of both cultures, a symbolic re-enactment of the Québécois revisionist history of French contact with Indigenous groups as one of mutual respect and hybridity.

Maïna thus reflects official ideologies of pluralism and accommodation, of Quebec as a model of building positive relationships with the Indigenous peoples within its borders. Despite its purportedly Indigenous subject matter, however, this film is not about Inuit and Innu, but rather about contemporary Québécois appropriating the pre-contact era into their own origin narrative, as critics identified it as "Québécois" via its setting, "le Grand Nord québécois" (Quebec's Great North).[18] In its defence, *Maïna* employs a cast largely comprised of Indigenous actors, features dialogue in Indigenous languages, and endeavours to construct viewer identification with Indigenous characters depicted as fully human, experiencing an array of emotions, including different ways of loving, laughing, and using aggression. *Maïna* also works towards erasing historical media images of "Indians" as a monolithic Other by differentiating between the lifeways of the two groups. And yet, as one critic notes, "the inevitable love story developed in *Maïna* proceeds from a vision that implicitly reveals the Western culture of its authors," as do the film's technical aspects: "at times you'd think we were in an episode of the television series *Xena*."[19]

Viewed through the lens of Bruno Cornellier's rigorous study *La "chose" indienne : cinéma et politiques de la représentation autochtone au Québec et au Canada*

(2015), despite its good intentions, *Maïna* participates in the continued reification and erasure of Aboriginal peoples as anchored in a lost past. It projects a desired self-image of contemporary Quebec as a pluralistic society, accommodating different cultures sharing its vast territory. The metaphorical link it establishes between Indigenous peoples and French settlers serves only the latter's agenda for Cornellier, who insists that: "in order to survive, morally and politically, its history and colonial heritage, the modern liberal State needs to some degree, but never completely, to make itself Indian. It has to imagine a certain filial relationship between settlers and First Nations."[20]

For Cornellier, stories like *Maïna*, told about Aboriginal peoples by the modern liberal settler nation of Quebec project representations of the "Indian" that do not reflect an authentic movement towards reconciliation, but instead remain implicated in colonial systems of power and knowledge. A similar appropriation of Quebec's Indigenous peoples, coupled with the representation of colonial antagonisms more typically thematized in Quebec national cinema, appears in the other historical film scenarized by Pierre Billon, *Nouvelle-France*.

Although its French-language title suggests a bona fide historical film, *Nouvelle-France / Battle of the Brave* (2004), the most ambitious work examined in this chapter, aims for the status of "heritage film." As theorized by Andrew Higson, heritage films display the past "as visually spectacular pastiche, inviting a nostalgic gaze that resists the ironies and social critiques so often suggested narratively by [them]."[21] An international co-production with a $30 million budget, touted as "the most significant cinematographic production in the history of Quebec cinema,"[22] the film's visual spectacle definitely trumps any pretence to historical accuracy.[23] Shot in both French- and English-language versions on location in France, England, and Quebec, including the historic Forteresse de Louisbourg on Cape Breton Island standing in for Quebec City, and featuring French, British, American, and Québécois stars outfitted in lavish costumes, *Nouvelle-France* invites a nostalgic gaze using historical cliché as a backdrop for an unlikely and doomed romance. The film was ostensibly engineered by producer Richard Goudreau (b. 1950), the entrepreneur behind the iconic *Les Boys* hockey comedy franchise, who tasked Jean Beaudin (1939–2019) as director. Among other epic elements, it includes an original song composed by Patrick Doyle and Luc Plamondon, "Ma Nouvelle-France," and performed by Céline Dion over the film's closing credits. Although *Nouvelle-France* proposes a generic melodrama,[24] it does so against the backdrop of Quebec's most significant *lieu de mémoire*, the fabled Conquest by the British. Clearly an origin story, described as depicting "a fundamental part of our history,"[25] it participates in the construction of national identity through its characterization of various participants in foundational moments as either good or evil. Critics, however, consistently panned the film:[26] "Jean Beaudin's last feature film has certainly achieved unanimity, Québécois critics condemning without appeal this expensive and insipid blueberry that has

committed the mortal sin of explaining nothing about one of the most significant events in the history of the French-Canadian nation."[27]

Set on the very eve of the British Conquest, between 1758 and 1761, with
a prologue and epilogue that occur some two decades later, *Nouvelle-France*
exploits the nation's historical imaginary through an array of clichés. Billon's
scenario draws from several literary sources, including "La Corriveau," a historical figure who inspired a folk legend,[28] and William Kirby's 1877 bestseller *The
Golden Dog*, which remains uncredited.[29] In addition to an array of caricatured
historical figures, including William Pitt (Tim Roth), Benjamin Franklin (Colm
Meaney), Madame de Pompadour (Micky Sébastian), and Voltaire (Philippe
Dormoy), the film's climax involves Quebec's most-invoked site of memory: the
French defeat at the Battle of the Plains of Abraham, outside the gates of Quebec
City, on 13 September 1759. Despite its numerous historical and literary allu-
sions, the film's primary narrative interest is the ill-fated love story between its
two fictional protagonists. Although it contributes to discourses about national
identity, it teaches little about the actual course of history,[30] at times leading
viewers astray with its inaccuracies and exaggerations. Indeed, to return to Higson's conception of the heritage film as being both nostalgic and a pastiche,
Nouvelle-France cobbles together as many random historical references as it can.
In many cases, its very ambition as an international co-production forced it to
compromise with historical truth, including the requirement to invent roles for
French and British actors.

Instead of depicting the glory of the French regime, as one might expect of
a heritage film, *Nouvelle-France* frames Quebec's origin story through loss: The
deaths of two father figures open its narrative; the loss of a war and a mother
and lover conclude it. It does so in part by focalizing the narrative through the
eyes of a young girl, a figure of innocence lost, a metaphor for the colony itself,
the symbolically named France Carignan (Juliette Gosselin). Looking back on
this key moment in her own and her nation's past as she attends the death of the
family priest, le père Blondeau (Gérard Depardieu), the now adult France (Isabel
Richer) introduces this notion in voice-over:

> 1759. Another lifetime, another world. I was only a child then, living in a country
> which, in the eyes of history, was still in its infancy. I had no idea that my country
> was about to be lost, but by the grace of God, I would survive this hostile, beautiful
> no man's land, ten times bigger than its mother country France, the same France
> that was about to sell us for a handful of islands in the sun. The English were prepa-
> ring to attack where I was born, and when the city of Quebec fell, England would
> seize the keys to a new outpost of her empire. That was our fate, and this is our story.

France's monologue invokes the cliché of Quebec's sense of betrayal "for a handful of islands in the sun," when France retained the profitable slave-labour sugar

islands of Guadeloupe and Martinique, instead ceding Canada to the British at the Treaty of Paris in 1763. *Nouvelle-France* thus rehearses the national family romance, popularized by historian Heinz Weinmann in the 1990s,[31] in which the infant country is abandoned by the bad mother (France) only to be raised by an ambivalent father (Great Britain). The film then jumps from one deathbed to another, "Twenty Years Earlier," as a title card instructs, and introduces the film's hero, François Le Gardeur (David La Haye), who arrives in Quebec to learn that his father has just died. Framed by death, the film's structure – as one big flashback – invites nostalgia as viewers follow France in memory back to her childhood, to the moment when her beloved mother, Marie-Loup Carignan (Noémie Godin-Vigneau), met and fell in love with Le Gardeur.

Nouvelle-France builds on the notion of the family romance through the images of dysfunction it portrays at the individual and collective levels; perhaps disgusted by their corrupt fathers, both implicated in European systems of power and economic exploitation, the film's hero and heroine seek more "authentic" models for their identity. By establishing close ties to the Innu for François and Marie-Loup, *Nouvelle-France* participates in the historiographical revisionism that posits present-day Quebec as founded upon the interaction between French Canadians and Indigenous peoples. Not only has Marie-Loup learned herbal lore from an Innu elder, she and her biological daughter, France, speak that language fluently with her adopted Innu daughter, Acoona (Bianca Gervais, in brownface). Reflective of the movement to embrace Quebec national identity as a Franco-Indigenous *métissage*, Marie-Loup's name and appearance combine distinctly French elements with Indigenous borrowings, like a totem animal, the wolf. Indeed, Acoona describes her as having white skin but the heart of an Innu. Similarly, Le Gardeur first appears in the film crossing the frozen North with his Indigenous sidekick, Owashak (William Merasty, Cree), and his ties to the Innu are reinforced in additional sequences. Depicted as an effective New World woodsman, Le Gardeur also studied political science in Paris; a fighter and a lover (he seduces the Intendant Bigot's mistress before falling in love with Marie-Loup), he is also an idealized father figure for the orphaned France Carignan. Both leads' wardrobes, soft brown like deerskin, and hairstyles, often loose and unkempt, associate them more closely with Indigenous characters, setting French Canadians apart from the continental French, epitomized by the elegant (even foppish) attire and mores of the French-born Intendant Bigot and his mistress, Angélique de Roquebrune. Marie-Loup and Le Gardeur represent ideals of Québécois strong femininity and woodsy masculinity, as well as figures of national independence. Marie-Loup underscores her role as a metaphor for Quebec, asserting her right to self-determination to Le Gardeur: "I know I am not important or influential, sir, but I am my own person."

Unfortunately, though, as a woman ahead of her time, forces beyond her control will deny her the sovereignty that she (and the nation she allegorically

Figure 2.1. Rugged New World identities and costumes for *Nouvelle-France*'s Marie-Loup (Noémie Godin-Vigneau) and Le Gardeur (David La Haye), along with her daughter France (Juliette Gosselin) and adopted Indigenous daughter Accona (Bianca Gervais).

represents) craves. Swept up in the whirlwind of larger political forces, the love affair between Le Gardeur and Marie-Loup is foiled by personal betrayals; believing herself abandoned, Marie-Loup settles for marriage to Xavier Maillard (Sébastien Huberdeau), who, having lost his position of privilege with the departure of the French administration, becomes drunk and abusive. The film's narrative climax derives from what has been called the "founding myth"[32] of La Corriveau. This polyvalent figure, based on the actual legal case of Marie-Josephte Corriveau (1733–63), has over the years been invoked to scare children into good behaviour, then appropriated as a figure of feminist oppression and resistance, as well as a figure of British injustice towards francophones.[33] Convicted of murdering her husband by British court martial during the military regime, Corriveau was paraded through Quebec City, hanged, and her caged remains displayed as a warning at the crossroads of Pointe-Lévy. Billon's screenplay (which he also novelized)[34] follows the revisionist image; when Marie-Loup's abusive husband is found dead, she is accused, tried, and spectacularly executed, the victim of British injustice and the Catholic Church's complicity with the new regime.

Overseeing an international co-production, *Nouvelle-France*'s producers were required to create roles for actors from France and the United Kingdom, forcing the construction of side narratives involving historical figures from Canada's two "founding nations." France's loss of its colony to the English provides an epic backdrop to the melodrama's foiled love affair, but *Nouvelle-France* nonetheless constructs a historical narrative that attributes that loss more to *ancien régime* corruption than to the storied military defeat on the Plains of Abraham.[35] Three significant historical figures personify France's abandonment of Quebec: the king's corrupt colonial administrator, Intendant François Bigot (Vincent Perez); Louis XV's powerful favourite, the Marquise de Pompadour (Micky Sébastian); and François-Marie Arouet "de"Voltaire (Philippe Dormoy). "Lining his pockets while men fight for a lost cause," Bigot is characterized as a sexual libertine, even a rapist, sullying the colony's beauties. His mistress Angélique de Roquebrune (Irène Jacob) also serves as his procuress, but warns Marie-Loup, who has caught Bigot's eye, "Don't use your nails or your teeth – unless you want them torn out." Bigot's reminder to François (and the film's viewers) that New France was not completely lost to the French until the Treaty of Paris in 1763 further reveals his lack of political loyalty: "Everything can be negotiated, Monsieur Le Gardeur, even a country." Sent to France on the eve of the British invasion by Canadian-born Governor Vaudreuil (Paul Savoie), Le Gardeur seeks Voltaire's assistance to gain the ear of Madame de Pompadour, since "France's foreign policy is run by the marquise." *Nouvelle-France*'s inclusion of the philosophe, known to be "violently opposed to the Canadian cause," provides a pretext for the recitation of a *lieu de mémoire* emblematic of Quebec's abandonment by France in the film, his oft-quoted description of Canada as "quelques arpents de neige" (a few acres of snow).[36] With his concluding effeminate giggle, Voltaire becomes an easy target for pastiche; as with Bigot, the effete and foppish affectations of the French, powdered and bewigged, in their brocade jackets and lace cuffs, their tights and high-heeled shoes, contrast with the simple manliness of the Canadian Le Gardeur, with his long but unpowdered hair, brown jacket, deerskin breeches, and boots. Similarly, Madame de Pompadour's narcissistic cynicism appears as she sits for a portrait in her luxurious chateau, hypocritically concerned about the expense of running a war on two fronts and refusing Le Gardeur's plea to "dismiss the crooks and the bunglers" governing New France. She retorts, "Eliminate the bunglers from the positions of power! Sheer genocide!" Le Gardeur's parting comment marks an ideological shift, implying that Britain's constitutional monarchy might be preferable to French absolutism: "The English! For a long time, I believed they were Canada's main enemies. They're the most visible, that's for sure, which makes them the least dangerous." Whereas this implicitly federalist comment might appeal to the Anglo-Canadian audience that the film clearly covets, historical figures from England and its American colonies fare no better than the French in *Nouvelle-France*'s characterization.

Three brief sequences, filmed in the spectacular location of the Painted Hall of London's Old Royal Naval College, standing in (as a title informs) for the "Royal Naval Command, England," with dialogue in English, invent an entirely fictional encounter between Benjamin Franklin (Colm Meaney) and William Pitt the Elder (Tim Roth), helmsman of the British Parliament during the Seven

Years' War.[37] Although Franklin was on a second mission to London from 1757 to 1762,[38] and published his views that England must maintain its hold on Canada,[39] his presence at the dinner that Pitt hosted in honour of General James Wolfe (Jason Isaacs) on the eve of his departure for Quebec – which actually took place – is a complete fabrication. Whereas Pitt's characterization suits that of a wise statesman, *Nouvelle-France*'s depictions of Franklin and Wolfe clearly fuel anti-American and anti-British attitudes. For example, Franklin demands "Canada's annexation by Britain," coupled with the assimilationist opinion that "We must rid ourselves of the Canadians and the Savages for good … by having them swear allegiance to the Crown of England."[40] Wolfe, depicted as a melancholy yet violent invalid, fares even worse, becoming a mere caricature of a figure frequently idolized as the hero of a battle that changed the course of North American history.[41] He interrupts an unnamed general, hysterically asserting, "Negotiate! You cannot negotiate annexation! Weakness! Annexation is won!" He insists that "Quebec must be taken before the river freezes. I have taken Louisbourg; with your permission, I will take Quebec and Montreal. If the city refuses to give in, I will torch it and chill it twenty-four hours a day; I will burn the crops; … I will destroy the farms; … I will leave a trail of famine and devastation behind me." Although an actual citation from his correspondence,[42] this tirade is undermined by the wheezing fit that concludes it, and this histrionic depiction of Wolfe verges on unintended comic relief. Even after his death, he becomes the object of Madame de Pompadour's ridicule, as she laughs, "Apparently, he recited a poem on the battlefield," invoking a well-documented anecdote that he recited Thomas Gray's "Elegy Written in a Country Churchyard" to his troops the night before the battle.[43]

Nouvelle-France proposes that, facing treachery on both sides from the Old World, New France must rely on its own wits and ideals to survive. Its portrayal of the French colony's only Canadian-born governor, Vaudreuil, reveals a nascent desire for self-government, echoing notions developing in the American colonies to the south. Dialogue establishes Vaudreuil's status as an authentic founding father, as Father Blondeau reassures him that "You can defend Nouvelle-France. The people here trust you." Vaudreuil explains why: "Probably because I'm a born and bred Canadian, like them. It is both my weakness and my strength." And Le Gardeur agrees, insisting that "It's high time that the born-and-bred Canadians took their destiny into their own hands." This statement reveals the ambivalence typical of popular texts that must appeal to a wide audience. On the one hand, viewers unaware that in the eighteenth century the term "Canadian" referred only to French Canadians might interpret the film's message as a federalist one, uniting all Canadians, French- and English-speaking, against the British Empire.[44] On the other hand, franco-nationalist and even sovereigntist viewers could just as easily interpret the statement as a call for Québécois self-determination.

Among the film's many disappointments is its elliptical treatment of the Battle of Quebec itself. Rather than staging a historical re-enactment of the iconic Battle of the Plains of Abraham, *Nouvelle-France* focuses on the preceding siege and bombardment, depicting even this through the lens of gothic melodrama, as clouds roll over the moon, accompanied by dramatic music. The camera tilts up over the rooftops of Quebec and out onto the view of British ships arriving up the St. Lawrence, and a first brief montage reveals the British batteries on the south shore slamming the city with heavy artillery, setting buildings on fire. The second battle montage shows a group of artillerymen (inaccurately clad in the stereotypical British red coats, rather than the artillery units' blue ones),[45] loading a cannon (before a rather poorly integrated green-screen woodland backdrop). Whereas Wolfe was given ample screen time, the French general who also died of wounds received on the battlefield that day, the Marquis de Montcalm, remains glaringly absent from the scenario. By focusing on the bombardment, rather than the battle, aside from the obvious budgetary restraints, *Nouvelle-France* maintains its focus on French Canadians as victims, instead of as active participants in the battle for their government.[46]

Despite its hodge-podge approach to historical fact and its failure as a heritage film, *Nouvelle-France* nonetheless contributes to popular constructions of contemporary Québécois identities with its New World hero's hybrid identity, combining Indigenous ruggedness with European knowledge. Despite its revisionist approach to La Corriveau, transforming her from history's mariticide and legend's witch into the beautiful Marie-Loup, a proto-feminist victim of patriarchal systems of justice and a founding mother figure for a New World French identity, *Nouvelle-France*'s heroine-victim also draws from a long national history of martyrs.[47] Focusing on the corruption of *ancien régime* France, it suggests that the colony might have flourished with better administration and remained French. Instead, it fell to the heavy hand of British colonial (in)justice. Indeed, Marie-Loup's execution holds political value for the colony's new English masters, as Governor Murray (Michael Maloney) explains that the "life of an illiterate French Canadian girl is a small price to pay for the wholehearted collaboration of the clergy." Paraded through the streets of Quebec City in an iron cage, her hair shorn, Marie-Loup invokes other martyr figures in Quebec's historical and fictional past, including the *Saints Martyrs canadiens* and *La petite Aurore, l'enfant martyre* (Jean-Yves Bigras, 1952). By focusing on Marie-Loup's demise in parallel with that of the French colonial regime, *Nouvelle-France* thus reinscribes Quebec's tradition of finding national heroes in martyrs. Whereas Indigenous studies critics would align its deployment of "sidekick" characters like Owashak and Acoona (who, incidentally, is killed in the bombardment sequence) with self-interested appropriations, *Nouvelle-France* does, at least, acknowledge the Indigenous presence in the colonial era, an aspect completely absent from the film adaptations of Fred Pellerin's *contes de village* (village tales).

Fanciful Imaginings of Quebec's Historical Capital:
Fred Pellerin on film

Maïna, Nouvelle-France, and even the colonial-era thriller *Rouge sang / The Storm Within* (Martin Doepner, 2013) clearly identify for viewers a concrete historical setting for their melodramatic or fantastical narratives. By adhering to the conventions of a certain genre of storytelling and with their clear engagement of a specific and collectively recognized period of history, they remain accessible to popular audiences in Quebec. These contrast markedly with the quirky and less generally accessible auteur films discussed in the third section of this chapter. Somewhere in between lie the vaguely historical adaptations of popular contemporary storyteller Fred Pellerin's *contes de village* (village tales), which nonetheless evoke a clichéd image of the national past. Reviving the lost art of the *conteux,* an itinerant storyteller who visited pioneer farms to entertain the *habitants,* in his stage shows, their recording on DVD, and publication as book-CD combos, Pellerin (b. 1976)[48] creates a fictional space, lost in time, but inspired by his real hometown of Saint-Élie-de-Caxton, projecting an imaginative vision of a Quebec that might have been but probably never was. Drawing on the oral tradition of French Canadian folktales to participate in a neo-nationalist reappropriation of this heritage, Pellerin's *contes de village* pastiche an already blurred, folkloric, and romanticized image of Quebec's rural, Catholic, homogeneously French Canadian past, lovingly poking fun at the various personality types, superstitions, and outmoded folkways of the *Anciens Canadiens,* updating these for the postmodern era, appealing to contemporary audiences of all ages hungry for a connection to their ancestors. Evocative of the image of rural Minnesota painted by Garrison Keillor in his syndicated radio segment "News from Lake Wobegon," Pellerin's works are also deeply and uniquely *québécois.*

Both nationalist artists, engaged in the promotion and preservation of Quebec's cultural heritage, it is not surprising that – prior to directing *Les rois mongols* (discussed in chapter 1) – actor Luc Picard found inspiration in Pellerin's outlandish tales, co-writing and directing their big screen adaptations, *Babine* (2008) and *Ésimésac* (2012). Their film aesthetic, designed by Nicolas Lepage, seemingly inspired by the bizarre imaginary worlds of French filmmakers Jean-Pierre Jeunet and Marc Caro in *Delicatessen* (1991) and *The City of Lost Children* (1995), nonetheless transmits a uniquely French Canadian sensibility. The charm of Pellerin's art lies in his extensive wordplay, which sometimes gets lost in the stories' translation into visual conventions; indeed, critics asked, "how can you transpose the marvellous onto the big screen?"[49] Although the film community recognized their efforts with seven Jutra nominations, *Babine* and *Ésimésac* only partially succeed at rendering concrete the mental pictures that Pellerin draws in words.[50] Pellerin's popular novels and their film adaptations continue to appeal to audiences later in the millennium; ten years after *Ésimésac,*

Francis Leclerc – son of musical icon Félix Leclerc – directed a new adaptation of Pellerin's *L'arracheuse de temps* (2020).

The very titles of *Babine* and *Ésimésac* reveal the process of adaptation to film conventions, each focusing on a single character to anchor the episodic anecdotes drawn from Pellerin's more cleverly titled story collections, *Dans mon village il y a belle Lurette* (2001), *Il faut prendre le taureau par les contes!* (2003), and *Comme une odeur de muscles* (2005).[51] The first film focuses on a Candide-like *ingénu*, Babine (Vincent-Guillaume Otis), "le fou de village parce qu'à cette époque-là chaque village avait son fou et chaque fou son village" (the village idiot because at that time every village had an idiot and every idiot a village), conceived when the Sorcière (Isabel Richer) had magical sex with the Forgeron Riopel (Gildor Roy). His name derives from his talent on the harmonica, the traditional instrument often called the *ruine-babines*, an iconic marker of Quebec's folk music heritage. Although the entire village, especially Le Vieux Curé (Julien Poulin), accepts and understands Babine, when Le Curé Neuf (Alexis Martin) arrives, a set of unfortunate circumstances leads to his persecution.

Concessions to the collaborative visual project of filmmaking involve Quebec's star system and linguistic simplification of the wordplay for a wider audience. Whereas Pellerin's listeners can hear, and readers can even more readily see wordplay on the page, thus creating their own mental image of these larger-than-life characters, in Picard's film viewers must *see* the star. Well-known, even beloved, actors play these characters with relish, make-up and costume partially transforming them into the stuff of myth, indicating the fairy tale nature of Pellerin's re-imagined pioneers of Quebec's second colonization of the *pays d'en haut*. Viewers immediately sympathize, then, with Le Vieux Curé, played by Julien Poulin, the beloved incarnation of Elvis Gratton, and Alexis Martin's past roles as a neurotic intellectual help render the Curé Neuf antipathetic. But the demands for a screen-friendly female star radically transform La Sorcière and with her viewer reception. Whereas Pellerin's tales draw on the fairy tale tradition of the wicked witch, describing her as old and unattractive, the films cast the younger and more attractive popular leading lady Isabel Richer in this role. Furthermore, in the interest of political correctness, her name is changed from the racially charged moniker "La Sauvagesse," in Pellerin's CD-books, to the less controversial La Sorcière. Ironically, this well-meaning change completely erases the Indigenous presence from this fanciful image of the national past. Similarly, when Luc Picard takes for himself a secondary character in Pellerin's *contes*, an inventor and shopkeeper originally named Brodain Tousseur,[52] the latter assumes a larger role in the film with a more conventional name, Toussaint Brodeur. Thus, while Québécois filmgoers recognize familiar figures from the province's star system, enhancing the film's marketability, this manoeuvre undermines the internal logic of Pellerin's tales.

Figure 2.2. Rendering the imaginary world of Pellerin into a visual image: The nostalgic depiction of a late nineteenth- or early twentieth-century pioneer village nestled into the Laurentian Mountains in *Babine*.

Babine and *Ésimésac* attempt to render the magic of Pellerin's *contes de village* concrete for viewers with establishing shots of a stylized frontier village set in, one presumes, the Laurentian Mountains, a significant site in the second colonization's land-clearing endeavours. Despite fantastical touches to costumes and architecture, the pioneer town contains the recognizable stock figures: a general storekeeper (Luc Picard), a blacksmith (Gildor Roy), a barber, a village priest, and so on. Both films' heroes result from prodigious, magical births, but these are sometimes altered for the *grand public* film, which adopts the language of accommodation absent in Pellerin's stories. Similarly, invoking the classic French fairy tale "Riquet à la Houppe,"[53] Babine was born with a hunchback, a physical trait the film does not reproduce. *Ésimésac* draws on the legendarily large size of French Canadian families; his mother, Madame Gélinas (Marie Brassard), already has an uncountable number of children and remains magically pregnant for years. Because he was carried so long in the womb, her prodigious offspring, adult-sized at the age of two, becomes the strongest man in the village. Indeed, a variation on Louis Cyr,[54] Ésimésac's (Nicola-Frank Vachon in his only lead role) trademark goggles also reference modern-day national hero Dédé Fortin of Les Colocs. His name (and the film's title) is a contraction of Onésime-Isaac Gélinas, a nod to both the biblical tradition and the unusual names taken in old-time Quebec, but it also resonates with regional toponyms taken from Indigenous languages, such as Lake Mégantic.

Despite their focus on the visual, *Babine* and *Ésimésac* also explicitly invoke the oral traditions from which they derive – Pellerin's own performances *and* the nineteenth- and early twentieth-century tales of Honoré Beaugrand, Louis Fréchette, Pamphile Le May, and others. *Babine* frames its narrative with Pellerin's own voice-over, signalling the "once-upon-a-time" of a near forgotten oral tradition: "L'histoire que je vas vous conter a se passé dans le temps où du temps, il y en avait encore, pour toujours, du temps, pour l'éternité et même après. C'était dans l'ancien temps … C'était dans le temps où on se racontait encore des histoires" (The story I'm gonna tell you happened in the time when there was still time, always, for eternity and even after). By situating their fairy tale "once upon a time" in an actual, physical time and space, these films operate a folklorization of the national past in a way that Pellerin's original tales did not. As Stéphan Gibeault notes, the *conteux* (storyteller) serves as a bridge between past and future;[55] Pellerin's stories, *as told*, are filled with wordplay that both idealizes and criticizes past and present together, interpellating contemporary listeners to value a sense of community that no longer prevails in post-national, neoliberal, globalized Quebec. Through his stage performances, oral recordings, and written words, the *conteux* Pellerin frequently brings the reader/listener back into the present during their telling, thus building a connection between past and present. This trait is far less present in the films,[56] which tend to distance the viewer from the characters and activities on-screen because they are so far-fetched. And yet, *Babine* and *Ésimésac* do foreground history as a form of storytelling set in a past time frame but also as pertinent to the present. Indeed, Le Vieux Curé's pocket watch is key to Babine's trials, and he knows that he must "prendre bien soin pour que le temps s'arrête jamais" (take good care of it so that time does not stop), suggesting movement and change rather than social stagnation. Indeed, as Zoé Protat observes, Pellerin offers "a tale, yes, but one that passes the limits of the fairy world with the ambition of offering a certain social comment."[57] The social message of both Pellerin's stories and their film adaptations is one of humanity, tolerance, and acceptance of difference: "Babine c'est le fou du village; faut prendre bien soin de lui. C'est un bien collectif" (Babine is the village idiot; we have to take good care of him. He's a collective asset). In contrast, Le Curé Neuf represents the close-mindedness of a bigoted, self-satisfied pre–Quiet Revolution Quebec. Similarly, *Ésimésac*'s message is one of building community through mutual aid, rather than seeking individual profit and gain, a critique that targets contemporary neoliberal Quebec.[58]

Yet, despite its nods to the acceptance of difference, the never-never land of Saint-Élie-de-Caxton remains homogeneously white and francophone. In an incisive analysis of contemporary adaptations of fairy tales, Cristina Bachilega asks, "who is reactivating a fairy-tale poetics of wonder and for whom?"[59] Despite the overt message of accommodation, in the identity politics of a so-called post-nationalist Quebec, Pellerin's project feeds the dying embers of ethnic nationalism, magically transporting audiences to a "simpler" time, when Québécois identity could still be conceived as homogeneously French Canadian. The nostalgic elements of *Babine* and *Ésimésac* reinforce communal and identitary ties between "died-in-the-wool" French Canadians, and Pellerin undeniably participates in the franco-nationalist project proclaimed on Québec's licence plate motto, *Je me souviens*. The paratextual material – epigraphical citations, prefaces, and a final track on the CD – as well as the tales themselves underscore the importance of *la mémoire*, memory, in community building. And yet, Pellerin's work – and to a lesser extent its film adaptations – offers a discourse of resistance and transformation that pertain both to the "yesteryear" and the clerico-nationalist traditional ideology of colonization associated with it, as well as to the contemporary dominant ideology of an increasingly post-national, neoliberal Quebec of today. This paradoxical attitude, which at once nostalgically exhorts viewers to remember national *lieux de mémoire* while at the same time criticizing Quebec society, past and present, recurs in a corpus of auteur films that stylistically draw upon and contribute to the historical imaginary.

Auteur (Re)visions of Sites of Memory: The Historical Fantasies of André Forcier and Olivier Asselin

Despite their quirkiness and largely because of Pellerin's popular success and Picard's cultural capital, *Babine* and *Ésimésac*, with their fairy tale structure and historical referents, nonetheless remain largely accessible to a general audience in Quebec. In contrast, several auteur directors have produced highly singular visions of the past, visions that clearly do not seek the lowest common denominator audience typical of the popular film, visions so quirky that they sometimes alienate even viewers convinced of the value of the art film (myself included). But Quebec's institutional critics, who privilege auteur over *grand public* cinema, consistently praise them, and Quebec's and Canada's film funding institutions continue to approve projects by the relatively less accessible directors André Forcier and Olivier Asselin.

A well-established, albeit quirky filmmaker, with the first of his fourteen fiction features dating back to 1971, André Forcier (b. 1947) continued to write and direct through the first two decades of the new millennium, including several films that engage various historical moments in sometimes acerbic and sometimes frivolous ways. A true *québécois* auteur, Forcier rejects the Hollywoodization of the national cinema,[60] largely defying genre conventions, eschewing techniques that draw viewers in and manipulate reactions, calling attention to the fact that what happens on-screen is *not* an exact reflection of any historical or contemporary reality. Indeed, Pierre Barrette describes Forcier's style as "multiform, irreducible, largely incomprehensible."[61] Johanne Sloan, writing of

The Countess of Baton Rouge (1997), set in 1968, observes of Forcier's period pieces that

> In these films … the past surges up, but veers between tragic and comic modes of emplotment and between realistic and dreamlike modes of pictorialization. If Forcier's films share something with the tradition of Latin American magic realism, it is in the sense that the surreal dimension of Forcier's work relates to the vagaries of collective memory and serves to illuminate Québécois cultural identity and history in a new way.[62]

Forcier's nostalgia for the 1940s and 1950s appears in his recent films. *Les fleurs oubliées / Forgotten Flowers* (2019) memorializes an iconic figure in the construction of Quebec as a territory through the denomination of its flora and fauna, Frère Marie-Victorin (né Conrad Kerouac, 1885–1944), founder of Montreal's botanical gardens and author of *La flore laurentienne* (1935). In an extreme expression of Forcier's whimsy, the botanist returns from beyond to encourage a present-day green activist (Roy Dupuis) and commits acts of eco-terrorism. This film constructs the environmental protector, Frère Marie-Victorin (Yves Jacques), as a *lieu de mémoire*, human, but also deeply ethical, refusing to act on his sexual attraction to his young female assistant. Conversely, *Embrasse-moi comme tu m'aimes / Kiss Me Like a Lover* (2016) exploits incestuous sexual desire to develop a somewhat perverse national allegory, invoking a nostalgic array of minor *lieux de mémoire*. It also engages the emergence of contemporary discourses on national identity, linking them to Canadian participation in World War II. In contrast, however, with Simon Lavoie's *Le déserteur* (2008), a social realist, historical dramatization of a real-life incident, focusing on the injustice of the shooting of a conscripted French Canadian who deserts the army, Forcier's carnivalesque approach distances viewers from his characters. Critics called attention to the auteur's engagement with the historical imaginary, describing this film as "history reinvented," but also depicting the past it invokes as somewhere "between reality and the imaginary."[63]

Like *Nouvelle-France*, Forcier's film invokes caricatures of real figures from history alongside idiosyncratic fictional characters. For example, *Embrasse-moi* casts iconic filmmaker Denys Arcand as French Canadian political economist Édouard Montpetit (1881–1954). His lectures on the relationship between economics and the national question at the Université de Montréal inspire a *prise de conscience* for the film's fictional hero, Pierre (Émile Schneider), and his love interest, the budding feminist Marguerite St-Germain (Mylène Mackay). Unfortunately, a series of over-the-top misadventures prevents their union, including Pierre's frequent hallucinations of his beautiful, but jealous and wheelchair-bound twin sister, Berthe. Her repeated (and often hysterical) requests for him to, as the title suggests, kiss her like a lover would – as he bathes her or reads Zola's *Nana* to her before tucking her into bed – are more disturbing because the role is played by Juliette Gosselin, a young actress whom viewers have watched grow up on-screen since she first appeared as the fey child France, Marie-Loup Carignan's daughter, in *Nouvelle-France*. Although Pierre is finally able to rid himself of Berthe's spectre, passionately kissing Marguerite at what appears to be the film's conclusion, Forcier leaves viewers instead with a final fantasy sequence depicting an able-bodied Berthe chasing Pierre's "truck" (as he calls it), jumping into its bed, glaring ferociously, almost like a feral child at the camera. *Embrasse-moi's* confused and confusing message appears to be that having rid itself of a crippled past, post-war Quebec's modern youth can now move forward to build the nation's future.

Forcier's carnivalesque depiction of "Montréal 1940," as a title card indicates, nonetheless engages an evolving national identity, partially figured through various characters' attitudes about Canada's role in World War II. At the film's opening, Pierre explicitly supports the war effort, expressing romantic notions about heroism on the battlefield; his attitude divides the family, as his wheelchair-bound twin, Berthe, reacts hysterically to his appearance in uniform. Their dialogue immediately sets the political backdrop for Forcier's surrealist Québécois family romance:

> BERTHE : Je veux pas que tu meures en guerre! Qui c'est qui mettras des fleurs sur ton tombeau? La conscription s'en vient.
> PIERRE : La conscription c'est pas pour demain. Mackenzie King puis ses Anglos ont peur de la guerre civile.
> BERTHE : Si t'es conscrit, jure-moi qu'on ira se cacher dans une cabane à chasse … Comme deux amoureux.

> BERTHE: I don't want you to die in the war! Who will put flowers on your grave? The draft is coming.
> PIERRE: The draft is not coming anytime soon. Mackenzie King and his Anglos are afraid of civil war.
> BERTHE: If you are drafted, swear that we'll go hide in a hunting cabin … Like two lovers.

Repeatedly designated as *folle* (crazy), Berthe is needy and manipulative, as well as openly seductive towards her brother, haunting his dreams as an able-bodied vamp; jealous and vindictive, her unregulated sexual desire causes poltergeist-like activity in their home. Even after she has found love and married a middle-aged Italian widower, Élio Morelli (Tony Nardi), she refuses to relinquish her hold on Pierre, sending her husband into her widowed mother's (Céline Bonnier) arms. Morelli's ethnicity provides Forcier a pretext for invoking the Italian presence in Montreal, Italy's role in World War II, and another minor *lieu de mémoire*, real-life

French Canadian tenor Raoul Francoeur (Marc Hervieux), tutored in Italian diction by Morelli.

Pierre's uniform, however, is not that of the Canadian Armed Forces, but rather that of a paramilitary drill unit led by Sergeant Boileau (Julien Poulin), a stereotypically ambivalent working-class, "colonized" Québécois, a local personality type that Poulin had incarnated in Pierre Falardeau's Elvis Gratton films. While indoctrinating the young men during drill, Boileau unwittingly reveals their true function in an imperial conflict: "Atta boy! On est des beaux et des bons Canadiens Français qui marchent pour l'Empire Brittanique ... Si vous voulez sauver votre peau, engagez-vous drette-là. Si vous attendez la conscription vous serez sur la première ligne pour servir à chair à canon" (Good boy! We're good and handsome French Canadians marching for the British Empire ... If you want to save your skin, join right now! If you wait for conscription, you'll be on the front lines serving as cannon fodder). In addition to suggesting the British Empire's treatment of its subjects like dogs ("Atta boy!"), his discourse manipulates young men to volunteer, at the same time revealing a critical awareness of colonial troops' ultimate purpose as cannon fodder. French Canadians' conflicted relationship to empire further appears at the official recruiting station, which sports a banner reading, "Braves Canadiens-Français! Enrôlez-vous pour sauver la mère patrie" (Brave French Canadians! Enlist now to save the mother country). Here, specifically *French* Canadians are interpellated through their sentimental connection to the former colonial metropole, their "mother country" ostensibly being France. Finally, Forcier invokes US cultural imperialism in his portrait of Marguerite's first suitor and Pierre's best friend, Ollier Allard (Luca Asselin), and his father, Elphège (Réal Bossé). Besides caricaturing an "authentic" working-class French Canadian masculinity, their love of baseball — which also invokes Gilles Carle's classic *Les Plouffe* (1981) — identifies them clearly as North American, but also perhaps as colonized in a different way. Their appreciation of a sport symbolic of the United States suggests their alienation as French Canadians, having internalized a continental discourse of American — that, is US — cultural superiority. Taxi driver Elphège dreams of a career in the American big leagues for Ollier, who met Joe DiMaggio at the Yankee's training camp. *Dompé* (dumped; an anglicism) by Marguerite, however, Ollier enlists and heroically sacrifices his life for his platoon mates by falling on a live grenade. Forcier's perhaps ambivalent depiction of his various characters blurs the intent and target of his social satire. On the one hand, as salt-of-the-earth types, the Olliers are more sympathetic characters than the film's leads; but on the other, they are also lampooned as naive bumpkins, deluded by political narratives that lead them to give up their lives for the colonial empire. Ultimately, Forcier's ambiguous approach leaves room for readings not just as parody, but also as pastiche, sometimes conceived of as a "loving parody." Through all these layers of distancing, however, Forcier still returns to such historical points of reference as the Conscription controversy, reminding contemporary viewers of the franco-nationalist narrative of British oppression, but doing so in an idiosyncratically ludic, rather than dramatic, manner. To his credit, Forcier refuses to manipulate viewer emotions in the manner of a Falardeau; rather, he rejects viewer immersion in his fiction, adopting instead the technique of a Brechtian *Verfremdungseffekt*, an estrangement to allow for critical distancing.

Marguerite also initially supports the war effort. A student at the École normale, she begins to strive for more than teaching young women the domestic curriculum to which they were limited. Above all, she seeks escape from her stereotypically working-class Montreal family; her mother (Pascale Montpetit) is an oppressed *dévote*, her father (Roy Dupuis) a worthless alcoholic. Her summer job at the Dupré & fils department store shows her a more privileged side of Montreal society and introduces another target for Forcier's critico-nostalgic depiction of pre–Quiet Revolution Quebec, the then prevalent ethnic nationalism that conceived of French Canadians as a "race." As an elevator attendant, Marguerite greets customers: "Bienvenue chez Dupré & fils, le plus grand magasin à rayons au service de notre race" (Welcome to Dupré & Son, the biggest department store to serve our race). Philippe Dupré (Patrick Drolet), the *fils* (son) of the store's name and founder, is in love with her, and he later enlists in the air corps to impress her. An earnest bore who speaks only in clichés, Dupré concludes their conversation asserting that "Une grande race a besoin d'un grand magasin" (A great race needs a great department store). His dictum offers a wordplay on the term *grand magasin*, which literally is "great/big store," but when used together means "department store." Incarnating francophone bourgeois elites who profit by exploiting the masses, when he returns from the front, a war hero who has lost his legs, Dupré helps assure the financial well-being of the Sauvageau clan. Pierre and Élio have invented together a high-tech wheelchair with a seat that raises its user to eye level with the rest of the world. Given the numerous casualties after Dieppe, Dupré orders seven hundred units, considering it his duty to "commercialiser vos fauteuils roulants géants pour les infirmes de notre race!" (market your giant wheelchairs for the infirm of our race). Once again, Forcier uses exaggeration to call attention to the naivety of those who listen to master narratives, while also highlighting the profitability of war.

Forcier's scenario, co-written with Linda Pinet, imagines Pierre escaping conscription first by finding a secret agreement between the mayor of Montreal and Mackenzie King to fund twelve new police officers among the conscripts. He joins the mounted police, temporarily assisting their mission, as stated by Capitaine Turgeon (Pierre Verville), to "débarasser Montréal des tapettes" (rid Montreal of faggots). Marguerite's brother Réal Antoine Bertrand is having an affair with the parish priest and so refuses to help Pierre get in touch with Marguerite, who fled Montreal after killing her father with a hot iron after catching him sexually abusing her younger sister (Émi Chicoine). When a disappointed Pierre again threatens to enlist, Berthe asks Élio to have her brother beaten by mafiosi, leaving him permanently crippled, needing a cane to walk. The trope of incest is clearly overdetermined in this film, appearing in multiple family relationships, and it results in abuse like this. Forcier embraces the mythology of the Quebec family romance, but his absurd treatment defuses some of its power.

Although his production company is named Les Films du Paria, Forcier's ability to gain funding for such a far-fetched product reveals that he is anything but a pariah-like outsider for Quebec's filmmaking institutions. Despite the extent to which he stretches the historical imaginary, his work remains deeply territorialized and, for all its idiosyncratic self-indulgences, is viewed as reflective of a certain collective self-image.[64] Eschewing the techniques of Hollywood and its genres, Forcier also eschews reaching larger, popular, mass audiences; playing to a small group of artistic and intellectual insiders, he perhaps plays devil's advocate. As Marcia Landy observes, just as they serve to construct the nation, "history and memory have also played a part in destabilizing conceptions of the nation."[65]

Although filmed earlier than *Embrasse-moi*, Forcier's *Je me souviens* (2010)[66] follows it chronologically, explicitly set in 1949 with a second sequence around 1956. Depicting francophone activism developing prior to 1960 in its stylized fictionalization of the Abitibi mine strikes that played a key role in the development of the contemporary nationalist movement, Forcier once again chooses a national *lieu de mémoire* as the target of his satire.[67] Filmed completely in black and white, an artistic choice that accuses the "black and white" thinking of the past and signals the *Grande Noirceur* as a colourless, bygone era, Forcier's *Je me souviens* exploits clichés about the period of Quebec's history just prior to the Quiet Revolution, paying at the same time homage to Claude Jutra's canonical *Mon oncle Antoine* (1971), set in the same place and time, also focalized through the eyes of a boy. But *Je me souviens* remembers Quebec's past leaders, political, economic, and religious, viewed in a fun-house mirror, with its parodies of "le Chef," as then-Premier Maurice Duplessis was known, wealthy anglophone mine owners, and the local bishop. Forcier depicts Duplessis (Michel Barrette), accused in real life of allowing foreign and anglophone interests to exploit Quebec's natural resources while refusing federal funding for social programs, as mercilessly browbeating his staff and opponents while rewarding obedient toadies. A conversation between the prime minister and (the apparently fictional) Mgr. Eugène Madore (Rémy Girard) following reports of unionizing activity in the Sullidor mine reveals the film's hyperbolic exaggeration of received images of historical figures:

DUPLESSIS : Eugène, je suis inquiet pour le Sullidor avec ce qui se passe à Asbestos.
Un syndicat et communiste. C'est votre devoir d'éduquer le petit peuple.

MGR. MADORE : Rassurez-vous, Maurice. J'ai suggéré à Monsieur Taylor d'engager
les orphelins comme mineurs apprentis … Les orphelins vont travailler corps et
âmes pour délivrer le Sullidor de l'enfer du communisme.
DUPLESSIS : Eugène, bravo au nom de la raison d'état. Enfin ces petits bâtards seront
utiles à la province.

DUPLESSIS: Eugène, I'm worried about Sullidor with what's going on at Asbestos.
A communist union. It's your duty to educate the little people.
MGR. MADORE: Rest assured, Maurice. I suggested to Mr. Taylor that he hire orphans
as apprentice miners … The orphans will work body and soul to save Sullidor
from the hell of communism.
DUPLESSIS: Eugène, bravo in the name of *raison d'état*. Finally, these little bastards will
be useful to the province.

This exchange, in addition to exploiting Duplessis's virulent anti-communism
and his counting on the church's traditionalist values to keep the people in
check, also refers to the scandal referred to as "Duplessis's Orphans."[68] Under
Duplessis's regime numerous orphans were placed in mental institutions so that
the state could cheaply ensure their care, and *Je me souviens*'s bishop proposes
to put them to work in the mine as scabs. His program fails catastrophically, as
one dies in a mine accident and another is eaten by a wolf, an example of the
film's elastic relationship with verisimilitude. Another orphan replaces the Seeing Eye dog of Mrs. Taylor (France Castel), the blind but *bonne vivante* wife of
the wealthy mine owner; like the dog, perhaps the strapping teenager will also
sleep in her bed, she suggestively asserts. Not only does Forcier parallel anglophone exploitation of francophones with child sexual abuse, but he also invokes
the trope of the mistreated child ever-present in Quebec film history, discussed
in chapter 3.

In addition to the cynicism of Quebec's francophone elites, *Je me souviens* parodies the anglophone capitalists with whom they are figuratively in bed. Belonging to the margins of the British colonial elite, Iram Taylor (Doris St-Pierre)
believes that South Africa is paradise on earth, signalling his racism through his
treatment of a Black servant. His status as foreigner in Abitibi is made clear when
his toady, the complicit French Canadian foreman Richard Bombardier (David
Boutin), proposes to take him moose hunting. Instead, Iram shows off the zebra
skin from his African safari. To underscore his film's anti-imperial sentiments,
Forcier parallels French Canadian oppression by the British Empire to that of
Ireland, involving far-fetched situations, including Roy Dupuis's character, Liam
Hennessey, speaking Gaelic and then teaching the Irish language to a disturbed
child, Némésis (Alice Morel-Michaud). Her biographical trajectory allows for
further references to other historical scandals recently portrayed on film, as the
child actress cast in the role of Némésis had portrayed the emblematic abused

child in *Aurore*, and the administration of electroshock and her otherwise brutal treatment by nuns invokes that of singer Alys Robi, institutionalized in a mental hospital staffed by nuns, depicted in *Ma vie en cinémascope* (discussed in chapters 3 and 4).

For Forcier, nothing is sacred; whereas *Je me souviens*'s pro-union, populist agenda is clear, it lampoons even sympathetic characters, including union activists Robert Sincennes (Pierre-Luc Brillant) and Roch Devos (Mario Saint-Amand), and other members of the "Parti ouvrier progressiste," thus named, the characters explain, because the Communist Party is illegal in Canada. Although loved by his wife (Hélène Bourgeois Leclerc) and idolized by his son, the focalizing child character to which many other nostalgic period pieces have recourse (see chapter 5), neither Sincennes nor Devos can resist the temptations of an attractive local widow, Mathilde Bombardier (Céline Bonnier). After her husband's ridiculous accidental death – he slipped and fell on a shard of glass from a broken champagne bottle as they celebrated his collaboration with Mr. Taylor – she swears vengeance and seduces the two otherwise upstanding union organizers, conceiving Némésis in hate rather than love.

It is difficult to take this film seriously, and, indeed, Forcier wants viewers precisely to laugh at *all* of Quebec's sacred cows, not just the usual ones. Despite its deployment of historical clichés, generally to parodic effect, *Je me souviens* focuses viewers upon the winds of change blowing prior to 1960, thus nuancing the myth of the Quiet Revolution as marking the abrupt advent of modernity in the province. Indeed, Marc-André Lussier praised the film as revealing "a hidden page in Quebec's history, that of the 1950s. A time of the Grande Noirceur [Great Darkness], but also a time when militantism began to buck in the harness."[67] Lussier's comment signals how, despite its exaggerations and idiosyncrasies, Forcier's cinema participates in the construction of the national historical imaginary, at least for the intellectual, artistic, and literary elite.

Forcier's excessive productivity, consistently supported by cinematic institutions, contrasts with the tiny corpus of another quirky auteur, Olivier Asselin,[70] whose two twenty-first-century films depict Québécois characters as actors on the international historical stage. A film professor, his works are exercises in cinematic style and photographic effects, spectacles that also engage in social critiques with a carnivalesque approach to characterization, like that of Forcier. His earlier historical fantasy, *Un capitalisme sentimental / A Sentimental Capitalism* (2008), opens self-referentially as its rather ordinary protagonist, Fernande Bouvier (played by Asselin's co-scenarist Lucille Fluet), crosses the Atlantic to become a market commodity in New York and is eventually involved in the 1929 stock market crash of Black Tuesday. Described as a "comédie philosophique"[71] (philosophical comedy) rather than a historical film, and even including musical numbers, *Un capitalisme sentimental* dialogues on the commodification of art and the capitalist system in general. Indeed, this film offers very little that is specific to Quebec, and perhaps that characteristic, which is reproduced across his body of work, partly explains the small size of Asselin's oeuvre, as funding institutions possibly opt for specificity over universality. Indeed, Marcel Jean underscores the director's idiosyncratic style.[72] Asselin's polished aesthetic, combining colour and black-and-white footage to evoke retro film styles ranging from Expressionism through film noir, privileges the visual image over narrative consistency or historical verisimilitude, and he continues in this vein in his next film.

Set in 1944 with flashbacks to 1927 and 1933, *Le cyclotron / The Cyclotron* (2016) directly engages World War II, but unlike Simon Lavoie's *Le déserteur* (2008), a historical film per se rooted deeply in the territory of Quebec, or even Forcier's Montreal-set parody of the Conscription era, *Embrasse-moi comme tu m'aimes*, Asselin sets his intrigue largely in Europe.[73] As in his previous film, Asselin takes liberties with historical fact, invoking various Western *lieux de mémoire* and linking the race for the atomic bomb with speculation about different possible outcomes to the conflict. Described as "somewhere between popular film and demanding experimentation,"[74] *Le cyclotron* offers a brilliant example of Québécois directors' technical mastery of the cinematic medium, combining historical stock footage and live-action sequences that actively play with framing and perspective, both integrated through sophisticated montage into certain decors requiring special effects to animate.

Opening titles set the context for *Le cyclotron*'s period thriller intrigue, indicating that "Le film qui suit est inspiré de faits historiques" (The following film is inspired by historical facts). Those historical facts include developments in theoretical physics, Einstein's theory of relativity, and Niels Bohr's quantum mechanics; in addition to fuelling the creation of the atomic bomb, these theories "bouleversent notre conception de la réalité" (upset our conception of reality). *Le cyclotron* itself will play with characters' (and viewers') conceptions of historical reality as scientist turned spy Simone (Lucille Fluet) and her target (and ex-lover), physicist Éric Scherrer (Mark Antony Krupa), convince a Nazi science officer, König (Paul Ahmarani), that the Berlin–Paris express train they ride carries an atomic device, armed via a tiny cyclotron set in a timepiece. König, believing that the train is bound for Paris, hopes to destroy the newly liberated French capital for the glory of the Third Reich. He descends with his SS assistants, taking Éric hostage and sending Simone to (as he believes) her certain death. Holed up in a bunker, using the famous parable of Schrödinger's cat[75] to illustrate how quantum mechanics allows for the simultaneous existence of parallel realities, Éric convinces his captors not only that they must remain isolated long enough for radioactive fallout to clear, but that until they emerge the possibility that Berlin, instead of Paris, might be destroyed remains valid. Side-by-side sequences support this hypothesis, showing alternate versions of Simone's arrival: one in Paris followed by newsreels of Hitler's victory, another in Berlin resulting in the Allied victory over the Third Reich. When the men finally emerge from the bunker, they learn the actual outcome of the war involving a third possibility, unanticipated by the Europeans: the Americans' development of the atomic bomb and destruction of Hiroshima. Éric's device had failed altogether.

An epilogue sequence in 1948 stages Simone's post-war encounter with König that signals US recruitment of former Nazis to develop Cold War atomic weaponry. The naive questions of her daughter, Anna (conceived on the train with Éric), underscores the subjective nature of reality and invokes the timeless problem of memory in Quebec through Simone's description of König as "un mauvais souvenir" (a bad memory). Anna also asks, "Où est-ce qu'elles vont les histoires?" (Where do stories go?). Her mother replies, "Elles restent dans nos têtes … comme les souvenirs" (They stay in our heads … like memories). This final colour sequence (there have been several throughout) cuts back to the film's dominant black-and-white imagery to a complex montage of thousands of images and stories all occurring at once, suggesting again the film's exploration of parallel realities, before the closing credits roll.

Set entirely in Europe and the United Kingdom, also referencing the United States, the Soviet Union, and Japan, *Le cyclotron* refuses to mention Canada or Quebec; Asselin thus resists the navel gazing often attributed to Quebec national cinema. At the same time, however, he engages its core questions of memory and possibility, suggesting his film's potential for a reading as national allegory, the status of Schrödinger's cat – dead or alive, dead and alive – a metaphor for Quebec's relationship to sovereignty. Above all, Asselin foregrounds the subjective nature of reality and the role that storytelling plays in its construction, using the magic of film to illustrate various possible outcomes, but also to denounce nationalist fanaticism of the variety deployed by Hitler and to implicate the ends-justify-the-means philosophy of the United States, as well. Because of their engagement with international events outside of Quebec, however, both of Asselin's films remain more accessible to an international art film audience than any of Forcier's. Well received for its technical mastery in Quebec,[76] unfortunately its extremely limited release also limits access outside Quebec to Asselin's unique filmic vision.[77] While few of the younger filmmakers of the *renouveau* have ventured away from social realist film techniques, seemingly returning to the nation's *cinéma direct* tradition after the *nouvelle génération* had strayed from it, Maxime Giroux's historical fantasy *La Grande Noirceur* in some ways echoes Asselin's imaginative approach to the period film.

Pour en finir avec la Grande Noirceur: Maxime Giroux's *La Grande Noirceur*

Having documented often grim realities about the alienation of the contemporary Québécois subject,[78] several young filmmakers of the *renouveau québécois* turned to the historical imaginary, tracing the origins of the national malaise. Whereas some of these have adopted realist or literary approaches to the past, like Simon Lavoie in *Le déserteur* (2008) and *Le torrent* (2017) and Mathieu Denis in *Corbo* (2014), their peer Maxime Giroux (b. 1976) looked to historical fantasy to engage a period of Quebec's past that has reached mythic proportions, as seen in the film corpus explored in chapter 3. The title of *La Grande Noirceur / The Great Darkened Days* (2018) refers to a period most directly associated with the mandates of conservative leader Maurice Duplessis as premier of Quebec (1936–9; 1944–59), but which has become mythologized to extend farther into the past. Literally translated as "the Great Darkness," the *Grande Noirceur* was reconstructed in Quebec's historiography as a sort of provincial dark age. According to this myth, which developed after the electoral triumph of the Liberal Party in 1960 and the modernizing reforms of the so-called Quiet Revolution, French Canadians had long clung to a backward-looking, traditionalist, rural way of life supported by the dominant clerico-nationalist ideology. The Catholic Church's strict morality fuelled their sense of inferiority, thus enabling their continued oppression and exploitation. Historians have, of course, since questioned the simplicity of the dual myth of the *Grande Noirceur* / Quiet Revolution,[79] but their lingering status as *lieux de mémoire* appears clearly in the twenty-first-century film corpus, particularly those considered in chapters 3 and 4. In contrast with Lavoie's rigorously documented *Le déserteur*, Giroux invokes this period directly in his fantastical account of a World War II–era deserter's adventures in the American West in *La Grande Noirceur*. Not only does Giroux's historical fantasy grapple with the national myth of French Canadian abjection and stage a moment of liberation; it also makes a scathing comment on the illusory nature of the American dream.

La Grande Noirceur opens, like so many films in this corpus, with a voice-over narration, in which the protagonist, Philippe (Martin Dubreuil), recites (in English with a French Canadian accent) an ethic for humanity that his experiences to come, set against the vague backdrop of World War II, will completely negate: "We all want to love each other … We all want to help one another. Human beings are like that." He does so over an extreme close-up as he paints a Hitler-style moustache on his upper lip; the following sequence, accompanied by eerily dissonant orchestral music by Olivier Alary, reveals that he is a participant in a contest for the best imitation of Charlie Chaplin, whose philosophical ideals he was quoting. Winning the contest, he is soon robbed of his ten-dollar prize by three American bullies who outstrip the naked French Canadian (he has paid a quarter for a shower) in size and aggression. As he removes the cash from his victim's hanging trousers, their leader (Buddy Duress) begins a pattern for the film, in which Philippe will be given advice by those he meets: "I'll show you how it works around here. From your pocket to mine." Although the plucky French Canadian gives chase to his tormenters through an indeterminate industrial facility, they leave him only a duffel bag containing his Charlie Chaplin costume and a thin blanket. The Chaplin costume opens the film out of its depiction of a "typical Québécois loser" and his struggle to survive, allowing it to engage with an array of forms of oppression from beyond the national borders. Chaplin's make-up invokes Adolf Hitler, but Chaplin himself was, of course, Jewish and parodied the Führer in *The Great Dictator* (1940); these references, however, can be turned back around to Quebec's own dictator, Maurice Duplessis, who has been compared to European fascists Francisco Franco and Benito Mussolini.

Bizarrely clad in the outsized wool jacket and trousers of Chaplin's signature attire, the draft dodger Philippe begins a trek through the American West, en route to shelter at an uncle's home in Detroit. As he travels, largely along the rails, through a backdrop of stunning rock formations and apparent ghost towns – stylishly shot by Sara Mishara in Nevada's high plains dessert – Philippe encounters individuals whose strangeness exceeds the limits of the historical imaginary, entering the realm of fantasy. The first of these, Hector Batignole (Reda Kateb), presents himself as a talent scout and offers Philippe a lift; on learning that his passenger is from Montreal, the Frenchman describes Quebec as "Ah, la Nouvelle-France. C'est l'Amérique là-bas aussi" (Ah, New France. It's America there, too), signalling his misconception of the French-speaking province as both still lost in the historical past, but also newly recolonized into a broader American culture. As Hector offers to help Philippe with his entertainment career, a radio news bulletin interrupts with a pastiche speech by General Patton (Bruce Dinsmore), characterizing "real Americans" as bullies who love to fight, winners intolerant of losers. Visibly upset by the aggression of this discourse, the determined French Canadian continues eastward alone. He wakes covered in snow and makes his way to an apparently deserted town; after finding an abandoned lunch pail, he eats but is later shot at by a mysterious figure. Finding shelter underground, Philippe encounters an even stranger individual than the larger-than-life Hector. Her arm in a sling and toting a firearm, Helen (Sarah Gadon) presents herself as a widow and introduces her pet dog, Rosie (Soko); instead of an animal, chained to the floor is a young woman in a bright red dress forced to perform this role for her captor. Playing along with the crazy woman's charade, Philippe attempts to escape with Rosie only to face a more formidable foe. The entire town appears to be a trap, ruled by the mysterious Lester, who, abetted by Hector and Helen, runs a business of kidnaping and selling humans for all purposes to the highest bidder. The invented situation invokes the slave trade and the concentration camp, perhaps aligning the hapless French Canadian with other oppressed groups throughout history.

Played by well-known French actor Romain Duris, Lester scorns French Canadians, sneering at Philippe's family photos: "Regarde-moi ces illettrés. Ces pauvres cons. C'est un minable votre Chaplin. On va jamais le vendre" (Look at these illiterates. Poor schmucks. Your Chaplin is pathetic. We'll never be able to sell him). Treated to a narrative meant to undermine his self-confidence and instill a sense of inferiority, Philippe's victimhood appears complete when, after failing to obey the rules laid out by Lester, he is tortured and then encased in clay up to his neck. Lester explains to Philippe that he was once like him, but he adapted, even flourished in America: "Ce pays me permet de faire tout ce que je veux. Il me donne tout. Il me rend tout. Il me permet de renaître. Il fait de moi son fils glorieux, violent et puissant. Il y a une certaine beauté … Il n'y a pas de limites ici. Pas de retenu" (This country allows me to do anything I want. It gives me everything. It returns everything to me. It allows me to be reborn. It makes me its glorious son, violent and powerful. There is a certain beauty … There are no limits here. No restraint). His discourse reveals that the American dream is for exploiters, perhaps also explaining Giroux's choice of setting, the limitless skies of the Western landscape, which figure these violent and barren possibilities. Despite the apparent hopelessness of his situation, Philippe determines to help Rosie, and when Lester frees him, although still covered in mud, the French Canadian resists. Removing from its hiding place in his sock a large-calibre rifle shell that he stole from Helen, Philippe stabs the hubristic Lester in the neck and flees. Not completely trodden down, he performs an act of resistance, attempting to take his destiny in his hands and escape this oppression.

After a black screen, *La Grande Noirceur*'s elliptic scenario, co-written by Giroux with Simon Beaulieu and Alexandre Laferrière, next jumps to Philippe walking through a railroad tunnel towards the sun. Arriving at a town near sunset, he sees a movie screen erected outside, on which – their faces filled with wonder – children watch images (assembled from World War I stock footage) depicting the horrors of war, including bombed cities, the exodus of refugees, and, finally, graphic close-ups of the *gueules-cassées*, French soldiers whose faces have been destroyed in the first fully technologized conflict. After calling his mother and breaking down under duress, but also expressing his determination to return home, Philippe has a final, strange encounter with a travelling salesman (Cody Fern). His briefcase full of "Treasure Chest" cigarettes (the package designed like that of the iconic Lucky Strike) promises the escape people need from their cares, a final comment on consumerism and addiction. In the film's only direct reference to its title, the salesman advises Philippe (in English) to "Embrace what's coming – the great darkened days of natural decay and everything will be just fine … Just let it go." Philippe resists: "But I don't want to let go. I want to see my people." Accepting the cigarette, nonetheless, he coughs and chokes, waking the next morning to find a magical gift: The salesman has restored his original ten dollars and left two packs of cigarettes. He now walks off with determination, even hope; stopping to wash the mud stains off his clothing, he strides through grassy plains, the mountains in backdrop against a bright blue sky. A penultimate shot of Philippe in his Chaplin suit invokes René Magritte's *Man in a Bowler Hat* (1964), and the film concludes as he sits in a train looking out the window at the mountains and desert, appearing finally to have found his way back east, towards home.

Rather than depicting Quebec itself during the *Grande Noirceur*, Giroux's historical allegory traces the steps from victimhood towards an uncertain enlightenment of an individual French Canadian who has tried to escape Quebec's inevitable engagement in world affairs. By evading the draft, Philippe has expressed a first form of resistance to colonial oppression from the European metropole, refusing to participate in war on behalf of the British Empire; he has fled, however, to a more insidious – because more morally ambiguous – locale in the mythical American West. Although he again shows courage and resistance to its more overt forms of exploitation and violence, Philippe appears to succumb to the more insidious lure of commercialism, accepting the salesman's gift. The film's ambiguously hopeful ending, in which the French Canadian emerges from the Great Darkness of colonial conflict and human oppression through violence into the light of the gentler enslavement that modern consumerism represents, comments cynically on contemporary Quebec as having simply exchanged one form of domination for another, with the Quiet Revolution's reforms later followed by the province's adoption of neoliberal consumer values. It nonetheless features a portrait of French Canadian resistance and survival in its protagonist. Martin Dubreuil's performance is superb, and his casting is meaningful, as well, for the actor has long played secondary roles and often ones that portray him as a typical Québécois loser or victim, and he does justice to this first lead role in a major production.

Conclusion

According to Denis Bachand and Annie Lise Clément, it is "a sign of maturity … [that] more and more genre films are being made in Quebec."[80] A further sign of the cinematic industry's maturity in twenty-first-century Quebec is the increasingly specialized subdivision of those genres, allowing for the production of, for example, a historical thriller like *Rouge sang* or a historical horror comedy like *Le poil de la bête*. The exponential increase in film production since the year 2000 affords filmmakers a new range of possibilities to explore the historical imaginary, playing with and personalizing for Quebec's audiences the full array of Hollywood genres and their hybrids. The risks taken by auteur filmmakers like Forcier, Asselin, and Giroux attest in a different way to the maturity of Quebec cinema. They reveal that producers and funding institutions feel that they can afford to support idiosyncratic artists whose films are likely to be unprofitable but will contribute to the prestige of the national cinema. The existence of films like *Le cyclotron* or *La Grande Noirceur* belies institutional film critics' recurring lament that a film's potential for profitability has become excessively important during the decision-making process about funding.

Whereas the number of rigorous historical films per se produced in Quebec remains limited, as seen in chapter 1, this chapter's exploration of how the historical imaginary fuels more fanciful cinematic reconstitutions of the past only begins to scratch the surface. The next two chapters reveal the extent to which Quebec's film industry invokes and even seeks to construct new *lieux de mémoire* that can form the basis for a twenty-first-century self-image for the nation. Undaunted by the failure of *Nouvelle-France* as a new form of Québécois heritage film, like their British and American counterparts had in the 1990s, Quebec's filmmakers turned to the literary adaptation, developing a successful formula for a uniquely local version of the costume drama. Finding inspiration in the local literary genre of the *roman du terroir*, early in the twenty-first century producers struck gold with adaptations of classic rural novels, whereas young auteurs revisited the almost mythical era of the second colonization, sometimes reframed as Quebec's Wild West, as well as its depiction as the *Grande Noirceur*, as we examine the corpus presented in chapter 3. Chapter 4 follows the rise of the biopic in Quebec, a genre closely related to the historical film for its reconstructions of the past focused on the life of a unique individual who has contributed to a sense of national greatness. Quebec film in the new millennium increasingly frames the nation's sports heroes and popular music stars as new, secular *lieux de mémoire*, thereby projecting a modern identity by way of winners whose success stories reassure viewers of Quebec's significance, but which also participate in a long history of national martyr-heroes.

3 Adapting the *Grande Noirceur* to the Screen: The *Roman du Terroir* and the Quebec Heritage Film

The feeling of nostalgia reshapes the past to address concerns and desires specific to the present.

Christine Sprengler[1]

[The scenario constitutes] a site of traces and memories that, refracting literature, reflect the cinema, like a matrix revealing the boundaries between literature and cinema.

Michel Larouche and Serge Cardinal[2]

Like the historical film per se, the adaptation to film of a nation's literary classics, texts typically written and/or set in the past, participate in a nation's historical imaginary, often linking past to present through nostalgia, as suggested by Christine Sprengler in the citation above. Instead of the shared memory of historical events and figures, adaptation films draw on audiences' memory of literary texts read (or often simply read about) in school. A nation's literary canon, as Benedict Anderson argues, informs and is informed by notions of collective identity, the construction of the "imagined community" that is the nation.[3] Indeed, some texts in the canon become so imbedded in the nation's historical imaginary that they become *lieux de mémoire* themselves. Because of their relationship to the canon and their engagement with the nation's cultural capital, some literary adaptations have been theorized by Andrew Higson as "heritage films"[4] and by Julianne Pidduck as "costume films."[5] Those scholars focus, however, on prestige productions from international film centres like Hollywood, Paris, and London. If we accept that Quebec's is, indeed, a "small nation cinema,"[6] lacking the financial resources, internationally known literary works, or world-changing historical events to inspire filmmakers, it seems logical that the heritage film has been slow to develop there.

Michel Larouche's assertion that "the relationship between cinema and literature in Quebec has always occupied a considerable space" notwithstanding,[7] literary adaptations have not always figured prominently in the province's cinematic history.[8] In 2003, André Loiselle asserted their relative rarity, explaining that "the generations of filmmakers who started making fiction films in the 1960s and created the canon of the 1970s were generally influenced by documentary and auteurist practices … [and] naturally drawn away from pre-existing texts, especially from drama, which imposes a rigid structure on the adaptor."[9] Furthermore, until recently SODEC's and Telefilm Canada's programs funding the screenwriting process privileged proposals for original screenplays.[10] Since the 1990s, however, Quebec filmmakers have increasingly turned to the perceived *valeur sure* (sure value) of the adaptation film, which includes not just film adaptations of literary and theatrical works, but also remakes of earlier films and reboots from popular television and even radio series, all of which adapt already familiar characters, plots, and settings for contemporary film audiences.

As Pidduck argues, "cinema can never offer an unmediated window onto the past,"[11] and this notion of mediation and reinterpretation of the past text for present-day audiences lies at the heart of adaptation theory. Robert Stam describes the adaptation as "an interested *reading* of a novel and the *circumstantially shaped* 'writing' of a film."[12] Although the question of fidelity to a source text remains a frequent focus of criticism, Stam argues that "the notion of fidelity is highly problematic … It is questionable whether strict fidelity is even possible."[13] Thus, this chapter focuses as much on what twenty-first-century adaptations say about contemporary Quebec as what they tell us about Quebec's past. It identifies the "memory-images,"[14] to invoke Pidduck's term again, that these films present and teases out how these "traces and memories," described by Michel Larouche and Serge Cardinal in the epigraph above, contribute to the construction of a shared historical imaginary.

The heritage film, however, is not an entirely new phenomenon in Quebec, and precursor texts exist for our twenty-first-century corpus, including Claude Jutra's adaptation of Anne Hébert's 1970 novel *Kamouraska* (1973), starring Geneviève Bujold, who had recently achieved international celebrity with her performance in Charles Jarrott's English heritage film *Anne of the Thousand Days* (1969). Stam acknowledges the significance of casting in a heritage film's success, arguing that "performers too become, in their way, the adapters and interpreters … as they mold characters through gestural details, ways of walking or talking."[15] Following Richard Dyer's theory outlined in *Stars* (1979), in addition to the actual performance, the actor's prior roles, off-screen media presence, and other factors that contribute to the creation of a "star persona" are equally significant.[16] Audiences' reception of a particular actor's embodiment of a familiar literary or historical character carries weight, and miscasting can lead to critical or box-office failure. The heritage film's recent success, then, is due in part to Quebec's well-developed star system;[17] producers' and directors' choice of actors shapes the "memory-image" that a given film seeks to recreate. For this reason, in this chapter and throughout this book, I acknowledge the actors' contribution to how a film text projects a particular image of the collective past for construction of national and individual identities for the present day.

Several early successes just after the year 2000 fuelled the rise of what Liz Czach calls the "Quebec heritage film."[18] She identifies three box-office hits – *Séraphin : un homme et son péché* (2002), *Aurore* (2005), and *Le Survenant* (2005) – as providing a model for further adaptations. The choice of which literary narratives inspire screen adaptations (or which film classics merit remakes or reboots) speaks to the construction of the nation's self-image in the same way as the choice of which actual historical events are commemorated in the historical film per se and even the historical fantasy. As Czach asserts, "the heritage film works to reaffirm, for older Québécois, or create, for newcomers and a younger generation, a collective shared memory of a colonized past (and by inference, present)."[19] Czach explains that in a time when neoliberalism and globalization threaten the long-standing conception of Quebec national identity as homogeneously French Canadian and Catholic, "the Quebec heritage film reaffirms a past in which Quebec identity was cohesive, shared, and binding."[20] Like its international counterparts, the Quebec heritage film deploys "strong allegories of specific national pasts addressed to national audiences."[21] Unlike French or even Chinese heritage films, however, which "have cross-cultural intertexts … that are legible to international audiences,"[22] Quebec's heritage films (or more modest adaptations) may not appeal to external audiences unfamiliar with its literary history.

In contrast with Great Britain's heritage films, exemplified by stunning adaptations of Jane Austen and E.M. Forster novels expressing nostalgia for the lavish lifestyles and/or imperial glory of the nation's past, Quebec's adaptations of local literary and film classics depict "an era of dispossession":[23] that of the so-called *Grande Noirceur*, the Great Darkness. Strictly speaking, this label has become associated with the mandate of the province's ultra-conservative Premier Maurice Duplessis, who governed from 1936 to 1939 and again from 1944 to 1959, the year of his death. Viewed as an oppressive dark age for a Quebec dominated by traditionalist, agricultural values and the strict morality of the Catholic Church,[24] some intellectuals began to see this period as extending back into the nineteenth century.[25] An imaginary equation linked the *Grande Noirceur* ideology to a second wave of colonization in Quebec; beginning as early as the 1870s and stretching as late as the 1930s, and promoted by figures like the now legendary Curé Antoine Labelle (1833–91),[26] French Canadians were urged to clear land in the so-called *pays d'en haut*, bounded by the Laurentians to the north and stretching west into present-day Ontario and the Great Lakes. The period is seen as one of oppression not only for its conservative ideology, but also because the territory being cleared and settled, such as the Abitibi region (which later became significant for its mines), was not fertile enough to support large Catholic families that had outgrown the cleared and productive southern lands along the St. Lawrence.

At the same time, the literary celebration of agricultural values fuelled the development of what is considered Quebec's only homegrown literary genre, *le roman du terroir*.[27] The classic *roman du terroir* dates to the nineteenth century with Patrice Lacombe's *La terre paternelle* (1860) and the thesis novels of Antoine Gérin-Lajoie and Pierre-Joseph-Olivier Chauveau,[28] but it lives on through the early twentieth century. In addition to the Frenchman Louis Hémon's *Maria Chapdelaine* (1914), Damase Potvin edited the journal *Le Terroir* (1918–38) and contributed his own novels, *Restons chez nous* (1908) and *L'appel de la terre* (1918), to the genre.[29] Reactions to the *roman du terroir*'s idealization of rural life, though, including social realist depictions of its hardships, appeared as early as Albert Laberge's *La scouine* (1918), and more mixed representations, which blurred nostalgia with negative images of the close-mindedness of small-town, Catholic, French Canadian society appear in Claude-Henri Grignon's *Un homme et son péché* (1933) and Germaine Guèvremont's *Le Survenant* (1945). During and after the Quiet Revolution of the 1960s, Quebec's writers help propagate the myth of the *Grande Noirceur*, almost unanimously adopting a stance that vilified the province's agricultural, Catholic past for several decades, as seen in Marie-Claire Blais's *Une saison dans la vie d'Emmanuel* (1965) and Gaétan Soucy's *La petite fille qui aimait trop les allumettes* (1995).

Although what Florian Freitag has alternatively called the "farm novel" certainly exists in other cultures,[30] the Quebec-specific *roman du terroir* became the inspiration for a local variation on the heritage film, recalling for contemporary Franco-Québécois their ancestors' trials and tribulations while building the nation. At the same time, these narratives, occurring in an ostensibly pre-modern, rural setting before 1960, allow contemporary Québécois to congratulate themselves on their social evolution since their grandparents' and great-grandparents' time. For this reason, twenty-first-century adaptations of the national literary heritage of the *roman du terroir* express an ambivalent nostalgia, at once validating the past as a heroic era and criticizing its values, reinforcing a present-day self-image of secular liberalism and the accommodation of difference necessary for a modern, pluralistic society.

This chapter, then, examines filmic representations of the *Grande Noirceur*, in its broadest definition from around 1870 through 1959, both through the literary adaptation or the readaptation of a film classic, and also in several original screenplays. Following Czach, it reveals how early in the new millennium heritage films feed a national foundational myth of victimhood, particularly in adaptations of the *roman du terroir* and responses to it, including Charles Binamé's

Séraphin : un homme et son péché (2002) and Luc Dionne's *Aurore* (2005). From blockbuster heritage films to independent films from rising young directors, we see an ambivalent nostalgia about the *Grande Noirceur*, as in Érik Canuel's *Le Survenant* (2005) and Catherine Martin's original screenplay for *Mariages* (2001). But we also see the beginnings of a discourse that questions the validity of that historical myth in Francis Leclerc's *Pieds nus dans l'aube* (2017) and Sébastien Pilote's *Maria Chapdelaine* (2021). This revisionist attitude includes a cycle of films that depict members of an institution frequently designated as history's villains in twentieth-century historical narratives from Quebec, an institution whose domination over Quebec culture was frequently blamed for the quasi-medieval attitudes said to prevail during the *Grande Noirceur*: the Catholic Church. The chapter thus analyses three prestigious filmmakers' depictions of priests and nuns as making positive contributions to Quebec society: Micheline Lanctôt's *Pour l'amour de Dieu* (2011), Léa Pool's *La passion d'Augustine* (2013), and Benoît Pilon's *Le Club Vinland* (2020). It closes on a discussion of Simon Lavoie's adaptation of Gaétan Soucy's stylized *anti-terroir* novel, *La petite fille qui aimait trop les allumettes* (2017).

Adaptation and the Quebec Heritage Film: *Séraphin : un homme et son péché, Aurore, Le Survenant,* and *Mariages*

I argue in chapter 2 that *Nouvelle-France* can be read as a failed heritage film; here, I follow Liz Czach to contend that this form succeeded in Quebec by turning away from the first colonial era to focus on the second. Early twenty-first-century Quebec heritage films adapted from the *roman du terroir* and its literary responses, or from "classic" radio, television, and film interpretations of the *Grande Noirceur*, critique an outmoded values system. But they also reflect a problematic longing for a time when Quebec society was homogeneous and patriarchal, and the Catholic Church dictated clear-cut behavioural norms. These films' negative representations of clerical fanaticism, abuse, or neglect, unjust paternal (or maternal) power, and the rejection of individuals who do not conform to dominant ethnic and social ideals associated with the national past are thus undercut by their nostalgic visions of a homogeneous local community.

Quebec heritage films, like the Anglo-American examples of *Pride and Prejudice* (Joe Wright, 2005) or *The Age of Innocence* (Martin Scorsese, 1993), draw upon classic texts from the literary or film canon that provide a historical reference point for contemporary audiences and engage the nation's foundational myths.[31] In populist Quebec, we have already seen the negative depiction of the French nobility in *Nouvelle-France*, developed to comic effect in *Le poil de la bête*. Instead of nostalgically depicting the luxurious costumes and dwellings of Regency or Belle Époque noble or bourgeois characters – the social and economic elites of English-language heritage films – Québécois heritage films invoke the *roman du terroir*, which glorifies the life of the common farmer, especially the pioneer. They feature plain farmers and small-time merchants in the archetypical setting of the remote frontier village. And although some of these films maintain the anglophone heritage film's frequent concern with a love story, given melodrama's status as Quebec's dominant filmic mode,[32] the protagonists' love affair generally ends unhappily. Above all, as in melodrama,[33] family dynamics lie at the narrative core of the Quebec heritage film, often involving abuse and even martyrdom of the child figure.

While what the French call the *film d'époque* had been out of favour in Quebec's film industry,[34] producer Lorraine Richard took a chance that paid off with *Séraphin : un homme et son péché / Heart of Stone* (2002), its success at the box office marking a turning point, triggering similar films in the coming years.[35] Critical responses were mixed,[36] but audiences appreciated the formula developed by director Charles Binamé (b. 1949), a team of writers including Pierre Billon and Antonine Maillet,[37] and producer Richard. Based on Claude-Henri Grignon's 1933 novel,[38] focused on the titular miser, Séraphin Poudrier, and his deadly sin of greed, *Séraphin* also drew on Paul Gury's classic 1949 film adaptation. These foundational texts had already begun to convey for an increasingly urbanized Quebec the sense that a bygone way of life should be preserved. Nostalgia, then, was already a key element in Grignon's highly mediated narrative, which was soon broadcast on radio. Gury's film adaptation developed secondary characters in Grignon's novel, the novel's oppressed *ingénue* Donalda, now a beautiful young woman, and transforming Alexis Labranche into a handsome young voyageur to build up a motif of forbidden love for the screen.[39]

Grignon grew up in the iconic northern town of Sainte-Adèle, set picturesquely among the Laurentian Mountains, the same region that the historical Curé Labelle encouraged French Canadians to colonize at the turn of the twentieth century as an alternative to emigration to the cotton mills of New England. These *pays d'en haut* (literally, the lands on high), the northwestern regions of the province spreading all the way to the Great Lakes, previously only explored by the *coureurs des bois*, represented Quebec's frontier. Visual representations of it – including a twenty-first-century television reboot of Grignon's now mythical narrative *Les pays d'en haut / True North* (2016–22) – have been likened to the American Western.[40] Produced early in the new millennium, however, *Séraphin* tempers its nostalgia with critical images of earlier generations' economic and social hardship as they faced the northern region's poor soil and short growing season, the dangers of the logging industry, and the rigidly defined social climate dominated by clerico-nationalist ideology.

Set in the 1880s, iconic sequences of *défrichage* (clearing the land) provide the backdrop for *Séraphin*, which reveals the ugly little secrets of rigidly Catholic, small-town life; as a character explains, they live in a "pays qui nous étouffe d'en dedans" (a country that suffocates us inside). Individual misery is compounded in the film by the titular villain's lack of empathy – the *Heart of Stone* of the film's English-language title – fuelled by an overweening greed. Referred to as "le diable en personne" (the devil in person), Séraphin controls the town as its mayor and only moneylender. In Pierre Billon and Charles Binamé's screenplay, his greed is psychologized as originating in a childhood trauma, becoming a perversion in adulthood, as he achieves erotic satisfaction running his fingers through bags of gold coins. Séraphin exploits the repressed sexuality that fosters unhealthy relationships in his society, blackmailing the syphilitic Curé Raudin (Normand Chouinard), threatening to tell the bishop about his "widow" mistress in Trois-Rivières, Delphine (Louise Portal). Furthermore, Séraphin rejects Simone (Catherine Trudeau), a young girl whom he has impregnated, and who dies after an illicit abortion attempt. Above all, he coerces the young Donalda to marry him in exchange for expunging her weak-willed father's (Rémy Girard) debt. Donalda's self-sacrifice forces her to relinquish a more appropriate fiancé, and not only does her husband deny her the joy of children because they cost too much, but he also overworks and eventually starves her to death.[41]

In addition to an iconic villain – Séraphin is played by the brilliant character actor Pierre Lebeau (b. 1954) – a blockbuster melodrama requires romantic leads. Binamé's team, therefore, transforms Grignon's moral parable of mortal sin into a story of frustrated love, casting a conventional leading man and lady in wholesomely pretty Karine Vanasse as Donalda and Roy Dupuis, *the* leading man in Quebec since the 1990s, as Alexis Labranche. Following Gury's lead, *Séraphin* transforms Grignon's middle-aged farmer into a dashingly handsome, romantic figure of wanderlust and backwoods adventure. The film's nostalgia, reinforced by a saccharine orchestral musical score by Michel Cusson, appears openly in conventional panoramic sequences that linger on the region's natural beauty during sequences of the lovers' trysts in the woods, their informal engagement, and Alexis's departure for the logging *chantiers* where he plans to make enough money to marry. Significantly, as the film's voice of the future, the hero argues for the need to think about more than just farms to build "un pays" (a country); *Séraphin* thus hints at the nation's impending modernization through the arrival of a railroad, but this, too, becomes another outlet for its villain's greed as he exploits insider information to call in debts, buying low and reselling land at a premium.

Although its villain eventually faces a just punishment, dying a horrible death trying to retrieve his gold as his house burns to the ground, *Séraphin* perversely denies sexual fulfilment to the legitimate lovers, Donalda and Alexis, granting this happy ending instead to a figure who has taken a vow of chastity, the *curé*. At the film's conclusion, he quits the priesthood to join Delphine. Whereas Donalda's lament to her lover, "Comment ça se fait, Alexis, qu'il n'y a pas eu une petite place pour nous dans un pays aussi grand?" (How is it, Alexis, that there wasn't a little place for us in such a big country?), indirectly accuses rural Quebec's intolerance, as it sacrifices the young woman on the altar of family duty, the *curé*'s scandalous behaviour points towards the province's secular future. As he takes leave of Donalda's grieving father, the *curé* admits, "J'aime une femme. Je veux vivre au grand jour. Ça prend du courage. C'était votre fille qui m'a donné ce courage-là" (I love a woman. I want to live in the open. That takes courage. It was your daughter who cave me that courage). Following the foundational myth of suffering and victimhood outlined by Czach,[42] the Quebec heritage film glorifies Donalda as a figure of saintly courage, but kills her off before change occurs, suggesting that martyrs are required for society to advance in the same manner we saw in chapter 1's historical films. Indeed, Marie-Claude Loiselle accuses *Séraphin* of exploiting the spectacle of Donalda's suffering so that contemporary viewers can feel good about having evolved a new, less oppressive system of values:

> Our past becomes here nothing more than a pure pretext to turn oppression and moral misery into a spectacle. The spectacle of a Quebec from which we have freed ourselves, and the film, with each shot, is the witness, the proof, the arrogant and cunning affirmation of this liberation. Binamé adopts this comfortable (and reassuring) height so we can contemplate that which no longer is about us, or concerns us anymore.[43]

But the popular success of *Séraphin* inevitably led to further exploitation of this formula. In fact, the town notable's admission of Donalda's martyrdom – "C'est notre silence qui l'a tuée" (It's our silence that killed her) – resonates with another tragic story of a daughter's martyrdom, that of Aurore Gagnon, newly adapted to the screen just three years later.

In his psychoanalysis of Quebec's foundational myths, *Du Canada au Québec : généalogie d'une histoire* (1987), Heinz Weinmann argues that in its family romance, French Canada perceives itself as a child abandoned by its parents, France and England.[44] Applying his theory to film history, Weinmann attributes the canonical status of Jean-Yves Bigras's *La petite Aurore, l'enfant martyre* (1952)[45] to audience identification with Aurore, a child who has lost her idealized birth mother and is then symbolically abandoned by her weak-willed father, who allows the abuse by a wicked stepmother to occur. Although a martyr, it is her very suffering, her endurance, that makes of Aurore "the first heroine, still negative, of course, of this Quebec being born."[46] Very much aware of this legend, filmmaker and writer Luc Dionne's (b. 1960) stated goal for *Aurore* (2005), his adaptation of a Québécois *lieu de mémoire*, is to return to the historical record of the real-life Aurore Gagnon case.[47] Following André Mathieu's[48] well-researched book, *Aurore : la vraie histoire de l'enfant martyre* (1990),[49] Dionne's film proposes to provide twenty-first-century audiences with a true account, thus echoing the truth claims of the historical film per se. And, although less obviously so than *Séraphin* and *Le Survenant*, it also adapts a book to the screen.

Aurore's production team, then, establishes a sense of historical verisimilitude in its recreation of Quebec from 1909 to 1920, depicting rural life and all its hardships in detail. One of the factual errors promulgated by Bigras's film – easily attributed to limited production values and the cinematic convention of simplifying the complex – is the notion that Aurore was an only child. Following the historical record, Dionne presents her with several brothers and sisters, including an infant brother who also died while in the care of their stepmother, and the director develops the bond that forms between the siblings. He retains the actual names of individuals, despite the possibility of confusion between Marie-Anne Caron (Stéphanie Lapointe), Aurore's biological mother, and her stepmother, Marie-Anne Houde (Hélène Bourgeois Leclerc). To build viewer sympathy for the martyred child and antipathy for her *marâtre*, the evil stepmother, Dionne begins Aurore's story prior to her mother's death from tuberculosis. Child actors who will become well known in the subsequent decade portray the blonde-haired and blue-eyed Aurore, a model of modesty and affection, at ages six (Alice Morel-Michaud) and ten (Marianne Fortier). In contrast, from the audience's first glimpse of her, the future stepmother is depicted as vain, greedy, and cruel, perhaps even diabolical, as one character describes her: "Elle est démoniaque. Elle a enfermé un de ses enfants dans la grange pis tout ce qui compte pour elle c'est l'argent. Ils disent que c'est elle qui a tué son mari" (She's demonic. She locked one of her children in the barn and the only thing that matters to her is money. They say she's the one who killed her husband).

As his consumptive wife remains bedridden after giving birth and is eventually institutionalized, Aurore's father, Télésphore Gagnon (Serge Postigo), invites his cousin, the recently widowed Marie-Anne Houde, to help in his household. Almost immediately after his wife's death, Télésphore marries Houde. In addition to the suggestion of incest, *Aurore* suggests that Houde has sexually bewitched her cousin, reproducing the reactionary binary that women are either saints or demons. Its ambivalent nostalgia thus reinscribes the very ideology it condemns, and, precisely because of its commitment to visual social realism, its spectacularization of the martyred heroine's suffering reaches levels previously not seen on Quebec's screens. Houde's tortures include pouring hot wax on the girl's nightdress, beatings, making her sleep in the attic, denying her food, and burning her. The camera lingers on images of Aurore's atrocious suffering, framing a bloody leg, then travelling up her body to a close-up of her crying face. *Aurore* disturbingly reprises an episode from Bigras's original film, appearing to share Houde's perverse pleasure in destroying the physical beauty of its child protagonist, in an iconic sequence in which her hair is burnt off with an overheated curling iron.

Figure 3.1. The apotheosis of the French Canadian martyr as images of Aurore's (Marianne Fortier) atrocious suffering climax with her death.

Indeed, Dionne frames Aurore's story precisely through the lens of martyrdom, opening with her mother relating the story of Philomène, the patron saint of their town, Fortierville, a virgin tortured after purportedly refusing to marry the Roman Emperor Diocletian. Not only does *Aurore* focus on its child protagonist's exceptionalism – her difference from the suffocating conformism of *Grande Noirceur* Quebec – it fosters an uneasy sentiment that its protagonist deserves or masochistically desires her punishments. Aurore confesses, for example, to the *curé* that even when she tries to conform to her stepmother's frequently unreasonable expectations to avoid punishment, "Je peux pas être comme les autres puisque je suis pas comme les autres" (I can't be like the others because I'm not like the others). She expresses her desire to die – "Je veux aller rejoindre ma mère" (I want to go join my mother) – and attempts suicide by throwing herself under a train. Finally, as Aurore lies nearly immobile on her attic pallet, dirty and wounded, her martyrdom appears complete as a ray of light shines through the window, and a dove flies in, accompanied by angelic music, scored by *Séraphin*'s composer, Michel Cusson.

While on the one hand, Dionne's film participates in the superannuated ideology linking violence and insanity to the demonic, on the other *Aurore* purportedly seeks to understand dysfunction, in keeping with twenty-first-century values. It suggests that Marie-Anne Houde's violence derives from some type of mental illness, aggravated by pre- and post-partum depression, since her pregnancy by Télésphore leads to greater animosity towards her stepchildren. Aurore's particular selection as the object of her stepmother's rage derives from an uncanny resemblance to her late mother but is also related to the child's difference. When Télésphore attempts to explain Aurore's seemingly rebellious behaviour as not just linked to her mother's death, he attributes it to her conception in sin: "Peut-être l'alcool a fait ça. Quand Marie-Anne pis moé avons fait cette-enfant-là on avait bu un peu trop" (Maybe alcohol did that. When me and Marie-Anne made that child, we'd had a little bit too much to drink). Houde later uses her husband's confession to influence the *curé*'s perception of the child as wilful: "elle a été conçu dans la boisson et la luxure ... C'est l'enfant du péché" (she was conceived in drink and lust ... She's the child of sin). According to this perverse logic, Aurore, ostensibly conceived in sin, somehow deserves the excessive punishments she receives. For contemporary viewers, brought up in secular, post–Quiet Revolution Quebec, of course, these expressions of antiquated superstition, rooted in unquestioning religious belief, further demonize Aurore's weak father and evil stepmother.

Aurore thus participates in the general trend of condemning the backwardness and hypocrisy of rural French Canadians, viewed as having been fostered by the Catholic Church, which dominated the pre-industrial, rural Quebec society associated with the myth of the *Grande Noirceur*. Church figures repeatedly thwart attempts to intervene in Aurore's situation by her maternal grandparents and Justice of the Peace Oréus, played by one of the province's best-loved actors, Rémy Girard. Fortierville's unsympathetic religious leader, Curé Leduc (Yves Jacques), both resents their ignorance and exploits it. Defensively asserting that "vous détestez ceux qui réfléchissez" (you detest those who think), he accuses them of anti-intellectualism, revealing the false motives behind many priestly "vocations" born not out of faith and a desire to serve but rather from intellectual thirst. Arrogant and resentful at being relegated to a rural parish, his sense of self-righteousness and power over his parishioners contributes to Aurore's abandonment, reinforcing the myth of the *Grande Noirceur*. Furthermore, *Aurore* couches the clash between secular and religious authority in terms of resistance to injustice versus acceptance of oppression as Oréus confronts the *curé*: "Les Curés, vous êtes jamais responsables de rien, vous. Avec vous, c'est le destin, la bonté de Dieu. Dieu-là, il s'amuse-tu à les faire pleurer là en haut? Ah, non, c'est vrai – ils brûlent en enfer. Pis la petite-là – c'est ça qu'elle a vécu, Monsieur le Curé, l'Enfer" (You priests, you're never responsible for anything. With you, it's destiny, God's goodness. Does it amuse God to make them cry up there? Oh no, it's true – they burn in hell. Well, that little girl – that's what she lived, Monsieur le Curé, Hell).

Invoking the community's failure to intervene in family matters, critic Pierre Ranger titles an interview with Dionne "Pour enfin briser la loi du silence" (To finally break the law of silence), referring to the filmmaker's stated goal of understanding the period in question and calling out the law of silence that surrounded abuse, condoned in part because of the church's teachings relating to patriarchal authority, but also linked to the then prevalent sentiment that

leniency would lead to weakness: Spare the rod, spoil the child.[50] At the same
time that *Aurore* presents a story of past behaviours that, in theory, are no longer
condoned, Dionne also posits that this code of silence regarding child abuse still
prevails in twenty-first-century Quebec: "even though *Aurore* takes place from
1909 to 1920, I found that its message was, after all, very current."[51] Dionne's
use of emotionally charged images, coupled with this discourse about child
abuse, represents a call to action, recalling Colman's description of the cinema of
recognition[52] that we have frequently observed of the Québécois historical film.

   Above all, in its revision of the *lieu de mémoire* established by Bigras's film,
Aurore memorializes the life of a *real* girl, not just a character in a notorious old
melodrama, engaging the question of memory after her death and her parents'
arrest. Dionne rejects the *curé*'s injunction to forget Aurore: "Tout de suite, après
ce sermon, doit commencer l'oubli. Ce grand déshonneur pour notre paroisse,
il faut commencer à l'enterrer afin qu'il disparaisse à jamais – à tout jamais – de
mémoire collective" (Right away, after this sermon, we must begin to forget.
This great dishonour to our parish, we must begin to bury it so that it disap-
pears forever and ever from the collective memory). The director gives the last
word to the secular authority, Oreus, who insists that remembering is necessary:
"moi, j'oublierai jamais" (*I* will never forget). Like many historical films, *Aurore*
closes with title cards that explain what happened to those involved, including
Marie-Anne Houde's commuted death sentence and death from cancer, and
Télésphore's life sentence, of which he served just five years. Despite the erec-
tion of a memorial tombstone for Aurore Gagnon where none had previously
stood,[53] critics remained sceptical of the film's positive impact, noting that "in
the film industry, the Québécois from back then … are rather the haggard witnesses who serve to confirm *our* morals today."[54] In addition, this comment
signals the institutional critic's scorn for popular genre films (cinema as industry), a perhaps justifiable criticism in relation to this film's spectacularization of
child abuse, but one that similarly exploitative art films – such as the bizarre
family romance in André Forcier's *Embrasse-moi comme tu m'aimes* (discussed in
chapter 2) – seem to escape.

   After the success of *Séraphin*, producers reconsidered a project to adapt another
literary classic that had attained *lieu de mémoire* status, Germaine Guèvremont's
Le Survenant (1945) and a popular television series based on it (1954–60).[55]
Pitched to them as early as 1989, including a scenario by Diane Cailhier,[56]
they hired rising filmmaker Érik Canuel (b. 1961) to direct *Le Survenant / The
Outlander* (2005). It depicts the arrival of an unnamed outsider in the small
town of Chenal-du-Moine, near Sorel on the St. Lawrence, who disrupts the
complacency of provincial-minded farmers and petits bourgeois. Although it
also offers another female martyr figure, it shifts focus onto a more positive
model for contemporary Québécois masculine identity in the hearty, life-loving
Survenant. On the one hand, Canuel's film adaptation reflects contemporary

Quebec's condemnation of old-fashioned values found in *Séraphin* and *Aurore*; on the other, its more openly nostalgic aesthetic and overarching celebration of male freedom and the natural environment blur its critical focus.[57]

Set in 1910, *Le Survenant*'s opening credits establish the film's nostalgic feel and prepare the viewer to be cast into a quaint but outmoded past world, featuring drawings by Frédéric Bach, invoking Guèvremont's own illustrations for her text,[58] accompanied by Michel Corriveau's saccharine musical score. Cinematographer Bernard Couture – one of the province's premier cameramen since the year 2000 – lyricizes the natural landscape in which Le Survenant (Jean-Nicolas Verreault) goes duck hunting with Le Père Didace Beauchemin (Gilles Renaud), for example. This imagery naturalizing male bonding and freedom clashes with claustrophobic images of lamplit parlours, underscoring the film's critique of the narrow-minded residents of Chenal-du-Moine, associating social constraints with the feminine domain of the household and village. With his hearty laugh, tall and blonde Jean-Nicolas Verreault (b. 1967) portrays the title character as an attractive man, in love with life, savouring every moment, cherishing above all his freedom.

The film opens with the wanderer's knock on the door of the Beauchemin farm, which has become an iconic moment in Québécois television and film. Looking for temporary room and board in exchange for work, the charismatic man is immediately embraced by the aging widower. Favoured over his own timid and conventional son, ironically named Amable (likeable/friendly; François Chénier), Le Survenant inspires jealousy and suspicion in the heir and his wife, Alphonsine (Catherine Trudeau). Although she also struggles with her sense of duty and the received ideas of her community, neighbour Angélina falls in love with Le Survenant. Lame and an old maid in Guèvremont's novel,[59] Angélina is played in Canuel's film by attractive leading lady Anick Lemay. Despite his growing attraction to her, Le Survenant obeys his wanderlust and eventually leaves town.

The villagers' xenophobia and the protagonist's openness to the world outside, a trait that much of twenty-first-century Quebec film will celebrate, appears in a key passage, in which the film borrows dialogue almost word for word from the source text. During an evening social gathering, locals ask Le Survenant about Le Père Didace's new love interest, a serving woman at a bar in Sorel referred to only as L'Acayenne (Dominique Pétin), a nickname that identifies her, too, as an outsider, an Acadian from beyond the Gulf of St. Lawrence. As Le Survenant describes her attractiveness, a local woman's reaction is that "Qu'elle reste donc dans son pays!" (She should stay where she comes from!). He then chides these provincials for their closed-mindedness:

> Vous autres, vous savez pas ce que c'est d'aimer à voir du pays, de se lever avec le
> jour, un beau matin, pour filer fin seul, le pas léger, le coeur allégé, tout son avoir

sur le dos. Non! vous aimez mieux piétonner toujours la même place, pliés en deux sur vos terres de petite grandeur, plates et cordées comme des mouchoirs de poche. Sainte bénite, vous aurez donc jamais rien vu, de votre vivant!

You all, you don't know what it's like to love to see the country, to get up with the sun, a beautiful morning, and to leave, all alone, with a light, a free heart, and all your belongings on your back. No! You prefer always walking in the same place, bent in two over your tiny lands, flat and furrowed like handkerchiefs. My word, you will never have seen anything in your whole lives!

Aptly named because of his provincial attitudes, Pierre-Côme Provençal retorts, "Tout ce qu'on avait à voir, Survenant, on l'a vu" (All that we need to see, Survenant, we've seen it).[60] These lines sum up *Le Survenant*'s message about the close-mindedness of the provincial past and a desire to open up to the world at large embodied by its eponymous protagonist, a message particularly appreciated by Canuel's generation. Indeed, Canuel describes his own admiration for the character since first reading the novel at age fifteen: "For me, Le Survenant is the man who arrives and brings something new, a new way to think, an open-mindedness, a certain modernity."[61] By focusing upon the figure of emancipation instead of one of martyrdom, just as Guèvremont's novel began to break with the traditional *roman du terroir*, Canuel's film marks a new development in the Quebec heritage film. Whereas *Aurore* and *Séraphin* suggest that suffering is "coterminous, indissoluble, and necessary for a shared sense of identity,"[62] *Le Survenant* shows a way out of the cycle of victimhood, albeit by leaving the unhealthy, stifling atmosphere of the community, but its discourse is also heavily gendered; whereas the man is free to leave, Angélina remains behind, her horizons limited. In contrast, Catherine Martin's *Mariages* (2001), an independent film with a limited budget and an original screenplay, offers a feminist counterpoint to these later popular successes, albeit an ambivalent one.

Catherine Martin (b. 1958) has proven to be a quiet but enduring auteur presence in the Québécois film scene since the turn of the millennium, and her first fiction feature, *Mariages* (2001), was nominated for Best Screenplay at both the Jutra and Genie Awards in 2002. Marie-Claude Loiselle singles it out as "the most beautiful and solid fiction film that our cinematography has seen in the last few years."[63] Set around 1885–90, Martin's explicitly feminist film predates the period-piece explosion soon to come; although it critiques the ideology of a bygone era, it affords its female protagonists greater agency within a nonetheless oppressive system, eschewing the melodrama's binary vision of saints and whores. Not technically a literary adaptation, it nonetheless draws on the Québécois literary traditions of both the *roman du terroir* and its subversive counterpart, the fantastic story. Despite its fantastic motif of a magically preserved corpse and ghostly apparitions, *Mariages* focuses on the internal and external conflicts of a young woman caught between socially expected subservience to family authority and her personal aspirations and desires within the framework of a painstaking historical reconstitution.

Mariages's young protagonist, Yvonne Pelletier (Marie-Ève Bertrand), leads a Cinderella-like existence in the home of her older sister, Hélène (Guylaine Tremblay), doing household chores and caring for her nieces and nephews. It has been agreed, or rather Hélène has decided, that Yvonne will return to the convent, where she had been studying, to take the veil. Two somewhat miraculous events, however, foil Hélène's well-laid plans for ordering her younger sister's future by relegating her to a nunnery. First, while moving the cemetery to a new location, a worker's carelessness reveals that their mother, Anastasie Dubé (Louise de Beaumont) – interred over a decade ago – has been perfectly preserved, transformed into a "statue de sel" (statue of salt), invoking the biblical imagery of Lot's wife. This miraculous phenomenon sets in motion a chain reaction of disruption, including her display in state, her ghostly apparition, and Yvonne questioning the received story of the circumstances surrounding her mother's death. Next, the return of a local prodigal son introduces a new bachelor into the community, further alienating the sisters. Whereas Hélène quickly arranges a marriage between her fifteen-year-old daughter, Thérèse (Mirianne Brûlé), and the eligible bachelor Charles Allison (David Boutin), Charles notices the more mature and sensual Yvonne. Despite the obstacles placed in the couple's way to happiness, the film suggests that Anastasie's ghostly presence, coupled with folk magic performed by the family servant, Maria (Hélène Loiselle), eventually work towards a fairy-tale ending for its protagonists. Despite its fantastic elements, *Mariages* comments realistically on women's roles in French Canadian society during the late nineteenth century. Its title, *Mariages*, in the plural, invokes a feminist narrative critical of the limited number of legitimate roles that French Canadian society offered for women, and Martin explores four generations of female experiences of love and marriage: those of the grandmother figure Maria, the former matriarch Anastasie, her daughters Yvonne and Hélène, and finally, the latter's daughter Thérèse.

The grandmotherly crone, Maria, a sixty-something widow who has served the Pelletier family as a nursemaid to Yvonne and Hélène, now keeps house for the sisters' consumptive stepmother, Noémie (Markita Boies). Due to social pressures in her youth, Maria experienced love, but not marriage, and bestows a cabin in the woods, the site of her past trysts, to her spiritual granddaughter, Yvonne. The next generation, that of Yvonne's late mother, Anastasie, and her posthumous rival, Noémie, also offers a troubled image of love and marriage. Although Auguste Pelletier (Raymond Cloutier) was bereft when Anastasie died, and their romance is described as a *fol amour* (mad love), "sans raison" (without reason) and "sans bon sens" (without common sense), he married Noémie only six months after his first wife's death. After Anastasie's disinterment, Noémie fears that her jealous apparition has returned to take Auguste away. While it seemed that Auguste and Anastasie "s'aimaient comme des fous" (loved each other like crazy), Yvonne also learns that her mother suffered from "melancholy" – what we would call today clinical depression – and had actually committed suicide, suggesting perhaps her dissatisfaction with the limited roles allowed her in French Canadian society.

The tragic circumstances surrounding Anastasie's marriage appear destined to impact her daughters and granddaughter as well. The elder, Hélène, is clearly unhappy, figuratively abandoned by her alcoholic husband and forced to take care of both business and home; almost a non-character and referred to only as "le notaire" (the notary – his profession), he is glimpsed just once and briefly, huddled under the bedclothes, apparently drunk. Whether severe by nature or forced into this role by her unhappy marriage, Hélène is a humourless, conventional nineteenth-century bourgeoise, ever anxious about appearances, her ambition limited to obtaining a good marriage for her daughter. To control the "qu'en dira-t-on" (literally, "what will one say," a.k.a. gossip) Hélène attempts to control the behaviour of the single women under her charge. Stressed and concerned, Hélène seems to wish that others share her unhappiness, constantly suppressing expressions of joy, desire, play, and imagination in favour of a strict Catholic, bourgeois moral code. Indeed, her plans for Yvonne and Thérèse seriously threaten their ability to lead happy, sexually fulfilled lives. Not only does she seek to condemn her sister to a life of celibacy in the convent, but Hélène also plans to send an unprepared teenager into a stranger's arms. Barely pubescent, uninformed about the facts of life, Thérèse embodies contemporary images of the repressed Victorian girl whose wedding night will be a traumatic moment and subsequent sexual relations viewed as a marital duty rather than a shared pleasure. When quizzed by Yvonne about how she feels about marrying Charles, Thérèse shows interest only in her trousseau.

The nuns themselves have told Hélène that the sensual and imaginative Yvonne is not made for conventual life; fortunately, supernatural forces intervene so that this Cinderella figure ultimately wins her handsome prince, but not before overcoming several obstacles. Although treated like a servant, Yvonne has caught Charles's attention when he visits the Pelletier home; a chance meeting in the lane allows him to express his interest and to offer her a handkerchief. This token becomes the centre of a folk ritual, through which Maria helps Yvonne attract Charles; Noémie helps arrange a secret marriage ceremony, and the couple – in defiance of paternal and sororal authority – consummate their relationship. *Mariages* critiques not only nineteenth-century treatment of women, but also patriarchal control over sons. For, as Charles explains to Yvonne, his father is forcing him to marry Thérèse as a condition of paternal forgiveness for a long-standing disagreement about his own adult destiny. Although he decides on his own to reject the arranged marriage, Charles refuses to tear Yvonne from her family by taking her with him when he returns to the city.

The couple's fate seems doomed, but the feminist tale offers a resistant vision of a young woman rejecting the role offered her by polite French Canadian society and assuming agency for her own destiny. After Charles's departure, Yvonne realizes she is pregnant, but her failed abortion attempt confirms Hélène's suspicions that her sister has become "une fille perdue" (a lost woman). Yvonne escapes from her locked room, planning to look for Charles in the city, finding work – like so many single French Canadian girls – as a domestic. Unable to locate her lover, but clearly as unsuited for life as a servant as she would have been as a nun, a flash forward reveals Yvonne living in Maria's cabin in the woods, visited occasionally by her married lover. Still unsatisfied, she resolves to find Charles, again seeking Maria's assistance, using a supernatural invocation. The film closes on her reunion with Charles and the image of the two lovers entwined, in a fairy tale ending that suggests a courageous woman might transcend the limited roles that French Canadian society of the time dictated for her: unhappy marriage, an unfulfilled life as a spinster, domestic servant, or as a nun. Its focus on the fairy-tale romance and conclusion with the constitution of the heterosexual couple, however, undermine its overall feminist message.[64] An independent film, *Mariages* nonetheless escapes the logic of martyrdom evident in the *grand public* heritage films of the early 2000s. In the next decade of the new millennium, the heritage film will develop even further, eventually eschewing the melodramatic aspects of its precursors, proposing a less ambivalent, more fully nostalgic vision of the pioneer past, questioning its very appellation as a *Grande Noirceur*. It will also offer, at times, more space for female protagonists to decide their own fate.

Later Heritage Films and the *néo-terroir*: *Pieds nus dans l'aube* and *Maria Chapdelaine*

From the compulsion to reject the national past prior to 1960 as an era whose clerico-nationalist ideology kept French Canadians in their place and oppressed by both church and state found in the heritage films of the early 2000s, a fond remembrance of the personalized, yet communal nature of village life develops in its second decade. *Pieds nus dans l'aube / Barefoot at Dawn* (2017) represents a new iteration of the Quebec heritage film that leaves behind the national myth of victimhood and celebrates rurality. Based on the eponymous autobiographical novel by his father, singer-songwriter and national icon Félix Leclerc (1914–1988), published in 1946, Francis Leclerc's (b. 1971) film adaptation of a nostalgic coming-of-age story, a fond eulogy to a lost childhood, presents a series of vignettes held together by visual images that draw the viewer back into the past, and into the *pays d'en haut*. With shots of a horse-drawn sled pulled through the wintry landscape, both *Le Survenant* and *Pieds nus dans l'aube* directly reference an urtext of Quebec cinema's nostalgic imagery of the province's rural past, Claude Jutra's *Mon oncle Antoine* (1971).[65] Indeed, co-written with Fred Pellerin, creator of *Babine* and *Ésimésac* (discussed in chapter 2), Leclerc's adaptation opens as patriarch Léo (Roy Dupuis) and his sons deliver firewood to a house surrounded by forest. The sequence establishes the notion that the prosperous should help those in need and creates a pretext for the budding friendship between its young protagonist, Félix (Justin Leyrolles-Bouchard, an avatar for the national songster), and the impoverished Fidor (Julien Leclerc) that provides the film its narrative scaffolding.[66] Set in La Tuque, on the Saint-Maurice River, in 1926–7, *Pieds nus dans l'aube* includes traumatic loss, unrequited love, and a sense of living in a time of change, elements more frequently found in films set in the 1960s than those set in the 1920s. It revises the *roman du terroir* plots seen earlier in the millennium, offering a cinematic re-imagining full of nostalgia, but also with hope for the modernizing society that has begun to reach into the heartland.

Although the poetry of Félix Leclerc's novel would be impossible to capture on-screen, Francis Leclerc attempts to do so with numerous lingering, even slow-motion sequences without dialogue, accompanied by a very effective musical score by Martin Roy and Luc Sicard. Evocative of the folk melodies of the time, the melancholy strains of a piano, guitar, and cello enhance without overpowering the sequences they accompany, and these contrast with the overly orchestrated scores of the heritage melodramas *Séraphin* and *Aurore*. The overarching storyline involves young Félix's last summer at home before leaving for the *collège classique* in Ottawa;[67] in addition to his friendship with Fidor, the adolescent begins his initiation into (painful) affairs of the heart and has his first brushes with death. Not only does the twelve-year-old develop a crush on Garde Lemieux (Marianne Fortier), a lay nurse whose horse he cares for, but he also witnesses a love-related tragedy. After overhearing the town's playboy barber Gaspard (Mickaël Gouin), also a transplant to the region, brutally reject the local blacksmith's wife (Marie Laurence-Lévesque), who had been his lover, Félix and Fidor find her body in the river. The film elides several other personal traumas narrated in the novel, including a massive fire that might have razed their house and sister Anne-Marie's marriage and subsequent death, an episode that seems to have inspired Leclerc's earlier period film, *Une jeune fille à la fenêtre* (2001).[68]

Pieds nus dans l'aube's nostalgia focuses largely on representing an idealized family life that contrasts soundly with the grim visions conveyed in *Séraphin* or *Aurore*. Félix's mother, Fabiola (Catherine Sénart), nearly always appears in the kitchen making something good for her large family to eat; she clearly loves her son, teasing him, but also discussing things he has witnessed, explaining adult behaviour, allowing him to be sad, and exonerating him from guilt. Although it is occasionally noisy, the large Leclerc home has plenty of space for the many children, as well as his Uncle Richard (Guy Thauvette), to read and play piano or board games. Their parents also love each other; their father is clear about moral principles, but kind and affectionate. For example, when Fidor is caught stealing at Monsieur Gravel's (Mathieu Lepage) general store, he is punished only with a lecture by Léo, their complicity established when Fidor calmed the blacksmith Bérubé's (Claude Legault) dog after it attacked him. In addition to their home in town, the family has a cabin in the mountains, which allows male bonding between the uncle, father, Félix, and his older brother Jean-Marie (Tristan Goyette-Plante). *Pieds nus dans l'aube* offers a revisionist image of family life in the *Grande Noirceur*, depicting a home filled with love and ideas.

One of Francis Leclerc's choices as adaptor occurs in his rendering of the Leclercs' hometown as much smaller than that of his father's novel, which already has its own factories for the exploitation of its valuable lumber resources. Hints of modernity's threat to this rural utopia, a village set along a picturesque river flanked by mountains, do appear here and there – for example in the "Old Chum" tobacco advertisement painted on a building and the seductive, big-city ways of the barber. Most obviously it appears during the visit of Uncle Rodolphe (Robert Lepage), who brings gifts for the children and describes the wonderful new technology of radio. He implicitly criticizes city life in comparison to the village, however, playing the *bonimenteur* to his own variety show: "C'est comment la ville? La ville, c'est le peuple rassemblé autour des usines. Des maisons collées comme un jeu de cartes … La ville, c'est du monde qui va à droite, du monde qui va à gauche. Mais ce monde qui va à droite ne connait pas ce monde qui va à gauche … La ville, c'est un cri que personne n'entend pas" (What's the city like? The city, it's people gathered around factories. Houses glued together like a deck of cards … The city is people that go right, then go left. But the people who go right don't know the people who go left … The city is a cry that no one hears).[69] And yet, its allure is unmistakable, and Félix's eventual journey there – as for so many young Québécois – appears as a necessary stage in personal development rather than an evil to be avoided at all costs.

In terms of national politics, *Pieds nus dans l'aube* pays lip service to the discourse of English-French conflict, but without the typical resentment depicted in Quebec national cinema. The management class, "les Anglais," live in a manor house where Félix and Fidor are treated to an evening of decadence because Garde Lemieux has given them tickets to a fundraiser ball, but Fidor's expressed resentment about the "riches" (rich people) soon evaporates, as he stuffs himself with goodies and champagne. The advantages of learning English are stated clearly for Félix, in a matter-of-fact rather than indignant manner, but he is also instructed to command respect for himself from others. When he says he can understand English, he is admonished softly, "Comprendre, oui. Mais il faut surtout que tu apprennes à répondre" (Understand, yes. But you must above all learn to answer back). This understated assertion insists that French Canadians should not just understand English to take orders, but that they must also learn to speak for themselves. Indeed, Félix's only worry involves his impending departure, after a government test administered at school has identified his intellectual gifts, to the *collège classique* in Ottawa, but this, too, as Uncle Richard tells him, is an important opportunity, one that will open up "toutes sortes de possibles" (all sorts of possibilities). And the viewer knows, of course, that things will turn out well for the future nationalist musical pioneer; the boy's departure on the train is narrated, in the only moment of voice-over in the film, through a recording of Félix Leclerc reading his poem "Le Départ."

The film's overall message is about freedom, relayed as a fable, in which animals stand in for people, as Fidor and Félix discuss the story of a fox who chewed off its foot to escape a trap. Fidor says naively, "Ça marche pas de capturer les bêtes. Ça les empêche de vivre" (It doesn't work to capture animals. That keeps them from living); like the fox, humans, too, need freedom. But unlike the tension felt between Le Survenant's wanderlust and pressures to settle down, *Pieds nus dans l'aube* is also about the land and belonging, naming a place as "Chez nous," as the boys' voices ask the echo in the mountain, repeated in the lyrics of the Leclerc song "Tu te leveras tôt," sung by Martin Léon over the film's closing credits, "C'est à toi, tout cela … C'est ton pays … Elle sera fière d'être de ce pays-là" (It's yours, all of this … It's your country … She will be proud to be from this country). Leclerc's film suggests, then, that one can have *both* a home, but also the freedom to leave it, marking a significant step in liberating Quebec national cinema from the foundational myth of victimhood.

A new adaptation of Quebec's most iconic novel, Frenchman Louis Hémon's *Maria Chapdelaine* (1914), takes the heritage film even further in its relatively unadulterated celebration of the pioneer era. Preceded by adaptations by French filmmaker Julien Duvivier in 1934 (starring French icon Jean Gabin as François Paradis) and Gilles Carle in 1983 (with Carole Laure in the title role), Sébastien Pilote's (b. 1973) *Maria Chapdelaine* (2021) subtly updates the iconic *roman du terroir*'s narrative of a farm girl's choice between three suitors, each incarnating a possible lifestyle for French Canadians in 1910. "Conscious of taking on a monument,"[70] with an announced $7 million budget and advance media hype over casting,[71] including nationalist rapper turned actor Sébastien Ricard (of Loco Locass) in the role of patriarch Samuel Chapdelaine, Pilote acknowledges that *Maria Chapdelaine* participates in a renewal of the heritage film. The only adaptation to be filmed entirely on location in the Lac Saint-Jean region, it aspires to authentic historical reconstruction; indeed, the set of the Chapdelaine farm appears to have actually been carved out of the boreal landscape, surrounded first by a ring of stumps and then by the woods itself.[72] Pilote expresses his deeply felt identitary connection to the film's woodland setting:

That woods, there – it's home. It's the sand drained from the Péribonka River for thousands of years. Saint-Ambroise, where I was born, Sainte-Monique, Péribonka: It's the same soil. I know it, intimately, just like I know the vegetation that grows on

Figure 3.2. The set of Sébastien Pilote's *Maria Chapdelaine*; the early twentieth-century pioneer farm appears literally carved out of the woods.

> it. I spent my childhood exploring that forest … It's a project that's held my heart for a long time and it's in keeping with my earlier films. It's a novel that obsesses me, that I've always loved for its great simplicity.[73]

Pilote belongs to the same generation of filmmakers as Rafaël Ouellet, another filmmaker whose work has been compared to a recent literary movement, described as the *néo-terroir*,[74] calling for a return to Quebec's roots, a tendency seen in the body of regional films developing in the 2010s. I argue that Pilote's adaptation of this foundational text participates in this *néo-terroir* movement.

Insisting that "my Maria Chapdelaine is a girl of her times," Pilote makes clear that he has not revised Hémon's ending,[75] but through subtle choices of casting and line delivery, he makes its conclusion a compelling one. Contemporary readers often find Hémon's ending, in which Maria chooses a staid and boring farmer for her future husband, based entirely on her sense of duty rather than any physical or emotional attraction, unpalatable, even anti-feminist. Pilote's *néo-terroir* approach brilliantly reframes the young woman's choice as the only way for her to remain loyal to herself, thus satisfying twenty-first-century viewers' expectations while remaining "faithful" to the source text. However, Maria's first love is the charismatic *coureur des bois* François Paradis (Émile Schneider). As a fur trader and logger, Paradis's ties to the woods and his family's relationships with Indigenous peoples link him to an earlier stage in Quebec's development, the romantic moment of exploration. Although he has agreed to settle down to marry her once he has saved enough money, his death in a snowstorm while trying to return from the logging camp to spend Christmas with Maria and her family forecloses the option of a romantic love match and fulfils the logic of the *terroir* narrative by insisting on settlement. Since their engagement had never become official, those around her can't understand Maria's grief; Pilote deftly handles aspects of Hémon's novel that stress the influence of the parish priest at this time by casting a younger actor associated with rebel roles, Danny Gilmore (b. 1973), as the *curé*. Remaining faithful to the novel's original dialogue, the *curé* scolds Maria for her inappropriate, exaggerated grief, as a "tourment profane et pas convenable" (profane and inappropriate torment) in society's eyes because Paradis "ne vous était rien," was nothing to her. While conveying the message that in 1910 Quebec society relationships between young men and young women existed *only* once they were condoned by their parents and the local priest, Gilmore's understated delivery avoids earlier films' more egregious portrayals of often villainous clerics, such as Yves Jacques's in *Aurore*.

Although still grieving privately, Maria must move forward with her life and decide between two remaining suitors: Eutrope Gagnon, a young farmer clearing land nearby, and Lorenzo Surprenant, who has returned from Massachusetts to sell his father's farm. In the novel's logic, the arguments for and against each suitor become arguments for and against two possible lifestyles for French Canadians. Gagnon represents, of course, the *terroir* ideology of remaining in Quebec to farm the land; Surprenant, in contrast, represents the exodus of French Canadians to the textile mills of New England, their adoption of modern, urban, consumer lifestyles in the city, and their feared assimilation to an *American* identity. The film's dialogue reproduces Lorenzo's arguments vaunting the attractions of city life to Maria, but casting, the subtleties of delivery, and the rest of the cast's reaction to his comments, including Maria's own, suggest that she really should turn down his proposal. Lorenzo insists that "Ici, c'est pas une place pour vous, Maria" (This is not a place for you, Maria), suggesting that a woman of her beauty deserves a life in the city, with all the modern conveniences, able to visit "des ben belles places pas pantoute comme icitte" (really beautiful places nothing like it is here). His tone remains matter of fact, rather than arrogant or argumentative, when he rejects the locals' assertions that there is nothing more beautiful than a cleared plot of land and the freedom of the agricultural life, but Maria can't help but feel the implied insult to her own family and their chosen way of life, particularly when her mother (Hélène Florent) becomes Lorenzo's verbal adversary. Not long before Lorenzo's return to Massachusetts, his uncle (Gilbert Sicotte) invites his neighbours to a *veillée*, a traditional evening party of music and dancing; the conversation becomes ideological as Lorenzo debates the relative charms of rural life with his uncle's guests. Insisting that the country life is not for him, French wordplay allows Pilote to make a statement about identity and Quebec's agricultural roots; a local suggests to Lorenzo something to the effect of, "So it's not your idea of the good life to live here with tree stumps," referring to the iconic image of the partially cleared farms of the Lac

Saint-Jean region at this time. Lorenzo agrees, matter-of-factly, that he is fine where he is in the States, "Parce que, non, il n'y a pas de souches" (Because, no, there are no stumps). While he literally refers to the fact that the land in New England was cleared long ago and there are no longer any tree stumps present, the term *souches* (stumps/roots) is heavily coded in Quebec. Indeed, old-stock ethnic French Canadians are referred to as being *de vieille souche*. Lorenzo thus inadvertently takes himself out of the running for Maria's hand precisely through his affinity for a modern, urban lifestyle, but also one in which roots and family are not important.

Casting, of course, plays a significant role in Pilote's strategy to lead viewers towards accepting that the least attractive of the novel's three suitors *should* win out in his *néo-terroir* film. A highly gifted actor, Robert Naylor (b. 1996), cast as Lorenzo, simply lacks the good looks and charisma of his rival, Eutrope Gagnon, played by the blonde and handsome Antoine-Olivier Pilon (b. 1997), already a familiar lead to Quebec film and television audiences. In the novel's logic that "au pays du Québec rien ne doit mourir et rien ne doit changer" (in the land of Quebec nothing must die and nothing must change),[76] Maria's somewhat forced choice of Eutrope reinscribes a traditionalist, Catholic ideology, in which the young woman sacrifices herself and her individual desires to fulfil her duty as a wife and mother. In his updated *néo-terroir* interpretation, Maria's choice of Eutrope is validated through certain twenty-first-century codes for individual identity and couple formation, allowing Pilote to remain faithful to his film's literary source text, but also to provide contemporary audiences with a satisfying conclusion. In this film adaptation, Eutrope's physical attractiveness rivals that of the dead beloved François and exceeds that of Lorenzo, but he is shy and remains in the background, while François and then Lorenzo take centre stage in the earlier "chapters" of the film. His ongoing interest in Maria, however, is made clear by the filmmaker through repeated reaction shots as Maria interacts with his rivals. When Maria's mother takes ill and appears to be dying, Eutrope volunteers to fetch the *curé*, travelling part of the way by foot in winter; his success at this task (one where the seasoned forester François had failed, perhaps because his winter journey was motivated by selfish desire for Maria), brings him closer to the Chapdelaine family. But it is Pilon's nuanced delivery of his impassioned proposal to Maria (lines that in the novel seem dryer than dirt and suggest Eutrope's relative unattractiveness in relation to Maria's other suitors), that wins both Maria and the viewer over to accept his suit. Although he begins a bit roughly, explaining that he never discussed his "amitié" (friendship) with her before because he guessed that she preferred François, "Puisqu'il est mort, je me suis dis que, moi aussi, je pourrais tenter ma chance. Je suis pas riche, mais j'ai deux lots, déjà payés, pis vous savez que c'est de la bonne terre" (Because he's dead, I thought that maybe I, too, could try. I'm not rich, but I have two lots, already paid for, and you know that it's good soil). As he talks about his land and his future plans, his enthusiasm grows and appears contagious as Maria begins to smile with him. He continues, moving from their mutual work ethic to his feelings for her: "Vous êtes vaillante, Maria, accoutumée à l'ouvrage, pis moi aussi … Alors, si vous voulez bien me marier, je vous aimerais bien. L'amitié que j'ai pour vous, cela peut pas se dire de même" (You are strong, Maria, accustomed to work, and I am too … So, if you would like to marry me, I would love you well. The friendship that I have for you, it can't be expressed like that). But he concludes with a clincher for twenty-first-century audiences, insisting both on her freedom of choice, but also closing his arguments with a comment about her identity as an individual: "Vous êtes libre, comme de raison … Vous seriez heureuse d'être la femme que vous êtes, avec moi, Maria" (You are free, as it should be … You would be happy to be the woman that you are, with me, Maria). Eutrope has watched and observed, and he knows Maria almost as well as she knows herself because he knows that the city woman that Lorenzo wants to make her into is not an identity in which Maria would be loyal to herself. By remaining on the farm, near her family, as Eutrope's wife, she will be herself. This assertion confirms something she said earlier to Lorenzo; although she admits that "J'aurais aimé être maîtresse d'école" (I might have liked to be a school teacher), indicating that she is educated and possesses a certain level of intellectual curiosity, when Lorenzo interjects that her parents shouldn't have asked her to give that up, Maria insists, "Ils ne m'ont rien demandé, Lorenzo" (They've demanded nothing from me, Lorenzo). Her assertion indicates that her loyalty to her family is her own choice, and that remaining on the farm is not a burden imposed on her by others.

Sébastien Pilote's adaptation of *Maria Chapdelaine*, then, is faithful to its source text while reinterpreting *terroir* ideology, including admitting many of its tragic aspects, to align with the twenty-first-century *néo-terroir* movement that revisits Quebec's rural past to embrace it as part of the national heritage and as informing the individual identities of twenty-first-century Québécois. Pilote refuses to elide some of the more unpleasant aspects of life in the pioneer regions of the Lac Saint-Jean region, allowing Lorenzo to voice the reality that − as hindsight has revealed − the winters are too harsh and the growing season too short to make agriculture truly profitable as a lifestyle that far north. In addition to Lorenzo's and the local doctor's (Gabriel Arcand) explicit critiques of the Chapdelaines' remote rural lifestyle, Laura Chapdelaine's death and Samuel Chapdelaine's admission of guilt after the fact represent implicit critiques that are present in the novel. Although, like her daughter, Laura has freely chosen this lifestyle, she has essentially been worked to death by her husband's behaviour. As readers of the novel know, a loving father and husband, the Chapdelaine patriarch has an unbridled pioneer spirit, a love of adventure that places him somewhere between François Paradis, the *coureur des bois*, and Eutrope Gagnon, the settled farmer. After Laura's death, Sébastien Ricard grimly delivers Samuel's eulogy for his wife's strength and loyalty despite his overweening need to repeatedly uproot his family to move farther north to "faire de la terre," to *make* land by clearing the forest. Of course, with each move, they had to start from scratch and so never reached a point of material prosperity as farmers, and so the eloquent, educated Laura (brilliantly played by Hélène Florent) died before they could realize her dream of living on cleared land with a village nearby. Although Pilote thus updates Hémon's female characters, his adaptation cannot escape the power dynamics of gender prevalent in early twentieth-century rural Quebec. Her husband's dream undeniably took precedent over Laura's. It appears, however, that Eutrope recognizes Maria's agency and their marriage will be more of a partnership.

Pilote's film aesthetic of poetic realism further aligns *Maria Chapdelaine* with the *néo-terroir* movement and brings the Quebec heritage film to a place beyond the melodrama of earlier films like *Séraphin* and *Aurore*. Reflecting a long film tradition of documenting the natural beauty of *la belle province*, numerous transition sequences linger on the snow-covered landscape, or the greenery of the forest, often dramatically lit at sunset. The historical reconstitution appears painstaking dialogue frequently accompanied by the sounds of farm animals, the drudgery of daily chores revealed – largely through Laura's lean figure, the strain of her work visible in the lines on Florent's face. At the same time, however, lighting and photography add a poetic, almost saintly dimension to the Chapdelaine family at work, iconic ancestors of today's Québécois. Michel La Veaux's cinematography, which effectively uses the close-up to reveal the inner workings of characters' psyches, also frequently employs backlighting so that characters are haloed in a nimbus of light as they go about the mundane tasks around the farm. Although it is set largely on a small, remote farm in northern Canada, and not in a Newport mansion or an English manor, with the restraint of its plot and performances and the rigour of its historical reconstitution, *Maria Chapdelaine* represents, perhaps, Quebec's first *true* heritage film.

Revisiting the *Grande Noirceur*: Revisionist Images of Catholicism in *Le Club Vinland*, *Pour l'amour de Dieu*, and *La passion d'Augustine*

In an overview of Quebec's historical films Pierre Véronneau asks, "what history of Quebec do we want to address across the history of Québécois cinema?"[77] As we shall see in chapter 5, twenty-first-century Quebec film clearly privileges representations of the 1960s, showing Quebec's so-called Quiet Revolution as a golden age,[78] and implicitly criticizes the preceding "dark ages" of the *Grande Noirceur*. Most Quebec heritage films depict the period from the 1880s to the end of the 1950s through the lens of this myth,[79] reflecting an ambivalent nostalgia for a simpler time of national homogeneity and the clear moral direction of the Catholic Church, all the while criticizing pre–Quiet Revolution values as backward. Several exceptions, however, offer a more nuanced image of this era. For example, Francis Leclerc's *Une jeune fille à la fenêtre* (2001), in which a young woman moves from the countryside to the city to study piano in the 1920s, and Bernard Émond's *La femme qui boit* (2002),[80] which traces an urban woman's descent into alcoholism across the early twentieth century, revisit the *Grande Noirceur* myth. They reveal that Quebec's urbanization, industrialization, and social and intellectual awakening had already begun much earlier than 1960, following a similar timeline to the rest of North America. These films, along with several biopics discussed in chapter 4, participate in a movement of historical revisionism, questioning the process of myth-making that surrounds both the *Grande Noirceur* and the Quiet Revolution.[81] This corpus includes a small group of films that re-examine the post–Quiet Revolution received image of the Catholic Church as being largely to blame for the nation's tardy advent to modernity, reframing the church's contribution to Quebec society before 1960 in a more positive light.

The secularization of the province's educational, health, and social services systems in the 1960s became part of a foundational myth for twentieth-century Quebec, which posited the so-called Quiet Revolution as a turning point in the modernization of French Canadian society. In the new millennium, however, a movement of historical revisionism centred on the myths of the *Grande Noirceur* and the Quiet Revolution developed; a key thrust of this movement has been to revisit the way in which the Catholic Church's earlier contributions in these areas had been devalued, demonized, or completely elided in both popular and historical discourses. As we have seen so far, twenty-first-century film generally reflects the received image that the Catholic Church was complicit with the British conquerors and instilled the notion that French Canadians were *né pour un petit pain* (born for a small piece of bread), encouraging them to remain in a position of submission in the Canadian hierarchy. Basically, as the standard narrative goes, Catholicism fostered the backward, provincial attitudes attributed to pre-1960 Quebec associated with the *Grande Noirceur*. As we have already seen, historical films, along with biopics (to be discussed in chapter 4), tend to depict parish priests as small-minded bigots or out-of-touch intellectuals, nuns as sadistic and judgmental, and the church hierarchy as corrupt and hypocritical. However, a handful of films have begun to revise these stock images, casting a more favourable light on the Catholic Church and its role in the development of Quebec society. Benoît Pilon's critically acclaimed popular success *Le Club Vinland* (2020), Micheline Lanctôt's *Pour l'amour de Dieu* (2011), and Léa Pool's *La passion d'Augustine* (2013) offer sometimes surprising new looks at the role of religion in French Canadian society during the *Grande Noirceur* and into the Quiet Revolution.[82]

Benoît Pilon (b. 1962) earned critical acclaim for his historical drama *Ce qu'il faut pour vivre / The Necessities of Life* (2008), about an Inuit man (Natar Ungalaaq) who is forcibly moved from his home to be treated for tuberculosis in a Quebec City sanatorium in the early 1950s.[83] It offers a balanced image of French Canadian attitudes in that era, with some blatantly racist and others open and respectful. But the nun in charge of the hospital, Soeur Luce (Louise Marleau), is insensitively efficacious in her interactions with the new patient, reflecting received images of religious caregivers as uncaring. His more recent film, *Le Club Vinland / The Vinland Club* (2020) revises this negative image of Catholic clergy. Set in 1949, it depicts the educator Frère Jean as a progressive and inspirational teacher who leads a group of students on a quest for origins: an archaeological dig investigating the possibility of a Viking settlement along the shores of the St. Lawrence. The actual existence of the quasi-mythical Vinland has, of course, since been established with the excavation and study of the UNESCO World Heritage Site at L'Anse-aux-Meadows, Newfoundland, discovered – as a closing title card reminds viewers – in 1961. By casting Sébastien Ricard, the charismatic nationalist hip hop artist and member of Loco Locass, in the role of Frère Jean, Pilon enhances his film's revisionist message, which memorializes the positive role of clerics in intellectual endeavours in Quebec prior to the Quiet Revolution, directly countering the received image that the Catholic Church was, instead, responsible for a national backwardness. Co-scenarized by the director with Normand Bergeron and Marc Robitaille, the author of two popular memoirs adapted to film (discussed in chapter 5), *Le Club Vinland* pays explicit homage to (Catholic) educators in a concluding dedication; indeed, Pilon recounts his personal inspiration by a similar figure at the Collège Paul-de-Varennes.[84]

Himself a product of the very school where he now teaches, Frère Jean has benefited from the sponsorship of the Catholic Church and studied in the United States; inspired by his American mentor, his interpretation of a new translation of the Viking sagas leads him to believe that Leif Erikson turned south along the coast of Labrador and into the St. Lawrence, landing on its north shore not far from the *collège*. With a group of students, he forms the titular "Club Vinland," sharing his theory and inspiring them to go on an archaeological dig. For balance, *Le Club Vinland* does include characters who represent the close-minded bureaucracy of the Catholic hierarchy and the petty jealousies that arise in communal life. The school inspector, referred to as Le Frère Visiteur (Guy Thauvette), severely admonishes Frère Jean for his hubris, comparing him to the famed botanist (featured in André Forcier's *Les fleurs oubliées*) Frère Marie-Victorin when he is invited to present his theory at a conference at the Université Laval. He upholds the theory that Christopher Columbus discovered the Americas, rejecting an earlier Viking presence as pagan and idle dreaming, without moral value. But the film's villain, the stereotypical petty, narrow-minded, self-satisfied cleric who abuses his power over young people, Frère Cyprien (François Papineau), engineers Jean's humiliation. Manipulating a younger, lonely student, Jérôme Dubé (Alexandre Perreault), Cyprien authorizes the theft of a package intended for Jean. Its contents are revealed only later, when Jean's American mentor, Professor James Thompson (Guy Sprung) of the University of Baltimore, sees the Viking brooch he had sent Frère Jean on display at the school. He reveals that the artefact, ostensibly "proof" of the Viking presence in Charlevoix, had been planted at the Club Vinland's dig site; only later do we understand that it was planted not by Frère Jean, but by well-meaning students manipulated by Cyprien, whose revenge is complete when Jean is fired from the school and sent to work in the order's archives.

By addressing the value of seeking new knowledge, *Le Club Vinland* creates a space for debate about national identity and aspirations through dialogue between Frère Jean, Le Frère Visiteur, and Frère Léon (Rémy Girard), director of the (fictional) Collège Saint-Antoine, which – unlike the *collèges classiques* that prepared Quebec's elites for university educations – serves the agricultural and rural classes. In response to Frère Jean's Christmas pageant, which posits a meeting between Algonquins and Leif Erikson followed by a duel between Erikson and Columbus, Le Frère Visiteur takes exception, declaring that learning should *not* be entertaining. He asserts the school's instructional mission: "Nos élèves sont les fermiers et les ouvriers de demain" (Our pupils are the farmers and workers of tomorrow), and thus need to learn basic skills, not "des idées frivoles" (frivolous ideas). He further raises the issue of social change and the need to uphold traditional church values, without which "les sociétés finissent par éclater!" (societies will end up by breaking apart). With the Asbestos mining strike as a backdrop, *Le Club Vinland* further engages the notion of social change, situating Quebec's advent to modernity as beginning already during the so-called *Grande Noirceur* of Maurice Duplessis, as seen in acts of popular resistance to the bourgeois, capitalist status quo. Indeed, sympathetic coverage of the strike by Pierre Elliott Trudeau helped galvanize opposition to Duplessis's conservative Union Nationale party, and it launched the careers of strike leader Jean Marchand and journalist Gérard Pelletier, men who would be instrumental figures in Jean Lesage's Liberal government elected in 1960 and deemed responsible for the Quiet Revolution.

In a later conversation, Le Frère Directeur reprimands le Frère Jean, insisting that

Notre société change. Il y a de quoi s'inquiéter. L'église perd du terrain. Les jeunes se détournent de la religion. On parle même du *Refus global*. Les provocateurs, les communistes sont partout. C'est une vraie menace. Je comprends tout à fait votre intérêt pour l'histoire et la science, frère Jean, mais nous sommes ici dans la province de Québec, pas dans un collège américain.

> Our society is changing. There are things to worry about. The church is losing
> ground. Young people are turning away from religion. There is even talk about the
> *Refus global*. The provocateurs, the communists are everywhere. It's a real threat. I
> completely understand your interest in history and science, brother Jean, but we are
> here in the province of Quebec, not in an American college.

Although he is later shown to be indulgent and reasonable, willing to change his
mind when the evidence is present, Le Frère Directeur is conservative enough
to worry about the winds of change already blowing in 1949. His speech refers
to a *lieu de mémoire* representative of those winds, *Refus global* (1948), the manifesto of a group of artists called the Automatistes, led by Paul-Émile Borduas.
It called for a "total refusal" of French Canadian social norms, viewed as close-
minded and petit bourgeois, and its publication is now viewed as heralding
the Quiet Revolution to come. Le Frère Directeur also specifically frames his
limiting discourse as being about Quebec itself, suggesting that here in Quebec
we do not have the ability to think and dream like Americans do. Le Frère Jean,
however, is quick to defend himself and his educational philosophy:

> Pendant que les jeunes Anglais s'éduquent, nous autres, on continue à gaspiller le
> talent de nos élèves en les sortant de l'école à la neuvième année pour les envoyer
> dans les champs, les mines, puis les usines! Mais pourtant ils ne sont pas moins forts
> que les autres. C'est à nous de leur dire que … c'est correct de rêver!

> While the young English [Canadians] are getting an education, we are continuing
> to waste our students' talent by pulling them out of school in the ninth year to send
> them into the fields, the mines, and the factories! And yet, they are no less intelli-
> gent than the others. It's up to us to tell them that … it's okay to dream!

Frère Jean thus directly accuses the local ideology of the Québécois being *né
pour un petit pain*, speaking like a prophet for the coming Quiet Revolution,
which would bring secular education to greater numbers, resulting in the transformation of Franco-Québécois society from an agricultural or urban working-
class society to the predominantly middle-class, white-collar one it has become.
Le Club Vinland thus participates in a revisionist historiography developing since
the year 2000 that pokes holes in the myth of the *Grande Noirceur*, underscoring
how Quebec was already well on the route to modernity before the perceived
hinge date of 1960.[85]

The film's discourse also addresses questions of courage and historical truth.
Frère Jean, even though he later admits that his desire for his theory to be true
possibly hampered his critical thinking skills, represents the courage to follow a
dream, wherever it may lead. In the opening pageant sequence, he reassures his
students who are nervous about going onstage: "le trac," fear, is normal, even

good to have, he says. "Le courage, le vrai courage …, c'est d'avoir peur, mais d'y aller pareille" (Courage, true courage …, is to be afraid, but to go ahead anyway). This phrase becomes a mantra for the smaller, isolated student Dubé, who finally uses it to stand up to his abuser, Frère Cyprien, at the film's conclusion. (The family-oriented, feel-good film remains coy as to whether or not this abuse was physical, avoiding the unpleasant subject of priestly sexual abuse.) Frère Jean's courageous assertion early on that "la vraie histoire, elle est là, dans ces sagas" (the true history is here, in these sagas), holding up a volume of the Viking sagas, of course, is later proven to be true with the discovery of the Anse-aux-Meadows Norse settlement. But his ultimate humiliation and admission of guilt also suggest that some dreams may be too grandiose to follow, hinting perhaps at a further allegorical comment on the FLQ's aspirations for national sovereignty. Directly defying Le Frère Visiteur's order to dismantle the Club Vinland and to stop talking about Vikings, Frère Jean brings the boys to the dig site, where they "discover" the planted brooch. As they arrive, he declaims, "En faisant des fouilles ici aujourd'hui, c'est comme planter notre drapeau. Tous les autres après nous vont savoir que nous sommes le premiers à croire que des Vikings s'étaient arrê-tés dans Charlevoix!" (Digging here today is like planting our flag. All the others after us will know that we are the first to believe that the Vikings had stopped in Charlevoix!). This talk of planting flags suggests aspirations to national glory, of grandiose dreams of independence. Later, when the subterfuge is revealed and Frère Jean humiliated, he apologizes to his students and colleagues: "Je sais que vous êtes déçus. Que vous m'avez suivi dans cette aventure. C'est moi qui suis coupable. Coupable d'avoir mis de côté mon esprit critique" (I know that you are disappointed. That you followed me on this adventure. I'm the guilty one. Guilty of having set aside my critical spirit). He then mentions that all we can do now is to learn a lesson from these events, but he never specifies what that les-son is. This expression of guilt and of a loss of critical thinking suggests that the lesson is that we must follow our dreams, but within reason, intimating perhaps that there are those who go too far with their dreams.

In addition to inspiring the Club Vinland to dream, Frère Jean also motivates Émile by giving him a movie camera, perhaps an autobiographical nod to Pilon's stated mentor, but also to the significant role that filmmaking played in Quebec's growing self-assertion. The film closes with an epilogue set in the hinge year of 1967. Now having left the order and teaching in a university, Jean receives a letter and a film from the now adult Émile, who followed the reasonable dream of furthering his education and participating in the archaeological digs at l'Anse-aux-Meadows, thus introducing the idea that le Frère Jean's Viking dreams were not unfounded. *Le Club Vinland* thus reminds contemporary Québécois of the significant role played by individual Catholic educators who inspired generations of leaders. Although it certainly plays upon some of the negative stereotypes attributed to the church hierarchy, it also acknowledges the presence of positive role models. Indeed, it makes a point of observing that during the Asbestos strike, Montreal Archbishop Joseph Charbonneau supported the miners, in opposition to Premier Maurice Duplessis, reversing Forcier's parodic depiction of collusion in *Je me souviens*. Furthermore, by invoking that iconic strike, it calls into question the myth of the *Grande Noirceur* by insisting that Quebec's social revolution had already begun in 1949.

Quebec film icon Micheline Lanctôt (b. 1947) similarly revisits the received image of teaching clerics in *Pour l'amour de Dieu / For the Love of God* (2011). Set in 1959, on the eve of the Quiet Revolution, it tells a story of frustrated love between two sincerely pious members of religious communities. Like many films eulogizing the 1960s discussed in chapter 5, Lanctôt focalizes the narrative through the eyes of a child, in this case eleven-year-old Léonie (Ariane Legault), whose life is touched in a positive way by one of the teachers in her convent school, Soeur Cécile (Madeleine Peloquin). Through her brother Maurice (Guillaume Boisbriand), also a member of a religious order, Cécile meets Father Malachy (Victor Andres Turgeon-Trelles); they fall in love and engage in a spiritual struggle, but ultimately renounce fulfilment as a couple because of their deep-seated belief in God and respect for their religious vows. Despite critics' evocation of the cliché depicting the *Grande Noirceur* as "a period populated by fantasies related to familiar iconography," *Pour l'amour de Dieu* nuances its depiction of clerics, revealing that "all teaching nuns were not tyrannically pious, all priests were not child rapists, and all parents were not bigots."[86] Lanctôt thus recasts the image of the Catholic Church as abuser found in *The Magdalene Sisters* (Peter Mullan, 2002) and *Indian Horse* (Stephen S. Campanelli, 2017), to name just two film examples from beyond Quebec. Instead, she shows Soeur Cécile working a positive influence on Léonie, an imaginative soul who seeks nourishment in religious beliefs and its aesthetic aspects, but who also needs practical encouragement to strive for the world beyond. A frame narrative involving the middled-aged Léonie (Micheline Lanctôt) reveals that she has become a successful journalist, breaking an educational, class, and gender barrier imposed by her humble working-class, French Canadian origins. Although she became a product of the Quiet Revolution's social and educational advances, *Pour l'amour de Dieu* implies that, without the influence of Soeur Cécile, Léonie may not have had the confidence to overcome a stifling family environment.

The film does not completely elide, however, all negative images of the church, suggesting that some of the dysfunction in Léonie's family derives from her brother's childhood abuse by a priest. A disruptive alcoholic, the young adult Jacques (Lawrence Arcouette) is a burden on the family, yet their mother, Pauline (Lynda Johnson), prefers her son to her potentially gifted daughter. On the one hand, *Pour l'amour de Dieu* adopts a conventional narrative, in which the small-minded, conventional French Canadian family fails to nourish the imaginative youth. On the other hand, it revises this narrative by proposing a member of the clergy as a positive mentor who understands and fosters individual growth and difference. Indeed, it marginalizes its anti-clerical discourse; the brother's abuse is a thing of the past and both Jacques and his mother are unsympathetic characters. For example, Pauline, complains about Léonie to her ineffectual husband (Marc Paquet) that "J'en ai assez de la voir fourrée dans les jupes des soeurs!" – literally translated as "I've had enough of seeing her stuffed in the nuns' skirts," but the term *fourrée* has a sexual connotation in Québécois French, thus implying an unfounded accusation of sexual impropriety to Léonie's relationship with Cécile, thereby undermining Pauline's credibility. Furthermore, Soeur Cécile's caregiving reflects modern standards, as she protects and defends the girl, in contrast with her unenlightened mother, who wants to punish Léonie for wetting her pants at school, reflective of traditionalist severity.

Instead of accusing clerical celibacy as impossible to maintain or simply inhuman, *Pour l'amour de Dieu* underscores the humanity of its religious protagonists and their struggle to remain chaste, devoting dramatic sequences to Cécile and Malachy's natural attraction to one another as healthy, attractive, young people with mutual interests, but also to their spiritual struggle to resist temptation and honour their vows. Admittedly, Lanctôt's film implicitly critiques the very doctrine of clerical celibacy, somewhat definitive of the Catholic Church, associating small-mindedness with some members of the clergy, since Cécile's own brother, Maurice, denounces the suspected lovers to their superiors. At the same time, however, it questions contemporary secular ideology that sexual love and partnership is the only route to individual fulfilment. Instead, Cécile and Malachy are true believers who ultimately allow their faith in God and their vocation to serve others to conquer their individual desires. When they meet again in old age, neither appears to regret the decision they made, and both have lived deeply meaningful lives.

Of a generation with Pierre Falardeau, Lanctôt's earlier films followed the ONF documentary style; for example, *Deux actrices* (1993) simply depicts two actresses self-consciously discussing their roles. In *Le piège d'Issoudun* (2003), she intercalates the realist yet somehow understanding depiction of an unbalanced mother's murder of her two children with stylized images of the stage rendering of a fairy tale, revealing her interest in experimentation. *Pour l'amour de Dieu* also reflects some magical realist techniques more typical of younger directors, with Jesus Christ (Rossif Sutherland) appearing physically to Cécile, dialoguing with her and with Léonie. In contrast with Léonie's powerless father, Jesus appears as a true father figure, comforting members of his flock. Reinforcing the paradoxical imagery of Christ as both the Good Shepherd and the Lamb of God, Lanctôt films a stray lamb wandering through a building and appearing to the middle-aged Léonie, who addresses her own spiritual crisis by helping the aging Cécile (Geneviève Bujold, whose venerable on-screen presence adds clout to the characterization) visit the elderly Malachy (Nelson Villagra). Like the lamb herself, middle-aged Léonie wanders alone through the halls of a convent, and, believing she hears God calling her, queries aloud, "Jésus?" Lanctôt concludes on the image of a middle-aged woman who, although she reached maturity in the secular climate of Quiet Revolution–era Quebec, could never have accomplished what she has in life (she has become a career-woman journalist) without a prior religious grounding, and who comes full circle to reconsider her (lack of) faith. As an exemplary individual, Léonie symbolizes Quebec itself; having rejected the Catholic Church in her youth (she played a role in the discovery of Cécile and Malachy's relationship), she now returns to re-evaluate the significance of the church's contribution to her life achievements and personal fulfilment.

Like Lanctôt's independent art film *Pour l'amour de Dieu*, Léa Pool's (b. 1950) bigger-budget, general-audience production *La passion d'Augustine / The Passion of Augustine* (2013) is partially focalized through the eyes of an adolescent and depicts the positive impact that a nun-teacher, Soeur Augustine (Céline Bonnier), has on her life. In contrast, though, this feel-good film, derivative of France's *Les choristes / The Choir* (Christophe Barratier, 2004), offers only a superficial revision in its attitudes towards the church, falling back upon familiar clichés about the Catholic hierarchy stifling individual initiative. It does, however, address the impact of Vatican II reforms upon the daily lives of nuns running a convent school. It thus contributes to the body of 1960s-set films, addressing a different aspect of the (r)evolutionary changes during that decade, including for women in religious orders. Pool nonetheless depicts Vatican II's reforms as superficial, a mere facelift; her fictional nuns' sometimes traumatic, sometimes joyful exchange of the traditional surplice and coif for more modern clothing allegorizes the liturgical updates meant to modernize the Catholic Church. In contrast with *Pour l'amour de Dieu*, *La passion d'Augustine* does not depict Augustine's (or any of the other nuns') vocations as very sincere, even trivializing the sacred notion of Christ's Passion by comparing Augustine's trials to it in the film's title. Indeed, her battle with the church hierarchy suggests that her personal love of music and her individualistic desire (self-interested but also generous towards her students) to promote elite-level musicianship among young French Canadians in the 1960s is rather egotistical, opposite to the church's core value of self-sacrifice and humility. Finally, the film's depictions of, for example, Augustine's mother superior rehearse familiar clichés of the petty jealousies and conservative attitudes believed to be prevalent in communal religious life. That said, *Pour l'amour de Dieu* celebrates the contribution made by the excellent musical instruction that occurred in church schools prior to the secularization of public education in Quebec. The film reinforces Quebec's self-image as a nation of entertainers, a people for whom music has long been a traditional pastime, but it also reminds contemporary viewers of the church's role in developing this cultural trait, a phenomenon we shall see in the musical biopics analysed in chapter 4.[87]

Adaptation and the *anti-terroir* Heritage: Simon Lavoie's *La petite fille qui aimait trop les allumettes*

Despite the development of a film vision that revises the master narrative of the *Grande Noirceur* in the 2010s, two young filmmakers, Mathieu Denis and Simon Lavoie (b. 1979), working together and separately seek to caution contemporary Québécois that failing to let go of their past can lead to tragedy. Their critically acclaimed *Laurentie* (2011) is a contemporary drama about a young man who figures the *misérabiliste* strain of resentment that still exists in Quebec today.[88] Prior to that collaboration, Lavoie wrote and directed a solid historical film per se, *Le déserteur* (2008), which memorializes the true story of Georges Guénette, who was shot in the back in rural Quebec for the crime of desertion on 7 May 1944. Lavoie subsequently adapted a classic Anne Hébert *anti-terroir* short story in *Le torrent* (2012),[89] whose tormented young protagonist Neil Bishop calls "an archetype of the French-Canadian."[90] His adaptation of *Le torrent*, like *Laurentie* (2011), displays the damaged male subject of the nation, not to glorify its victimhood, but rather to accuse it of assuming this problematic position. Lavoie takes this stance a step further in his adaptation of postmodern Québécois novelist Gaétan Soucy's[91] *La petite fille qui aimait trop les allumettes* (1998).[92]

Infused with the gothic atmospheres of Anne Hébert and Marie-Claire Blais, *La petite fille qui aimait trop les allumettes / The Little Girl Who Was Too Fond of Matches* (2017) obliquely relates a tale of familial horror, including accidental death, incest, and suicide.[93] Set in rural Quebec in the 1920s,[94] the film introduces viewers to the Soissons family, whose patriarch (Jean-François Casabonne) has raised his children in isolation from the rest of the world, allowing them to be read as an allegory for the myth of the *Grande Noirceur*'s depiction of Quebec. It is clear that a family tragedy occurred sometime in the past, and his response has been so extreme that even he calls his sanity into question. Referring to them only as "Fils," the "Père" maintains his offspring in total ignorance, forbidding them numerous things; the elder son (Antoine L'Écuyer) accepts his father's authority without question, but the younger – who is actually a daughter – questions and explores, reading aloud to herself from Pascal and Saint-Simon.[95] Told that her penis fell off when she was little, "La jeune fille" (Marine Johnson), as she is identified in the film's credits, is raped by her brother and becomes pregnant. Haunted by strange dreams of a happy family life, she suffers from a repressed traumatic memory that resurfaces after her father's suicide, and she and her brother are left to fend for themselves. That memory explains both the film's title and the dark family secret: an inarticulate monster-child kept caged in a shed by the father, referred to only as "le Juste châtiment" (Laurie Babin-Fortin), the just punishment.

Described as "librement adapté" (freely adapted), Lavoie's film successfully transposes Soucy's postmodern gothic novel onto the screen; its black-and-white imagery suggests a time past, invoking fairy tale elements, in some ways evocative of Jean Cocteau's classic *La Belle et La Bête* (1945). Set in and around the Soissons family's seigneurial stone farmhouse, the film's narrative – like its literary source text – invokes Charles Perrault's classic tales, including "Cinderella," "Bluebeard," and "Little Red Riding Hood."[96] Like various fairy tale heroes and heroines, *la petite fille* remains ignorant of her identity, but searches for answers, particularly after her father's death, when she can explore the manor's various previously forbidden locked rooms. When her brother – who continues to address her as "Frère" (Brother) – tries to stop her, she asserts, "Je veux savoir qui on est, moi! Ça te dérange pas que tu te tiens dans le noir? Ça ne te fait rien? … Tu vois qu'il ne nous racontait que des histoires toutes nos vies, hein?" (*I* want to know who we are! Doesn't it bother you that you're in the dark? That means nothing for you? … You see that he's been telling us stories our whole lives, don't you?). In contrast with her brother, who upholds the *Grande Noirceur* status quo of paternal authority, *la petite fille* questions the master narrative that they have been raised with, seeking the truth about her identity and a greater measure of self-determination. The sequestered princess is even rescued by a Prince Charming figure, Paul-Marie (Alex Godbout), a mine inspector who first sees her while trying to deliver a message to her father, and who later helps her escape both the villagers and her enraged, grieving brother.[97] These elements appear much more explicitly in Soucy's novel, which also eventually names the title character and her twin, Ariane and Alice, invoking classical mythology and the heroine of Lewis Carroll's Wonderland.

Lavoie's effective use of lighting (or rather, lack thereof) underscores the metaphor of light versus dark as related to knowledge and ignorance. Several sequences involve the father or the daughter walking through the dark with just a lantern, and viewers – like the Soissons children – frequently remain in the dark about precisely what is happening on-screen. The filmmaker also uses camera angles to conceal visual information, as well, lending *La petite fille qui aimait trop les allumettes* an air of the art horror film. Indeed, the Soissons family manor is a house of horrors concealed, to be fully revealed to the light of day only at the film's conclusion when *la petite fille* recovers her memory, burns down the house and its horrible contents, escapes capture by a horde of villagers who have come to investigate, and gives birth to the child she conceived after her brutish brother raped her. The film's powerful dream/memory sequence – a departure from Soucy's novel, which alludes only to a dress and suggests that Ariane was the author of her own physical pain – reveals the full horror of the dysfunctional situation prevailing in the Soissons family home, explaining the tragedy that has so far only been hinted at. The "justly punished" monster is *la petite fille*'s twin sister, and it wasn't she who caused the fire that left her burned and mutilated and killed their mother, but rather the protagonist herself; jealous of her sister's joy and the attention she receives while playing with a sparkler, she touches a lit match to her twin's cotton dress. As horrible as this memory is, with the self-realization that it brings also comes a form of liberation, as *la petite fille* overcomes the paternal interdiction that represses truth and knowledge, which she had read from the *Mémoires du Duc de Saint-Simon* earlier in the film: "de sorte que la mémoire de lui sera à jamais éteinte" (so that her memory of him will never be extinguished). Instead of extinguishing the memory of the fire, she brings it back to light.

La petite fille qui aimait trop les allumettes lends itself to psychoanalytic readings, given its concern with origins and reproduction, as well as its mise en scène of incest, a story of castration, attempted fratricide, twins and doubling, and an attempt to supplant the father. Sexual repression is overdetermined as the father keeps his "sons" ignorant about their origins, including telling them that, God-like, he had made them from clay. To deal with his loss, he represses the very existence of their beloved mother, whose corpse he keeps – his deranged version of a Sleeping Beauty – enshrined in a locked room. Indeed, he represses the female sex altogether, convincing *la petite fille* that she is a boy, in a bizarre reversal of a castration narrative. The absent mother, abusive father, and ignorant children – one of which searches for answers and identity – reflect the prevalent "family romance" as national allegory. Furthermore, the film and its source text propose dark commentary on the period of the *Grande Noirceur*, in many ways following the clichés of Quebec's obscurantism during an era coded as pre-modern. Religion plays a significant role in the film, particularly after the father is revealed to have once been a priest; he maintains a strange altar in the home, dictating the biblical story of Jesus raising Lazarus from the dead to *la jeune fille*. Sin, punishment, rights, and interdictions figure at the core of the drama, which condemns a sometimes arbitrary and clearly mad patriarchal authority that quashes youthful curiosity and desires. And whereas the Soissons father is, of course, an exceptional figure of such authority, Lavoie depicts the "normal" society of the villagers as not much different, thus condemning the backwardness and intolerance of French Canadian society. Perceiving the innocent and ignorant *petite fille* as a threat to social order, they first tie her up and later arrive at the isolated manor as an angry mob to investigate her father's death. Lavoie focuses particularly upon the village priest, showing in close-up his mouth, twisted into a grimace of disdain, suggesting that the society that produced Soissons is just as mad as he is.

Janet M. Paterson's feminist reading of the novel informs my interpretation of the film as national allegory; it identifies the remembered period when the mother was alive as a sort of prelapsarian *paradis perdu* of familial bliss and gender equality, followed by the father's post-Fall reign of terror. *La petite fille*'s ultimate destruction of the domain resulting in "un monde patriarchal en ruines" (a patriarchal world in ruins) allows for the construction of a new order.[98] If we read the Soissons family *domaine* as a microcosm of Quebec, an isolated site of sequestration and abjection at the film's opening, we can consider the prelapsarian regime during the mother's lifetime as, perhaps, the French regime of New France. Her tragic death in flames allows for the establishment of the father's reign of terror, a symbolic reimagination of both the British regime and the Catholic Church's rule; finally, *la petite fille*'s liberation at the film's conclusion points towards Quebec's sovereignty, bought with the lives of "Le Frère" and "Le Juste Châtiment" (whom *la petite fille* has killed to put out of its misery, but also to stifle perhaps this reminder of her own guilt). With the birth of her child at the light of day, *la petite fille* attains adulthood and self-governance; nonetheless, the villagers remain nearby, and the possibility of her discovery, capture, and institutionalization as both an orphan and an unwed mother undermines the film's hopeful conclusion. Thus, whereas both the novel and its film adaptation frame the Quebec condition through the trope of pain and victimhood[99] – in contrast with the more nostalgic heritage films analysed by Liz Czach – they refuse to enshrine this position as inevitable. Unfortunately, the protagonist's revolt fails to achieve for him/her an untainted happiness, a pattern seen in the other film adaptations of *anti-terroir* novels, Simon Lavoie's *Le torrent* and Karim Hussein's adaptation of Marie-Claire Blais's *La Belle Bête* (2006).

Conclusion

Twenty-first-century revisions of the *roman du terroir* take a somewhat evolutionary trajectory, with ambivalent projections of contemporary Franco-Québécois' ancestors and their values appearing early in the millennium, with more favourable, fully nostalgic films appearing towards the end of its second decade, with *Pieds nus dans l'aube* and *Maria Chapdelaine*. These Quebec heritage films, big-budget studio productions targeting the general public, contrast with independent films that unequivocally condemn the *Grande Noirceur* ideology, presenting characters in revolt, thus replacing the fetishization of the victim with a call to life affirming action. Frequently, the auteur films discussed throughout this book offer a counterpoint to the more complacent narratives of *le cinéma grand public*, a certain strain of which attempts to break with the ideology of pain, posing Québécois as winners at home and participants in the world's affairs abroad, as we shall see in many of the biopics discussed in chapter 4. With twenty-first-century post-national, neoliberal Quebec society viewed by certain artists and intellectuals as just as indoctrinated as the mythical French Canadians of the *Grande Noirceur*, these stories of personal resistance interpellate younger viewers to reinvest in the nationalist cause at a time when *la québécitude* appears to be once again under threat.

4 Creating New Sites of Memory: The Rise of the Biopic in Twenty-First-Century Quebec

In making the lives of the famous fit particular contours – and thereby controlling normative boundaries of actions and lives – [biopics] cultivate … a world view that naturalizes certain lives and specific values over alternative ones.

George F. Custen[1]

The genre's charge … is to enter a biographical subject into the pantheon of cultural mythology, one way or another, and to show why he or she belongs there.

Dennis Bingham[2]

Historical films memorialize a collective past upon which a national identity can be based, and literary adaptations contribute to the nation's historical capital as they bring to life past eras. Similarly, as George F. Custen and Dennis Bingham assert above, biographical films function as a means of remembering significant figures who have contributed to the nation's sense of self expressed through its political and cultural heritage. Indeed, the choice of individuals whose lives appear film worthy contributes to the construction of national identity in that such creative judgment calls establish a canon of exemplary figures, those people who have made "us," in this case the people of Quebec, who "we" are. Pierre Nora's conception of the *lieu de mémoire* does not limit the site of memory that holds special meaning for the collective to literal places and monuments.[3] Exemplary individuals can be invested with such significance, as well, as Benoît Melançon argues, for example, in *The Rocket* (2009), his cultural history of French Canadian hockey icon Maurice Richard.[4] In the Quebec context, obvious candidates include colonial founders like Jacques Cartier and Samuel de Champlain, or political leaders like Louis-Joseph Papineau and René Lévesque. The filmed biography, or "biopic," tells the life story (or sometimes just key portions of that life) of an individual recognized for their social, political, or cultural contribution to national society; that contribution may be positive or negative, depending on the individual. As a meaning-making form of popular culture, biopics contribute to the construction of the imagined community of the nation. By recalling the lives of iconic figures, as well as offering up new, sometimes surprising, models, they propose updated *lieux de mémoire* that hold meaning for the nation in its evolving sense of self. The biopic, previously rare in Quebec – Andrée Fortin identifies only three titles in this category prior to the year 2000 and seventeen after[5] – has become a rising genre in this period of cinematic maturity, with filmmakers documenting, more or less faithfully, the lives of exceptional Québécois from the realms of music, sport, and even crime, proposing new cultural icons for the twenty-first century. The biopic's visual and narrative imagining of the past through the life of a significant individual inevitably engages the nation's "historical imaginary" and works towards the construction of collective memory, as Andrée Fortin has recently argued about the rising genre that she refers to in French as the *biofiction cinématographique*.[6] Her term "biofiction" calls attention to the constructed nature of the biopic, also linking it to the literary adaptation since many of the biopics examined here developed from published biographies.

This chapter outlines how the *biopic québécois* focuses on the lives of individuals who have contributed to the nation's advent to modernity, beginning in the late 1920s and 1930s with the demographic and economic shift from the rural life of agriculture to the urban life of manufacturing. As a body, these films track the course of Quebec's modernization in the early twentieth century through the *Grande Noirceur* and into the Quiet Revolution of the 1960s, thus intervening in the evolution of those historical myths, either to uphold received ideas about these periods or to question them. This discussion sets the stage for the final chapter's analysis of an even larger body of nostalgic fictionalized memoirs and semi-autobiographical films set in the 1960s, a decade viewed as the golden age for Quebec's developing nationalist and sovereigntist aspirations. Beginning with a biopic about an iconic athlete and entertainer, Louis Cyr, going on to examine films documenting the lives of musical performers, it concludes with a discussion of notorious figures who achieved fame in the 1960s and after. Although Liz Czach identifies several of these films as heritage films,[7] as we shall see, the biopic in Quebec develops a slightly different set of conventions than the literary adaptations discussed in chapter 3. As Andrée Fortin observes,[8] these "biofictions" frequently work to establish truth claims about their subject matter, as do the historical films per se discussed in chapter 1.

National Memory and the Sports Hero: Daniel Roby's *Louis Cyr, l'homme le plus fort du monde*

The cultural significance of Quebec's National Hockey League franchises, the one-time Quebec Nordiques and the Montreal Canadiens, has been well documented.[9] Sport films and sport biopics, in particular, link national identity to excellence on the playing field, invoking collective memory of outstanding athletes as unifying figures that bring together the diverse inhabitants of the modern, pluralist nation-state.[10] Quebec's pantheon of national heroes includes star hockey players like Guy Lafleur, Jean Béliveau, and, above all, Maurice Richard. Indeed, multiple analyses have shown how Charles Binamé's "super-production"[11] *Maurice Richard / The Rocket* (2005) frames the sports hero as a precursor to the political leaders of the Quiet Revolution, using his fame to protest French Canadian oppression.[12] Long before Maurice Richard, however, French Canadians looked to a sports hero who combined amazing strength with a sense of showmanship for which Quebec has been increasingly recognized: turn-of-the-century strongman and circus impresario Louis Cyr.

Only recently, since the fantastic success of Cirque du Soleil, have cultural historians begun to uncover the lost history of an ongoing tradition of French Canadian circus and to celebrate Quebec's influence in the development of the contemporary *cirque*.[13] Indeed, Louis Patrick Leroux argues that "contemporary circus with its combination of artistic activity and sports ethos has permeated Quebec society in ways that cannot be ignored," and that it has been "presented as a distinctive hybrid model for creativity emerging from a distinct society."[14] Leroux concludes that "circus has allowed Quebec, a small, self-conscious nation, to have its artists travel the world, to be recognized and applauded for its creativity, know-how, entrepreneurship, and innovation."[15] Given the cultural significance of *cirque*, it is not surprising that a biopic of the pioneering strongman Louis Cyr (1863–1912) participates in the twenty-first-century film movement to construct new *lieux de mémoire* for contemporary Quebec.

As Leroux documents, "the trope of the strongman has historically been associated with French-Canadian resilience in the face of difficult circumstances."[16] Quasi-mythical characters, larger-than-life heroic figures from the epical period of timber clearing and agricultural colonization have been the subject of literature and popular songs, like Claude Gauthier's "Le grand six pieds" (1964) and Félix Leclerc's "La drave" (1967). These French Canadian legends, like Jos Montferrand and even Paul Bunyan, are often based on real-life individuals.[17] "The founder of the first fully Quebec-run circus,"[18] Cyr Brothers Specialty Company (1892–6), Cyr achieved international fame by touring with John Robinson's and the Ringling Brothers circuses in the later 1890s. Humiliated by his treatment as spectacle, Louis Cyr returned to Quebec and founded the Cirque Cyr-Barré in early 1899 with fellow Ringling Brothers performer Horace Barré, who was (falsely) hailed as French from France by his promoters. *Louis Cyr, l'homme le plus fort du monde / Louis Cyr* (2017) successfully draws on Hollywood biopic tropes to memorialize a forgotten national hero, an outsized but ultimately real-life figure who symbolizes the feats of Quebec's pioneers and prefigures the province's future as a producer of international entertainers.

Directed by Daniel Roby (b. 1970) with a screenplay by Sylvain Guy, based on Paul Ohl's 2005 biography,[19] also involving nationalist writer and public intellectual Victor-Lévy Beaulieu, *Louis Cyr, l'homme le plus fort du monde* pays homage to this circus pioneer. Brilliantly scored by experimental rock cellist Jorane,[20] the film effectively pulls viewers into Cyr's life story, told in some ways like a fairy tale, yet at the same time focused on the authenticity of its historical reconstitution. Like other historical films, title cards guide the viewer in time and space, but also – for the famous strongman – document the world records that he continues to hold. A parable about the resilience of the grandparents and great-grandparents of today's Québécois, the film clearly situates itself in a time *before* the opportunities now available existed, recounting how one extraordinary man overcame the odds and followed a unique destiny, thereby proving that French Canadians could achieve greatness. Like Charles Binamé's earlier rendition of the life of Maurice Richard, *Louis Cyr* offers contemporary Québécois film audiences an image of historical winners rather than losers.

Framed through the eyes of Cyr's daughter, Lili (Eliane Gagnon), the film opens with her resentment, as his business partner and fellow strongman Horace Barré (Guillaume Cyr) delivers a letter to her Catholic boarding school meant to justify his life choices. Barré's narration reveals that her father sacrificed much to provide Lili with the opportunities she now enjoys, carrying viewers back in time through flashback to Cyr's humble origins and rise to fame, with occasional returns to this narrative frame. His story begins – as a title card indicates – in Lowell, Massachusetts, in 1878, a time when numerous French Canadians had migrated south to work in New England's textile mills: "Tout ça pour réaliser le rêve de tous les Canadiens Français à l'époque: arrêter de survivre et vivre un peu" (All that to fulfil the dream of every French Canadian at the time: to stop simply surviving and to live a little bit).[21] *Louis Cyr* establishes their oppressed condition as an Irishman insults Cyr's little brother, Pierrot (Charles-Olivier Pelletier), "French Canadians, eh! Scum of the earth," but Louis (Antoine Bertrand) defends the honour of his race by lifting an enormous stone. He humbly rejects entrepreneur Mac Sohmer's (Cliff Saunders) first offer to manage his career as a showman but later accepts so he can buy a proper-sized coffin for his sister, who has died of consumption. These early sequences establish Cyr's modesty, family values, and honesty. In part because of these internalized values, the hero requires adjuvants on his journey to greatness, beginning with his brother Pierrot, who coins the phrase, "l'homme le plus fort du monde" (the strongest man in the world). Embarrassed, Louis shakes off the compliment, but his future wife, Mélina (Rose-Maïté Erkoreka), finds it natural; "Il est fier de son frère. C'est bien, je trouve" (He's proud of his brother. That's good, I think). Pride in his accomplishments becomes a leitmotif, underscoring the film's message of national pride. Mélina motivates Louis to discover the world beyond the mills of Lowell, but the hero faces obstacles on the way to his destiny, the biggest of which may be the ingrained notion that French Canadians are *né pour un petit pain*, reinforced by his father's assertion that "C'est icitte, ta place, avec nous autres" (Your place is *here*, with us). To improve himself, to find more in life, Louis must leave that which he holds most dear, his family.

Cheated by Sohmer,[22] Louis and Mélina manage their own affairs until, his confidence growing, Louis attempts to book Montreal's Mechanics' Hall. Once again, he needs assistance navigating the big city system, and Gustave Lambert (Gilbert Sicotte) becomes his manager. The film covers the stages of Louis's rise elliptically, but effectively; from early countryside shows in a barn to the red-and-gold luxury of Mechanics' Hall, Cyr learns a sense of showmanship and the importance of deploying the media without compromising his principles. *Louis Cyr* introduces a second leitmotif, the uncanny, almost supernatural nature of Cyr's lifting abilities, as Lambert asks a physician to examine his protégé. Comparing Cyr to Barré, "Doc Sargent" (Neil Kroetsch) notes that there is "something much bigger than strength here. Something more difficult to assess." Louis explains his ability as deriving from his own willpower, his drive for something better, a notion underscored by his lack of weight training and the obvious difference between his portly figure and that of body builders like David "Baby" Michaud (Simon Boudreau) and Eugene Sandow (Dave Simard, a real-life Canadian champion).

As his recognition across North America grows, including shows in New York with his new promoter Richard Kyle Fox (Gil Bellows), Quebec Premier Honoré Mercier (Alain Lépine) recognizes Cyr's "contribution à la promotion de la nation canadienne française" (contribution to promoting the French Canadian nation). His ambition now is to conquer Europe, but the very drive that brought him fame and fortune will lead to his downfall. Guilty of hubris, Cyr becomes obsessed with beating Eugene Sandow, who refuses his challenge, likely knowing that he can't beat Cyr with the trickery then common, a plot element that also contrasts French Canadian honesty with American show business. After a magnificent sequence in a London theatre, documenting his unbroken world records via superimposed titles, the film depicts Cyr as compelled to prove his superiority to Sandow in New York. On Fox's invitation, he attempts something never done before: a tug of war with horses. A stunning, although clichéd, slow-motion montage rehearses the spectacular four-horse pull performed in Portland, Maine. As sublime vocals chant, blood runs out of Cyr's ears and nose, signalling his superhuman effort; one pair of horses collapses, and just after the requisite one minute, so does Cyr. This feat brings him to the hospital, where he is diagnosed with acute kidney disease and given six months to live. The hero, of course, overcomes this challenge too, living another ten years. Forced to retire to his farm, his experience in the spotlight, including betrayal by his managers, convinces him that his daughter should not lead such a life, as a "bête de cirque," revealing the source of Lili's anger. She, too, had a talent for lifting,

Figure 4.1. Louis Cyr's (Antoine Bertrand) famous four-horse pull as depicted by Daniel Roby; the blood pours from his nose, but he refuses to give in, sacrificing himself to give his family a better life.

and even performed with her father as a child; when she wishes to pursue this career, offered a contract with Ringling Brothers, the patriarch Cyr refuses. Haunted by his own illiteracy, he insists that she should have a better life. Liz Czach argues that "the film functions as a reminder of a suffering national figure, an *aide-mémoire*, to reaffirm the hardship that is, and by extension continues to be, the condition of the Québécois people."[23] But *Louis Cyr, l'homme le plus fort du monde*'s celebration of Cyr's accomplishments and the manner in which it stresses the father's self-sacrifice to improve his child's quality of life also signals a new direction in Quebec popular cinema that foregrounds the nation's winners. Offering positive role models for a new generation poised for success, these films also acknowledge the previous generations' struggles that led to the younger generation's privileges.

Reviewers in Quebec clearly identified the film's contribution to collective memory and the (re)construction of identitary models. Jérôme Delgado's description as "the story of Cyr, a real Québécois,"[24] posits the strongman as a role model for today, even though he lived during a time when the now outdated terms *Canadien* or *Canadien-français* still applied. Insisting that contemporary Quebec has forgotten its pre–Quiet Revolution past, Delgado notes the "near forgotten state" in which this national hero has fallen and views Roby's film as fulfilling "a duty of memory" with Cyr incarnating "the hopes of a community."[25] Antoine Godin reiterates the film's national significance, but rather to critique twenty-first-century Quebec's production of "a diverting, popular cinema, without a political or cultural message."[26] Evocative of Custen's description of the Hollywood biopic's role in constructing a certain history for national viewers,[27] Godin rejects this new tendency to idolize entertainers rather than serious historical figures like the "Sieur de Roberval, Louis-Joseph Papineau ou

Wilfrid Laurier."[28] As seen in chapter 1, Pierre Falardeau's *Le 15 février, 1839* certainly memorializes just such a figure, Chevalier de Lorimier, but the sheer number of films collected in this chapter confirms Godin's observation that, like it or not, in its quest for new *lieux de mémoire*, twenty-first-century neoliberal Quebec prefers figures that unite, rather than divide, and that above all make the nation feel good about itself.

Maurice Richard and *Louis Cyr, l'homme le plus fort du monde* participate in a new trajectory for Québécois popular film: the deconstruction of the "typical Québécois loser" and the construction of Québécois winners. Just as in Charles Binamé's biopic Maurice Richard becomes an exemplary model of national Québécois identity, a "personage linked to a period, one of Quebec's awakening,"[29] Louis Cyr frames the possibility of French Canadian valour in an even earlier time frame. Like these sports heroes, musical entertainers from the twentieth century also offer the nation uncontroversial sites of memory in the twenty-first.

The Musical Biopic in Twenty-First-Century Quebec[30]

Given that Quebec's best-known citizen may well be singer Céline Dion,[31] it is not surprising that since the year 2000 the musical biopic has developed into a bona fide subgenre. Indeed, quality biopics of Quebec's musical icons span the province's twentieth-century history, beginning with *La Bolduc*'s (2018) depiction of its early years to *Ma vie en cinémascope* (2004) documenting the 1930s to the 1950s, *Gerry* (2011) covering the 1960s and 1970s, and *Dédé, à travers les brumes* (2009) bringing viewers into the 1990s. These films pay homage to their subjects as national geniuses, but they depict genius as coming at a price, frequently defining it within the framework of the *poète maudit*, which conforms to the portrait of the artist as a young (mad)man (or mad woman) found in their precursor text, Robert Favreau's *Nelligan* (1991).[32] Québécois biopics also share a common narrative arc that attributes greatness to a combination of innate talent and dedicated hard work. The artist's biographical trajectory involves a period of apprenticeship, punctuated by the appearance of various demons that will haunt him/her, followed by the rise to fame, a tragic fall, and often concluding with an early demise. These musical biopics follow certain visual and narrative conventions: sequences in which the artist learns his/her craft, often in childhood; apprenticeships with teachers and collaborators; images of the artist composing and honing his or her skills. In addition, concert montages include shot-reverse shots to reveal the artist's interaction with the crowd and fans' adulatory response; studio recording sequences document the creative or performative process. Sequences underscoring the mediated nature of the artist's life, including, for example, images of news clippings or the artist's own appearances on radio and television document critical responses to the artist's work.

As Charles Stéphane Roy observes, "the biopic bears witness … to the culture of a people allowing for the rehabilitation of ambiguous figures or those ignored by official history."[33] The musical biopic in Quebec rehabilitates controversial figures and memorializes recognized stars. Born with innate talent and charisma, endowed with an overweening ambition and an accompanying work ethic and obsession with perfection, these musical icons rose to fame, but all too frequently plummeted to an early demise, usually linked to the excessive trait that fuelled their rise to glory. Violaine Charest-Sigouin describes this model as framed by "the myth of fame, of this overweening will … which in the end can only prove destructive."[34] Rejecting the inherited French Canadian model of being *né pour un petit pain*, these artists reached for the stars, but also paid the ultimate price with an early demise, their individual struggle for recognition an allegory for the collective dream of national self-determination.

Precisely because they memorialize a life completed, these films take place in the past, participating in the construction of the nation's historical imaginary, using both visual and narrative cues to situate viewers in the geographical and historical context of the artist's rise to fame. Not only do they situate their subject in a specific time frame; biopics also territorialize the lives of their subjects within the geographical context of Quebec. Furthermore, as a cinema of recognition, they exploit the powerful affective charge of music. Because of budget constraints, these period pieces frequently rely on stock footage montages to situate their protagonists in time and space, but these also blur the line between historical or biographical "fact" and the film's fictionalized portrayal. Collectively, biopics situate Quebec within the march of global history, allowing viewers to experience visually key moments like the Great Depression, World War II, and the moon landing, linking world events back to their impact at home. Sites of memory charged with meaning for a collective identity in formation, the national icons whose lives they present thus emblematize the populace as a whole.

The *Grande Noirceur* in the Musical Biopic: *La Bolduc, L'enfant prodige,* and *Ma vie en cinémascope*

After Céline Dion, Mary Rose-Anne Travers Bolduc (1894–1941), known simply and fondly as La Bolduc, represents Quebec's most iconic musical figure. Described by her biographer as "la turluteuse du peuple,"[35] La Bolduc appropriated the folk songs of her Québécois and Irish ancestors from the Gaspé region, developing an original musical form that responded directly to the needs of popular audiences during the Great Depression.[36] A major production, François Bouvier's (b. 1948) *La Bolduc* (2018), written by Benjamin Alix and Frédéric Ouellet, pays homage to her life and career, rehearsing her legend for contemporary audiences, recalling a bygone era with nostalgia. It engages Hollywood biopic conventions, transposing these onto a specifically Québécois subject and setting, contributing to La Bolduc's status as a *lieu de mémoire*.

Told in flashback, its opening lines establish the singer as representative of working-class Quebec, as her adult daughter, Denise (Rose-Marie Perreault), explains in voice-over that *La Bolduc* recounts "comment une femme comme elle a pu devenir une légende de la chanson. La porte-parole des gens du peuple. La plus grande vedette que le Québec ait jamais connue" (how a woman like her became a legend in song. The spokesperson of the little people. The greatest star that Quebec has ever known). Title cards guide viewers through time, tracing the star's rise from humble origins, and how she overcame obstacles to fulfil a societal need with her music. Her original contribution to Quebec's musical tradition united past forms and present conditions into a unique song style, which drew on folk melodies and *turlutte* (tracing a melodic line with nonsense syllables like jazz's scat), coupled with original lyrics inspired by daily life in Depression-era Quebec. In addition to celebrating her individual accomplishments, *La Bolduc* offers a feminist-lite message, underscoring tensions between the traditional roles of wife and mother assigned to her by French Canadian Catholic society, the personal fulfilment she gained from her art and its success, and the need to provide for her family. Above all, her story engages the collective narrative of Quebec's transition from a traditional to a modern society.

Like *Louis Cyr*, *La Bolduc* frames its narrative through a child's resentment and eventual forgiveness, suggesting this notion's pertinence for contemporary audiences comprised of baby boomers and their adult children. Denise Bolduc follows the opening lines cited above with the admission that in 1940 she can now forgive her conservative mother for her refusal to allow her daughter to follow her own nonconformist career path. Throughout the film, Mary is reminded that her career violates social expectations, as seen in a priest scolding her before a show in Rivière-du-Loup: "Madame Bolduc, le rôle d'une femme est de s'occuper de ses enfants et de son mari. J'ai bien peur que vous ayez abandonné votre foyer aux mains du Malin" (Madame Bolduc, a woman's role is to take care of her children and her husband. I am quite afraid that you have abandoned your home to the hands of the Devil). External pressures to conform result in internal struggle and conflict with others as Mary attempts to fulfil her responsibilities as wife and mother, while at the same time carrying out professional duties as an artist, bringing joy to the common people of a region stricken by an international economic disaster.

Flashbacks establishing the artist's origins include young Mary's 1913 arrival in Montreal, invoking the rural exodus and struggle of single young women to make ends meet temporarily on a domestic servant's or a garment worker's salary, with the ultimate goal of finding a husband and starting a family. When she marries Édouard Bolduc (Émile Proulx-Cloutier), the young wife faces the tragic reality of high infant mortality. As World War I breaks out – revealed by a shot of a newspaper on her back steps – Mary goes into labour with a first, stillborn child. Later, as the young mother brings her three surviving children to visit a graveyard plot bearing six small wooden crosses, *La Bolduc* reveals a collective history of serial pregnancies, some resulting in surviving children, others in miscarriages, stillbirths, and infant death. Over her lifetime, the real-life Mary Travers Bolduc raised only four children (one of whom died at the age of three) out of thirteen pregnancies.[37]

Another medical tragedy, however, forced Mary out of the home and into the spotlight. Just as the family prospers enough to buy a piano, Édouard is temporarily disabled. *La Bolduc* elliptically depicts the patriarch's chronic toothaches, his wife dramatically told of an "accident," and a doctor describing her husband's precarious health after massive blood loss resulting from a botched dental extraction.[38] The family's bad luck, however, leads them to greater fortune as its matriarch parlays a musical talent developed as a form of everyday sociality into a professional career. Mary seizes the opportunity to fill in as a violinist for stage producer Conrad Gauthier's (Germain Houde) popular revue, "Les Veillées du Bon Vieux Temps" (Evening parties from the good old days). She appears onstage in a white wig, a nostalgic representation of the French Canadian tradition of *la veillée*, evenings of music, dance, and storytelling held on long winter nights by the province's early *habitants*. The film rehearses her discovery by the recording producer Roméo Beaudry (Serge Postigo) of Starr-Guénett Records,[39] her rise to popularity, her career touring the province, and daughter Denise's role as her accompanist. It exposes Édouard's resentment over Mary's newfound fame, which provides for the family when he cannot. Not only is Édouard teased by friends about who wears the pants in his family, but he also begins to lash out at his wife, frustrated by their unnatural, world-upside-down situation: "tout va revenir dans le sens du monde!" (literally, "everything will return to the direction of the world" – that is, return to normal). In addition to the injury Mary feels at her now alcoholic husband's lack of support, she suffers insult in the form of married women's legal status as minors and her need to declare herself a *marchande publique* (public merchant) in order to manage her own finances. Despite the fact that she performs as "Mme Édouard Bolduc," dresses in a sober black dress onstage, and calls her family from the road, doing everything she can to be a proper wife and mother, La Bolduc – a nickname she didn't like – is consistently haunted by her Catholic upbringing. She openly rejects the role of emblem for women's struggles during an (apocryphal) encounter with women's rights pioneer Thérèse Casgrain (Mylène Mackay). When Denise wins a Hollywood screen test in a local talent contest, her conservative parents, seconded by their future son-in-law (Yan England), forbid the young woman to pursue her own dream of stardom, finally explaining Denise's anger at the film's opening.

As La Bolduc's fame grows, her children become more self-sufficient, and Édouard's status as provider is restored when he finds work in the Baie-Comeau, documenting yet another important step in Quebec's modernization via its self-defining hydroelectric projects; life appears to stabilize, albeit unconventionally. But, of course, the star pays the price for her success; extensive time on the province's sometimes bumpy, sometimes icy back roads eventually result in a serious car accident.[40] While being treated for a broken leg and a head injury, however, she receives a more serious diagnosis: X-rays reveal a cancerous tumour. Heroically facing innovative radium therapy and stoically fulfilling her concert responsibilities despite increasing pain, the star is eventually struck down.

Paving the way for and influencing the careers of other national entertainers, particularly women, La Bolduc has been praised for her "vanguard career as Quebec's first singer-songwriter."[41] In addition to its historical touchstones, *La Bolduc* revisits national cultural traditions, including the vaudeville-style theatrical reviews like "Les Veillées du Bon Vieux Temps," the church-organized "tombola" that provided an opportunity for young Catholic singles to meet, and musical afternoons and evenings among family and friends. It thus signals music's role in the construction of Quebec's identity. Although it fails to explore her regional origins in the Gaspé Peninsula, including the fact that Mary Travers's mother was Louis Cyr's cousin,[42] *La Bolduc* stresses the importance of local culture, lampooning a priest's encouragement of art songs from France when young people prefer the regional reels and jigs that the *chansonnière* will incorporate into her style. It shows her inspiration and artistic practice as she spontaneously composes the lyrics for her first big hit, "La cuisinière," while cooking with her daughter. Scholars have documented the social and political significance of her songs,[43] but the film gives this line to suffrage activist Thérèse Casgrain to Denise: "Jamais avant votre mère une femme n'a osée prendre la parole en public" (Never before your mother has a woman dared to speak in public). Talented and successful but devoted to family values, La Bolduc represents, in a sense, an updated mother figure for the nation. A winner despite her struggles, she revises the image of victimhood found in *Nouvelle-France*'s Marie-Loup Carignan, for example, or even in a more related figure, Alys Robi, depicted in another musical biopic from earlier in the new millennium.

La Bolduc adopts the mild feminism found in an earlier big-screen biopic about a near contemporary of Travers's daughter, big band chanteuse Alys Robi (1923–2011). Robi's tragic career trajectory perhaps justifies La Bolduc's desire to spare her daughter the controversial lifestyle of the starlet. Denise Filiatrault's (b. 1931) *Ma vie en cinémascope / Bittersweet Memories* (2004) memorializes "Quebec's first star,"[44] its title invoking Luc Plamondon's tribute, "Alys en cinémascope," performed by Diane Dufresne in 1979.[45] Perhaps inspired by a line in Robi's memoir, *Un long cri dans la nuit* (1990), in which the singer recalls that her entire life flashed before her eyes as she was being wheeled into the operating room to undergo a lobotomy,[46] Filiatrault's screenplay frames Robi's biography – told in flashback – through this traumatic moment. Pascale Bussières,

Figure 4.2. Alys Robi's (Pascale Bussières) incarceration in the Saint-Michel-Archange mental asylum likens the fallen star to other French Canadian martyrs.

cast in the lead role, interprets the nervous breakdown, which led to five years in the Saint–Michel-Archange mental asylum, electroshock, and drug therapies, as deriving from career-related stresses, compounded by a sexual neurosis, the result of an internal conflict between a strict Catholic upbringing and her adult sexual relationships with two married men. A somewhat repetitive melodrama, the big-budget, heavily subsidized film received scathing commentaries from institutional critics Marie-Claude Loiselle and Pierre Barrette as inauthentic and derivative of Hollywood films.[47] Evocative of *Frances* (Graeme Clifford, 1982), a biopic of lobotomized writer Frances Farmer (Jessica Lange), *Ma vie en cinéma-scope* proposes a mildly feminist agenda in its depiction of Robi's internment, but its anti-lobotomy stance contradicts the singer's own memoirs, which portray the procedure as essential to her recovery from mental illness.[48]

Despite its adoption of Hollywood biopic conventions, *Ma vie en cinémascope* clearly situates its heroine within the province of Quebec and its history, but it also marks an important development as she crosses national boundaries to play a role on the international stage. Stock newsreel footage documents the Depression and World War II abroad, while staged sequences reveal these international crises' impact at home. Born Alice Robitaille in 1923, the future starlet began her career out of necessity; a signboard at a theatre box office shows the decreased price, from one dollar to ten cents, for a double feature film *and* live entertainment, signalling the economic crisis and explaining her performer father's difficulty making ends meet.[49] Key references to local history include the Conscription debates as iconic local radio station, CKAC, interviews Montreal Mayor Camilien Houde (Martin Larocque). His release from prison for anti-conscription rhetoric coincides with Robi's return from a concert tour, during which she played her part in the war effort by entertaining troops. In a unifying gesture, the film visually imagines both sides of the wartime controversy meeting, as Robi and Houde, carried triumphantly on the shoulders of adoring fans, shake hands. But it also signals her impending mental crisis as the overwhelming attention brings on a panic attack. In the 1950s, her nightclub career plays out against stock footage of neon on Montreal's "Main," as its entertainment strip, Saint-Laurent Boulevard, is known. Place and date title cards identify less obvious references, such as the site of Robi's internment: "Institut Psychiatrique / St-Michel Archange / Québec 1952." Just as published memoirs and biographies specifically link the artist to the nation, biopics construct the artist as specifically French Canadian or Québécois, both visually and with dialogue. As a child, Robi performs on the Dufferin Terrace outside Quebec City's landmark Château Frontenac hotel; her departures from the famous Victorian sandstone monument, Montreal's Gare Windsor, and her vaudeville tour of small-town churches, their distinct architecture marking their *québécitude*, link her to various aspects of the province's geography. When she seeks fame in the wider world, she admits, "I miss Quebec very badly," and expresses joy on returning home to Quebec City, "ma ville natale" (my birthplace).

Ma vie en cinémascope situates Robi's career within contemporary musical trends; a child star referred to as "l'enfant prodige de la paroisse" (the parish's child prodigy), she appears first in vaudeville shows, associated with historical figures in the Montreal entertainment world, such as Rose "La Poune" Ouellette (Nathalie Mallette), Jean Grimaldi (Normand Chouinard), and her first lover, Olivier Guimond (Serge Postigo).[50] Discovered by band leader Lucio Augustino (Denis Bernard), also her eventual lover, Robi plays a pivotal role in introducing Latin sounds to Quebec in post-war Montreal's nightclubs. She establishes an international reputation performing in Las Vegas and Hollywood, referred to as "The French-Canadian bombshell, Alys Robi!" *Ma vie en cinémascope* includes montages with pin-up photos and entertainment magazines with the media darling's image on the cover. Robi's career coincided with the rise of radio, and the film signals this new medium's presence in Quebec with sequences of studio concerts, her mother listening to a priest's homily, and Montrealers attentive to the anti-conscription speech that resulted in Houde's arrest. Filiatrault thus plays with *mise en abyme*, featuring the starlet contemplating her own image (as the iconic actress Pascale Bussières contemplates her own image on these photos while playing the role of Robi), inserting fake newsreel footage of Robi entertaining the troops, and staging her pioneering appearance in London on the BBC's first television broadcast.

Indeed, since genius is linked to innovation, Robi's television appearance is one of the many famous "firsts" ritually replayed in these biopics, but genius is also linked to difference, exceptionalism, and even madness. Robi is considered "la première 'star' québécoise," the first French Canadian entertainer to launch an international career. First, she performed in Toronto on CBC radio with Lucio Agostini's "Latin American Serenade"; then she was "la première canadienne francaise dans le domaine populaire à enregistrer à New York" (the first French Canadian in popular music to record in New York). She was also the first French Canadian to perform in Las Vegas and was slated for a screen test in Hollywood when a car accident intervened, also perhaps triggering the first signs of mental illness as she subsequently freezes up onstage. *Ma vie en cinémascope* depicts Robi's demons as rooted in her humble origins. Having been exploited as a child entertainer to contribute to the family economy, she watches as an illness, presumably polio, leaves her brother Gérard an invalid Alys's care for him even after her rise to fame aligns with appropriate feminine roles. Under the strict sexual mores of pre–Quiet Revolution Catholic Quebec, her guilt over her affairs leads to neurosis, the film implies. Her career introduced Robi to her first lover, who becomes jealous of her success, which then triggers an affair with the married Agostini. Viewed increasingly as a temperamental artist, Robi is exploited and overworked by her agents, leading to mental exhaustion and moodiness, for which she initially agrees to check into a "rest home," not realizing that, once interned, she will not be allowed to leave until deemed cured. Although the film resists conspiracy theories according to which Robi's financial managers robbed her of her fortune by extending her internment,[51] Filiatrault does infer that as a nonconformist woman, Robi was in some sense punished for her behaviour and success by a society not yet ready for change. Despite its suggestion that "the heritage biopic … portrays their [protagonists'] suffering as a precondition for becoming a true Québécois and a national icon,"[52] *Ma vie en cinémascope* depicts the nation's nascent modernity, as does the independent film, *Jack Paradise (Les Nuits de Montréal) / Jack Paradis: Montreal by Night* (Gilles Noël, 2004), which also memorializes Montreal's night club era in a fictionalized account of jazz pianist Bob Langlois.[53] By bringing back to light the glory days of a forgotten icon, it also reminds twenty–first-century viewers of past French Canadians in order to inspire future contributions and shifts focus from stock images of rural Quebec found in the heritage film to the urban landscape.

Another child prodigy like Robi, but in the field of classical music, is the subject of *L'enfant prodige / The Child Prodigy* (2010), written and directed by *Aurore*'s Luc Dionne, developed in large part through the efforts of concert pianist Alain Lefèvre to "rehabilitate the work" of virtuoso and composer André Mathieu (1929–68).[54] Dionne received mixed reviews for his account,[55] derived largely from J. Rudel-Tessier's 1976 biography, itself based on extensive interviews with the artist's mother, Mimi Mathieu.[56] Frequently referred to as "le petit Mozart canadien" (the little Canadian Mozart), Mathieu pursued an international career as a concert pianist, but this *biopic québécois* lingers on the young adult's failure to become Rachmaninoff's musical heir as a composer. Patrick

Drolet portrays the tormented genius as haunted by his lost childhood success, dysfunctional family relationships, unrequited love, and his ambition to be recognized as a composer rather than a pianist. Fuelling periods of depression and mental instability, including a suicide attempt, with alcohol, Mathieu suffers a seemingly inevitable early demise.

L'enfant prodige follows the conventions of the musical biopic, situating Mathieu's career in time and space, first in the territory of Quebec with stock period footage of Montreal monuments like Dorchester Square and the Oratoire Saint-Joseph. Later images of Expo 67, for example, trace the passage of time. Foreign locations are also signalled for the viewer, but due to economic constraints, Sofia, Bulgaria, stands in for the Parisian landscape. During an important sequence establishing the artist's international success, however, a shot of the sign marking Paris's Maison des Étudiants Canadiens identifies a *lieu de mémoire* in the French capital where Mathieu, along with other significant national figures including André Laurendeau, had stayed.

L'enfant prodige also situates the French Canadian genius within a broader musical context, offering comparisons, catch phrases, and using a system of name-dropping that compares the local hero to better-known international heroes, thus creating a relationship of genius by association. Working in the milieu of classical music, and referred to as "Rachmaninoff's heir," Mathieu's compositional style is inspired by Romantic and impressionist music, later shown in conflict with the rise of modern and concrete music. Taught first by his father, Rodolphe Mathieu (Marc Labrèche), a composer in his own right, the film's André is told by Rachmaninoff (Itzhak Finzi) himself, "Vous êtes le seul musicien digne d'être mon héritier" (You are the only musician worthy of being my heir).[57] Mathieu also studies in Paris under Arthur Honegger (Marc Béland), a major twentieth-century composer, but his musical affinity with the aging Russian Romantic and his refusal to embrace contemporary compositional trends thwarts his success, as he admits, "La modernité, c'est pas pour moi ... j'suis complètement dépassé" (Modernity is not for me ... I'm completely left behind). The local hero's association with prestigious world figures elevates the entire nation, and this type of name-dropping, linking Quebec to international trends, becomes a hallmark of the *biopic québécois*. *L'enfant prodige*'s depiction of the child Mathieu as in synch with his times, but his inability to keep up with contemporary trends as an adult fuels the notion of his arrested development. Caught in the glory of the past, his situation allegorizes the nation itself struggling with the rapid modernization of the 1960s, inevitably leaving some citizens at a loss, feeling out of place. Although Dionne elides this aspect of Mathieu's political engagement, his flirtation with *Duplessisme* as an adolescent and young man supports this interpretation of the artist.[58]

Like *Ma vie en cinémascope* before it, *L'enfant prodige* depicts the media's role in the construction of the star, superposing images of archival newspaper coverage onto shots of the young genius in concert. It recites Mathieu's famous firsts as a French Canadian virtuoso and composer, including his first concert at Montreal's Ritz-Carlton Hotel in 1935 at the age of five; his Young Composers Prize celebrating the one-hundredth anniversary of the New York Philharmonic in 1941, and his 1943 concert at Paris's Salle Chopin-Pleyel 1943. But it documents failures as the artist's downturn begins. For example, desperate to reach a larger audience and recover the adulation he knew in his youth, Mathieu controversially participates in a new fad, the pianothon. But the seeds for his early demise were already sown in his childhood: family pressures, a dysfunctional sex life, an unreceptive French Canadian public, his growing self-perception as a failure, and the use of alcohol to handle these stressors.

Despite his middle-class origins, his parents' modest economic circumstances as musicians align Mathieu with Quebec's other musical heroes, most coming from poor, working-class families. Whereas La Bolduc and little Alys Robi sang just to put food on the table, the bourgeois aspirations of André's parents exacerbate economic pressures on him, but they also live vicariously through him. In addition, his overbearing mother Mimi's (Macha Grenon) interference in his relationships with women further isolates him. His genius attracts the mature Colette Ostiguy (Isabel Richer), but she ultimately rejects him. When he finds an age-appropriate love object, marrying Johanne Lecompte (Catherine Trudeau), she dominates him, and he evidences little sexual desire. One particular demon follows Mathieu throughout his career: the public's desire to see him as a French Canadian child prodigy coupled with the critical establishment's later rejection of him as a composer. Finally, his early alcoholism – already as a teenager, Mathieu drank heavily – damages his career, before it most likely causes his death. Still hopeful for a comeback, Mathieu was invited to perform at Expo 67, but the invitation was withdrawn as officials feared he might show up drunk. Although hardly a role model, Mathieu's character development situates him as an individual at once ahead of his time and somehow behind the times as well. Biographers and *L'enfant prodige* blame Quebec audiences' lack of preparation for his, at first, innovative music as a major source for his demons. In this respect, Mathieu represents the post–Quiet Revolution modern subject born too early to be properly appreciated. In the end, *L'enfant prodige* invokes for contemporary Québécois an example of a French Canadian's success on the international stage, coupled with his rejection at home. A transitional figure between the *Grande Noirceur* and the Quiet Revolution, Mathieu's portrait remains that of the *maudit Canuck*, a reminder of the nation's struggles for recognition. In contrast, the rebellious attitudes of two rock musicians correspond with Quebec's image of itself as a modern society, fully belonging to the American continent, but also a unique part of it because of its francophone culture and independent, even anti-authoritarian attitude in relation to the rest of Canada.

Musical Artists after the Quiet Revolution: *Gerry* and *Dédé, à travers les brumes*

Just as the sports biopics posit their male heroes as models for French Canadian valour (*Louis Cyr*) and even a nascent Québécois nationalism (*Maurice Richard*), two musical biopics explicitly align the artist with the developing sovereigntist movement from the 1960s through 1995. Indeed, singer-songwriters like Félix Leclerc (1914–88) and Gilles Vigneault (b. 1928) used their music actively to promote francophone culture and the sovereigntist movement, and they would be followed by subsequent generations of performers, from Robert Charlebois (b. 1944) to contemporary artists like Daniel Lavoie (b. 1972).[59] One of Charlebois's contemporaries is the subject of a biopic that contributed to a spate of period films devoted to the 1960s (discussed in chapter 5). Alain Desrochers's *Gerry* (2011) brings back to life the charismatic lead singer of the 1970s rock group Offenbach, described in the film as "les [Rolling] Stones du Québec." Mario Saint-Amand charismatically reincarnates Gerry Boulet (1946–90), brought down not by his rock-star lifestyle but by colon cancer, yet Nathalie Petrowski's[60] scenario nonetheless depicts the self-destructive aspects of the sex and drugs regularly associated with rock and roll. Described as "a Québécois version of Oliver Stone's *The Doors*,"[61] *Gerry* follows Mario Roy's biography of the artist,[62] packing numerous micro-incidents into some ninety short sequences. From Boulet's insistence on moving the group's musical trajectory away from the derivative, often English-language pop sounds of *yéyé* towards a harder, blues-based rock and roll, coupled with powerful lyrics in French that reference local, working-class, and youth realities, *Gerry* presents its titular artist as a new type of national hero. Saint-Amand's physical similarity to his model – not handsome but cocky and lithe and overtly heterosexual – corresponds to accepted images of French Canadian machismo, and the representation of Quebec's contributions to world culture through spectacle and music fits its twenty-first-century self-image. The entertainment icon reinforces the construction of Montreal as a "ville festive" (festival city) and Gerry's career mirrors on a smaller scale that of Céline Dion or Cirque du Soleil.

Representing on-screen a period more readily accessible to viewer memory, *Gerry* uses more subtle techniques to signal its time frame than the stock footage or title cards found in biopics set in earlier eras. For example, close-up shots of licence plates indicate the date of 1966; bearing the pre–*Je me souviens* tagline, *la belle province*, they signal that the modern province was still in development. A bicycle plate dated 1976 bearing the Olympic rings and campaign posters in favour of a "OUI" vote for the 1980 referendum cleverly mark advances in time, also referencing key events in nationalist politics. Set in this historically Catholic province, *Gerry* documents the evolving social context of Vatican II reforms, the rise of secularism, and the counterculture's significance in 1960s and early 1970s

Quebec.[63] The film depicts Offenbach in concert with the Quebec flag flying behind them or waved by fans, clearly linking them to the nation and nationalist attitudes, and Gerry Boulet's working-class accent and vernacular Québécois French mark him as *d'ici* (from here). *Gerry* explicitly engages debates over singing in English or French, even addressing the question of what *kind* of French – debates integral to national identity. For Quebec's (and even France's) popular musical artists, singing in English has long seemed a requirement for success; the choice to sing in French thus represents a political stance. Furthermore, *la Querelle du joual*, a polemic over the use of vernacular Québécois French or Standard International French, raged in the 1960s.[64] The counterculture rock band, of course, sides with *joual*, as band member Pierre Harel (Éric Brunet) rejects the long-standing "colonized" mentality of French Canadians who felt culturally inferior to France or the United States, proudly proclaiming the new national identity, just beginning to be labelled "Québécois." Exaggerating his own accent, he incites the crowd: "Vous voulez qu'on chante en francais? Les Stones, eux, ils chantent pas en français; le français, ça se parle en France. Icitte, on est au Québec! Pis on parle Québécois! Et on chante Québécois!" (You want us to sing in French? The Stones, they don't sing in French; French is spoken in France. Here, we are in Quebec! So we speak Québécois! And we sing in Québécois!).

Gerry Boulet, and André "Dédé" Fortin after him, participated in debates over the direction of popular music in Quebec, and both insisted that Québécois musicians write lyrics in French rather English. Gerry's career began during the *chanson* versus *yéyé* debates,[65] which saw French-language popular music move from the model of the folk- or crooner-style song typified by Félix Leclerc (in Quebec) and Charles Trenet (in France) towards band-based popular music, the *yéyé* modelled on the Beatles. In the late 1960s and 1970s, this debate evolved with Robert Charlebois combining a *chanson*-like approach to composition with a rock aesthetic. Boulet took this a step further, insisting on heavier, blues-based rock and roll. Not only does the film's dialogue declare that Offenbach is "les Rolling Stones du Québec," but Gerry also distances himself from the pop stylings of fellow nationalist Robert Charlebois, exclaiming, "Je ne suis pas Charlebois!" Boulet's relatively modest career, including a brief stint in France to tour and make a documentary film,[66] largely remains tied to the territory of Quebec. Unlike the subjects of earlier artists' international careers, the biopic convention of associating the subject with other, more famous individuals remains limited to local celebrities like poet Denise Boucher (Louise Bombardier) and singer Marjo (Maxime Morin).

Like other biopics, *Gerry* references Offenbach's notable firsts, including a landmark in the decolonization of popular culture, which is dominated to this day by English-language artists, writers, and filmmakers. Offenbach was the first French-Canadian band to play in the Montreal Forum, a major concert venue usually reserved for internationally acclaimed anglophone acts like the Beatles or

Queen. Dialogue reminds younger viewers of this event's significance: "On est les premiers à avoir fait le Forum, comme les Américains! On l'a eu, tabarnac!" (We're the first ones to do the Forum, like the Americans! We've made it, dammit!) They also participated in Québec Rock, "la plus grosse tournée rock que le Québec a jamais eu là" (the biggest rock tour that Quebec has ever had), and Boulet's leadership of Offenbach led to a signal performance of a rock opera–style mass in the Oratoire Saint-Joseph. Like other innovative Québécois artists, however, such visionary works often met with negative critical responses, suggesting the province's ongoing lack of readiness for unique genius.

Boulet also faces obstacles, including his working-class origins, with his father rejecting the profession of musician as inappropriate for his son. Traits that contribute to the larger-than-life image of the heroic subject include Gerry's massive sexual appetite, coupled with female fans' availability to the charismatic star, which make it difficult for him to remain faithful to a single woman, thus destroying both of his significant relationships. Whereas Robi and Mathieu were exploited and the latter overprotected by his family, Boulet's bandmates frequently abandon him, simply lacking his drive for success. Drugs and alcohol certainly played a role in the artist's self-destruction, but instead of the madness associated with artistic genius in the *biopic québécois*, like La Bolduc, Boulet was attacked from within by a different, physical demon: cancer. His personal drive allegorizes the nation's growing confidence and self-determination; even his early demise suggests his synecdochic, part-for-the-whole relationship to Quebec's failed campaign for sovereignty. This motif is even further developed in a biopic about a 1990s music star, André Fortin.

Dédé, à travers les brumes / Through the Mist (2009), written and directed by Jean-Philippe Duval (b. 1968), depicts the life and death of André Fortin (1962–2000), lead singer of the iconic 1990s rock band Les Colocs who took his own life via the Japanese ritual of seppuku. Casting Sébastien Ricard from the nationalist rap group Loco Locass to play "Dédé" underscores Fortin's separatism, as does the suggestion that the failure of the 1995 referendum on sovereignty represented a turning point in Fortin's downward spiral. Widely praised by critics for its animation and stop-motion transition sequences, this is certainly the most auteurish of the *biopics québécois*; concerns were nonetheless raised about its role as a collective catharsis and about its troubling *mise en image* of Fortin's suicide.[67] Aesthetically, critics likened it to "a series of music videos illustrating an artist's work" rather than a coherent biography,[68] perhaps because it lacked a sustained written account of its subject's life upon which Duval could base his scenario.[69] And yet, this film suggests that the personage of "Dédé," sporting his hallmark early aviator's goggles and helmet, has become a new site of memory in Quebec.

Whereas *Gerry* features the 1980 referendum, *Dédé* is overdetermined by its title character's experience of the 1995 referendum, restaged through campaign signs featured prominently and a key sequence depicting a party organized, it was hoped, to celebrate the victory of Quebec's popular bid for sovereignty. Instead, it depicts Dédé's heartbroken reaction to the vote's outcome. Unlike other musical biopics that relate more distant historical periods, *Dédé* relies on costuming, make-up, and furniture to indicate its time frame, but nonetheless territorializes *Dédé* within the national space in obvious ways, including exterior shots of the Colocs' actual former apartment on the Plateau-Mont-Royal, as well as more subtle ones, such as the film's opening sequence invoking the northern landscape and the motif of hockey;[70] similarly, tour sequences include shots of road signs indicating the distance to Montreal and Quebec City.

André "Dédé" Fortin is explicitly connected to Montreal through a creative maquette of the city, including the landmark Olympic Stadium, that stylistically documents his arrival by bus from Lac Saint-Jean, where he grew up. Inside the iconic apartment, which provided the group with its name (*les colocs* = the roommates), his pride in national culture appears in a poster for *Les bons débarras* (Francis Mankiewicz, 1980), and a Montreal Canadiens jersey bearing the number 2 (retired in honour of defenceman Doug Harvey) hangs in a closet. Furthermore, *Dédé* explicitly invokes Fortin's nationalist position in dialogue. To Belgian bandmate André Vanderbiest (David Quertiniez), confused about French Canadian identity, Fortin declares himself firmly as "Québécois." With dialogue in English when he first meets future Coloc Mike Sawatzky (Josef Mesiano) at a meal, Fortin admits, "I do share with strangers from the other loneliness," comically referencing through his mistranslation the concept of Canada as "two solitudes." But he also admits that if the anglophone wants to join the band: "There's a problem. I'm a nationalist sovereignist."

In terms of musical innovation, just as Gerry Boulet promoted the notion that Québécois could sing and play authentic, blues-based rock and roll, Dédé was instrumental in opening up Québécois popular music, dominated by the national *chansonnier* tradition, to the possibility of French-language alternative rock. Whereas Gerry rejected the (to him) outmoded Charlebois, Dédé embraced the appellation "le nouveau Charlebois!" He also introduced the rising category of "world music," collaborating with the Senegalese-born Diouf Brothers, contributing to an idea of Quebec as a pluralistic society. Concert sequences include the iconic Montreal nightclub the Quai de brumes, on the Plateau-Mont-Royal, the Spectrum, and the Plains of Abraham; these venues situate *Dédé* squarely at the origins of Quebec's current alternative/indie rock scene and Les Colocs are a touchstone group for later acts, like Loco Locass.

Like Gerry, Dédé's dedication to his art, exacerbated by an expanding ego, results in conflicts with bandmates and sexual infidelity. But an ongoing record of depression, depicted as first occurring while a student in film school, but also exacerbated by the 1994 death of bandmate Patrick Esposito (Dmitri Storoge), who likely contracted AIDS as a by-product of his heroin addiction, constructs the fractured dream of national independence as a pivotal disappointment that pushes an already teetering individual over the edge. Furthermore, the unique form that Fortin's suicide takes, drawn from his obsession with Japanese film and culture – including admiration for the writer Yukio Mishima (1925–70), who committed suicide by seppuku – further inscribes Dédé as a paradoxical national visionary whose very individuality and difference, although often misunderstood during his lifetime, ultimately leads to hero status. Although *Dédé, à travers les brumes* clearly celebrates the artist's triumphs, depicting him in many ways as a winner, it ultimately erects him as a victim-martyr for the lost cause of sovereigntist nationalism.

Overall, rejecting their place as *Canadiens-français, un peuple né pour un petit pain*, the musical artists memorialized in these *biopics québécois* reflect glory on their home province; yet while they serve as cultural ambassadors, some also suffer the condemnation and betrayal of their own people during their lifetimes. Jean Beaunoyer underscores how "before becoming a myth, Alys Robi was the favourite target of gossips, calumniators and rumour mongerers."[71] As a victim, he argues (along with Liz Czach), Robi has paradoxically become interesting to a Quebec that has still not had enough of *La petite Aurore, l'enfant martyre*, and the success of the 2005 reboot, *Aurore*, attests to the accuracy of this assertion. Citing Maurice Richard's elevation from sports figure to "l'idole d'un peuple," Beaunoyer proposes that "for the last fifty years, the Québécois have preferred victims to idols whose weight they couldn't support."[72] Arguably, Alys, André, Gerry, and Dédé join *la petite* Aurore, along with earlier national martyr-heroes, including the *Saints Martyrs canadiens*,[73] Dollard des Ormeaux, Chevalier de Lorimier, Louis Riel, and René Lévesque. To achieve greatness, these artists struggle with various demons, and the ability to overcome these (if only temporarily) represents the strength and resilience of the Québécois people. Eventually succumbing to them, however, paradoxically also allows for their memorialization as martyred victims.

In their search for new, more relevant franco-nationalist but non-partisan,[74] and above all secular, *lieux de mémoire*, twenty-first-century filmmakers have turned to sports figures and entertainers to remind younger generations of Québécois who did not experience French Canadian oppression first-hand of the obstacles overcome before contemporary Quebec could develop. Sometimes these films simply congratulate contemporary viewers on the progress made towards self-affirmation as a pluralistic, modern democracy. More radical films suggest that the current dominant position of French language and culture in Quebec is not assured, and that the struggle continues.[75] Because, more than any other factor, the French language, in particular vernacular Québécois French – often referred to by the shorthand *joual* – represents the national identity, these musical icons have been memorialized on film precisely because of their role in maintaining the French language through popular culture. The construction of new secular and apolitical *lieux de mémoire* for the nation, however, is not unanimously well received by institutional film critics who raise concerns about "quick and easy profit from icons who have become the spontaneous pillars of an immediate heritage."[76] And yet, as Beaunoyer remarks on the recent rehabilitation of lost cultural icons, "While accepting themselves, the Québécois have accepted their stars."[77] Critics may well be content with such treatment of sportsmen and entertainers when we compare them to another significant group of historical figures seemingly raised to the status of *lieu de mémoire*: criminals whose temporary public notoriety has made them the subject of a biopic in the twenty-first century.

Clever Criminals as Culture Heroes: *Le piège américain* and *Monica la Mitraille*

In its search for new, apolitical *lieux de mémoire*, Quebec cinema in the twenty-first century has turned to some unlikely suspects, including well-known criminals and other controversial figures. Generally films destined for a popular, rather than art film, audience, these films appeal to Quebec's flirtation with illegality, derived on the one hand from a Gallic *esprit frondeur*, an appreciation for individualists who break with the conventions of mainstream, conformist society, and on the other from a nationally specific sense of Quebec's own marginal status as a nation, a province that resists the restraints of the official political establishment, something already seen in the discussion of the memorialization of members of the FLQ, for example, in chapter 1. As with other forms of the biopic, Quebec's producers and directors have found inspiration in touchstone Hollywood films, like Arthur Penn's *Bonnie and Clyde* (1967). Perhaps significantly, a more recent model from France, Jean-François Richet's two-part blockbuster *Mesrine, Part 1: Killer Instinct* (2008) and *Mesrine, Part 2: Public Enemy #1* (2008), about continental heist artist Jacques Mesrine (Vincent Cassel), was a co-production with Canada (Quebec) and Italy. Like its contemporary cultural metropoles, France and the United States, Quebec is not without its criminal heroes whose transgressive nature fits the national image of populist resistance to social elitism. Some of these were born or began their careers during the *Grande Noirceur* but then peaked during the 1960s Quiet Revolution or later. Films like *Le piège américain* (2008), about mobster Lucien Rivard, and *Monica la Mitraille* (2004), which depicts bank robber Monica Proietti as a Robin Hood figure, invoke the historical imaginary since (although some of their subjects are still living) their main intrigue occurs in a bygone era. Others, such as *Le dernier tunnel* (2004), *Piché : entre ciel et terre* (2010), and *L'affaire Dumont* (2012), document the lives of more recent figures who achieved notoriety because of their relationship to criminality, as either perpetrators or victims of injustice.[78] More recently, Daniel Roby's English-language *Target Number One* (2020) was inspired by real-life journalist Victor Malarek's investigation into the unjust imprisonment of a French Canadian in Thailand, Alain Olivier.[79] Two more films memorialize the careers of Québécois hitmen: Luc Picard's *Confessions* (2021), based on the memoirs of Gérald Gallant, and Raymond St-Jean's *Crépuscule pour un tueur* (2023), about Donald Lavoie (b. 1942), who worked for Montreal's Dubois Gang. The analyses that follow explore how two of these controversial figures fit into the construction of new *lieux de mémoire* for twenty-first-century Quebec, and how their directors and writers envision the past for present-day audiences.

Charles Binamé's last French-language feature, *Le piège américain / The American Trap* (2008), dramatizes a key moment in the life of what Élie Castiel describes as one of "these national antiheroes that history seems to forget,"[80] mobster Lucien Rivard (1914–2002), active across the 1940s, 1950s, and 1960s. This comment calls attention to the biopic's function of uncovering lost history and constructing for public consumption new *lieux de mémoire*. In the notorious individual biopic, however, the focus is on anti-heroes, viewed nonetheless as emblems of national identity, largely through their status as figures of resistance to the forces of order, which in the Quebec context are frequently associated with anglophone authority (Canada, England, the United States) or francophone economic, political, or religious elites complicit with it. Although *Le piège américain* focuses on a very brief episode of Rivard's life, like others memorialized through the biopic, the gangster's story, as Élie Castiel, long-time editor of *Séquences*, asserts, "places Quebec on the world chessboard. The national territory is no longer isolated. Things happen. Quebec is no longer a country recognized only for its culture, its language, its heritage and its politics, but also for the more doubtful practices of certain individuals."[81]

Rivard's crime empire flourished in the 1940s and 1950s through a string of nightclubs in Fulgencio Batista's Cuba; after Castro's coup, he fled and, with the help of Canadian officials, temporarily avoided extradition to the United States for drug trafficking. His escape from Quebec's Bordeaux Prison in 1965 launched him back into the headlines. A target of Robert F. Kennedy's fight on organized crime,[82] Rivard was apprehended and prosecuted in the United States for his role in the French Connection drug smuggling ring. *Le piège américain*'s scenario, by Fabienne Larouche and Michel Trudeau, links Rivard to Cold War intrigues and conspiracy theories surrounding the assassination of John F. Kennedy, invoking for viewers an "episode in Quebec's socio-political history not well known by the general public."[83] Furthermore, by casting fan favourite Rémy Girard in the role, "Charles Binamé has made Lucien Rivard a popular hero."[84] Indeed, Binamé – director of Quebec blockbusters *Séraphin* and *Maurice Richard* – comments on his success with the historical film, invoking the national motto, *Je me souviens*, claiming that, "for me, history is the ideal tool for exploring the depths of memories from the past."[85] But he also admits that *Le piège américain* is not meant to be "a veridical documentary" as much as "a viewpoint on the unhealthy relationship between the mafia and politics."[86] Binamé's film technique, however, blurs the lines between fact and fiction, inserting images of actor Girard into stock footage sequences, for example. Besides those of the biopic, *Le piège américain* invokes the conventions of the Mafia film and Oliver Stone's conspiracy drama *JFK* (1991). In addition to a local anti-hero, it also memorializes a little-known but central figure in conspiracy theories: Rose Cheramie, a woman who purportedly notified authorities about Kennedy's imminent assassination on 20 November 1963, but who was later found dead.

The title of *Le piège américain* refers to Rivard's ultimate capture; this focus on the Québécois's American connections serves a dual purpose. First, Rivard's story participates in a significant current in twenty-first-century Quebec national cinema that seeks to locate Québécois characters (both historical and fictional) as players on the world stage.[87] This trend validates the national subject in the global context and rejects stereotypes of the French Canadian as immured in the past, with his/her horizons limited to the provincial borders. Then, the film reveals Quebec's ambivalence towards the United States. On the one hand, Rivard is interesting because of his connection to the great figures of American politics; his story allows Québécois to have a stake in the Kennedy assassination, a world-changing event that also personally touched those who remember it, even in Canada. Indeed, as Binamé suggests in an interview, the Québécois perceived that with that assassination something of the American dream had died.[88] Here, the American dream refers to the national ideals of freedom and equality. On the other hand, *Le piège américain* implicitly condemns the American government and secret services for covering up the truth about the assassination. Furthermore, the American "trap" is not just the literal one laid for Rivard to secure his arrest, but also, perhaps, the one awaiting Québécois who, like Rivard, fall into the trap of forgetting their roots and identity to pursue another sort of American dream, that of material success at all costs.

The biopic of another anti-hero, or rather anti-heroine, Monica Proietti (1940–67), described as "Canada's Bonnie Parker,"[89] bears similar testimony to the development of high-quality popular genre film in Quebec. Based on the novelization of her life, *Souvenirs de Monica* by Georges-Hébert Germain,[90] *Monica la Mitraille / Machine-Gun Molly* (2004), directed by Pierre Houle from a screenplay by Luc Dionne and Sylvain Guy, memorializes a notorious figure from the national past. With pretensions perhaps to heritage film status, its $7,375,000 budget[91] and star-studded cast ensured the film's success at the box office. Michel Cusson's score, with its recognizable trademark jazz and contemplative, Southwest-sounding guitar tracks, also invokes the trio Dionne-Houle-Cusson's collaboration on *Omertà* (1996–8), a highly popular Mafia-themed television series and its eponymous film reboot (Luc Dionne, 2012). The film combines nostalgia for the 1950s and 1960s, fuelled by elegant art direction by Michel Proulx, with deep territorial roots in the working-class neighbourhoods of Montreal's East End. Popular period musical hits like "Love Me Tender" and

"Wild Thing" accompany a story replete with love, sex, and the rush of nonconformist behaviour, a dash of humour thrown in along the way, as well as light lip service paid to the discourse of francophone oppression.

Despite the change of its anti-heroine's name to Monica Sparvieri, *Monica la Mitraille* adopts biopic conventions that suggest its "truth" value, including stock footage in black and white over a background of period-specific jazz music to bring viewers back in time, and the wrecking balls demolishing slums near the Sparvieri family's East End home invoke a past era of urban renewal in Montreal. Despite their Italian name, the Sparvieris appear to be fully assimilated Québécois, but *La famille Plouffe* they ain't: Eldest son Mario (Hugolin Chevrette-Landesque) is a pickpocket and aspiring pimp, spunky Monica is an on again, off again prostitute – in her words, "su'la game quand ça me tente ... pas su'la game quand ça me tente pas" (hooking when I feel like it ... not hooking when I don't). Embodied by Céline Bonnier, one of the province's best-known spunky female leads, she asserts her *québécitude* by insisting on being called Monique, a move through which the filmmakers distance their protagonist from her Italian identity and the Mafia, aspects exploited in Germain's book.[92] Her best friend and cousin Sylvana (Isabelle Blais), whose name is also Gallicized to Sylvaine, is an aspiring night club singer and part-time hooker, as well. Monica's beauty and spunky personality, however, earn her the attention of an up-and-coming Scottish newcomer to the East End crime world, Michael Burns (Frank Schorpion). Their marriage is the break she needs to avoid the downward spiral that eventually overwhelms her cousin, and it allows her to overcome the odds stacked against her by her East End background in a different way from that of the standard culture hero.

Frustrated with the domesticity that the men in her life repeatedly impose on her, Monique wants to participate in her husband's work; later, when he is jailed, she turns to his former collaborator, Gaston Lussier (Patrick Huard), to help make ends meet. Despite her Italian origins, constructed as a Franco-Québécois not content with her *petit pain*, Monique asserts her equality, even superiority, to the men around her in intelligence and character, as well as in ambition and sex drive. This level of agency renders her character a charismatic folk hero and also reflects the mildly feminist agenda *de rigueur* in twenty-first-century Quebec historical films. Although a relationship with a man once again forces Monique into a domestic role, as her new lover Gaston buys a house in the suburbs where she can raise her children, Monique manipulates him to take an active role planning "jobs," gaining in confidence, but also in recklessness. Whereas he takes their "work" seriously, for her a heist is always exciting, and she becomes addicted to "cette rush-là" (that rush). When Gaston is arrested, she finally meets her match in terms of antisocial recklessness in Gerry Simard (Roy Dupuis),[93] participating in increasingly dangerous bank robberies. Finally, in the iconic year of Expo 67, Monica's activities catch up with her; more easily recognizable after a newspaper feature and now targeted by the police, she gets lost driving a getaway car with

Gerry and his brother Bob (Mario Jean), and a chase ensues, which ends in her death. The filmmakers underscore the pathos of her demise by framing it through an act of excessive force; her injuries clearly fatal after her car collides with a city bus, police nonetheless shoot her point-blank. The film's final shot shows her laid out dead on the pavement, yet another victim-martyr to the establishment and its unjust treatment of the common man or woman, just trying to get by.

Although clearly not model citizens, the criminals eulogized in these (fictionalized) biopics make statements about a certain type of Québécois identity. *Monica la Mitraille* establishes the poverty and oppression in Montreal's pre–Quiet Revolution East End as an environment likely to foster either desperation or rebellion. Her stereotypical Italian father's womanizing, coupled with her own rejection of the dominant model of feminine submission and self-sacrifice that her mother incarnates, exacerbate the hostility of young Monica's environment. A tenement fire, which seriously burns Paula and kills her mother and a sibling, steels her will to *not* return to that life, recalling perhaps aspects of Alys Robi's determination in *Ma vie en cinémascope*. Maurice Morrissette (Rémy Girard), the sleazy local crime boss and Sylvana's boyfriend-pimp, Maréchal (Alexis Bélec), embody the neighbourhood's endemic criminality. The film documents a climate of oppression, exploitation, and abuse particular to women in French Canada, a problem that other twenty-first-century films reveal in many ways to be unchanged from the 1950s.[94] It suggests that given Monica's background, the *only* possible roles open to her are either that of the long-suffering spouse and mother, constantly struggling to make ends meet given the endlessly growing number of her children, or earning a living in a profession associated with disrespectability or servitude: nightclub singer, barmaid, or prostitute. As a bank robber, she escapes this fate to enjoy life, if only for a short time.

Le piège américain, *Monica la Mitraille*, and *Le dernier tunnel* (Érik Canuel, 2008; about bank robber Marcel Talon), elevate Quebec's most famous criminals into subversive national heroes, even *lieux de mémoire*, humanizing the violent subject and eliding the repercussions of their acts. Such narratives appeal to the *esprit frondeur* of the average Québécois for whom the police are *les boeufs*, oppressive figures of authority, often as corrupt as the system they serve, even out to get the common man or woman. *Monica la Mitraille* offers the familiar feminist-lite subtext of Monica's desire to escape the gender roles laid out for her; certain parallels can be seen between aspects of her life story from the 1960s and 1970s and that of a more contemporary figure of notoriety who, at one point in her life, also made a living as a sex worker, the feminist writer Nelly Arcan.

The Controversial Literary Figure: Anne Émond's *Nelly*

At the dawn of the new millennium, Isabelle Fortier,[95] writing under the pseudonym of Nelly Arcan, was rocketed into the international literary spotlight after the publication of her first novel, *Putain* (2001), a *succès de scandale* that drew on her life experience as a sex worker. The pressure to repeat that success and the criticisms of her life and works that ensued merely exacerbated the damage done to her ego, and less than a decade later, in September 2009, she committed suicide, an act obsessively prefigured throughout her oeuvre. "Librement inspiré de la vie et de l'œuvre de Nelly Arcan" (Freely inspired by the life and works of Nelly Arcan), as much literary adaptation as it is biopic, Anne Émond's (b. 1982) *Nelly / Nelly: This Is Her Life* (2016) memorializes the writer, translating to film the spirit of her autofictions. Like Arcan's literary output, Émond's scenario belongs to what Patricia Smart describes as "a category of works close to the autobiographical novel, but which proudly display their refusal to submit to generic boundaries. Neither novels nor autobiographies, they are a combination of the two, thumbing their nose at readers who look for signs of the pact guaranteeing the referential truth of the text."[96] Rather than a conventional chronology, or even a life story told in flashback, Émond's *Nelly* projects an image of the "écrivaine maudite" (damned writer)[97] through a series of avatars based on her life and characters, accompanied by direct citations from her works in voice-over and dialogue.

A collection of intercalated episodes, the film's structure reflects the fragmented ego exposed in Arcan's autofictions, shaped by dysfunctional family structures that informed pre–Quiet Revolution Quebec society and then trapped in the ideological contradictions regarding female subjectivity. Like its literary sources, *Nelly* represents "the product and symptom of an age in which the old hierarchies have collapsed, ... [and] makes a spectacle of a self in free fall."[98] Both Arcan's fiction and Émond's film reveal the impact on developing female psyches of contemporary media's unattainable spectacle of female "perfection" and postmodernity's emphasis on image.[99] This identity crisis is exacerbated in Quebec because of its historical relationship to Catholic values that posited humility, renunciation, and self-sacrifice as the hallmarks of femininity.[100] Significantly, however, Émond's autofictional biopic elides key elements of Arcan's oeuvre that explicitly link it to the national epic;[101] by doing so, however, she universalizes the systems of oppression that Arcan sought to expose, perhaps explicitly to appeal to audiences beyond Quebec's borders.

Like the autofictions it acknowledges through an opening title card crediting Arcan's French publisher, Éditions du Seuil, Émond's *Nelly* openly resists the truth claims of biography in its refusal to disentangle fact from fiction in its depiction of the Québécois literary personage of "Nelly Arcan." Émond frames her fictionalized account of the life of Nelly Arcan (Mylène Mackay) the writer, along with the fictional characters she created, through the notion of performance, not only in the construction of a public persona, but also in the articulation of an individual, gendered personality.[102] Furthermore, its non-linear, episodic structure resists the reconstruction of a clear developmental trajectory.

Instead, it presents its fragmented subject as a series of personae, some more heavily fictionalized than others, nonetheless tracing a general arc that leads from Arcan's beginnings as a sex worker (sourced largely from *Putain*), her discovery and controversial success, through her well-known demise. Underscoring the notion that the self is generated in relation to an Other, Émond's various avatars for *Nelly* frequently appear in relation to a significant figure in her life or works. Like other Quebec biopics' construction of the artist as a damned genius, *Nelly* suggests the childhood origins of the psychic tensions that fuel creativity and a rise to fame, but the film remains haunted throughout by the artist's fall from grace.

Nelly opens with a teenaged girl performing the iconic theme of nostalgia, "Le temps des roses" (also a hit in English as "Those Were the Days"), in lip synch with French pop artist Dalida's 1968 version; as her enthusiasm for the performance builds and she begins to sing along out loud, she is shushed by her mother in the front row. Émond thus signals how family expectations and concern with appearances effectively silence a young woman in search of her voice. The film closes on a parallel image of an adult Nelly, walking tentatively onstage, taking the microphone and singing the same song, but this time in a hesitant, almost strangled voice. Having now told of the writer's revolt – a struggle not just for self-expression but actually to find herself through writing – *Nelly* concludes that the forces that suppressed her youthful enthusiasm, resulting in an overbearing sense of oppression as an adult, have triumphed, effectively silencing her voice with her suicide. The conventional titles that conclude a biopic after the film's penultimate image of an older Nelly climbing onto a chair with a rope confirm this notion: "Isabelle Fortier a mis fin à ses jours le 24 septembre 2009, à l'âge de 36 ans. Elle a publié quatre romans, dont un à titre posthume" (Isabelle Fortier put an end to her days on 24 September 2009, at the age of thirty-six. She published four novels, one of them posthumously).

Depicting the thirteen-year-old Isabelle (Milya Corbeil-Gauvreau), Émond outlines the origins of the adult's dysfunction in four sequences, mostly drawn from the short story "Peggy."[103] As in the prologue, Nelly's childish enthusiasm is stifled by a parent; excited to have her future told via a Tarot reading by her aunt (Roxane Bourdage), Isabelle cries out but is shushed by her father (Martin Boily) because her mother is asleep in the next room. Émond thus establishes the mother's absence, a recurring trope in Quebec literature and film,[104] as elaborated in *Putain*.[105] Émond elides, however, references to Catholicism, key attributes of Arcan's protagonists' father (in *Putain*) or grandfather (in *Folle*). Instead, she draws from *Folle*'s description of the failed attempt at predicting a life that, the film implies, will be cut short, signalling both the inscrutability of Nelly as subject and her uniquely absent destiny as a future suicide. Voice-over signals the lack that will become a hallmark of her subjectivity: "Quelque chose en moi n'a jamais été là" (Something in me was never there). Subsequent sequences show her as a relatively normal adolescent, a shy though stunningly pretty, blue-eyed blonde, but Isabelle is consistently outshone by her brunette best friend, Marie-Julie (Audrey Anne Tremblay).[106] When Marie-Julie describes her new boyfriend Félix (Xavier Roberge), Isabelle is galvanized, perhaps excessively curious, as she presses for details. Voice-over by the adult Nelly accompanies the next image of Isabelle watching voyeuristically as Marie-Julie and Félix kiss, and experiencing an intense sensation, a *brûlure* (burning), from her solar plexus on down. The final teenaged sequence depicts Isabelle at a party, dancing with a boy her age to Modern English's "I Melt with You," significantly, a song about the loss of ego in sexual desire. This hopeful image of normality, however, soon gives way to the intensity of Isabelle's jealousy as she sees Marie-Julie dancing, sandwiched between her own boyfriend and the boy Isabelle liked. Hurt and angry, she marches home, as a voice-over explains both her budding sexuality and the excessive emotional impact of this double rejection:

C'était un nouveau monde et ça me captivait. Dans ma capture, j'ai souffert un martyre. Quelque chose s'est brisée en moi. Quelque chose s'est fendue en deux comme un arbre frappé par la foudre en son milieu. Je vous jure qu'en ce moment j'ai entendu son craquement en douleur.[107]

It was a new world, and it captivated me. In my captivity, I suffered like a martyr. Something broke within me. Something cracked in two like a tree struck by lightning at its core. I swear to you that in that moment I heard it cracking in pain.

Arriving home to seek the safety of her bed, the young Isabelle, crying, consoles herself by masturbating. Émond thus suggests her protagonist's dysfunctional relationship with sexuality, something intensely felt but also associated with rejection and pain rather than joy.

Nelly opens with the chronologically first avatar of the writer as a young woman in a series of segments largely pulled from *Putain* (*Whore*, 2001) working as call girl using the pseudonym "Cynthia." This sequence establishes her obsession with image, as she primps before the arrival of a client, later reinforcing the character's narcissism as she looks into the mirror while stroking his penis (which remains off camera), a wry smile developing on her lips. Initially, Cynthia enjoys the role she plays as a sex worker and is gratified by positive online reviews of her performance. Contrary to the book's description of older men, her clients in the film are youngish, white, and decent-looking, and they compliment her on how beautiful and sexy she is, an image reinforced by the perfection achieved for Mackay by Émond's costume, hair, and make-up team. Cynthia also has a social life in these sequences, a group of friends comprised of other escorts who drink, dance, and talk about their work to let off steam. These episodes become increasingly disturbing, however, revealing the dark side of the sex trade: First, a client, Rock (Karl Farah), pays extra to sodomize her, an act that is visibly painful; then, another, Patrick (Mathieu Lepage), abuses her physically; and, finally, an older, anglophone client, Trevor (Jason Cavalier), hesitates, stating that she looks older than her online photo, but that she's "okay." The ugly reality behind the glossy image of porn and the sex trade is revealed when Cynthia undergoes a medical examination; with no make-up and long, straight hair, she appears older, even worn out. Voice-over quotes from *Putain* comment on the number of people needed for the subject to maintain the image of beauty that has begun to slip: "Voilà pourquoi je vis seule … , je préfère l'accumulation des médecins et des psychanalystes, chacun sa spécialité, chacun s'affairant sur l'une ou l'autre de mes parties … , un seul homme dans ma vie serait dangereux, trop de haine en moi pour une seule tête, j'ai besoin de la planète, de l'étendu du genre humain" (Here's why I live alone … , I prefer the accumulation of doctors and analysts, each with his speciality, each working on one or another of my parts …, a single man in my life would be dangerous, too much hate in me for a single head, I need a planet, the entire human race).[108] Although she evacuates much of Arcan's narrators' spleen from her film, preferring to depict her as a victim, Émond reveals this emotional neediness in sequences with a plastic surgeon (Jean-Moïse Martin), a psychoanalyst (Marc Béland), discussed below, and the young writer's French publisher, Mathieu (Francis Leplay).

The first "Cynthia" sequence concludes on the image of the prostitute, alone after serving a client, on the bed of a downtown high-rise, Montreal lit behind her at night, writing in a journal, thus introducing the young writer. This avatar, also young, blonde, and beautiful, but more conservatively dressed, suggests her double life during this phase, as she types on a computer in a nicely appointed home office. In voice-over, she recites the opening lines from *Putain*: "Oui, la vie m'a traversée, je n'ai pas rêvé ces hommes, ces milliers, dans mon lit, dans ma bouche, je n'ai rien inventé de leur sperme sur moi, sur ma figure, dans mes yeux, j'ai tout vu et ça continue encore, tous les jours ou presque" (Yes, life ran through me, I didn't dream of these men, in the thousands, in my bed, in my mouth, I didn't invent their sperm on me, on my face, in my eyes, I saw it all and I still continue, every day, or almost).[109] Émond introduces other avatars in the meantime, distancing the university student and promising young writer from the prostitute as, about fifteen minutes in, the film climaxes, in a sense, with the key phone call announcing the publication of her manuscript in France. Mathieu compliments her on the maturity and density of her style but indicates that "votre texte a créé un onde de choc au comité de lecture" (your text created a shock wave with the editorial committee), and he inevitably asks if it is based on her life. With the ambiguity typical of the autofiction, Nelly replies, "Certaines choses sont vraies. D'autres non" (Some things are real. Others aren't). But she also reveals the underlying tragedy of her work: "En dehors de l'écriture, je suis rien" (Outside literature, I am nothing). With this line, Émond encapsulates

Patricia Smart's thesis that Arcan's work represents an attempt to "write herself into being" and move from the status of object to become a fully actualized subject.[110] *Nelly* explains her tragedy later, as her older avatar admits, "J'ai inventé Nelly pour protéger Isabelle, mais je pense que cela a fait le contraire, finalement" (I invented Nelly to protect Isabelle, but I think that this did the opposite in the end). As a subject who only exists in writing, even after her stunning success, and largely because of it, Nelly remains a hollow shell; unable to fill that void, she eventually implodes.

The third avatar of the writer to appear in *Nelly* invokes the protagonist of her second autofictional novel, *Folle*, but is the first to be specifically referred to as "Nelly Arcan." Ostensibly recounting the period in the author's life immediately following the *succès de scandale* of *Putain*, Émond differentiates this addictive personality from the writer's other film avatars with long, dark hair and heavy eyeliner, thus blurring where these events occurred in relation to the others, even suggesting that the brunette is the only really *fictional* character in the film.[111] Indeed, shot in an entirely different colour palette, including nostalgic, almost sepia tones, *Nelly* suggests that its obsessive love story may have occurred before she became a prostitute, even before she began writing, as voice-over addresses her lover: "Tu précèdes déjà tout" (You already precede everything). It immediately signals, however, the downward trajectory to come, while at the same time framing the dysfunctional affair as a case of ill-fated love at first sight: "On ne pouvait rien contre notre désastreux rencontre" (Nothing could stop our disastrous encounter).[112] At a party, it depicts – as do turn-of-the-millennium films like *Maelström* and *Un crabe dans la tête* – the urban hipsters of the Plateau-Mont-Royal, caught in a whirlwind of drugs, alcohol, and partying. Although this Nelly's addictive behaviours eventually get the better of the relationship, and her increasing jealousy and selfish tantrums lead her lover, François (Mickaël Gouin), to throw out the accusation, "tu es folle" ("you're crazy"), Émond has sanitized aspects of the relationship as depicted in *Folle*. Whereas *Nelly* frames this "phase" as a potentially conventional love story – François even proposes marriage and expresses the desire for children – destroyed by addiction, Arcan's novel recounts a much darker relationship of emotional and sexual abuse. Indeed, *Folle* depicts "a mad love affair that reduces the narrator to abjection," "the confirmation of a fundamental lack of substance which is literally enough to drive her mad."[113] The film codes François as Québécois, but the novel depicts the young Québécoise writer "Nelly Arcan" falling in love with a French freelance journalist whose purported "research" on Internet pornography masks his own sexual dysfunction. Furthermore, the novel explicitly develops a colonial dynamic, as "Nelly's feelings of inferiority in relation to France are one of the recurrent themes of the book."[114] Émond evacuates this aspect of the relationship from her film, a move indicative of the waning pertinence of Quebec's national narrative of colonial victimhood. Distanced from Arcan by a key generation, instead of rehashing old rancours very specific to Quebec, Émond focusses on the universal, feminist aspects of Arcan's life and work.

Another avatar of the writer at the height of her fame, one that moves subtly from the writer's double life (as prostitute and university student) to the media's objectification of the beautiful young writer coupled with market pressures to produce cash, suggests that Nelly is simply engaged in another type of prostitution. Like Cynthia, the young writer at first enjoys positive attention, basking in the compliments paid by a photographer and an interviewer, but over time, as she loses control of her image, the darker side of literary fame is revealed. In a fourth avatar of the author to be introduced over the course of less than fifteen minutes, Nelly appears at the height of her literary success, but the sequence more clearly establishes a parallel between the prostitute and the writer, who will also be "sold" to the public by those around her. Again, positioning her facing a mirror, Émond reveals Nelly sitting in an elegant bathroom, perfectly coiffed in a chignon and wearing a glamourous cocktail dress. As she applies lipstick, daubs it off, and then applies it again, the first hint of Nelly's insecurity appears, as does her excessive need to be reassured by those around her. But there is also an ambiguity as she meets "Suzanne" (Sylvie Drapeau), a middle-aged woman who might represent a call girl agency, but who turns out to be her literary agent. This episode resumes later, as Nelly makes an entrance at an elegant cocktail reception, but having drunk too much champagne, her behaviour soon becomes extravagant, and the ensuing rejection by fellow writer Guillaume Rival (Emmanuel Schwartz) further fuels her insecurity.

The objectification she experiences both as a prostitute and as a mediatized writer, but also her inability to overcome patterns that she understands and criticizes in her writing, appears in sequences featuring a flawlessly beautiful Nelly, clad in a luxurious winter-white sweater and trousers. They reveal her, however, lying on a psychoanalyst's couch. Transitioning from voice-over to diegetic dialogue, Nelly explains her identity crisis in these episodes that draw from *Putain*:

Tout ça arrive à quelqu'un qui semble d'autre que moi. J'suis juste à côté de moi. J'assiste aux choses, mais c'est pas vraiment moi. Je la regarde … parler, boire, danser, baiser, rire, pleurer. Je vois bien cette femme blonde couché sur le divan face à son psy … Mais je suis pas cette femme. Je joue très bien cette femme, par contre. J'ai besoin d'être vue, mais c'est pas moi que je montre. Donc, je disparais un peu … J'apparais pour disparaître.

This all happens to someone who seems other than myself. I'm just beside myself. I attend things, but it's not really me. I watch her … talk, drink, dance, fuck, laugh, cry. I certainly see this blonde woman lying on a sofa before her shrink … But I'm not

> that woman. I play the role of that woman really well, however. I need to be seen,
> but who I show isn't me. So, I disappear a little … I appear in order to disappear.

Relating her problems becomes just another role for Nelly, but instead of condemning, Émond attempts to explain, albeit ambivalently, her protagonist's dysfunction. Like a sex addict, she appears turned on by her own narrative, touching herself suggestively as she tells her analyst (Marc Béland), "J'avais besoin d'appartenir à quelqu'un. J'appartiens à ceux qui me prennent" (I need to belong to someone. I belong to those who take me). In a sequence purely of Émond's invention, since this episode does not (to my knowledge) occur in Arcan's fiction, Nelly attempts to seduce her analyst; he resists her advances, but, of course, this rejection further fuels the cycle of insecurity.

The chronologically final avatar of the writer appears a bit older, conservatively dressed wearing her unbleached, naturally sandy-blonde hair up. Although only in her early thirties, Nelly appears almost middle-aged in these sequences not long prior to her death; Émond underscores her isolation, frequently depicting the writer alone. She nonetheless interacts with others in two sequences that further reveal her insecurities as a writer and the devastating impact of the Other's criticism on the fragile self. In one of these, a delivery girl (Karelle Tremblay), who is also a fan, brings a box of novels titled *Nelly* (presumably a fictionalization of *Folle*), but her admission that the author's first novel remains her favourite signals the pressure to follow it up with another bestseller. This concern recurs in two sequences in which the writer is interviewed by a journalist (Francis Ducharme); in the first, he appears fan-like in his admiration, but in the second, indicative of the media's increasingly shrewish treatment of Arcan, he asks directly, "Comment vivez-vous avec le fait que vous n'avez jamais refait l'exploit de votre premier roman?" (How do you live with the fact that you haven't ever repeated the success of your first novel?) This episode draws on the writer's real-life public humiliation on the Québécois version of the talk show *Tout le monde en parle*;[115] he brings up the public's curiosity about the autobiographical aspects of her work, implicitly undermining their literary merit.[116] The film's final sequences indicate her further isolation, pain, and self-distancing from her own reality, accompanied by voice-over revealing her shame, the sense that her life, and even her words, have been killing her. Her concluding lines seem to explain her irrevocable, final act: "j'aimerais ça, passer à autre chose maintenant. J'aimerais ça, que ça aille mieux" (I would like that, to move on to something else now. I would like it for things to go better).

Émond's *Nelly* thus memorializes Arcan as a creative genius, but one whose genius derives largely from pain, an insurmountable sense of hopelessness, a lifelong struggle to fill a void, to find a voice, concluding that when that voice was found, it, too, merely covered an empty shell. It successfully translates the author's life and works onto the big screen, blurring the lines between fact and fiction, like Arcan's novels themselves. Certainly, Arcan merits a biopic as a "symbol of our literary success,"[117] but Émond evacuates the specifically national aspects of the writer's life and works, suggesting that Quebec national cinema has begun to move beyond the obsessive drive to assert its *québécitude*, seeking instead a connection with the world at large, a trend begun by the *nouvelle génération* directors like Denis Villeneuve and Jean-Marc Vallée, who answered the call from Hollywood, and carried on by Xavier Dolan, for example, with his largely French production *Juste la fin du monde* (2016).

Conclusion

The stylistic variety of the films explored in this chapter reveals the extent to which Quebec's filmmakers have appropriated the Hollywood genre of the biopic while also making it their own. Directors adept at producing *cinéma grand public* like Charles Binamé, Luc Dionne, François Bouvier, and Daniel Roby produced high-quality, mainstream biopics of well-known national icons in *Maurice Richard*, *L'enfant prodige*, *La Bolduc*, and *Louis Cyr*. Others have hybridized aspects of the biopic with other genres, most specifically the conspiracy or the crime film, as seen in *Le piège américain* and *Monica la Mitraille*. Whether they exploit figures from recent headlines or remind contemporary viewers of past national heroes, Quebec's biopics contribute to the construction of national identity through their focus on the transmission of memory, as Andrée Fortin observes.[118] Whereas early in the twenty-first century, like the heritage film literary adaptations discussed in chapter 3, they frequently focus on victimhood, suggesting their heroes as standing in allegory for the nation itself, they nonetheless also focus on individual Québécois who have attained success in the arenas of sports, music, or even criminal activity. Several other films, not treated here for reasons of space, memorialize other real-life Québécois's brushes with the justice system, including *Piché : entre ciel et terre* (Sylvain Archambault, 2010) and *L'affaire Dumont* (Daniel Grou, 2012);[119] even these notorious figures, remembered because they were victims of injustice, are celebrated as survivors, offering up parables of national fortitude. The *biopic québécois*, then, offers images of success and/or strength in the face of adversity, constructing new sites of memory for a nation perceived as increasingly apolitical, sports heroes and musical icons like Louis Cyr and La Bolduc, Maurice Richard and Gerry Boulet. Without completely leaving behind a sense of national victimhood, the film depiction of Les Colocs' André Fortin suggests perhaps that his emotional investment in the project of national sovereignty was unhealthily excessive, and that of Nelly Arcan elides the national narrative that underlies the writer's work. Given its title, *À tous ceux qui ne me lisent pas* (2018), Yan Giroux's film devoted to poet Yves Boisvert (Martin Dubreuil) similarly perpetuates the misunderstood writer trope, but it reminds viewers that a national talent should be celebrated rather than forgotten.[120]

Taken as a body, the *biopic québécois* retells the nation's history through individual lives as evolving from the scorned French Canadian, the "damned Canuck," of the pre–Quiet Revolution era, leaving behind the certain but perhaps oppressive values of the clerico-nationalist ideology, to embrace the modern world. As Andrée Fortin so eloquently concludes her article on *biofictions cinématographiques*,

> If, then, Quebec's cinematographic biofictions are, when taken together, thesis films, these theses are not about the people whose lives they tell, but rather about Quebec as a whole: the history of Quebec is full of collective battles, nationalism to begin with, but also feminism, and several people whose life stories are told have to fight to attain autonomy, even becoming victims of this fight. History is marked by political, juridical, religious, and cultural institutions that we must let go of, something that the characters of these biofictions don't always succeed in doing. This history must be transmitted, and this occurs not only by the films, but inside them.[121]

Above all, the *biopic québécois*'s celebration of sports, musical, and criminal culture heroes reveals Quebec's advent to modernity and the attendant consumerism and mediatization of daily life.

Further memorializing the nation's advent to modernity, mythologized as its Quiet Revolution in the 1960s, is the function of the films analysed in the next chapter, a corpus related to the biopic and the literary adaptation as it revives the nation's past visually through the mise en scène of a fictional narrative frequently based on a previously published autobiography or personal memoir. The period pieces examined in chapter 5 participate in the historical imaginary as they bring to the big screen not necessarily sites of memory – although national milestones are certainly evoked – but rather "sights of memory," as they invoke personal, individual visions of the collective past.

5 "Enthralling Narrative[s] of Bittersweet Reminiscence": Memoirs and Period Pieces

Nostalgia is a productive strategy by which to generate traumatic historiography, as it can draw, or one might say lure, the spectator into the enthralling narrative of bittersweet reminiscence.

André Loiselle[1]

The autobiographical story is the act of memory taking shape.

Luc Chaput[2]

Autobiographical films based on memoirs and even fictional works that invoke times past feed a sense of collective memory, documenting what may be referred to as *la petite histoire*. These "small" histories, as opposed to History with a capital aitch, nonetheless draw on and feed the historical imaginary as they invoke the bigger events in Quebec and the world around it. For example, films set in the late 1960s commonly reference the Woodstock music festival and Neil Armstrong's 20 July 1969 moonwalk, as well as Quebec-specific events like Expo 67. Like historical and biographical films, which claim to be based upon "real" or "actual" events, but which are always already reconstructions of the past filtered through a contemporary perspective, autobiographical and other "period" films transport the viewer back in time through decor, costume, and music. At the same time, their more openly subjective nature as constructions of memory, suggested by Luc Chaput in the epigraph above, frees them of the constraints of historical objectivity, allowing for a more whimsical, creative approach to the past. Several auteurs rising after the turn of the millennium produced critically acclaimed works in this category, such as Louis Bélanger's *Gaz Bar Blues* (2003), Jean-Marc Vallée's *C.R.A.Z.Y.* (2005), and Philippe Falardeau's *C'est pas moi, je le jure* (2008).

As with the historical film per se and the biopic, which tend to represent collective traumas or exceptional individuals whose lives come to a tragic end,

Quebec's frequently autobiographical period films engage painful childhood memories, but typically conclude on a hopeful message of trials overcome. The least overtly historical, perhaps, of the films studied in this book, they are also perhaps the most nebulous in their definition. For the purposes of this study, memoirs and period pieces are films based on published memoirs, autobiographical novels, or filmed from original scenarios that have autobiographical content, that stage the national past as perceived through the lens of a private individual experience, but one also connected to the collective historical backdrop.

This chapter studies nostalgic autobiographical films that tend towards the longing for a simpler past, but which also acknowledge that growing pains mark essential rites of passage in individual – and by extension, national – development. Filmmakers' fictionalizations of lives caught by destiny engage the nation's historical imaginary as they stage the specific context for those lives, but also as the individuals depicted allegorize the nation. Scholars like Christine Sprengler directly link nostalgia to notions of homeland and the modern nation,[3] and Pam Cook describes how "in film criticism, the distinction between nostalgia, memory and history has become blurred."[4] First coined by a seventeenth-century Swiss physician diagnosing the malady he found in homesick young soldiers serving abroad, the term "nostalgia" was later linked to "the homogenizing requirements of the modern nation state in the face of ethnic and cultural diversity."[5] Svetlana Boym argues that "in counterpoint to our fascination with cyberspace and the virtual global village, there is a no less global epidemic of nostalgia, an affective yearning for community with a collective memory, a longing for continuity in a fragmented world."[6] This theorization of nostalgia resonates with the films discussed in this chapter, almost all of which feature largely white, Franco-Québécois casts, thus signifying Quebec's nostalgia for its self-image of a homogeneous past, one already imaginary because such a vision of the nation elides Indigenous priority on the French Canadian home territory.

Not surprisingly, given the baby boomer demographic and the province's narrative of collective self-realization, the Quiet Revolution of the 1960s[7] represents Quebec's golden age in a series of filmic memoirs of a lost childhood released in the new millennium. Significant directors produced a body of films set in the 1960s or involving sequences of flashbacks to that decade, including Robert Lepage's *La face cachée de la lune* (2003) and Francis Leclerc's *Mémoires affectives* (2004). But Jean-Marc Vallée's breakout success *C.R.A.Z.Y.* (2005) inspired a spate of films by less well-known directors set in this hinge decade. This chapter outlines how these films construct the 1960s as a golden age of change for the better, often through implicit critiques of values, attitudes, and behaviours associated with the myth of the *Grande Noirceur*, a conservative past that should be rejected in favour of progressive, modern values. But it also looks at how a younger generation of filmmakers has begun to memorialize the 1980s and even the early 1990s as a new golden age, as seen most notably in Ricardo Trogi's *1981* (2009) and its sequels. The chapter concludes with an analysis of Xavier Dolan's representation of the 1990s in *Laurence Anyways* (2011), which links gender to national identity.

Nostalgia for Lost Pasts: Memorializing the Golden Age of the 1960s (and 1970s)[8]

As critics have noted, one of the major movements in Québécois cinema since the turn of the millennium has been the mythification of the 1960s Quiet Revolution as Quebec's golden age.[9] Indeed, perhaps *the* breakout Québécois film of the new millennium signals this current, as Jean-Marc Vallée's (1963–2021) *C.R.A.Z.Y.* (2005) broke box-office records and received widespread critical acclaim, ultimately leading its director to a career in Hollywood. The film's depiction of a working-class Montreal family through the 1960s and 1970s resonated with popular audiences, while Vallée's technical mastery and nostalgic soundtrack appealed to critics in Quebec and around the world.[10] Above all, the film held up a mirror to the nation's collective self, showing it an image not only of "who we were" but also of "who we aspire to be." Its (partial) resolution of the conflict between the macho and homophobic *pater familias* Gervais Beaulieu (Michel Côté) and his imaginative and charismatic son Zac (Marc-André Grondin), struggling to come to terms with his queer identity, seems to offer a positive national allegory for the province. As Robert Schwartzwald observes, "the goal of reconciling homosexual desire with paternal and social acceptance is presented as a somewhat atypical condensation of Quebec's struggle for autonomy and self-acceptance."[11] But Gervais's inability to embrace Zac completely on his own terms also mitigates that success, suggesting ongoing tensions in the national project regarding difference.[12] Vallée's film suggests that, like Zac, younger generations of Québécois embrace their own difference, unapologetically celebrating their francophone identity in North America. Like Gervais, however, the older generation has accepted the presence of difference in a Quebec that is no longer the homogeneous, Franco-Catholic province it once was only begrudgingly or by looking the other way.

Like many of the films discussed in this chapter, based on the memories and experiences of Vallée's gay co-scenarist François Boulay, *C.R.A.Z.Y* is rooted in autobiography, but not one told in a mundane manner. It is also significant because of its innovative approach to the visual and aural representation of a protagonist's life trajectory, including "abundant recourse to fantasy, reverie, and dream, supported in turn by anti-naturalistic forms of editing."[13] Like Denis Villeneuve in *Maelström* (2000) and Jean-François Pouliot with *La grande seduction / Seducing Dr. Lewis* (2003; remade in English as *The Grand Seduction* [Don McKellar, 2013]), Vallée participates in the twenty-first-century vein of visually stunning and technically experimental filmography in Quebec. From Villeneuve's talking-fish narrator to Vallée's Zac Beaulieu's daydream sequences, a major creative strain in the work of Québécois auteur directors involves blurring the lines between the real and the imagined, calling into question the ontological status of events depicted on-screen. While on the one hand, this thrust participates in a worldwide movement around the turn of the millennium seen in such films as *Como agua para chocolate* (Alfonso Arau, 1992) to *American Beauty* (Sam Mendes, 1999) and *Amélie* (Jean-Pierre Jeunet, 2001), its direct precursor in Quebec is another foundational autobiographical period piece, Jean-Claude Lauzon's *Léolo* (1992). As Jim Leach observes, Lauzon's films sought to break down the barrier between the real and the imaginary,[14] and this fluidity between levels of reality, a sort of magical realism, inspired *nouvelle génération* filmmakers Villeneuve, Bélanger, Briand, and Philippe Falardeau.

In addition to their common backdrop of the Quiet Revolution, these films also blur boundaries with the literary adaptation, based as they are on autobiographical recollections published as memoirs and autofictions, the French term for novelistic autobiographical writing. Mostly focalized through a child's or adolescent's perspective, these films look nostalgically at the 1960s as a period of change for the better, and many thematize to one degree or another the changing role of women and family structures in Quebec society. Less overtly interested in politics than the historical films discussed in chapter 1, they nonetheless engage the historical imaginary in their often very precise material reconstructions of a past era. An extremely talented cast of professionals working in the areas of production design/artistic direction/set design and decoration (Jean Babin, Patrice Bengle, Nicolas Lepage, François Séguin, Patrice Vermette) and costumes (Carmen Alie, Francesca Chamberland, Ginette Magny) supports the creation of this illusion.

Creative Re-Imaginings of the Past: *Emporte-moi, Maman est chez le coiffeur, C'est pas moi, je le jure,* and Their Followers

Not quite a decade into the new millennium and closely following on the success of *C.R.A.Z.Y.*, three highly popular films by significant directors set in the 1960s appeared in 2008. Léa Pool's *Maman est chez le coiffeur*, Philippe Falardeau's *C'est pas moi, je le jure*, and Francis Leclerc's *Un été sans point ni coup sûr* have been the object of significant academic studies that argue that the *Bildungsroman* of these films' child protagonists function as allegories for the nation.[15] Like these child protagonists, the allegorical reading goes, Quebec has successfully passed through the adolescent crises of the 1960s, arriving on the eve of the 1970s with a new maturity, forming the basis for an independent adulthood with the rise of the Parti québécois and the nation's aspirations for self-determination. Rather than rehearse arguments already made about these films as national allegory, I focus on these autofictions' basis in personal memory, their engagement of nostalgia, and their status as "narratives of bittersweet reminiscence," a term coined by André Loiselle in the epigraph above. Two of the three films released in 2008, *Maman est chez le coiffeur* and *C'est pas moi, je le jure* originate in memories of a single real-life family with direct connections to the historical events in progress. Scenarist Isabelle Hébert and novelist Bruno Hébert – the children of Jacques Hébert (1923–2007), writer, Liberal Party politician, and friend of Pierre Trudeau – coincidentally released films adapted from their writings in the same year. Isabelle Hébert wrote the scenario for Pool's film, and Falardeau based his screenplay on Bruno Hébert's autofictions *C'est pas moi, je le jure!* (1997) and *Alice court avec René* (2000).[16] These films, however, follow in the path of another significant precursor.

On the eve of the new millennium, Quebec's most recognized woman director, the Swiss-born Léa Pool, had already produced a nostalgic, autobiographically inspired film set in the early 1960s, *Emporte-moi / Set Me Free* (1999), which has become a classic of international women's cinema.[17] Although the vast majority of the 1960s nostalgia films discussed here feature young boys as protagonists, Pool directed not two (*Emporte-moi* and *Maman est chez le coiffeur*), but three films in this category focalized by young girls and women, including *La passion d'Augustine* (discussed in chapter 3). Because of its international significance and its status as a precursor text, Pool's 1999 film bears mention, particularly as it establishes the 1960s as a time of change and hope for an adolescent protagonist. Although she faces painful struggles, including an apparent lack of love from her adored mother and conflicted feelings about her budding sexuality, the film's conclusion offers hope to the teenage Hanna (Karine Vanasse). Hanna has choices for her future, in contrast with her unnamed mother (Pascale Bussières), who sacrificed her professional aspirations to support her husband's pipe dream (writing a great novel) and to feed her two children.[18]

With *Maman est chez le coiffeur / Mommy Is at the Hairdresser's* (2008), Pool revisits the 1960s through the eyes of an adolescent female protagonist, Élise Gauvin (Marianne Fortier); set during a pivotal summer, the film engages nostalgia's "bitter" aspects, invoking its etymological links to trauma and pain.[19] Élise's family situation is dramatically disrupted when her mother, Simone (Céline Bonnier), overhears a phone conversation revealing that her (unnamed) father (Laurent Lucas) is involved in a homosexual affair. A journalist, Simone accepts an assignment abroad, leaving her husband alone with the children, who cope with the maternal absence to varying degrees of success. As the father continues to work, he calls his own mother for assistance, but the children are still frequently left on their own; the film's title derives from their stock response to visitors: "Mama's at the hairdresser's." The sweet aspects of the film's nostalgia involve its elegiac moments depicting Élise's freedom in Quebec's countryside, including learning to fish after befriending the local "village idiot" figure,

Monsieur Mouche (Gabriel Arcand). The elder of her two brothers, Coco (Élie Dupuis), spends time with friends tinkering on a go-cart, but the younger, Benoit (Hugo St-Onge-Paquin), does not fare so well. Although a very engaging child, he clearly suffers from some learning delays and potentially serious psychological trauma because of his mother's absence. Indeed, he becomes increasingly disturbed, even self-destructive. After he is found having locked himself in a cupboard, banging his head against the wall, his father begins proceedings to send Benoit to a special school.

Maman est chez le coiffeur depicts 1960s Quebec society in evolution, a transitional period for women who were beginning to escape the previously prescribed roles of wife and mother, finding new outlets for personal fulfilment. But it also shows the price they pay to do so, as the film opens with iconic actress Céline Bonnier juggling her character's professional career with her private roles. Nostalgia, in its usual sense of a longing for the good old days, appears – as it does in the other films in this section – in the film's detailed reconstitution of the historical moment through make-up, costume, set design, and props. The mother, perfectly dressed and coiffed throughout these sequences, plays piano while also entertaining Benoit at her feet, then bakes a perfectly layered and frosted birthday cake, putting the finishing touches on an article in the meantime. Pool's film expresses a collective longing for the perfect, beautiful mother, a memory tinted not in tones of sepia but rather in the robin's-egg blue, mustard yellow, olive green, and burnt orange so typical of the late 1960s and early 1970s. Pool implicitly criticizes the small-minded, judgmental attitudes of the waning traditionalist Catholic society in its depiction of the clergy and its characters' nosy neighbours. The father's homosexual affair allows Pool to develop a queer agenda – another trend in twenty-first-century Quebec film[20] – revealing the damage done to families and relationships when homosexuals are forced to hide their sexuality in a tyrannically Catholic, heteronormative society.

As with Hanna in *Emporte-moi*, the bitter moment of Élise's abandonment by her parents affords her the sweet freedom to grow; for her brother Benoit, however, the trauma proves nearly irreparable. Through Élise's eyes, the father's plans to institutionalize Benoit become even more traumatic than her mother's absence. Her resistance prevents the father from carrying out his plans, and at the film's conclusion Simone returns from abroad to retrieve her children. Whereas Pool's film, although beautifully shot, remains within the realm of sociological realism, Philippe Falardeau (b. 1968) stretches the bounds of realism by allowing his unconventional inner life to be seen by the audience through the magic of cinema and injects these bittersweet memories with a sense of the absurd.

C'est pas moi, je le jure! / It's Not Me, I Swear (2008) reprises some of the events related in *Maman est chez le coiffeur*, this time narrated from the viewpoint of Isabelle Hébert's younger brother Bruno in his autofictions.[21] Himself the problem child, Bruno's narrative defuses some of the more troubling behaviours of his protagonist, Léon, taken seriously in his sister's characterization of Benoit for Pool's film.[22] Set in the summer of 1968, it also focuses on the traumatic departure of an idolized mother, Madeleine (Suzanne Clément), to Greece. The film's opening sequences illustrate Falardeau's creativity, his talent for "often disconcerting films in which the unrealistic flirts with the possible and deceptively careless writing tricks the spectator."[23] They also illustrate his use of humour to defuse trauma, borrowing Hébert's ludic use of language. As we view the stunning image of a Greek island in a deep blue sea filmed by master cinematographer André Turpin, Léon tells us in voice-over,

> Dans la Bible c'est écrit, "Au commencement était le Verbe." J'sais pas pour vous, mais, moi, le commencement n'avait pas de verbe, ni rien du tout. Je dormais tranquille à 20,000 lieux sous la mer. C'était avant le Verbe.
>
> Un jour, Dieu a tout gâché. L'eau de la mer s'est vidée d'un coup sec, ma tête s'est écrasée puis ma vie m'est apparu au bout d'un tunnel. Le docteur a dit que tout était beau, que j'étais un enfant normal.
>
> Moi, Léon Doré, un enfant normal?[24]

> In the Bible it's written, "In the beginning was the Word." I don't know about you, but for me the beginning wasn't the word, or anything at all. I was sleeping peacefully 20,000 leagues under the sea. It was before the Word.
>
> One day, God ruined everything. The sea water suddenly poured out, my head was smashed, and my life appeared before me at the end of a tunnel. The doctor said that everything was fine, that I was a normal child.
>
> Me, Léon Doré, a normal child?

These surreal musings occur as Léon loses consciousness after attempting to hang himself from a tree; his mother frantically rushes forth to free her son, reassuring him. Despite its very auteurish mise en scène, *C'est pas moi*'s subject matter, production values, advance publicity, and post-release success allow critic Robert Daudelin to categorize the film as belonging to "this mainstream cinema that from now on is one of the obvious components of Quebec cinema."[25] Evocative of Jaco van Dormael's *Toto le héros* (1991), instead of appearing as disabled or a "special needs" child, as did Benoit in Pool's film, Léon is absolutely extraordinary, but his curiosity and intelligence nonetheless lead him into numerous, tragi-comic scrapes. As the film's title suggests, Léon is a consummate liar, denying or talking his way out of trouble. His various interactions with neighbours, including breaking into and vandalizing their homes, nostalgically details a former Quebec, now memorialized through these films' reconstitution of the decor typical of 1960s family homes. Just as Falardeau admits of his own childhood, "we all have fairly precise memories of this period in our lives. It can be pleasant, as an adult, to revisit this period,"[26] similarly, 1960s period films allow baby boomers and Gen Xers to remember its impact on their own development, but they also construct a collective memory of a key era to be shared with younger generations.

As in *Maman est chez le coiffeur*, although the adored mother literally abandons her children, *C'est pas moi, je le jure* blames the father for her departure. For example, it underscores familial dysfunction during a family dinner, a type of sequence that will become a trope in later nostalgic period films. *C'est pas moi*'s self-important father, Philippe Doré (Daniel Brière), plays toady to a self-sufficient priest (Jean Maheux), their dinner guest. The two men's preoccupation with the bread and wine on the table (also an allegory of the Catholic communion) reveals their shallowness. Although they are political activists involved in the fight for French Canadian / Québécois recognition and self-determination, they are also the object of the film's lampoon, revealed as the underlying irony pierces through Léon's naive description of his father in voice-over: "Papa est ce qu'on appelle une personnalité connue. Un héros national. Un défenseur des droits de l'homme. Il ment jamais. Il est parfait. Il est avocat" (Papa is what you call a known personality. A national hero. A defender of the rights of man. He never lies. He's perfect. He's a lawyer). As Robert Daudelin interprets it, "It's the moment when, in this society where everything is unstable, the intellectuals that are said to be on the left came out of l'Action catholique and, like Léon's father, were identified with the review *Cité libre* … Through the character of Léon … there is a portrait of Quebec – of a certain Quebec in the process of waking up."[27] In addition to the strange paradox of Quebec nationalism, which brings together conservative Catholics and political liberals, the film exposes the inauthenticity of Quebec's professional middle class and its pretentious language politics,[28] as the father pedantically corrects his son's vernacular Québécois French.

C'est pas moi clearly questions masculine prerogatives, building viewer sympathy for the artistic mother by casting Suzanne Clément, one of the province's most appreciated leading ladies, against Daniel Brière, an actor whose limited number of big-screen roles include the unsympathetic gasoline franchise inspector in Louis Bélanger's *Gaz Bar Blues* (2003). Although Chantal literally abandons her son when she decides to leave the marriage, the rebellious Léon idealizes her courage and creativity, seeing through his father's hollow image. Philippe Falardeau's coming-of-age film sidesteps the issue of trauma, revealing Léon as already different even before his mother's departure. Reading Léon as an allegory for Quebec, this film celebrates a province that has certainly had its moments of "acting out," of rebellion against authority, but that also possesses a unique creativity and charisma, as it continues to grapple with the metaphysical question of "to be, or not to be." Old guard film critics, however, eager to see a serious, politically engaged tradition of Quebec national cinema be carried forward into the new millennium, criticized Falardeau and other *nouvelle génération* filmmakers precisely for this perceived apolitical turn.[29]

Riding on the coattails of *C.R.A.Z.Y.*, *Maman est chez le coiffeur*, and *C'est pas moi, je le jure!*, three more, unevenly successful 1960s-set nostalgic films, also focalized through the viewpoints of adolescent characters, were released: *Histoire de famille*, *Une vie qui commence*, and *Frisson des collines*.[30] Michel Poulette's *Histoire de famille* (2006), originally a six-hour television miniseries, was also released in a nearly three-hour theatrical version, casting *C.R.A.Z.Y.*'s Danielle Proulx as the Gagné family matriarch. Highly derivative, it develops plot elements as the pretext for mentioning national political and cultural touchstones and uses stock footage to situate the family saga within the national context. A 1962 conversation, for example, asserts that "C'est fini les Canadiens-français qui se plient avant tout le monde … Chacun est maître de son destin" (It's over now, French Canadians who bend over for everyone else … Each of us is the master of our destiny) – a thinly veiled reference to Jean Lesage's electoral slogan, *Maîtres chez nous* (itself borrowed from clerico-nationalist historian Lionel Groulx). And characters comment editorially on events, as when the unemployed patriarch (Luc Proulx) watches Pierre Trudeau talking about the *War Measures Act* and quips, "La suspension des droits de l'homme? Et batince. Join the club" (The suspension of human rights? Shoot. Join the club).

Written and directed by Michel Monty (b. 1964), a screen actor and theatre instructor at the Conservatoire d'art dramatique de Montréal,[31] *Une vie qui commence / Life Begins* (2010) follows the now familiar pattern of an adolescent boy who experiences a traumatic loss. In this case, though, the film explores two generations of trauma in 1963: At the age of twelve, Étienne (Charles-Antoine Perreault) loses his idealized father, Jacques Langevin (François Papineau), a death directly linked to family dynamics from the father's youth. In contrast with other films in this category, *Une vie qui commence* establishes complicity between its 1960s father and son; his father's death, possibly a suicide, leads Étienne to behave increasingly strangely. The generational conflict here occurs instead between the adolescent's father and grandfather (Raymond Cloutier). It might be tempting to read the latter, clearly the film's villain, as representing outdated *Grande Noirceur* values, but *Une vie qui commence* (like *C'est pas moi, je le jure*) connects him instead to the urban professional class that likely supported Jean Lesage's Liberal Party victory in 1960. It makes clear that the father of its troubled teenager was raised in an unloving, pressure-filled environment, as revealed during a family dinner at the grandparents' house that criticizes the hypocritical pretentiousness of French Canadian bourgeois elites to which the Langevin belong. However, *Une vie qui commence* (like *Frisson des collines*, discussed below) offers a retrograde image of its central female character. Étienne's mother, Louise (Julie Le Breton), played by a beautiful actress, appears as a 1960s fantasy wife before her husband's death, immaculately clad as she does housework and sexually eager at bedtime. Although her inability to cope financially after her husband's death comments on the limited opportunities for women and their lack of preparation for any other roles than those of housewife and mother, Monty's portrayal generally undermines Louise's agency. Her refusal of financial help from her in-laws appears irrational, and her recitation of platitudes and increasing authoritarianism in the face of Jacques's need for affection and understanding render her unsympathetic. The subtly anti-feminist film initially denies Louise the ability to meet challenges on her own, as she seeks help sorting out her life with another man not long after being widowed, but – as in *Un été sans point ni coup sûr* – she eventually grows and is shown as independent at the film's conclusion. Overall, although the child actor handles his role well, *Une vie qui commence* lacks the charm and imagination of *C'est pas moi, je le jure*, which it echoes with its idiosyncratic boy character, a successful feature exploited in yet another period piece, *Frisson des collines*.

Like Philippe Falardeau's nostalgic film, journeyman director Richard Roy's *Frisson des collines / Thrill of the Hills* (2011) introduces a charismatic young actor, Antoine Olivier Pilon (b. 1997). His incarnation of the oddly nicknamed adolescent protagonist, Frisson, largely carries what is essentially a hipper version of *Histoires d'hiver* (discussed below), establishing complicity between the boy and his motorcycle-riding uncle, Tom Faucher (Guillaume Lemay-Thivierge), who eventually takes him to Woodstock. This semi-autobiographical film was inspired by Roy's childhood in Saint-Agapit in the Lotbinière/Chaudière-Appalaches region. As in *Une vie qui commence*, Frisson loses an idolized father (Patrice Robitaille), an electricity lineman; also as in the Monty film, his mother (Anick Lemay), at first lost in her grief, abandons him, until she is "rescued" by the local veterinarian (Paul Doucet). In addition to their reinforcement of the 1960s as a moment of bittersweet memory for contemporary Quebec, these minor films also attest to another phenomenon related to the industry's growth: An increase in the number of films released each year allows for such derivative projects to see the light of the projection room. But it also testifies to the commitment of producers and public funding bodies like Telefilm Canada and SODEC to the neoliberal value of profitability, as they favour projects considered to be *valeurs sûres*. Combining sports with nostalgia seemed equally profitable, as seen in another body of related films that memorialize the 1960s.

Sports and Childhood Memory: *Histoires d'hiver, Un été sans point ni coup sûr,* and *Il était une fois les Boys*

Just two weeks after the premier of *Emporte-moi*, another 1960s period piece, this time focusing on a young boy's development, debuted: François Bouvier's (b. 1948) *Histoires d'hiver / Winter Stories* (1999), an adaption of Marc Robitaille's hockey-themed memoir *Histoires d'hiver, avec des rues, des écoles et du hockey* (1987).[32] Set in the winter of 1966–7 and thematizing the national sport of hockey, *Histoires d'hiver* offers a nostalgic revisitation of Quebec's transition to modernity,[33] another precursor, text for twenty-first-century films. Its protagonist, Martin Roy (Joël Dalpé-Drapeau), provides a model for similar boy characters and reappears in Francis Leclerc's *Un été sans point ni coup sûr*, also based on a Robitaille memoir.[34] These two films, released a nearly a decade apart by directors from different generations, can be read fruitfully in tandem because of their contrasting treatment of Quebec society's evolution, particularly regarding women's roles. A *Mon oncle Antoine* for generations after that of Claude Jutra, *Histoires d'hiver*'s apparent nostalgia is reinforced by the film's saccharine musical score by Michel Rivard (b. 1951) of the iconic rock group Beau Dommage. Its voice-over narration by Michel Leboeuf further underlines the film's engagement of memory, allowing commentary about the period – both of the protagonist's life and the province's historical trajectory – from an adult perspective. In this largely conventional film, which received lukewarm reviews, Bouvier nonetheless introduces elements of the fantasy or dream sequences, influenced by Lauzon's *Léolo*, that herald twenty-first-century Quebec film's departure from the social realism of *cinéma direct*.[35]

As Robert Proulx observes, the Roy family in *Histoires d'hiver* stands in as a microcosm for Quebec society, with the young Martin torn between his charismatic, working-class uncle Maurice, and his more straight-laced, white-collar father.[36] These brothers represent, respectively, the heroes of a bygone era and those of the new; the uncle's given name references two notable Québécois: hockey hero Maurice Richard and the political icon for Quebec's insular backwardness, Maurice Duplessis. Martin shares a deep sense of complicity with this favourite uncle, Maurice (Denis Bouchard), a fellow hockey fan who symbolizes the values of a dying generation. Indeed, his death represents a bitter, traumatic moment that nonetheless triggers forward movement in the boy's development. His father, Hervé (Luc Guérin), on the other hand, figures the province's future, the outward- and forward-looking technocrats who engineered the Quiet Revolution's trend towards professional advancement, for better or for worse. Hervé learns English to earn a promotion at work and attempts to socialize with his (albeit sympathetic) anglophone boss, Ron Richardson (Alex Ivanovici). The film's treatment of Anglo-Canada is relatively apolitical; Ron is somewhat nutty, his surname suggesting an anti-Semitic stereotype (son of the rich man). But because of his minority status as Jewish, he is also shown as sympathetic to French-language culture. Specifically set in a season in which the Toronto Maple Leafs, the Montreal Canadiens' archrival and emblem of Anglo-Canada, won the Stanley Cup, the film nonetheless uses the hockey rivalry to engage in the discourse of francophone defeat. And yet the film's ambivalent nostalgia concludes in 1967, the year of the great Expo, a major symbol of francophone achievement.

Above all, as they acquire a television and other appliances, the Roy family reflects the new consumer society, as do the neighbourhood children's activities of purchasing candy, swapping trading cards, and riding bikes. *Histoires d'hiver* reveals a glimmer of the developing changes in gender dynamics as well, but Bouvier reveals attitudes from an earlier generation (than that of Leclerc and other *nouvelle génération* filmmakers) in his trivialization of homemaker Jacqueline Roy. The casting of comic actress Diane Lavallée reinforces Bouvier's nostalgic portrayal of a typical stay-at-home mom of the 1960s. Self-conscious and unsophisticated while hosting anglophone elites, she does seek self fulfilment beyond motherhood by dabbling in arts and crafts. Although she evolves from paint-by-number kits to original artwork, her talent remains limited as she composes from a family photo. This caricatured depiction of the mother contrasts significantly with Leclerc's adaptation of another Marc Robitaille memoir.

Whereas in Bouvier's film the uncle's death allows the son to grow closer to his father, adopting a forward-looking attitude, in Francis Leclerc's *Un été sans point ni coup sûr / A No-Hit, No-Run Summer* (2008) the protagonist's father (Patrice Robitaille) represents the values of the past. Here, Martin (Pier-Luc Funk) asserts in voice-over, "L'ancien temps est fini. Mon père, il comprend pas ça" (The olden days are over. My dad doesn't get that). The generation gap between the two directors appears in their different adaptations of the same base characters drawn from Robitaille's two memoirs. Situated squarely in twenty-first-century trends, Leclerc decentres the father's authority and depicts the mother figure as more fully self-actualized. In contrast with *Histoires d'hiver*'s trivialization of its maternal figure, *Un été* focuses almost as much on the mother's growth as that of her son, as her need for personal fulfilment represents a significant subplot. Mutual conflicts with the traditionalist father establish mother-son complicity, and images of Mireille (Jacinthe Laguë) evolve over the course of the film, initially signalling her visible boredom, but concluding with her employment outside the home. The film further engages changing gender roles in its adolescent female character, Sophie (Frédérique Dufort); a tomboy raised by her single father, she is united with Martin by a mutual interest in baseball. Explicitly engaging social pressures for Sophie to perform a normative femininity, the film allows her to maintain an independent sense of self. Whereas *Histoires d'hiver* unquestioningly depicts the father as a blithe adherent to the trend towards modernity, *Un été* depicts the need for men's growth as well, so that by the end of the film Charles sets aside his petty jealousy and old-fashioned ideas, accepting Jacinthe's desire to work outside the home.

Set in 1969 and beginning two years after *Histoires d'hiver*, *Un été sans point ni coup sûr* thematizes the summer sport of baseball, linking the *petite histoire* of Martin's experiences on a seemingly hapless little league team with national history in the form of the debut of Montreal's one-time Major League Baseball franchise, the Expos. The Expos work particularly well as a nostalgic emblem of a time gone by, as the irony of a fan's assertion that "une équipe de baseball. C'est là pour la vie" (a baseball team is here for life) cannot escape today's viewers who recall that the Montreal franchise played its final season in 2004, becoming thereafter the Washington Nationals. *Un été*'s closing voice-over reveals how memory frames the tale:

> Quand je vais avoir l'âge de mon père, je ne sais pas comment je vais être … mais je sais que je vais me souvenir du premier été des Expos, que je vais me souvenir de mon match sans point ni coup sûr, que je vais me souvenir de mon père qui, cet été-là a pris conscience que j'étais son fils pour vrai.

> When I'm my father's age, I don't know what I'll be like … but I know that I'm going to remember the first summer of the Expos, that I'm going to remember my no-hit, no-run game, that I'm going to remember my dad, who that summer realized that I really was his son.

Although it looks longingly back at the past and childhood as carefree times, it is also forward-looking, underscoring twelve-year-old Martin's belonging to the generation of the future, as in his opening voice-over narration: "Ma mère dit que nous, les jeunes, on ne sait pas la chance qu'on a … Il y a du monde de mon âge qui s'inquiète pour son avenir … pas moi" (My mom says that we young people don't know how lucky we are … There are people my age who worry about their future … not me). At school, a teacher lectures his students out of frame, "Les hommes et les femmes de l'avenir sont vous autres" (You all are the men and women of the future). Meanwhile the camera focuses on words on the blackboard, "Un nouvel ère" (A new era), along with a poster stating, "Le futur sur la lune" (The future on the moon). The moon becomes a recurring motif in the film, leading up to the moonwalk, a trope frequently deployed to signal Quebec's participation in continental American modernity. The teacher's lecture also engages the tension between Americanization and Americanicity after his students admit they will spend their summer watching the Expos:

> Le baseball, c'est le sport national des Américains. Je ne vois pas pourquoi on a besoin de ça ici. Déjà on a le *Ed Sullivan Show* dans tous nos télés le dimanche. Mais si vous et vos copains peuvent me prouver qu'on apprendra quelque chose en regardant un match de baseball, on le regardera.

> Baseball is the national sport of Americans. I don't know why we need baseball here. We already have the *Ed Sullivan Show* on our TVs every Sunday. But if you and your friends can prove to me that we will learn something by watching a baseball game, we'll watch it.

Martin's intellectual friend Yvon Larochelle (Léo Caron) explains how in "les Amériques," stressing the plural to include Quebec, baseball offers new immigrants a common topic of conversation, "un point d'intégration dans la société" (a point of integration into society). His father had told him, "si je voulais comprendre le corps et l'âme de l'Amérique, il fallait que je comprenne le baseball" (if I wanted to understand the body and soul of America, I would have to understand baseball). Quebec's participation in US culture recurs when Martin's small but chubby teammate La Crevette (*1981*'s Jean-Carl Boucher) lists the television shows he is going to watch over the summer, including *Gilligan's Island* (1964–7).

Like other filmmakers of his generation, Leclerc shows Quebec as engaged with the world outside; in particular, while many films depict the United States and the idea of the Americanization of French Canadian culture negatively, Leclerc's film embraces Quebec's Americanicity.[37] Above all, the sport of baseball figures Quebec's specificity as a French-speaking but distinctly North American culture, a phenomenon established in Gilles Carle's depictions of baseball in *Les Plouffe* (1981). Like *C.R.A.Z.Y.*, which very distinctly uses American popular music in its soundtrack,[38] Leclerc's film also uses English-language popular music, but its thematization of the Apollo 11 moon landing on 20 July 1969, as characters anticipate and then watch it together on television, most clearly signals the nation's engagement with technological advances and North American achievements. Although the film takes place well prior to these, *Un été* makes references to the 1980 and 1995 referenda on sovereignty, deploying baseball as national allegory. An early sequence stages a scene in which a "OUI/NON" vote is significant, concluding on the message that it is not whether you win or lose, but rather fact that you played the game at all that matters.

In addition to referencing Bill Stoneman's no-hitter for the Expos on 17 April 1969, the film's title, *Un été sans point, ni coup sûr* refers to Martin's team's inability to score a run or even to make a hit on the field, but the lesson they learn, of course, is one of resilience. Reminiscent of the *Bad News Bears* (Michael Ritchie, 1976), Leclerc's feel-good film contributes significantly to revising the image of Quebec as a nation of victims and losers. But to underscore the contrast between Quebec values about participation with the implicitly US notion that winning, in and of itself and no matter the means, is the ultimate goal, Leclerc's "villain" is Gilbert Turcotte. Roy Dupuis plays the disciplined, *pur et dur* (hardcore) coach of the elite team, Les Aristocrates, whose name invokes the seigneurial elites rejected in populist Quebec national cinema, and from which Martin and his friends are excluded. Significantly, instead of casting Quebec cinema's most recognized (and classically handsome) face as his adult lead, Leclerc opts for the goofy-looking Patrice Robitaille, known for comedic roles as an obnoxious loudmouth, to play Martin's dad. Because this story is precisely about those who have been considered losers showing up to at least play the game, Dupuis's image is *too* perfect, too much that of a winner to represent the Québécois Everyman. Finally, *Un été* adopts a discourse found elsewhere in Quebec sport films, from *Les Boys* to Manon Briand's TV biopic about Anglo-Canadian swimmer Marilyn Bell, *Heart* (2004) – namely, that *heart* is the key quality necessary to play. Martin thus relates in voice-over during a climactic game sequence, "Il paraît que le talent, c'est pas tout, et que le coeur compte pour beaucoup" (It seems that talent isn't everything, and that heart counts for a lot).

While also a celebration of Quebec's transition to modernity, *Un été*'s critique of the developing consumer society is more acerbic than *Histoires d'hiver* in its depiction of a spoiled rich child, with voice-over providing meta-commentary to frame on-screen events. Its characters also appear more well rounded and less caricatured, and Leclerc employs techniques that had already become standard, it would seem, in his generation's filmmaking, including fantasy sequences. For example, in his imagination, Martin converses with a magically materialized Expos star, African American left-fielder Mack Jones (Phillip Jarret). The player's race both nods to Montreal's role in the career of Jackie Robinson,[39] but also represents, albeit in a tokenistic way, the insertion of a person of colour into the landscape of the Quebec historical imaginary.

Certainly, as Jane Moss argues, these films depict the Québécois family as "less patriarchal, less xenophobic, and less homophobic"[40] than what appears in the corpus of literary adaptations described in chapter 3. The very fact that *Maman est chez le coiffeur*, *C'est pas moi, je le jure!*, and *Un été sans point ni coup sûr* focus their narration (often with recourse to voice-over) through the eyes of a child or adolescent undermines the father's role as the centre of family life. In their plots and dialogue, these films explicitly call into question paternal authority as representative of outmoded values that must be rejected for Quebec to achieve modernity. But father-son reconciliations also occur, as seen in Richard Goudreau's nostalgic look at the childhood days of some of the nation's most beloved cinematic characters in another sports-themed film, *Il était une fois les Boys*.

Given the success of these sports-themed childhood memoirs, it is not surprising that the producers of the *Les Boys* franchise would get in on the action, with Richard Goudreau's (b. 1950) *Il était une fois les Boys / When We Were Boys* (2013).[41] Elsewhere, I document at length the role of the *Les Boys* films within the project of defining Quebec's national identity through hockey.[42] Although begun in the late 1990s, the series' success extended well into the new millennium, marking a key moment in the Hollywoodization of Quebec's film industry as it (with Pierre Falardeau's *Elvis Gratton*) revealed the profitability of the sequel. "One of the most successful Canadian films ever,"[43] *Les Boys* (1997) introduced viewers to a gang of typical Québécois losers who become winners through their sense of team loyalty and tricksterism. Directed by Louis Saïa (b. 1950), who co-wrote the scenario with Christian Fournier, *Les Boys* unites a cast of beloved actors that represents in microcosm Quebec's various male character types. These include bar owner Stan (Rémy Girard), playboy Bob (Marc Messier), statistics dork Fern (Paul Houde), gangster Méo (Pierre Lebeau), macho gay Jean-Charles (Yvan Ponton), stoner and rocker Julien

(Roc Lafortune), working-class heart-throb Mario (Patrick Labbé), and shy yuppie Ti-Guy (Patrick Huard). Sequels appeared at regular intervals, based on a set formula, with variations on a theme, including a trip to Europe in *Les Boys II* (Louis Saïa, 1998), a match against the Canadian Olympic women's team in *Les Boys III* (Louis Saïa, 2001), and a Canadiens Legends team in *Les Boys IV* (Georges Mihalka, 2005).

Writing on the eve of the new millennium, after the release of *Les Boys II*, Carlo Mandolini asked whether it is worth investing public resources into a creation that is "grossly commercial to the end of its fingertips,"[44] signalling an ongoing polemic in the evolution of Quebec national cinema. Despite his complete pan, Mandolini identifies how these films directly engage questions of national identity, defusing (but also productively identifying) the anxieties of contemporary Québécois men through humour. He observes that "while the first film showed us the difficulty in affirming masculine identity, *Les Boys II* showed the Québécois man's unease in his relationship with the *Other*";[45] similarly, the third and fourth films address, respectively, (heterosexual) male discomfort with liberated women and gay sexuality. Documenting the various ways in which the franchise responds to a certain need within the collectivity, Yves Picard describes the entire series as "a fairy tale for adults" with the special ability to "mentir vrai" (lie truthfully).[46] *Les Boys* has, indeed, attained the status of a cultural myth, and it has done so precisely by thumbing its nose at institutional stakeholders who maintain that cinema in Quebec should be an elite art practised by auteurs. That elitist attitude, however, contributes to "an unfavourable prejudice"[47] against Quebec national cinema, viewed as slow-moving and depressing, filled with loser characters – in a word, inaccessible to a general public that has long preferred Hollywood fare to home-grown art films. The development of popular genre and comedy films in the 1990s, and especially in the early 2000s, changed this image and lured the "average" Québécois into theatres. While I agree with institutional critics who claim that every year Quebec produces a good number of dumb and bad movies, I disagree that this turn towards accessibility is, in and of itself, a bad thing. On the contrary, it is an essential development in twenty-first-century Quebec national cinema, fostering growing levels of productivity with the financial support of box-office hits subsidizing auteur films that will not turn a profit. Indeed, Picard argues for the importance of such films, insisting that "the *Les Boys* film series has played a key role in our cinematography" by establishing a dialogue "between the big screen and the audience."[48]

Given the nation's hunger to hear this story told and told again, it is no wonder that a fifth instalment to the franchise was developed, a nostalgic reflection by the older members (and fans) of *Les Boys* upon their teenage years in the 1960s. Producer Richard Goudreau wrote and directed *Il était une fois les Boys* himself, its title's iconic reference to the French rendering of "once upon a time" suggesting the prequel's fairy-tale nature. Opening credits link past and present directly as the names of actors who played its most recognized characters appear on screen over images of 1960s homes and cars, followed by those of the actors portraying their younger avatars. The film stages an origin story for the iconic team, depicting their family lives, codifying the character traits that distinguished them as adults as already present in their youths. Stan Ouellet (Simon Pigeon) is a trickster; Bob Chicoine (Samuel Gauthier) is a charmer; Marcel Bilodeau (Derek Poissant) is a cross-eyed goof; Fern Rivest (Jassen Charron) is a stats nerd; and Jean-Charles Taillefert (William Legault-Lacasse) is first in his class. Of course, Méo (Maxime Desjardins-Tremblay) is already a thug, albeit a charming one (the prequel overwrites the original film's villain to conform to his later integration into the team in the franchise's story arc). A *Les Boys* film would not be the same without the adult actors who have incarnated these characters for the Quebec public for over a quarter of a century. *Il était une fois les Boys* thus casts these aging actors as family and community members. As in other 1960s nostalgic memoirs, family situations fuel the narrative's dramatic tensions. Stan's uncle, Mononc' Fred (Rémy Girard), owns a restaurant and runs the outdoor ice rink; Bob's father (Marc Messier) ignores both wife and son, spending his time instead with an elaborate model train; Jean-Charles's father (Yvan Ponton) expresses the anti-homosexual sentiments of the time; and Marcel (Luc Guérin) is the good-natured nerd his son will become. Since the young Méo has no family, Pierre Lebeau plays the team's coach, Jimmy, and actors who portray the younger generation of present-day "Boys" (too young to be teens in the 1960s) appear as community members. Roc Lafortune is the local cop, and Patrick Labbé the science teacher.

Following the formulaic structure of the other films, including practice sequences and games leading up to a championship match, *Il était une fois les Boys* pits the young team against Les Étoiles. Always the underdogs, the film reflects the series' franco-populist attitude since anglophone factory owner, Mr. Madison (Trevor Momesso), sponsors Les Étoiles, coached by the factory's manager and the film's villain, Jean-Guy Racette (Jeff Boudreault). This elite team is stacked with the town's best players, but Les Boys come from behind and win, inspired by rousing locker room speeches and employing trickster tactics on the ice. Like other nostalgia films, it includes a painful moment of loss that the group must experience together to solidify the lifelong relationships they establish. Introducing an expendable new character, Ben Bouchard (Maxime Gibault), Les Boys' charming blonde teammate tragically falls through the ice before the final match. Playing on the hockey motif of the "Phantom of the Forum," the ghost who helps the Montreal Canadiens during games,[49] Ben's apparition materializes on the ice to rouse his teammates to victory. Another fairy-tale moment, linking nostalgia to fantasy and wish fulfilment, occurs when Jean Béliveau appears at the rink to play with Les Boys, a treat arranged by Mononc' Fred through his friend, a Zamboni driver for the Canadiens, played

Figure 5.1. Although still called "Les As," the future Les Boys sport their iconic uniform colours of red, gold, and black. Captain Bob (Samuel Gauthier) gives them a pep talk before the big match, both ritual elements of the hockey film played with nostalgia for the 1960s and 1970s here.

by Michel Charrette, another familiar face from the series as Stan's son Popold. But a crowning moment for viewers occurs when, having held a school dance as a fundraiser, Les Boys debut their new uniforms; throughout the film they have been wearing blue jerseys with vintage lace-up necks, but at its conclusion they don the entertainment franchise's iconic colours of black, gold, and red.

Unlike the other 1960s nostalgia films, and in keeping with its fairy-tale nature, *Il était une fois les Boys* does not connect its mythical town to actual events in Quebec history. It signals itself as a period piece in other ways, including an opening voice-over of a weather forecast on AM radio, announcing that Jean Béliveau (who retired in 1971) is captain of the Montreal Canadiens. Iconic cars, including a black Shelby Mustang and a red Mustang convertible, play a similar role, as does the boys' hockey gear, including a Jacques Plante–style mask worn by the Étoiles' goalie. The film engages some social issues, however, including two dramatic subplots featuring the team leaders' mothers: Stan's widowed mother (Catherine Sénart) is being sexually harassed by her boss, Racette, and Bob's mother, Rachel (Joëlle Morin), is a nurse who temporarily leaves her neglectful husband. The Catholic Church still plays a central role in the daily lives of these families, as seen during a magnificent Christmas Eve mass, but the *curé* (François Léveillée) becomes the object of an anti-clericalism typical of twenty-first-century Quebec film. He tells altar boys Fern and Marcel to keep pouring wine into the communion chalice, smokes cigars, leers at women, but above all, spreads wicked gossip about Bob's mother. Nostalgia for a lost sense of community nonetheless appears as teammates and their parents all gather for a Christmas party at the Bilodeau home.

Despite its high production values, *Il était une fois les Boys* cannot be fully appreciated outside its context within the franchise; its many gags, but also its emotional moments, draw on insider nods to character foibles and team traditions. Ultimately, like all the films in the series, it is about how a group of misfit Québécois losers rise to victory because of their motto, "Tous pour un et un pour tous" (All for one and one for all). Furthermore, as with many sports stories from Quebec, although practice and hard work are required, *heart* is the key to victory, as Jimmy says to Mononc' Fred, "onze coeurs qui battent ensemble … ça peut faire des ravages" (eleven hearts beating together … that can do some damage). As is also typical of period films, music plays an essential role in establishing viewer nostalgia, both through a sentimental original film score and the diegetic and extradiegetic injection of popular songs from the period. Whereas earlier *Les Boys* films had called on iconic Quebec rockers Éric Lapointe and France D'Amour for songs like "Les Boys Band Blues," this film recruits acclaimed tenor Marc Hervieux to sing "Oh, Holy Night" at the midnight mass, the King Melrose Band for covers of period pop classics throughout the film, and then Bryan Adams, Roch Voisine, and Garou join in for an adaptation of Adams's "All for Love," reworked as "Tous pour un," for the film's closing credits. Like the musical biopics discussed in chapter 4 and other films that evoke a specific time period through music, *Il était une fois les Boys* contributes to its own nostalgic effect through fondly remembered classics, in the same way that the franchise's earlier films exploited music to engage viewers. Indeed, this prequel film is even meta-nostalgic in that viewing the film not only invokes a certain period in Quebec's history and viewers' lives, but also their experience of watching the earlier *Les Boys* films in the late 1990s.

Les Boys represents a true multimedia franchise in its deployment of visual media, including film and television, music, but also merchandise such as hockey jerseys, coffee mugs, and other paraphernalia sporting the fictional team's logo. Such products inserted into daily life allow fans to perform a certain identity, and in some ways, as critics would point out, these fan identities come to substitute for national identity. In the case of Quebec and *Les Boys*, a media franchise that is so iconically Québécois, performing a fan identity and performing a national identity amount to much the same thing. In *National Identity, Popular Culture and Everyday Life* (2002), Tim Edensor argues that, in fact, popular culture and daily life make a much more significant contribution to identity building and a sense of shared national culture than are the products of cultural elites, including independent art films. He argues that "[a] sense of national identity … is not a once and for all thing, but is dynamic and dialogic, found in the constellations of a huge cultural matrix of images, ideas, spaces, things, discourses and practices."[50] In my view, Quebec's popular film successes, like the *Les Boys* franchise, but also the heritage films and biopics discussed in chapters 3 and 4, contribute, for better or for worse, much more to a sense of shared national identity than do the independent art films viewed by a handful of critics and cinephiles in Montreal. By offering a homegrown alternative to Hollywood genre films, Quebec's cinema as an industry (perhaps rather than as an art) projects a positive image of collective self.

Revisiting the 1960s in the Art Film: *La chasse au Godard d'Abbittibbi*

In contrast with the highly popular films discussed so far this chapter, Éric Morin's (b. 1969) first feature film, *La chasse au Godard d'Abbittibbi / Hunting the Northern Godard* (2013) also looks with nostalgia on the 1960s, but from a quirky, self-conscious, art-film stance. As its title suggests, it whimsically memorializes the real-life event of Jean-Luc Godard's visit to Quebec in the late 1960s,[51] also signalling its fanciful aspects by misspelling Abitibi, an iconic region in Quebec's territorial imaginary. It reminds viewers of the signal event it engages with title cards: "À la fin des années soixante, un grand cinéaste a visité une contrée éloignée. Ce fait d'hiver a inspiré le conte qui suit" (At the end of the 1960s, a great filmmaker visited a distant country. This historical trivia inspired the tale that follows). Through an untranslatable wordplay (*fait d'hiver / fait divers* – literally, "fact of winter" / "news item"), the coy reference (*un grand cinéaste*), outdated language (*une contrée*), and direct statement (*le conte qui suit*), the film immediately establishes its tongue-in-cheek, ludic, fairy-tale nature. Sequences alternate between two main narratives, one more realistic, the other more fanciful. The latter parodies Godard's arrival, accompanied by an assistant and an actress, then coursing through the wintry wilderness on snowmobiles in pursuit of capturing some "authentic" images of Quebec, but instead staging ridiculous *mises en scène* that satirize continental French folkloric preconceptions of Canada, including a Halloween-style Indian princess costume.

Going beyond the meta-cinematic reference to Godard, French New Wave film, and its influence in Quebec, *La chasse au Godard*'s main narrative thrust involves a group of young people who film their attempt to "hunt down" Godard in order to make their own film in December 1968. The film's central character, Marie, played by the luminous Sophie Desmarais (b. 1986), incarnates a frequently expressed desire to leave her small town to find something more: "J'aimerais ça partir. Sortir de là. Voyager. Voir le monde. Faire des choses sans que du monde pense que je me prends pour une autre" (I'd like that, to depart. Leave here. Travel. See the world. Do things without people thinking I'm stuck up). The arrival of a Montreal filmmaker, Paul (Martin Dubreuil), an avatar of real-life experimental filmmaker Pierre Harel,[52] in Rouyn-Noranda catalyses this desire, and Marie and her boyfriend, Michel (Alexandre Castonguay), join Paul in the search for Godard. Michel is a caricature of the 1960s Québécois idealist suffering a clichéd *prise de conscience* that "On est des osties de colons"

(We're damn hillbillies). A student, he embraces Marxist ideals, but his comically exaggerated northern accent is nearly incomprehensible; like his intellectual models from the 1960s, he talks a lot, but in the end does absolutely nothing. Despite many frequent close-up shots that linger on Marie's exterior calm and stillness, at *La chasse au Godard*'s conclusion she is the one who acts on her dreams, leaving for Montreal to chase her destiny. Her complete name, Marie Laforêt-Kissnabiche, reveals her significance as an allegory for feminine identity in Quebec, combining French and Indigenous elements. Her first name, evocative of the Virgin Mary and of Louis Hémon's iconic *Maria Chapdelaine*, was also for a long time the most common female name in the province; she thus represents an Everywoman, albeit an exceptionally beautiful one, for Quebec. But Marie's last name also suggests the problematic notion of Québécois identity as hybrid, and sequences clearly refer to her Indigenous grandmother's practices and teachings.

Morin conveys nostalgia for a period in which he did not live, but which has become iconic for younger generations of politically engaged Québécois as a period (in contrast with the post-national present) when things were happening. Morin relies on stock devices like title cards, a meticulous reconstitution of period decor and costumes, and the reproduction (or use of authentic) print and broadcast media to reference notable events. Period-accurate advertisements for various made-up products announce the advent of consumer society, as do the brilliant pastiche sequences of ONF documentary film projects from that decade. Engaging the rise of the educational institutions that will form Morin's own generation, the relatively recently formed CÉGEP system,[53] Paul, Marie, and Michel begin a series of experimental documentary shorts meant to reflect young people's attitudes. Student interviewees utter revolutionary platitudes with a subtle parodic twist; for example, one girl states her dream "d'avoir une république libre du Québec" (to have a free republic of Quebec). Further interviews include individuals implicated in Quebec's economic exploitation of resources in the Great North: factory workers, lumberjacks, and the women who support them. When Marie interviews her mother and other women at a local gathering to discuss the *condition des femmes*, the assertion that "de plus en plus les femmes ... prennent la parole" (more and more women ... have begun to speak) obliquely references the ONF feminist documentary series *En tant que femmes*.[54] Individual and collective dreams, often broken ones, appear as a leitmotif, as characters are repeatedly asked to reveal theirs; for example, a mine worker insists that "mon père m'a dit que ça sert à rien, les rêves" (my father told me that dreams are good for nothing). The young filmmakers' efforts are nonetheless humorous, as, for example, when Michel introduces the segment "Parole aux travailleurs forestiers" (Speaking for forestry workers): "On s'en va voir des hommes. Des vrais. Ils sont pas tous beaux. Ils sentent pas tous bons" (We're going to see some men. Real men. They're not all handsome. They don't all smell good). Morin's tongue-in-cheek approach to his characters' earnestness represents a breath of fresh air when compared to other, emotionally bleak independent art films released at regional and international film festivals in the second decade of the new millennium.[55] And he avoids the nostalgia apparent in 1960s-set films that target a general audience.

Above all, perhaps, Morin's disrespectful treatment of the iconic filmmaker Jean-Luc Godard is enlightening, acerbically true in one sense, but possibly misleading in another. On the one hand, aspects of Morin's representation of Godard's visit and its impact reflect historical fact, as Germain Lacasse recounts in his detailed analysis of Morin's film,[56] and Julie Perron's ONF documentary on Godard's visit, *Mai en décembre (Godard en Abitibi)* (2000), depicts the French director as arriving in Abitibi in good faith to interview locals. Furthermore, a team of young Abitibiens did follow his lead to produce their own films, and the annual Abitibi-Témiscamingue International Film Festival has become a significant venue for independent film viewing. On the other hand, Morin targets French hypocrisy through the contrast between his fictional youths' filmmaking efforts, which genuinely put them in touch with *actual* people, and his fictionalization of Godard as pursuing a fantasy-based wild goose chase across the countryside. Furthermore, Morin gives voice to Godard's establishment critics, as the narrator (playwright René-Daniel Dubois) quotes from a vitriolic article written by Jean-Pierre Bonneville in the local paper *La Frontière* in January 1969: "Et notre grand cinéaste, il a traversé le monde pour rien. Quel était son véritable but? Nous ne le saurons jamais" (And our great filmmaker, he travelled the world for nothing. What was his real goal? We'll never know).[57] Morin's art film depicts the French visiting Quebec, positing the French Other's lack of authenticity. And indeed, another film that establishes the authenticity of Quebec's popular culture against the institutional norm of valuing a French canon, Alain Desrochers's *Cabotins* (2010), also turns nostalgically to a new decade for inspiration: the 1980s.

Nostalgia for the 1980s in *Cabotins*, *Gaz Bar Blues*, and Ricardo Trogi's *1981* Series

Leading up to the year 2000 a *nouvelle génération* of filmmakers born in the 1960s rose to the fore; twenty years later, Quebec's increasingly prolific film industry has fostered the careers of the largest number of filmmakers ever to be active in the province. Furthermore, unlike some professions (like academics, for example) in which young candidates must wait for their elders to retire,[58] Quebec's producers and funding bodies seem to be willing to take a risk on new talent. Furthermore, new digital technologies and entrepreneurial attitudes have also allowed young filmmakers to self-produce films. Guillaume Lafleur, for example, observed in 2011, "le renouveau du cinéma québécois et sa reconnaissance internationale sont le fruit du travail de quelques cinéastes dans la trentaine et la quarantaine" (the renaissance in Quebec cinema and its international recognition are the fruit of the work of a few filmmakers in their thirties and forties).[59] Just as their baby boomer and Gen X predecessors nostalgically revisited their childhoods in the 1960s and 1970s, increasingly younger Gen Y and millennial filmmakers began to express nostalgia for the 1980s and even the 1990s.

A director of commercial films, it seems fitting that Alain Desrochers should take on a project that engages discussions about the value of popular entertainment forms in Quebec. *Cabotins / The Comeback* (2010), scenarized by Ian Lauzon (*Piché, De père en flic*), expresses nostalgia for a lost past, reviving it in the present on two levels. Its aging vaudeville actors regret the good times they spent onstage in 1950s and 1960s popular variety shows; at the same time, the film's 1980s setting allows baby boomers to revisit a time when they were in their prime. Its cast, studded with aging A-list Québécois stars, including Rémy Girard, Dorothée Berryman, Yves Jacques, Gilles Renaud, and Gaston Lepage, invites this reflection to cross over from on-screen discussions about the failure and revival of the variety stage show to off-screen reflections about the value of popular genre film in the new millennium. The production crosses generations by also casting younger actors, Pierre-François Legendre and Marie-Ève Milot, whose characters comment on their elders' taste in entertainment, and to engage the father-son relationship, a frequent theme of twenty-first-century films.[60]

Cabotins' premise is simple: Retired performer and theatre owner Marcel Lajoie (Rémy Girard) is bankrupt, facing the seizure of his belongings. To raise some quick cash, he decides to revive his stage show, calling on former stars to perform with him in the barn theatre, La Grange à Marcel, which he still owns in rural Saint-Côme. There is only one problem: Many still nourish grudges from past treatment by the roguish producer and comic actor. They eventually come around, however, and the show's development and rehearsals occupy most of the film. These sequences nostalgically rehearse a form of entertainment perceived as lost to the nation but also worthy of revival, making *Cabotins* a self-referential play-within-the-film production. But resistance to Marcel's project allows for explicit meta-commentary on this and other home-grown forms of entertainment as well. To fully understand the film, one must understand theatre history, particularly the tradition of the *les variétés*, Quebec's version of vaudeville, stage entertainments depicted in an earlier period in musical biopics like *La Bolduc* and *Ma vie en cinémascope*. These involved a combination of short acts, including song, dance, magic acts, sketches, and so on; the humour was often physical and broad.[61] *Cabotins* reminds the viewer of this history via its opening credits, which represent a scrapbook filled with cuttings from the 1950s, 1960s, and 1970s, ending in 1980, referencing the highs and lows of two venues, La Grange à Marcel and a Montreal theatre, the Variétés, directed by the symbolically named Lajoie, a man who brought joy to popular audiences.

These clippings refer to other events during that era as well, including Jean Drapeau's campaign to clean up Montreal's night life scene in the 1960s, Paris in May 1968, and the construction of Montreal's Olympic Stadium. Although the Variétés's popularity had peaked in the 1950s and 1960s, headlines on a page dated 1977 state clearly that "C'est la fin d'une époque. Variétés Marcel ferme ses portes" (It's the end of an era. Marcel's Variety closes its doors). Hanging on until 1980, so that the national theatrical institution can be paralleled with the nation's aspirations for independence, headlines reporting the failure of the referendum in 1980 take second billing in Lajoie's scrapbook to the news that "L'union des artistes interdit à ses membres de jouer au théâtre Gilles Latulippe. Les théâtres de variétés ferment" (The actors' guild forbids its members to play in Gilles Latulipe's theatre. All the variety show theatres close). The film mentions Latulippe, an actual theatrical performer and impresario, to introduce his later cameo appearance.

Cabotins' 1980s setting allows for some spectacularly kitschy decors, including Marcel's mansion, replete with floral wallpaper and ornate furnishings, but it also allows for a certain attack on the neoliberalism of contemporary Quebec society, parallelled with the Reagan-Mulroney era. Announcing that "la comédie est terminée!" (the show's over!), the mayor and banker who calls in Marcel's loans, Stéphane Granger (Louis Morissette), is an uptight, bottom-line, sexually ambiguous young entrepreneur and city mayor whose office is adorned with a portrait of Ronald Reagan, but also with stuffed badgers. As he insists on his local public access television show, instead of supporting the theatre and its "vulgarité artistique" (artistic vulgarity) to bring potential income to the declining community economy, he wants to establish a museum for *le blaireau d'Amérique* (the American badger). The film deploys an over-the-top, caricatural sensibility derived from the Québécois sketch comedy that originated in the *variétés*. As precisely the type of film that institutional critics decry, this notion of vulgarity resonates with the film's meta-commentary on the cultural value of popular entertainment forms.

In addition to Granger, others describe the *variétés* as vulgar, most particularly the film's *ingénue*, an aspiring student at the Conservatoire d'art dramatique, Mélanie (Marie-Ève Milot). She provides some nostalgic (in its etymological sense of painful) wardrobe choices for viewers who grew up in the 1980s with her half-top and short jogging shorts, and her youthful ignorance provides *Cabotins* a device to revive audience memory and instruct younger viewers unaware of the cultural heritage. Her characterization lampoons a different sort of *mentalité colonisé*. Whereas *colon* usually refers to someone as ignorant, uncultivated, a redneck even, it can also refer to Quebec's (pseudo-)elites or nouveaux riches who reveal their status as colonized by preferring metropolitan French Culture (with a capital *C*) and language (viewed as artificial) to local, Québécois cultural forms and language (viewed as authentic). Not only does

Mélanie, the small-town girl with big ambitions, reveal herself to be the first type of *colon*, by referring to *tapettes* (faggots), but her initial attitude towards the show also mirrors the second type of *colon*. She is rehearsing Alfred de Musset's *On ne badine pas avec l'amour*, now a French theatre classic but ironically itself a maligned popular form when first performed in 1834. When Marcel helps her rehearse, she notices that he doesn't need to look at the script to cue her, remarking "Je pensais que t'étais un comédien de variétés déchu" (I thought you were a down-and-out vaudeville actor). At this moment, both Mélanie and the viewer realize that the scorned *variété* performers are just as rigorously trained as those performing high-brow theatre, a situation reflective of Quebec's contemporary film industry, as many popular film and television actors attended the institution to which Mélanie aspires and pursue simultaneous careers on the stage and screen.

Cabotins' other younger character, Pédro (Pierre-François Legendre), is Marcel's son; their relationship is in a shambles, in part because as a child and adolescent Pédro appeared onstage with his father but now suffers psychological scarring and an inferiority complex. Marcel's disdain for his son continues throughout the film, but a cathartic moment occurs onstage at the film's conclusion; yet another "meta" moment, it invokes Aristotle's theory of theatre's function as catharsis. Even this broad comedy, then, includes pain in its nostalgia, the bitter that must accompany the sweet. Significantly, however, whereas Marcel's aging colleagues regret the bygone era of their glory days, his father's image cast a shadow over Pédro's youth. Desrochers thus suggests his own generation's haunting by its forefathers, the lionized political heroes of the Quiet Revolution and/or, for filmmakers specifically, the nearly mythologized generation who invented Quebec national cinema at the ONF like Michel Brault. Desrochers's *cinéma grand public* film, however, did not capture film critics' attention to the extent that another bittersweet look at the late 1980s produced by *nouvelle génération* filmmaker who sought to continue the national tradition of socially engaged fictional filmmaking, Louis Bélanger.

Louis Bélanger's (b. 1964) sympathy for the working-class man appears as a leitmotif across his oeuvre, already evident in *Post Mortem* (1999)[62] and later in the English-language 1960s-set period piece *The Timekeeper* (2009). It recurs as a theme, as do the blues, in his breakout film, *Gaz Bar Blues* (2003),[63] a nostalgic portrait of a lost Québécois institution, the neighbourhood service station, apparently inspired by his own childhood memories.[64] Set in the pivotal year 1989, the film cross-cuts between the rise of the self-service gas station and the fall of the Berlin Wall. François Brochu (Serge Thériault, who earned the Best Actor Jutra for his performance) is an aging widower in the early stages of Parkinson's who has raised several children to varying degrees of success; his dream is for his sons to take over the titular *gaz bar*, the Champlain station that he runs in a working-class Montreal neighbourhood. Daughter Nathalie

(Fanny Mallette) has left the family home, but three sons still live there: Réjean (Sébastien Delorme) has dreams of being a photographer; Guy (Danny Gilmore) drops shifts to play blues gigs; and fourteen-year-old baseball fan Alain (Maxime Dumontier) can't wait to work in the shop but still has some maturing to do. An ensemble cast of misfits comprises the station's habitués, typified by the carless Jos (Gaston Caron), who just comes there to socialize. Although largely episodic in structure, with vignettes about the neighbourhood's various residents, the narrative is held together by an opening frame, in which a gunman holds Alain hostage, surrounded by police in a hold-up-gone-wrong scenario. The film eventually resolves the scene without a tragic death occurring, but it represents the last straw for François, who closes the doors of his failing business for good, marking the end of an era, the end of a neighbourhood institution, in essence, the loss of community.

The *gaz bar* is a largely masculine institution, and the father-son tensions so frequently thematized in Quebec film are central to Bélanger's narrative, as the sons do not share their father's dream, which in the prevailing economic climate appears as unrealistic as their own aspiring careers in music and journalism. But the *gaz bar* represents a site of community, with the masculine interactions occurring there involving care, but also betrayal. The gruff mechanic Gaston Savard (Gilles Renaud) generously helps Nathalie, Alain, and a local girl with a flat bicycle tire; when regular Normand Patry's (Gaston Lepage) teasing of the elderly bachelor Jos becomes too pointed, he is asked to leave; Ti-Pit (Claude Legault), although something of a trickster, rarely leaves the company of the blind Nelson (Réal Bossé). Through the frequently counter-productive ethos of caring that prevails at the *gaz bar*, Bélanger proposes an alternative to the neoliberal, utilitarian ideologies rising in the 1980s. Customers take advantage, however, of François's practice of giving credit, as they do his trust. The hold-up artist of the frame sequence is revealed to have a familiar face, and *gaz bar* regular Yves Michaud (Daniel Gadouas) has been using a hook to fish bills out of a hole in the safe. The response to this discovery reveals that the community also has its own sense of justice. Instead of being banned or turned over to the police, Gaston and Ti-Pit make Yves spend a certain number of hours each day in the station's ice freezer. As Chantale Gingras observes, "it's above all the respect for traditional values that come out of this film, in particular those of the family ... and of work well done."[65] At the same time as the film expresses nostalgia for a lost sense of community, it also explores the younger generation's desire to leave Quebec, and through them it connects the province to world events, another *nouvelle génération* preoccupation; thus, "Bélanger also situates his film in History."[66]

Eldest son Réjean, an idealist, leaves for Berlin precisely out of the desire to be a part of something bigger, of massive social change. His reports home, however, gradually become cynical, even bitter, as he sees the film's target, neoliberal commercialism, appropriating the fallen wall. In the end, he sympathizes with East Germans, but in a sort of backhanded manner; seeing parallels between Quebec and East Germany, Réjean's nostalgia is for the now and suddenly bygone era of totalitarian communism. Drunk one evening, he begins to rebuild the wall, hoping to restore to the East Germans the peace he believes they once had; of course, he is arrested and shipped home by the Canadian embassy. Upon his return, he explains to his puzzled father, "'Garde, pa, Berlin, là, c'est comme une station-service. À l'ouest, c'est le gros libre-service modern …, mais à l'est c'est comme le gaz bar. C'est les gros libres services qui va gagner" (Look, dad, Berlin, there, is like a gas station. In the West, it's the big, modern self-service …, but in the East, it's like our *gaz bar*. It's the big self-service stations that are going to win). Thus, Bélanger's film expresses nostalgia for the community of a more idealistic, more Marxist Quebec, prior to the Reagan-Mulroney-Bourassa neo-liberal era, before globalization and the rise of televisual media and computers, technologies that keep us inside our homes instead of seeking the company of neighbours.[67] While it is a particularly Québécois story, *Gaz Bar Blues* offers a universal message, as Manon Tourigny explains: "the director asks about the loss of our ideals and the benefits – real or imaginary – of progress and change that touch us all."[68]

Bélanger revisited the period of the 1970s and 1980s in his coming-of-age dramedy *Vivre à 100 milles à l'heure* (2019), but a more extended vision of the 1980s occurs in the work of Ricardo Trogi (b. 1970). Just a few years younger than Bélanger, Trogi belongs to another group of filmmakers to rise in the new millennium who infuse popular genre cinema with a sense of fun but also something of an auteur sensibility, although many of the "arty" devices they adopted were by then becoming standard film practice. Trogi's dramedies deal with the absurdities of life in twenty-first-century Quebec for younger adults, but his breakout popular success began a nostalgic series of films with heavily autobiographical elements.

Described as "one of the most important Québécois directors of his generation,"[69] Trogi casts a nostalgic eye on the recent past in his popular autobiographical tetralogy, its instalments transparently titled *1981 / The Year I Became a Liar* (2009), *1987* (2014), *1991* (2017), and *1995* (2024). Blurring the lines between reality and fiction, his focalizing protagonist is also named Ricardo Trogi, engagingly incarnated by actor Jean-Carl Boucher, who viewers watch grow up with the film cycle from a pre-teen to adulthood. In addition to their charm, the most significant aspect of Trogi's period films is their introduction of a new character type: Fully Québécois in his self-conception, Trogi's avatar is also the son of an Italian immigrant, adding diversity to the predominantly *pure laine* image of Quebec found in the films discussed so far. Throughout his cycle, Trogi pays homage to his Italian roots, pokes fun at *Québécois de souche* attitudes, signals the ironies of growing up in post–Quiet Revolution Quebec, and comments lightly on the increasing role that consumer goods play in constructions of identity. His films also reveal the cultural value of comedy, a frequently disparaged entertainment form.

The three films discussed here directly engage Ricardo's Italian origins, invoking, as well, Lauzon's fantasized Italian self in *Léolo*. For example, *1981* opens with a playful fantasy sequence set in an imaginary "Italie du nord 1944" (Northern Italy 1944). The wartime setting, filtered through the lens of his father's recollections and his own childish imagination, depicts "les maudits allemands" (the damn Germans) as a villainous force of oppression; a German officer (Claude-Michel Bleau) – comically speaking French with a Québécois accent and interjecting his discourse with idiomatic swear words *tabernak* and *ostie* – interrogates the townspeople about a stolen radio. Reprising a classic cinematic scene, when he demands that the thief, Benito, step forward, all the children, including Ricardo's boy father, do so. The joke is on the German: All the children in town were named Benito after Mussolini. Subsequent fantasy sequences punctuate the film, commenting on Ricardo's naive efforts to understand the world around him. His difference is signalled the first day in his new school as he must correct everyone's pronunciation of his surname, Trogi, and this becomes a running gag, fondly poking fun of the dominant culture's growing pains as it moves from a largely homogeneous to an increasingly diverse society. Ricardo also discusses diversity within Quebec through his mother's origins as a small-town girl who arrives in the big city. A cutaway shows a young woman by the side of the road with a suitcase, and the voice-over narration (performed by Ricardo Trogi himself) explains that she had the misfortune of being "pognée dans une famille pauvre" (stuck in a poor family) and so left the Côte-Nord in 1965. Claudette Trogi (Sandrine Bisson) embodies a certain type of rural Québécois identity, but her machine-gun fire, deeply enracinated popular Québécois French discourse is coupled with a readiness to break out into hysterics at any moment, suggesting a stereotypical Italian matriarch. Reversing the received cultural image, her Italian husband (Claudio Colangelo) is calm. In an interview the director comments that, during casting, he rejected actors who played the loud Italian because, growing up, "C'est ma mère qui parlait fort à la maison" (It was my mom who spoke loud at home), signalling the autobiographical nature of Trogi's *1981* film cycle.[70]

In *1987* Trogi reprises his engagement with Italian-ness; now a teenager completing secondary school and forced by his father to get a job, Ricardo works at the Italian restaurant where his father is an accordionist. The trickster figure finds it difficult to maintain a position of responsibility; in need of cash, Ricardo discovers through a chance event how easy it is to steal car stereos. Although he had earlier rejected "les osties de jobs d'immigrants" (damn immigrant jobs), a conversation with his friends that directly comments on identity targets Québécois small-mindedness and media stereotypes of Italians. Dialogue about the implications of their first theft then triggers Ricardo's adult reflections in voice-over narration (performed by Trogi himself, as in *1981*):

> BOIVIN : Trogi, c'est toi l'Italien, pas nous autres.
> RICARDO : Écoute, j'suis même pas italien. C'est mon père qui est italien, pas moi.
> BOIVIN : Donc, logiquement, ça fait de toi un Italien.
> [NARRATEUR :] J'étais pas frustré que mes chums pensait qu'Italien ça fait plus voleur que québécois. C'était fou parce que moi aussi, je pensais ça, on dirait. Et c'est sûr que si c'était des Italiens qui sont reconnus comme criminels; c'était peut-être quand même pas dû au hasard. [He mentions films like *The Godfather*] Je me suis un peu énervé et je me suis dit qu'à partir de cette heure je serais un peu plus italien que québécois.

> BOIVIN: Trogi, you're the Italian, not us.
> RICARDO: Listen, I'm not even Italian. It's my dad who's Italian, not me.
> BOIVIN: So, logically, that makes you Italian.
> [NARRATOR:] I wasn't frustrated that my buddies thought that Italian meant more of a thief than Québécois. It's crazy, because that's what I thought too. And it's certain that if Italians were well known as criminals, it probably wasn't just a coincidence … I was a little annoyed, and I said that from now on I'm going to be more Italian than Québécois.

A jump cut reveals Ricardo slicking back his hair – a poster for the film *The Untouchables* ironically accusing him from the background – and leaving the house in his father's sportscoat, the sleeves rolled up, his own parody of a mafioso's garb. The text hardly needs commentary; its statement about host countries' received ideas about immigrants are apparent, as are children of immigrants' hybrid sense of self. But its assertion pertains particularly to the Italian community in Quebec, repeatedly represented on the nation's small and big screens as mafiosi.[71]

Finally, *1991* sends Ricardo on a study-abroad trip to Italy while a film student at the Université du Québec à Montréal. Like the first episode in the series, it opens with a historical frame, this one set in 1916 Italy, where his grandfather had fallen in love; he wins the grandmother's hand with his mushroom risotto, but perhaps also because he is one of the few male survivors of World War I in the village. Finally meeting people who can pronounce his name correctly on the first try, the young Québécois, who speaks only a few words of Italian, faces a series of innocent-abroad-type adventures. But his film school training also comes in handy as a second series of fantasy sequences imagines him winning the heart of his beloved (Juliette Gosselin) through the lens of a black-and-white 1960s Italian film pastiche. The trip to Italy also serves as a pretext for Ricardo to assert his *québécitude*. While his parents accompany him to the airport, his voice-over expresses excitement, as he is about to experience "l'aventure vraie" (the true adventure) of a foray into the wide world: "L'Italie, mes amis. Un vrai pays avec des vraies affaires à visiter, pas le criss de Château de Frontenac" (Italy, my friends. A real country, with real stuff to visit, not the shitty Château de Frontenac). His tongue-in-cheek observation about Quebec's status as not really a *pays* also reveals the naive preconception that North Americans have about Europe and its authenticity, further targeting the marketing of Quebec City as a historical European city in North America. In addition to the touristic commercialization of the Vieux Québec, the assertion targets the Château Frontenac's explicit construction as a faux historical monument; although its architecture invokes a Renaissance chateau from the colonial period, it was built by the Canadian Pacific Railway in 1893.

Once in Italy, Ricardo loses his passport and must go to the Canadian embassy, triggering further commentary on Quebec's particular status as a nation within a nation, and on his own identity:

Même si j'ai ben aimé René Lévesque, j'étais plutôt content que le Réferendum de 80 ait foiré. J'étais vraiment content d'être canadien. J'suis encore fier d'être québécois mais ce jour-là, j'avais l'impression que, j'sais pas, si l'ambassade québécois avait existé, ç'aurait sûrement été dans un condo, là, pas une maison de même.

Even if I really liked René Lévesque, I was pretty glad that the referendum of 1980 had failed. I was truly content to be Canadian. I'm still proud of being Québécois, but that day, I had the impression that – I don't know, that if the Quebec embassy existed, it would probably have been a condo, not a nice house like that.

Impressed with the appearance of the embassy building, he contrasts it with what he imagines a Quebec embassy would look like.

Having grown up in post–Quiet Revolution Quebec, Ricardo comments perceptively throughout the series on life in a highly bureaucratized, seemingly forward-looking society, pointing out its contradictions. As a child in *1981*, he arrives at his new school, École Saint-Exupéry; the name suggests both official Quebec's ongoing desire to remain connected to the francophone motherland by signalling the well-known writer, while at the same time indicating the average Québécois's ignorance of this heritage. As they drive up, Ricardo asks his father, "Qu'est-ce que ça veut dire, Saint-Exupéry?" (What does that mean, Saint-Exupéry?) His Italian father answers, "Ça veut dire 'école'" (It means "school"). References to *Le petit prince* (1943) riddle the film, as Ricardo's teacher asks him if he has read it; later, after reading Saint-Exupéry's novel, he imagines himself and his classmates, interrogated by the German officer from the opening sequence, on the prince's planet. In *1987*, an opening frame sequence followed by several cutaways engages the seventeen-year-old Ricardo with members of the Assemblée nationale, as he questions the arbitrary nature of various policies regarding young people. First, he recalls to viewers that the government had recently changed the educational system: "Au Québec, pour que tout aille ben, fallait choisir ce qu'on allait faire dans la vie au secondaire" (In Quebec, in order for everything to go well, you had to choose what you are going to do in life in high school). He then pokes fun at the inadequacy of the ministerial test administered to young people to aid in their career choices; when told he would be good in human resources, he asks to have his test back to change his answers. Further commentaries address the arbitrary nature of the legal drinking age, observing that if seventeen-year-olds were qualified to choose their lifetime occupation, they could certainly choose what drink they wanted. His brief stint as a car stereo thief allows for commentary on the legal age when one's criminal record remains permanent. Caught by the police, though, Ricardo is more afraid of his mother: "La prison, je m'en crissais. Mais ma mère …" (I didn't give a damn about prison. But my mother …). As he gives up his life of crime, he admits his real sense of cultural belonging: "la Mafia de Sainte-Foy a officiellement fermé portes. J'suis redevenu québécois" (the Mafia of Sainte-Foy officially closed for business. I became Québécois again).

In addition to his place of birth and the territory he grew up in, Ricardo's mother is a *québécoise pure laine*; he shares a common history, language, and culture with the other children and young adults he encounters in Québec. These factors, and not the accident of his father's genetics, contribute to his sense of self. At the same time, the filmmaker pokes fun at, while also acknowledging, the role that consumer goods have come to play in North American identity formation, as well as the general broadening of the social category of the "middle class." In *1981*, almost directly after the opening frame in the imaginary wartime Italy, the eleven-year-old Ricardo introduces himself to viewers by naming and showing on-screen all his possessions, including his stereo, hockey gear, moon boots, and "l'estie de Rubik Cube" (damn Rubik's Cube). Because of these items, he says, "j'appartenais à la class moyenne." (I belonged to the middle class). Looking to make friends, he spies a group of boys all wearing matching red K-Way windbreakers; his goal, then, is to obtain a similar jacket and thus fit in, not with any natural affinities, but rather through an external symbol of belonging derived from consumer culture. This and Trogi's other films thus signal the "middle-classification" of Quebec, its move away from a predominantly rural, then working-class French Canadian Catholic identity before the Quiet Revolution. They reveal the tensions between social aspirations and the need to prove belonging via the outward signs of possessions essential to a middle-class identity in which professional lines no longer necessarily determine self-perceptions of class. As the adult Ricardo narrator tells us early in *1987*, "C'était la belle époque-là. Où c'était ton attitude qui te définissait – pas ta job" (That was the golden age. When it was your attitude that defined you – not your job). In *1981*, the Trogi family had recently moved into a large home in the suburbs, although the father works in a restaurant and the mother is a barmaid. At a certain point in the film, Ricardo tells his mother, "Tu vis au-dessus de nos moyens" (You're living above our means). Financial pressures of a recession force the family to sell their home, and in *1987* they live on the upper floor of a working-class Sainte-Foy duplex. The way people signal their identity through external signs like wardrobe and accessories, but also through the technology they deploy, becomes a constant device in Trogi's oeuvre, begun in *Québec-Montréal* (2002), which identified each character with an on-screen title stating their name, age, and profession. In *1987* he reprises this device to introduce the seventeen-year-old Ricardo's friends, indicating their names, professions (of course, things like lawn mowing appear here), and particular styles, such as "preppie" and "Le Bay," a reference to Canada's iconic department store, which originated as the Hudson's Bay Company. Social tensions over his background and his parents' means continue to be a source of conflict, as seen in Ricardo's embarrassment over his father's job, an issue in both *1981* and *1987*.

In its representation of a subject who is both fully Québécois in his self-conception, but only partially Franco-Québécois in his family origins, Trogi's *1981* tetralogy represents an important intervention into Quebec's identity politics. The 1980s was a key decade in public debates about national identity and the need to transcend the ethnic nationalism of the *pure laine* French Canadian, and to include migrant identities within the conception of contemporary Quebec. In the new millennium, across North America, gender identity would move to the forefront of public debates as the so-called millennial generation would come of age and begin to express themselves and their concerns on film. One of Quebec's best-known filmmakers to rise in this period, Xavier Dolan, released an important film that addressed gender identity within the framework of a nostalgic depiction of the very recent past.

Gender Identity and Millennial Nostalgia for the 1990s: Xavier Dolan's *Laurence Anyways*

More than any young director to rise in the new millennium, wunderkind Xavier Dolan (b. 1989) has seized the attention of audiences, institutional critics, and academics.[72] While fascination is unanimous, praise has not always been so.[73] Having worked in Quebec, Hollywood, and France, and even mesmerized audiences in India,[74] his is a truly international career. His period film *Laurence Anyways* (2012), a pioneering account of a man's journey towards becoming a woman,[75] retains our attention in this chapter for its nostalgic depiction of the 1980s and 1990s. Dolan's third feature film is also the evolving love story of a couple, tracing literature professor Laurence Alia's (Melvil Poupard) gender transformation alongside the more emotional and intellectual trajectory of his partner, Fred Bellair (Suzanne Clément). Few critics discuss the film as a period piece, but some liken it to *C.R.A.Z.Y.* because of its theme (gender identity) and nostalgic reliance on music and fashion.[76] But this film's subject matter foregrounds the role of fashion in identity formation much more directly through Laurence's external transition from man to woman via clothing, remaining more discreet on the surgical transition (mentioned only elliptically) that he undergoes before the end of the film. Rather, the film suggests that like Laurence Alia, we all perform our identity through the exterior that we present to the world. Thumbing his nose at earlier filmmakers' insistence on the disjuncture between interior and exterior, and at film critics' privileging of *fonds* over form, for the millennial Dolan, the surface *is* the essence. Pierre-Alexandre Fradet aptly replies to those who criticize Dolan's emphasis on the stunning image by insisting that "these idiosyncrasies are not ineptitudes; they demonstrate the true will of a filmmaker to work *from the basis* of surfaces to captivate the gaze and build up a discourse."[77] It is through the creation of a *visual* illusion of the past that *Laurence Anyways*, "a film that deploys vintage styling as part of its affective mode," works so well in its transmission of a sense of nostalgia even to viewers who were – like Dolan – barely born when the film opens on the eve of the 1990s.[78]

Dolan plays with the image of his title character in the film's opening sequence, as viewers see a series of reaction shots by a child, old ladies, various men to a figure that we see only from behind. The head of an immaculately coiffed individual, clad in a striking light-blue woman's suit with high heels, slowly turns, but Dolan delays the reveal, jumping immediately back in time, per a title card, to "10 ans plus tôt" (10 years earlier). We meet Laurence, then, when he is still a man living with a woman, as a domestic scene involving laundry suggests their playful relationship. The couple's wardrobe and a night at the disco, where they dance to the iconic sounds of the Cure, clearly situate them in the late 1980s and early 1990s. Songs like Jean Leloup's "1990" likewise punctuate domestic scenes, such as a dinner with Fred's sister Stéfanie (Monia Chokri). From work to disco to parties, theirs seems the typical hip young professionals' lifestyle. Only through the visual motif of rain does the film hint at Laurence's melancholy, until finally it cuts to an interview sequence, via which a voice-over indicates his radical identity change: "dans les années 90 vous êtes devenue ce que vous êtes" (in the 1990s you became what you are).

The couple's crisis allows for direct discourse about transgender identity and its distinction from homosexuality, as Laurence announces his true self to a hurt and puzzled Fred, "Je ne suis pas homosexuel. J'aime pas les hommes" (I'm not a homosexual. I don't like men) but also that "ça fait 35 ans que je vis comme ça" (for 35 years I've been living like that), indicating that this hidden desire has been a lifelong one. Clément's brilliance as an actress (and Dolan's ability to pull a performance out of actors almost all of whom are his seniors) appears as the tiniest expressions of her face reveal in turn hurt, incomprehension, and an honest

Figure 5.2. Laurence (Melvil Poupard) walks away from the camera and into the mists of her destiny in the opening sequence of Xavier Dolan's *Laurence Anyways*.

attempt to process Laurence's revelation and what it means for their life as a couple. In a similar sequence, he reveals his pending transformation to his mother, Julienne (Nathalie Baye),[79] who is not surprised, but neither is she understanding: "Tu te transformes en femme. Ou tu te transformes en con" (You're transforming yourself into a woman. Or you're transforming yourself into an idiot). A meeting in the metro after Laurence begins dressing as a woman underscores a generation gap in attitudes, but also perhaps the fact that Julienne is simply a bitch, as she asks, "Tu te déguises depuis combien de temps?" (How long have you been wearing a costume?). The idea that, by dressing as a woman, Laurence is wearing a costume brings to mind the relationship between gender, history, and nation linked in Pidduck's notion of the "costume film." In its own way, although it takes place in the very recent past, Dolan's *Laurence Anyways* echoes certain aspects of the heritage film, casting iconic actresses, the camera lingering on carefully conceived decors, and inserting a meta-textual discourse about appearance and identity.

Laurence Anyways stresses the courage required to come out as transgender in 1990, holding up a significant reminder to the younger Generations Y and Z that take gender fluidity as a given (at least those in liberal urban settings). Just as other filmmakers remind viewers of past national struggles, Dolan's oeuvre – this is a significant element of the thriller *Tom à la ferme* (2013) as well – invokes the struggle for freedom to express gender identity as an individual desires, not as biology or society requires. Dolan lingers on the physical transformation, with shots not just of Laurence applying make-up and arranging locks of hair, but also of Fred watching him do so. The transitional nature of change appears in a first step; since Laurence owns no wig and his hair has been kept short, he nonetheless jauntily walks down a hallway at the college wearing a woman's elegant business suit and yellow heels (albeit sensibly low). Again, Dolan shows the importance of others' response in the process of identity formation with a sequence of reaction shots from students and faculty. Laurence's colleague Michel Lafortune (Yves Jacques, an openly gay actor who played a drag queen in *Cabotins* but more famously incarnated Claude, the gay professor in Denys Arcand's *Les invasions barbares*), reacts verbally as they lunch together: "C'est une révolte!" (It's a revolt!).

At first, Fred's own rejection of conventional lifestyles and her apparently unconditional love for Laurence allows her to support a radical change that will inevitably affect her life as well. She lovingly gifts him a beautiful wig, saying, "La première fois que je t'ai rencontré, j'ai su que j'allais vivre une expérience extraordinaire avec toi" (The first time I met you, I knew that I was going to live an extraordinary experience with you), a line that points forward to the film's final scene, which stages their first meeting in 1987. Fred's pregnancy and subsequent abortion indicate that the couple remains sexually active together, but it also signals a coming crisis and social consequences for Laurence's non-conformist behaviour. He is called in to his superior's office, shown an article about a coalition formed to protest his presence, invoking the continued definition in the American Psychiatric Association's *Diagnostic and Statistical Manual IV* of transsexuality as a form of mental illness. Society's lack of acceptance continues as Fred loses her job, and Laurence is beat up in a bar. Walking down the street with a bloodied face, no one will help him until another trans person, Baby Rose (Emmanuel Schwartz), comes to his aid. These pressures wear on the couple's relationship as well; Fred increasingly withdraws, and she ultimately admits infidelity and leaves Laurence.

Laurence's continued love for her, however, is clear, as a few years later (a title informs us it is Trois-Rivières in 1995) Laurence appears to be stalking Fred, spying on her in her new home with her son, Léo. Fred's "normal" life contrasts dramatically with that of Laurence and his new friends, the visibly eccentric Rose family. Although his life goes on – even his mother eventually admits, "Dis-donc, t'es belle, hein!" (Well, you're beautiful, eh!) – Laurence's loneliness is evident, but so is Fred's lack of fulfilment in the heteronormative lifestyle she thought she desired. In a utopian sequence, the former couple go together to, as a title informs, "1996 l'Île au Noir."[80] Here, one of the film's most iconic visual sequences occurs as they walk outside and confetti-like, brightly coloured clothing rains down from the sky. But their temporary utopia is interrupted; not only has Fred lied to her husband about where she had gone, but she learns that he has also been unfaithful to her. But even more difficult for Fred is Laurence's announcement that she wants her transformation to be complete via surgery.[81] For Fred this becomes an insurmountable obstacle to their coupledom, and the two break up definitively. The film closes its opening frame by concluding the "Montréal 1999" interview, which reveals that Laurence has become a celebrated writer and is in the United States; completely confident and comfortable with her new self, Laurence refuses to cower or hide, calling out a clearly anglophone interviewer for her evident contempt.

Film scholars Bill Marshall, Jim Leach, and Andrée Lafontaine read Dolan's film through the lens of Quebec's unique national and cultural status. Leach invokes Richard Cavell and Peter Dickinson's assertion that "the stories we tell about our sexualities are one of the ways in which we articulate our sense of nationhood,"[82] but asserts conversely that "issues of gender and sexuality" are "shaped by [one's] cultural roots."[83] As Laurence spends most of the film's diegesis in a sort of "in-between" state, Leach reads Dolan's film as particularly resonant within notions of Québécois identity, citing Laurence's opening assertion in the film that "I am looking for someone who understands my language and speaks it." Laurence's language is one that will reject the judgments of (hetero) normativity; Leach pertinently discusses the film's ambiguous use of language and its ambiguous distinctions between Quebec English, Quebec French, and metropolitan French as mirroring Quebec's own in-between cultural status, as existing between the two worlds.[84] Andrée Lafontaine's discussion of Dolan's controversial practice of code-switching in his dialogues as "strategically used to break down interpersonal and emotional boundaries"[85] reinforces this interpretation. Like Leach, she invokes the opening lines of *Laurence Anyways*, connecting the search for an authentic identity to language, discussing Laurence's eventual ability to embrace a gender identity outside predetermined norms, which contrasts with the inauthenticity of Fred's mother, Andrée (Sophie Faucher), a colonized Québécoise who "not only puts on a French accent but also 'pretends she's French.'"[86] Thus, despite their apparent interest in very personal and individual stories of gender identity, the desire for authentic self-expression and the traps of family and societal expectations, *Laurence anyways* and Dolan's other films, including *J'ai tué ma mère* (2009) and *Tom à la ferme* (2013), are also engaged with notions of national identity, memory, and (albeit to a lesser extent) the historical imaginary.

Conclusion

In *Cinema of Pain: On Quebec's Nostalgic Screen* (2020), Liz Czach and André Loiselle insist upon the nostalgic nature of Quebec national cinema in the twenty-first century: "contemporary Quebec cinema, in all its multifaceted richness, does exhibit strong nostalgic tendencies that cut across visual styles, narrative themes, and modes of address."[87] The films discussed in this chapter, and throughout this book, blur past and present through the lens of nostalgia, and to the corpus addressed here, we might add even more films whose primary intrigue occurs in the present day, but which deploy flashbacks to a significant degree. These include minor auteur films like Julie Hivon's *Crème glacée, chocolat et autres consolations* (2001) and Anjo B. Arson's *Tous les autres, sauf moi* (2006), critically acclaimed art films that also benefited from larger releases like Robert Lepage's *La face cachée de la lune* (2003) and Francis Leclerc's *Mémoires affectives* (2004), Jean-Marc Vallée's under-appreciated follow-up to *C.R.A.Z.Y.*, *Café de Flore* (2011), an adaptation of a minor literary work in Gabriel Sabourin's *C'est le coeur qui meurt en dernier* (2017), and even the social satire *L'Empire Bo$$é* (2012). Nostalgia also figures in a growing body of regional films, set in the present day, but depicting sites within the territory of Quebec associated with lost or fading ways of life, as seen in Bernard Émond's *La neuvaine* (2005) and *La donation* (2009), Catherine Martin's *Une jeune fille* (2013), and Sébastien Pilote's *Le démantèlement* (2013). Memory and its loss play a central role not just in the nation's historical imaginary but also in films about and fully set in the twenty-first century, underscoring the ongoing pertinence of the national motto, *Je me souviens*, but also revealing its problematic nature.

Conclusion

The vast diversity of the corpus analysed here – nearly fifty films by three dozen directors released between 1999 and 2022 – shows that Quebec national cinema has reached an astonishing level of maturity. Even by limiting the focus to works set in the past, these films reflect the full array of genres, from standard historical films to biopics, from horror comedies to literary adaptations, from heist films to quirky independent art films. Situated between Hollywood and the world, Quebec's film industry has developed successful strategies that allow it to produce popular box-office hits, but it has not forgotten its roots in art film. With the help of government subsidies, it continues to release independent films that invoke its historical origins in the French Unit of the ONF, but its young directors also strike out into new territory. Above all, despite the relative waning of independentist nationalism, Quebec cinema remains a "national" cinema, reflecting past and present realities while also contributing to the construction of a national identity apt for the twenty-first century. The films considered here focus in particular on the construction of the national "historical imaginary," contributing to the sense of a collective past upon which that identity can be built for the future. Although they frequently express nostalgia for what is perceived as a lost past of cultural homogeneity, viewing Quebec as the homeland of the French Canadian nation, many of the films discussed here project revised images that propose a national identity that can include diversity, from the original, Indigenous peoples already on the land when the first French settlers arrived, to the many other cultural communities, from the Anglo-Celts to the Jewish, Italian, Haitian, Lebanese, and many others, that have arrived in Quebec since the eighteenth century.

Reviewing the body of historical films produced in Quebec reveals the persistence into the new millennium of many of the nation's foundational narratives, but it also reveals a certain discomfort with some aspects of the national past and a desire to rewrite these in order to promote positive interaction among the increasingly diverse subjects who call themselves "Québécois." The significance of the French language as the defining characteristic of Quebec's contemporary culture originates, of course, with the arrival of French colonists along the St. Lawrence River. As a settler nation, Quebec must come to terms with the violence of French contact, conquest, and settlement on territory already occupied by Indigenous peoples. Its relative discomfort with the inglorious aspects of its past is reflected, perhaps, in the paucity of films that deal with the earliest days of French colonization and the elision of many of the founding myths popularized in the nineteenth and early twentieth centuries, such as the exploits of Jacques Cartier and Samuel de Champlain, the struggles of the Jesuit missionaries, and the colourful adventures of the *coureurs des bois*. Instead, Quebec national cinema has made space for Indigenous filmmakers to revise the narrative of contact, as seen in the state support of films developed by Zacharias Kunuk's Igloolik Isuma production company and the Wakipone Mobile project. Significant Franco-Québécois directors have also attempted to reframe traditional contact narratives, as seen in Benoît Pilon's *Ce qu'il faut pour vivre* (2011) and François Girard's *Hochelaga, terre des âmes* (2017). Despite their perhaps well-meaning intentions to honour the region's Indigenous peoples, however, attempts by popular cinema directors and production companies to depict this period have been less successful, as seen in *Maïna* (2013). The rare attempt at envisioning early settlements in New France, *Le poil de la bête* (2010), avoids the Indigenous question and defuses the period's violence with satire, depicting French elites as murderous beasts preying even upon their own kind, the *habitant* peasant settlers.

Elites' betrayal of common French Canadians also frames narratives about the end of the French regime in Quebec and the arrival of the British conquerors. Despite the fact that French is the only official language in Quebec, and the province's French-language majority clearly established its political power in the late twentieth century, narratives of victimhood at the hands of the English linger in the twenty-first century, beginning with the failed heritage film *Nouvelle-France* (2004). Jean Beaudin's historical melodrama rehearses time-worn narratives of France's mistreatment and abandonment of its northern New World colony through its depiction of corrupt and effete colonial administrators. It asserts the establishment of a distinct, French Canadian identity that developed in relation to the North American landscape and Indigenous peoples, although its depiction of these remains stereotyped and ancillary to its French-origin hero. Rather than linger on the perceived national defeat with the English Conquest in 1763, however, twenty-first-century Quebec national cinema memorializes key moments of national resistance to the English presence, as seen in two significant historical productions focused on the Patriots Rebellions of 1837–8: *Quand je serai parti ... vous vivrez encore* (1999) and *Le 15 février, 1839* (2001). Although the rebellions did not result in independence from the British Empire for either Upper (i.e., English) or Lower (i.e., French) Canada, these films keep alive a certain resentment about the history of anglophone privilege in Quebec. But they also foster a narrative of survival, the survival of the French Canadian "race," as it was framed in the nineteenth and early twentieth centuries by the province's first "national" historians, like François-Xavier Garneau and Lionel Groulx. This memorialization of the Patriots, who proposed a liberal, democratic politics, also reframes received narratives of clerico-nationalist ideologies as leading francophone resistance, proposing secular heroes for the (post) modern nation of Quebec.

Indeed, as the development of the Quebec heritage film in the twenty-first century shows, a major agenda of films that engage the historical imaginary has been to criticize the belief system of the French Canadian, Catholic past while at the same time expressing a certain nostalgia for a simpler time when values were expressed in the black-and-white terms of clerical garb and the nation was ethnically homogeneous. Films like *Séraphin : un homme et son péché* (2002), *Aurore* (2005), and *Le Survenant* (2005) condemn as small-minded and conformist the ideology of rural, Catholic Quebec, revealing how communities rejected or abandoned individuals who were different, who did not conform to social conventions. Although they memorialize local literary classics for contemporary audiences, critics of Quebec heritage films suggest that they allow today's audiences to congratulate themselves for their open-mindedness, secularism, and political correctness. Without completely rewriting the received idea that contemporary Québécois have evolved to embrace new members of their community and have left behind a perceived Catholic judgmentalism, a body of biopics have sought out new, secular cultural heroes who rose above the victim status of heritage film protagonists. Turning to non-political figures, biopics like *Louis Cyr, l'homme le plus fort du monde* (2013), *Maurice Richard* (2005), and *La Bolduc* (2017) celebrate French Canadian figures of strength and success, establishing new *lieux de mémoire* for the nation. Although certain local stars are remembered as victims, as seen in *L'enfant prodige* (2010) and *Ma vie en cinémascope* (2004), they, too, are invoked as icons of national greatness, individuals who represented Quebec on the international stage.

Another major project of Quebec national cinema in the new millennium has been to demonstrate that, despite its status as a small nation, with francophones a minority in North America, Quebec's citizens have participated in global events. Instead of the long history of Quebec depicted as a backward, rural, enclaved society that reflected the values of the seventeenth century well into the twentieth, historical films and biopics consistently show the French Canadian province in relation to the outside world. Although its rare depictions of World War II focus more on resistance to French Canadians' recruitment to die for the British Empire, as seen in *Le déserteur* (2008) and *Embrasse-moi comme tu m'aimes* (2016), other films trace the activities of French Canadians abroad, as seen in *La Grande Noirceur* (2017) and *Le cyclotron* (2016). Although the 1940s and 1950s appear as relatively neglected periods in the historiography traced by

Quebec national cinema, another group of films focuses on revising the myth of the *Grande Noirceur* painted in the Quebec heritage film, pointing towards the nation's incipient modernity, but also sometimes revisiting the negative image of the Catholic clergy that it shows. Films like *Le Club Vinland* (2020), *Pour l'amour de Dieu* (2011), and *La passion d'Augustine* (2015) revise images of Quebec's religious figures as making positive contributions to the development of individuals and the collective.

Analysis of the body of films produced since the year 2000, though, reveals that contemporary Quebec national cinema has above all sought to depict the 1960s as Quebec's golden age. Film after film set in that period expresses nostalgia for the era of the Quiet Revolution, mythologized as the moment of Quebec's advent to modernity that laid the groundwork for contemporary Quebec's French-language society and culture to flourish. Above all, autobiographical, memoir-type films depict this era with nostalgia through the eyes of a child protagonist, as seen in several notable films like *C'est pas moi, je le jure* (2008) and *Maman est chez le coiffeur* (2008), but also in several minor films like *Frisson des collines* (2011). Rather than focus on the political figures who engineered the very real series of economic, political, and social reforms responsible for francophone dominance in Quebec today, these films focus on the everyday lives of individuals experiencing a society in transformation. It is not coincidental that many of these adolescent protagonists were born at the same time as the baby boomers who dominated the early twenty-first century; their own nostalgia most likely fed into these films' conception, funding, production, and popularity upon release. A handful of films, however, also sought to remind young people that the Quiet Revolution was not won without any bloodshed; thus, the role of the terrorist FLQ is invoked, frequently with more sympathy than condemnation, in films like *La Maison du pêcheur* (2013) and *Les rois mongols* (2017).

As the baby boomers reached retirement age, handing the film industry over to younger generations, the more recent past became an object of nostalgia in the second decade of the new millennium, as seen in Ricardo Trogi's *1981* tetralogy (2009–24), Louis Bélanger's *Gaz Bar Blues* (2003), Xavier Dolan's *Laurence Anyways* (2011), and the biopic *Nelly* (2017). Even more recently, the early 2000s Norbourg financial scandal was memorialized on film by Maxime Giroux in *Norbourg* (2022). Musical biopics eulogized more recent popular culture icons as fallen heroes, as seen in *Gerry* (2011) and *Dédé, à travers les brumes* (2009), and the national past was remembered in a more whimsical fashion in the film versions of Fred Pellerin's *contes de village*, *Babine* (2008), *Ésimésac* (2012), and *L'arracheuse de temps* (2021).

The first two decades of the new millennium reveal the continued relevance for contemporary Québécois of the province's motto, still borne on its licence plates, *Je me souviens*. Not only has the number of historical films increased exponentially, but the variety of ways in which directors engage the past has also exploded. Analysing this cross-section of films that address various historical periods and generations in Quebec, we also see a handing off of the filmic art and industry from one generation to the next. This volume began with an analysis of films by Michel Brault, a director engaged in the very birth of modern Québécois cinema in the 1960s, and Pierre Falardeau, one of the first baby boomer filmmakers to carry on the ONF tradition of political engagement while simultaneously embracing Hollywood narrative styles, film techniques, and genre conventions because of their ability to bring his message to a larger audience. Jean Beaudin and Charles Binamé laid the groundwork for the development of the Quebec heritage film, bringing local legends, literature, and heroes to the big screen in high-quality mainstream productions. In contrast, André Forcier continued Quebec's traditional respect for the auteur film, his idiosyncratic vision largely supported by funding institutions rather than commercial success.

Although some members of this old guard worked well into the second decade of the 2000s, at the turn of the millennium a *nouvelle génération* of directors born in the 1960s and early 1970s was heralded. Perhaps inspired by the success of Denys Arcand abroad, young filmmakers like Denis Villeneuve, Philippe Falardeau, and Jean-Marc Vallée began producing a new kind of film in Quebec and seemed to be more interested in conveying an aesthetic vision than a political statement. Perhaps because they were educated after the battles of the Quiet Revolution were won, they rejected the trope of the "Québécois loser" and aspired to international careers. Sadly, although Villeneuve's prestige continues to grow with his Hollywood mega-productions, Vallée's career was cut short when he was just fifty-eight. While these directors pursued an auteur aesthetic, others of their generation mastered the art of manipulating Hollywood genre conventions and adapting these to local tastes to reflect local social and political issues. Thus, Érik Canuel and Daniel Grou carved out successful careers with popular films, as did several directors born in the early 1970s, like Ricardo Trogi, Ken Scott, Daniel Roby, and Francis Leclerc.

By the mid-2010s, however, the *nouvelle génération* comprised of the last baby boomers and early Generation Xers was already being replaced by a newer, younger "nouvelle vague" or *renouveau* in Quebec's film scene. For many reasons, including the difficulty of assembling the budget needed to make a historical film, some of Quebec's most significant younger filmmakers – including Denis Côté and Sophie Deraspe – have thus far eschewed the historical film per se, and so are not discussed in this book. That said, this *renouveau* includes several directors firmly committed to engaging the historical imaginary from a new perspective, especially Simon Lavoie, Mathieu Denis, Sébastien Pilote, and Maxime Giroux. Despite concerns arising in the last decade over changing modes of delivery for visual narrative, exacerbated by the COVID-19 pandemic and its impact on the film industry, Quebec's young filmmakers appear committed to carrying on the tradition begun with the French Unit of the ONF of presenting their compatriots with images and stories relevant to their lives and identities from the past, into the present, and on to the future.

Notes

Introduction: Quebec National Cinema in the New Millennium

1 Anderson, *Imagined Communities*, 5–7.
2 Nora, "Between Memory and History" and *Les lieux de mémoire.*
3 Two recent essay collections make similar arguments: Gott and Schilt, *Quebec Cinema in the 21st Century*, and Carruthers and Tepperman, *Canadian Cinema in the New Millennium.*
4 See Nadeau and Barlow, *The Story of French.*
5 As opposed to the pejorative "Americanization," an eroding homogenization of the specificities of local, French Canadian culture, *l'américanité* can be conceived as a positive appropriation of Quebec's difference from France as a specifically North American society. See Lamonde, "Quebec's Americanicity."
6 Gervais et al., "Quebec Models."
7 Séguin, "Battle for Hollywood North."
8 Examples include episodes of *The Hunger* (1997–2000), *Big Wolf on Campus* (1998–2002), and *Vampire High* (2001–2) variously directed by Jean Beaudin, Érik Canuel, Alain Desrochers, and Daniel Grou (a.k.a. Podz).
9 Formerly the Prix Jutra, the award's name was changed in 2017 after Yves Lever's 2016 biography of the provincial icon included, albeit understated, allegations of Jutra's affairs with adolescent boys, provoking a controversy. See Lever, *Claude Jutra*, 153–4; CBC News, "Québec Film Awards."
10 For a succinct overview of this period, see Zubrzycki, *Beheading the Saint*, 5–15.
11 Lafleur, "Bouches cousues"; Sirois-Trahan, "La mouvée et son dehors."
12 The film's critical reception further identifies it as a "French" film, and its rating sparked a controversy in France, documented in Frédéric Ambroisine's film *Martyrs vs Censorship* (2008); West, *Films of the New French Extremity*, 151; Mellier, "Sur la dépouille." Québécois film critics discussed it in relation to the horror genre and French controversies, rather than in relation to Quebec's film canon or trends. Gravel, "Métaphysique de la douleur"; Grenier, review of *Martyrs.*

13 See, however, Adam Rosadiuk, "*Thirty Two Short Films.*"
14 See Longfellow, "*The Red Violin.*"
15 A. Smith, "Images of the Nation," 45.
16 Some argue that the 2019 enactment of Bill 21, *An Act Respecting the Laicity of the State*, puts the notion of accommodation at risk. See Celis et al., *Modération ou extrémisme?* Its proponents argue otherwise. See Ferretti and Rocher, *Les enjeux d'un Québec laïque.*
17 Marshall, *Quebec National Cinema*, ix.
18 Marshall, x.
19 CBC News, "Quebecers Form a Nation."
20 Hedetoft and Hjort, *The Postnational Self*, xvii–xxiii.
21 See, for example, various essays in Spencer and Wollman, *Nations and Nationalism*; Bloemraad, "Who Claims Dual Citizenship?"
22 Gott and Schilt, *Quebec Cinema*, 3–5.
23 Higson, "The Concept of National Cinema."
24 Rosen, "History, Textuality, Nation," 44–5.
25 Hayward, *French National Cinema.*
26 Higson, "The Concept of National Cinema," 141.
27 For both its original mandate, cited here, and its current iteration, see "The NFB's Mandate over the Years," Government of Canada, last modified 16 February 2023, https://www.canada.ca/en/national-film-board/corporate/about/history/mandate-timeline.html.
28 Marshall, *Quebec National Cinema*, 3.
29 Elsaesser, *European Cinema*, 20.
30 Colman, *Deleuze and Cinema*, 151.
31 Statistics from "Record Population Growth in Québec in 2019, but Significant Slowdown in the First Months of 2020," Institut de la statistique du Québec, 9 December 2020, https://statistique.quebec.ca/en/communique/record-population-growth-quebec-2019-significant-slowdown-first-months-2020.
32 Falkowska and Giukin, *Small Cinemas*, vii.
33 The category was renamed "Best International Feature Film" in 2020.
34 Lafontaine, "Introduction."
35 On Côté's significance, see Ransom, "Violence and Uncertainty"; Schilt, "Denis Côté"; Sirois-Trahan, "*Le cinéma à l'estomac.*"
36 Falkowska and Giukin, *Small Cinemas*, vii.
37 Hjort, *Small Nation*; Martin-Jones, *Scotland.*
38 Hjort and Petrie, *Cinema of Small Nations*, 2.
39 Bordwell, "Art Cinema."
40 Gittings, *Canadian National Cinema*, 96. See also Raboy, "Public Television," and Skinner, "Television in Canada," for discussions of Telefilm Canada and its policies.
41 Galt and Schoonover, "Impurity of Art Cinema," 6.
42 Marshall, *Quebec National Cinema*, 133–71.

43 Gittings, *Canadian National Cinema*, 87–8.

44 Edensor, *National Identity, Popular Culture and Everyday Life*, 20, 23.

45 Marshall, *Quebec National Cinema*, 173.

46 See, for example, Coulombe and Jean, *Dictionnaire*; Lever, *Histoire générale*; G. Marsolais, *Cinéma québécois*; Véronneau, *Histoire du cinéma*.

47 "Si les origines les plus lointaines du cinéma québécois remontent aux débuts de l'activité cinématographique au Canada, l'existence d'un cinéma québécois distinct, affichant clairement sa différence, s'est imposée avec évidence à la fin des années 1960. Aucun critique autorisé n'ose mettre en doute aujourd'hui l'existence d'un cinéma québécois ayant sa personnalité propre." G. Marsolais, *Cinéma québécois*, 16. Translations from the French are my own, unless otherwise indicated.

48 The late Janis Pallister's pioneering work, though admirable, has been largely superseded. Histories of Canadian film also provide limited coverage of Quebec. Jim Leach's edited volume, *Film in Canada* (2006), offers readings of seminal films, as does Jerry White's *The Cinema of Canada* (2006). Christopher Gittings's *Canadian National Cinema* (2002) devotes about fifty of its three hundred pages of text to Quebec, and David Pike's important study of more recent film, *Canadian Cinema Since the 1980s: At the Heart of the World* (2012), devotes a similar proportion of its pages to Quebec. George Melnyk has also contributed excellent studies of Canadian film that astutely deal with Quebec, including *100 Years of Canadian Cinema* (2004) and *Film and the City: The Urban Imaginary in Canadian Cinema* (2014); and his edited volume, *Great Canadian Film Directors* (2007), includes chapters on Jutra, Lauzon, Arcand, Lepage, and Pool.

49 MacKenzie, *Screening Quebec*, 72–3

50 MacKenzie, 72–3.

51 See Véronneau, *"En pays neufs."*

52 See Ravary-Pilon, *Femmes, nation et nature*; Wójcik, "(Re)visions télévisuelles."

53 See critical interpretations of this film by É. Beaulieu, "Le murmure," 49–51; A. Loiselle, *Stage-Bound*, 39–54; Tremblay-Daviault, "Avant la Révolution tranquille," 38–41; Weinmann, *Cinéma de l'imaginaire*, 27–50.

54 Note that Fyodor Otsep is credited as Fédor Ozep in his French-language films. See A. Loiselle, *"La Forteresse / Whispering City."*

55 Zéau, "L'office national du film"; G. Marsolais, *L'aventure du cinéma direct.*

56 See Araujo and Marie, *À grande allure*; Clandfield, *Pierre Perrault and the Poetic Documentary.*

57 See A. Loiselle, *Cinema as History.*

58 See Clandfield, "The Fatal Leap"; Leach, *Claude Jutra*; Lever, *Claude Jutra.*

59 See Bertrand, "De Gilles Groulx"; Bocage, *Gilles Groulx.*

60 See Y. Laberge, "Rapports réels et imaginaires"; Renaud, "Jacques Godbout."

61 See Carle, *La nature d'un cinéaste*; Leach, *Film in Canada*, 63–8.

62 See Leach, *Film in Canada*, 95–9.

63 See A. Loiselle, *Denys Arcand's*; A. Loiselle and McIlroy, *Auteur/Provacateur*;
Pike, *Canadian Cinema*, 79–106; Véronneau, "Denys Arcand."

64 For a full account of its international development and Quebec filmmakers' role in
it, see G. Marsolais, *L'aventure du cinéma direct revisitée*.

65 Marie, "Le direct et la parole," 8, qtd. in A. Loiselle, *Cinema as History*, 41.

66 A. Loiselle, *Cinema as History*, 61. See also Gittings, *Canadian National Cinema*, 87.

67 Gittings, *Canadian National Cinema*, 87.

68 Gittings, 87–8; Euvrard and Véronneau, "Direct Cinema," 72–93.

69 Scheppler, "*Pour la suite du monde*."

70 See Green, "Claude Jutra"; Moffat, "*À tout prendre*."

71 See Hebding, "Interroger le réel."

72 See Dubois, "De Roberto Rosselini."

73 Marshall, *Quebec National Cinema*, 25–53.

74 For a full account of the films of this period, see Lever, *Le cinéma de la Révolution
tranquille*.

75 For an extended discussion of these films, see Leach, "Double Vision" and *Claude
Jutra*.

76 See Shek, "Lemelin sur film."

77 See Levin, "Le roman à l'écran"; J.-M. Paquette, "Maria sous trois regards"; Simons,
"Gilles Carle."

78 Marshall, *Quebec National Cinema*, 85. See also Morris, "Canadian Gothic."

79 See Sullivan, "Work It Girl!," for an incisive assessment of *Valérie*.

80 "Le triste documentaire québécois misérabiliste": Coulombe, *Entretiens avec Gilles
Carle*, 49.

81 Coulombe, *Entretiens avec Gilles Carle*, 35–6.

82 "Un film consacré à une période qui m'est étrangère … , j'ai accueilli ce film
et ses personnages … comme si je les connaissais depuis toujours, comme s'ils
m'appartenaient au propre": Coulombe, *Entretiens avec Gilles Carle*, 9.

83 "Unique et profondément québécois": Coulombe, *Entretiens avec Gilles Carle*, 9.

84 Claude Jutra had produced *Kamouraska* (1973), but Yves Simoneau's *Les fous de
Bassan* (1987) – both adaptations of Anne Hébert novels – followed in Carle's
footsteps, as did Jean Beaudin's *Le matou* (1985), based on Yves Beauchemin's
eponymous novel. See Pallister, "*Les fous de Bassan*"; Vernier, "*Le matou*."

85 See Véronneau, "Denys Arcand"; Leach, "Two Canadian Auteurs"; Pike, *Canadian
Cinema*, 79–106; Moyes, "*On est au coton*."

86 See Harcourt "*Le Déclin de l'empire américain*"; A. Loiselle, *Denys Arcand's*; Testa, "The
Decline."

87 See Melnyk, *Film and the City*, 27–49; Simons, "Denys Arcand," among the many
articles dedicated to this film.

88 See Leach, "It Takes Monsters"; Melnyk, "Quebec's Next Generation"; Toles,
"Drowning in Love"; and Pike, *Canadian Cinema*, 144–70.

89 Leach, *Film in Canada*, 82.

90 Pierre Falardeau will be discussed in chapter 1.

91 See Desroches, "Suspicions and Castrations"; P. Gauthier, "The Role of Orality."

92 Pool's work will be discussed in chapters 3 and 5. See also Cairns, "Mères manquantes"; J. Gauthier "Living In/Between"; Grandena, "Léa Pool"; Green, "Léa Pool's *La femme de l'hôtel*"; Leach, *Film in Canada*, 105–6 and 154–8; Pike, *Canadian Cinema*, 144–70; Simons, "Léa Pool"; Stefanelli, "Queering Spectatorship"; Vaillancourt, "*La femme de l'hôtel*," and "Sorties du placard."

93 See Tschofen's "*Le Confessionnal*"; Pike, *Canadian Cinema*, 144–70; Leach, *Film in Canada*, 151–4; and Dickinson, "Double Take."

94 Pike, *Canadian Cinema*, 4.

95 Marshall, *Quebec National Cinema*, 43.

96 LeBlanc, "Elvis Gratton."

97 See chapter 1's discussion of more recent films on the 1970 October Crisis.

98 See Cornelius, "Robert Lepage's *Le Confessionnal*"; Massicotte, "Hantise et architecture"; Tschofen, "*Le Confessionnal*."

99 See Dunderjovic, *The Cinema of Robert Lepage*; Gibson, "The Truth Machine."

100 See Leach, *Film in Canada*, 83–6.

101 D. Baillargeon, *A Brief History*; Lamoureux, "Paradoxes."

102 See Nicole Giguère's film *Entretien avec Anne Poirier* (2005), available at https://www.onf.ca/film/entretien_avec_anne_claire_poirier/.

103 See Bruce, "Querying/Queering."

104 See the essays in Carrière, *Femmes et cinéma québécois*; Ramer, "*Mourir à tue-tête*"; Detchberry "*Sonatine*."

105 See A. Loiselle, "*A Scream from Silence*," and "Despair as Empowerment"; Ramer, "*Mourir à tue-tête*."

106 See discussions of Lanctôt in chapter 3 and Pool in chapters 3 and 5.

107 See also Gott and Schilt, *Quebec Cinema in the 21st Century*, 1–6.

108 G. Marsolais, *Cinéma québécois*, 9.

109 Chartier, "Cinéma du pays," 145; Lever, "Cinéma québécois," 87.

110 Ransom, "Deterritorialization."

111 Chartier, "Le cinéma du pays," 145; Lever, "Cinéma québécois," 87; Poirier, "Le cinéma québécois," 33n12.

112 Coulombe, "De quelques histoires," 35.

113 Literally translated as a "renewal of Quebec cinema"; a translation as "Quebec cinema renaissance" would not be inaccurate.

114 Fradet, review of *À trois, Marie s'en va*, and *Philosopher à travers le cinéma québécois*.

115 See Gendron, "Prophètes d'ici."

116 Dolan's work has already garnered a considerable body of academic work for such a young director. See M. Baillargeon, "Joy, Melancholy" and "Romantic Displacement"; Lafontaine, "Introduction"; Urquhart, "Displacement."

117 There is also an inequity in studies of women filmmakers from Quebec, apart from the many articles on Léa Pool.

118 See, for example, Ransom, "Men in Pain."

119 Olibet, "Chloé Robichaud and Sophie Deraspe," 94–7. See also the essays collected in Ravary-Pilon and Contogouris, *Pour des histoires audiovisuelles des femmes*.

120 For a sophisticated discussion of terminology for films by and about Quebec's more recent immigrant experiences, see Santoro, "Does It Matter Who Directs?"

121 See, for example, a special issue of *Nouvelles vues* (no. 22, 2023) on migrant cinema (M. Baillargeon and Bertrand, *Rencontres interculturelles*); Ransom, "What Is the Libano-Québécois?"; Santoro, "Does It Matter Who Directs?"

122 See, for example, Santoro, "The Rise of First Nations' Fiction Film" and "Reel Visions"; as well as articles in a special issue of *Québec Studies* (no. 75, 2023) guest-edited by Joëlle Papillon and Tania Grégoire. See also Bertrand, "Arnait Video Productions" and "Indigenous Women's Cinema."

123 See K. Smith, "(In)visible Borders."

124 See A. Loiselle, "Subtly Subversive."

125 Attebery, *Strategies of Fantasy*.

126 Elsaesser, *European Cinema*, 20–1; Nora, "Between Memory and History" and *Les lieux de mémoire*.

127 Elsaesser, *European Cinema*, 20–1.

128 Hobsbawm and Ranger, *The Invention of Tradition*.

129 Nora, *Les lieux de mémoire*.

130 Nora, "Between Memory and History," 7.

131 Nora, 8.

132 Lacoursière and Philpot, *A People's History*.

133 Linteau et al., *Quebec: A History, 1867–1929*; Linteau et al., *Quebec Since 1930*.

134 Létourneau, *A History for the Future* and *La condition québécoise*.

135 Czach, "The Quebec Heritage Film."

1. "Faithful" Representations of the Past

1 "Le cinéma fabrique une vision de l'histoire, participe à la construction de sa représentation": Véronneau, "Quelles représentations," 145.

2 Renan, "What Is a Nation?"

3 Anderson, *Imagined Communities*.

4 "Peu de reconstitutions d'époque, peu de films biographiques, peu d'œuvres qui articulent l'histoire, au sens collectif et objectif du terme, avec la mémoire collective, qui la mettent en représentation, autrement dit une pratique qui se distingue de la très grande majorité des cinématographies mondiales importantes": Véronneau, "Quelles représentations," 170.

5 A. Loiselle, *Cinema as History*, 153.

6 Sorlin, *The Film in History*, 15–16.

7 Landy, *The Historical Film*, 43.

8 Sorlin, *The Film in History*, 16.

9 Hughes-Warrington, "History on Film," 4.

10 Davis, "Any Resemblance."

11 Nora, *Les Lieux de mémoire*, 23–43; translated as "Between Memory and History."

12 See Filteau, *Histoire des Patriotes*; Greer, *The Patriots and the People*. Two earlier fiction films depict these events: Marcel Carrière's *St-Denis dans le temps* (1969) and Denis Héroux's *Quelques arpents de neige* (1972).

13 A. Loiselle, *Cinema as History*, 1, 2.

14 De Lorimier, "Testament."

15 Colman, *Deleuze and Cinema*, 151.

16 Davis, "Any Resemblance," 28; original emphasis.

17 Davis, "Any Resemblance," 29; original emphasis.

18 Indeed, André Loiselle criticizes Falardeau for taking the people out of the film: *Cinema as History*, 174.

19 Anglo-Canadian militia who aided the British imperial military in stopping the uprising.

20 De Blois, "L'accueil médiatique."

21 Barrette, "L'Histoire comme engagement," 46; Desmeules, "Un pur produit," 99.

22 See my introduction and Coulombe, *Entretiens avec Gilles Carle*, 49.

23 White, "Pierre Falardeau and Michel Brault," 45. See also Cambron, "Cinéma, histoire et pédagogie"; Cuillerier, "Le cinéma historique"; and Sanaker, "Hétérolinguisme," 74–7.

24 White, "Pierre Falardeau and Michel Brault," 45, 46. In contrast with the Anglo-Canadian White, Québécois Pierre Barrette praises Falardeau's open polemics and classicism, linking the latter to the three Aristotelian unities of Greek tragedy. See Barrette, "L'Histoire comme engagement," 46.

25 Marco de Blois also critiques Brault's film as excessively polemic in "Leçon d'histoire," 54.

26 White, "Pierre Falardeau and Michel Brault," 50.

27 White, 58, 60n8; de Blois, "L'Affaire Falardeau-Téléfilm"; M.-C. Loiselle, "Téléfilm Canada"; Perreault, "Le portraitiste," 21.

28 "À l'ère du cinéma de vitrine, où les institutions envoyaient fièrement des films supposément audacieux aux quatre coins de la planète, Falardeau nous présentait un Québec monstrueux, mais plus vrai que nature": Privet, "Pierre Falardeau," 8.

29 "Il est un auteur au sens fort et plein du terme": Barrette, "L'Histoire," 46. "Un des cinéastes les plus importants au Québec": M.-C. Loiselle, "Téléfilm Canada."

30 Marco de Blois cites an article by Lever published in *L'Actualité* in March 2001. See de Blois, "L'accueil médiatique," 41.

31 Falardeau's interview with Philippe Gajan and Marie-Claude Loiselle reveals his goals, including to reach Québécois youth – and not just the educated middle class – to create an accessible, popular-style film that instructs as it pleases, and to reveal the universal at the heart of the local. Gajan and M.-C. Loiselle, "Entretien," 43–6.

32 A. Loiselle, *Cinema as History*, 176.

33 "Parce qu'on n'en parle jamais": Brault qtd. in de Blois, "Leçon d'histoire," 54.

34 "Est apparu comme une œuvre lourde de sens, qui rappelle brutalement que la question du Québec n'est toujours pas réglée": de Blois, "L'accueil médiatique," 41.

35 See Clandfield, "Perils of the Unsaid"; A. Loiselle, "Michel Brault's *Les ordres*"; White, "Pat Murphy's *Maeve* and Michel Brault's *Les ordres*."

36 See White, "Pierre Falardeau and Michel Brault." Sylvain Garel provides a list of fiction and documentary films dealing with the FLQ through 2000 in "Le Front de libération."

37 In addition, several television miniseries engaged the topic, sometimes as part of a larger biographical project. English-language telefilm *Trudeau* (Jerry Ciccoriti, 2002), starring respected Canadian actor Colm Feore in the title role, covers the October Crisis. A six-episode miniseries, *René Lévesque* (Giles Walker, 2006), dealing with the national hero's career from 1958 through 1970, and starring respected character actor Emmanuel Bilodeau, addressed the crisis in episode 6. The CBC television miniseries *Octobre 1970* (Don McBrearty, 2006), filmed in English but with a largely Québécois cast, also strove for a documentary, true-to-the facts feel, but cast police investigator Julien Giguère (Patrick Labbé), who saves kidnapped British diplomat James Cross's life, in the role of hero. More recently, a documentary, *Les Rose*, about the Rose family, and directed by Félix Rose, was also released in 2020.

38 "Recréation des événements": Ramond, "De grandes espérances."

39 Duchesne, "*La Maison du pêcheur*."

40 His physical resemblance to Paul Rose is touted by reviewer Charles-Henri Ramond, "De grandes espérances."

41 Chartrand's father was Michel Chartrand (1916–2010), a celebrated union activist who played a significant role during the Quiet Revolution.

42 Chartrand, *Chartrand, cinéaste*, 19. The film is available at https://www.onf.ca/film /perce_on_the_rocks_en/.

43 Linteau et al., *Histoire du Québec contemporain*, 2:714.

44 "Alain Chartrand fait resurgir ce moment capital de notre histoire, en nous rappelant que les grands changements naissent parfois de la volonté d'une poignée d'idéalistes": Ramond, "De grandes espérances."

45 "Combler un trou de mémoire collectif": Duchesne, "*La Maison du pêcheur*."

46 Dubuc, "Maison rose."

47 Bauch, "Canada Survives."

48 Bélanger, *Salut, mon roi mongol*.

49 "Une allégorie de la crise d'octobre": Collard, "Un avant goût."

50 In this respect, Bélanger's novel invokes French Resistance member, teacher, and grandmother Lucie Aubrac's acclaimed *La Résistance expliquée à mes petits-enfants* (2000).

51 Falardeau draws on personal conversations with Francis Simard and on Pierre Vallières's *L'exécution de Pierre Laporte*, but we will never know for certain how Pierre Laporte interacted with his kidnappers.

52 This "charmante adaptation" seeks to "raconter aux jeunes un tragique moment historique, mais aussi de rappeler que malgré ses acquis – l'assurance-maladie, la DPJ, la loi 101 – la société d'aujourd'hui n'est pas si loin de celle d'hier": Dumais, "Il était une fois."

53 Thirteen students and one staff member were killed: Geneviève Bergeron, Hélène Colgan, Nathalie Croteau, Barbara Daigneault, Anne-Marie Edward, Maud Haviernick, Maryse Laganière, Maryse Leclair, Anne-Marie Lemay, Sonia Pelletier, Michèle Richard, Annie St-Arneault, Annie Turcotte, and Barbara Widajewicz. Blais et al., *Retour sur un attentat*, 10.

54 For a full account of this tradition and its influence, see Zéau, "L'office national du film"; G. Marsolais, *L'aventure du cinéma direct*.

55 In contrast with Quebec's national film tradition of *le direct*, which sought to reflect "real life" directly – that is, without the glamourous filters of Hollywood visual style – Villeneuve and others of his generation were frequently criticized as superficial, focusing too heavily on the image. Neither were their postmodern narrative approaches appreciated by institutional critics. See Barrette, "Le désert de l'âme"; M.-C. Loiselle, "Au-delà des apparences"; A. Lavoie, review of *Maelström*. In contrast, Denis Bachand makes a convincing argument for the influence of documentary film on Villeneuve and others. See Bachand, "Du national au transnational."

56 "Un travail de mémoire collective"; "l'articulation d'une blessure nationale à un féminisme populaire dans la société Québécoise": M. Gauthier, "Le film *Polytechnique*," 33.

57 See Lamoureux, "*Polytechnique*," and the other essays collected in Blais et al., *Retour sur un attentat*; Blais, *J'haïs les féministes*. On *Blade Runner 2049*'s anti-feminism, see Murphy, "Cyberpunk's Masculinist Legacy"; Stewart, "You'll Love the New *Blade Runner*."

58 Villeneuve twice cast actor Maxim Gaudette in roles of characters with Middle Eastern ancestry; in *Incendies* Gaudette plays Simon Marwan, the Quebec-raised son of Nawal who escaped the horrors of the Lebanese Civil War. See also Ransom, "What is the Libano-Québécois?"

59 D. Baillargeon, *A Brief History* and *To Be Equals*.

60 One of the external reviewers of this manuscript perceptively noted that Jean-François has a poster of *Pour la suite du monde* in his bedroom, observing that Perrault's film offers just the type of model of Québécois masculinity that Villeneuve's film sets out to critique.

61 See Dupuis-Déri, *La crise de la masculinité*.

62 "La tuerie est présentée comme une tragédie de l'histoire moderne du Québec, une blessure de la société québécoise au complet incluant les hommes et les

femmes (pas seulement les victimes, … leurs familles et leurs amis)"; "parfois …
rendre visible cette blessure, l'explorer, est un moyen de le guérir": M. Gauthier,
"Le film *Polytechnique*," 33.

63 Not only was a monument erected in memory of the victims, but the event's
anniversary has also become Quebec's "National Day of Remembrance and
Action on Violence Against Women." Furthermore, stricter gun laws and the
development of more effective responses to such events are attributed to the
Polytechnique Massacre. See Mélissa Blais, *J'haïs les féministes*, and the essays
collected in Blais et al., *Retour sur un attentat antiféministe*. See also Rosenberg,
"Neither Forgotten nor Fully Remembered," for an account of the media's
representation and memorialization of the events on their tenth anniversary.

64 This unpublished analysis was first presented in French as "Représentations
des premiers peuples dans le film Québécois," at the annual conference of the
APLAQA (Association des Professeurs des Littératures Acadiennes et Québécoises
de l'Atlantique), held in St. John's, Newfoundland, in October 2019.

65 Létourneau, *A History for the Future*.

66 See the discussion of migrant and Indigenous film in my introduction.

67 D. Harvey, "Toronto Film Review."

68 Davis, "Any Resemblance."

69 See Aldred, "Plastic Shamans"; Churchill, "Spiritual Hucksterism."

70 Trujillo – more recently known for his role in *Mayans M.C.* – was also cast as an
Indigenous leader, Kiotseaton, in Bruce Beresford's *Black Robe* (1991).

71 Here, I cite the English subtitles for the Algonquian dialogue; translations of
French dialogue are my own.

72 More than mere survival, *survivance*, as theorized by Gerald Vizenor, is a form of
Indigenous resistance against assimilation and/or folklorization, an insistence upon
the vibrancy of Indigenous cultures maintaining their own values while at the
same time adapting and appropriating what is necessary for the present and future.
Vizenor, "The Aesthetics of Survivance."

73 See, for example, Burelle *Encounters on Contested Lands*; Cornellier, *La "chose"
indienne*; D. Leroux, *Distorted Descent*.

74 Although past justifications explained the prestigious English-language university's
team moniker as simply referencing the team's red uniforms, it undeniably invokes
other appropriations of Indigenous people's historic prowess in battle in other
team names like the MLB's Atlanta Braves or Cleveland Indians, the latter now
changed to the Guardians. See Deer, "McGill Dumps Redmen." Furthermore,
as one of Montreal's wealthiest anglophone families, its capital accumulated on
the backs of French Canadian workers, the Percival Molson Stadium's name also
carries symbolic weight in the film's economy of cultural critique. The Molson
family's neocolonial role in Montreal's development has frequently been a target of
franco-nationalist intellectuals.

75 McGill University, "The McGill Redbirds."

76 The Musée virtuelle de la Nouvelle-France explains that this illness was probably
typhus, an outbreak of which occurred in 1687. See "Vie quotidienne : santé
et médecine," Musée virtuelle de la Nouvelle-France, Canadian Museum of
History, accessed 12 May 2025, https://www.museedelhistoire.ca/musee-virtuel
-de-la-nouvelle-france/vie-quotidienne/sante-et-medecine/. Earlier outbreaks of
typhus occurred in 1659 and 1665. Lacoursière and Philpot, *A People's History of
Quebec*, 38. Diderot and d'Alembert's *Encyclopédie* includes an entry on the "fièvre
pourprée."

77 I will address how this notion has been critiqued later.

78 The song "Québec History X," by hip hop artist Webster, attests to this. Ransom,
"Québec History X."

79 My translations of the French subtitles here.

80 It is not certain that Cartier used force, but most likely he used ruse, and his
captives/guests died. There are some details of chronology that appear problematic
in Girard's account if one consults the relatively well-documented Wikipedia
entry. See Wikipedia, "Stadacona," last modified 31 December 2024, 05:24 (UTC),
https://en.wikipedia.org/wiki/Stadacona.

81 The phrase refers to eight Catholic missionaries – René Goupil (1642), Isaac
Jogues (1646), Jean de Lalande (1646), Antoine Daniel (1648), Jean de Brébeuf
(1649), Noël Chabanel (1649), Charles Garnier (1649), and Gabriel Lalemant
(1649) – tortured by Indigenous people whom they sought to convert, but who
(rightly) saw the monks and priests as harbingers of unwanted cultural change.

82 Angenot, *Les idéologies du ressentiment*.

83 Many comedies and melodramas depict the average Québécois as middle-class
suburbanites. See, for example, *Le grand départ* (2008); *Le mirage* (2018); *Le trip à
trois* (2017); *Les 3 p'tits cochons* (2007; 2016).

84 Raheja, *Reservation Reelism*.

2. Stretching the Historical Imaginary

1 Nora, "Between Memory and History," 8, 19.

2 Pidduck, *Contemporary Costume Film*, 4.

3 See Dickinson, *Screening Gender*, 82–6; Gittings, *Canadian National Cinema*,
198–202.

4 See, for example, D. Bouchard et al., *De Kebec à Québec*.

5 Nora, "Between Memory and History," 8.

6 See Sugars, *Canadian Gothic*; Sugars and Truscott, eds., *Unsettled Remains*.

7 Dominique Demers (b. 1956) is a popular author, particularly of the youth
literature series upon which two films directed by Richard Ciupka, *La mystérieuse
Mlle C.* (2002) and *L'incomparable Mlle C.* (2004), were based.

8 Both the author and Demers's publisher Québec Amérique make claims that it has
been rigorously researched. See Demers, *Maïna*, 11, and the publisher's description

at https://www.quebec-amerique.com/livres/collections/litterature/tous
-continents/maina-306.html.

9 Cameron, *Far Off Metal River*. Walls documents similar conflict between Inuit and
the Chipewyan Dene on the western shores of Hudson's Bay in the post-contact
era. Walls, *Caribou Inuit Traders*, 16–19.

10 "Leur rencontre fut le théâtre d'un grand choc culturel qui engendra de
nombreux et fructueux échanges technologiques mais mena aussi parfois au
racisme et à la violence. De tout temps, semble-t-il, les êtres humains ont craint la
différence et se sont méfiés de l'Autre": Demers, *Maïna*, 12–13.

11 Gittings, *Canadian National Cinema*.

12 Although it casts Inuit as secondary characters and extras, *Agaguk*'s leads are played
by Filipino American actor Lou Diamond Phillips, Jennifer Tilly (of Chinese, Irish,
and Finnish extraction), and Japanese star Toshirô Mifune (1920–97). Philipps
appears to have been directed to play the Inuk character like a cave man, grunting
inarticulately or appearing puzzled by the events around him. See Dickinson,
Screening Gender, 87–91.

13 H.P. Lovecraft (1890–1937) has been labelled a racist writer, based on passages
in his correspondence and his fiction's frequent encounters between white male
protagonists and unspeakable "Others." He has had a significant influence in
Quebec and expressed his fondness for French Canadian society. See Ransom,
"Lovecraft in Quebec."

14 The casting of Graham Greene (Oneida) and Tantoo Cardinal (Métis), two notable
Native American/First Nations actors, as, respectively, Maïna's Innu father and
foster mother is symptomatic of *Maïna*'s lack of concern for autorepresentation.
Apart from several Inuit actors, including Natar Ungalaaq of *Atanarjuat*, the
production team displays little concern for matching actors to their characters'
specific identities on-screen. Indeed, Peter Miller (b. 1968), an anglophone from
Chibougamau best known for his role in the *Lance et compte* reboots (2009, 2012),
plays Manutabu, the heroine's first love interest. Miller's other roles include
playing a Hispanic in *Angle mort* (2011), but also a French Canadian *habitant* in the
historical thriller *Rouge sang*, set on New Year's Eve 1799.

15 The French-language DVD offers viewers three versions of the film: the original
English version, which includes dialogue in Innu, Inuktitut, and English-language
subtitles and voice-over narration by Maïna; the "original" French version, which
substitutes the English-language subtitles and voice-overs in French (but which
also must subtitle the opening title cards, since it is clear that the English version is
the true original); and a French-dubbed version, in which all dialogue is dubbed in
French, ostensibly an attempt to reach popular television audiences.

16 See John Feeney's 1958 NFB documentary *Living Stone*.

17 The extent of French Canadian adoption and appropriation of Indigenous cultures
and ethnic *métissage* remains controversial; Indigenous studies scholars question

it as a neocolonial practice of cultural appropriation. See Burelle, *Encounters on Contested Lands*; D. Leroux, *Distorted Descent*.

18 S. Marsolais, "Du livre au film."

19 "L'inévitable histoire d'amour développée dans *Maïna* procède d'une vision qui révèle implicitement la culture occidentale des auteurs"; "on se croirait par moments dans un épisode du feuilleton télévisé *Xena*": Desjardins, "Voyage au pays des glaces."

20 "Afin de survivre moralement et politiquement à son histoire et à son héritage colonial, l'État de peuplement libéral moderne a besoin en quelque sorte mais jamais complètement, de se faire lui-même indien. Il lui faut imaginer une certaine filiation entre les colons (*settlers*) et les Premières Nations": Cornellier, *La "chose" indienne*, 37.

21 Higson, "Re-Presenting," 109, qtd. in Sprengler, *Screening Nostalgia*, 89.

22 "La plus importante production cinématographique de l'histoire du cinéma québécois": "L'Histoire au grand écran."

23 For more discussion (in French) of the film's historical inaccuracies, see Ransom, "La représentation de *Nouvelle-France*."

24 For extended discussions of melodrama, see Mercer and Shingler, *Melodrama*; Ransom, "Men in Pain."

25 "Un pan fondamental de notre histoire": Desjardins, review of *Nouvelle-France*.

26 Luc Chaput refers to "l'insuccès de *Nouvelle-France*" in his review of *Sans elle*.

27 "Le dernier long-métrage de Jean Beaudin a, chose certaine, fait l'unanimité, les critiques québécois condamnant sans appel cette bluette coûteuse et insipide qui commettait le péché mortel de ne rien expliquer d'un des épisodes les plus marquants de l'histoire de la nation canadienne-française": Michaud, "Historia 101."

28 Indeed, *Nouvelle-France* began as a more modest production entitled "La Corriveau," based on a Gilles Carle script about a legendary female bogeyman. Kelly, "He Shoots."

29 A bestseller, the English text was translated by Pamphile Le May as *Le chien d'or* (1884–5), and later annotated by Benjamin Sulte, both eminent figures in Quebec's nationalist folklore revival. See Kirby, *Le chien d'or*.

30 Denis Desjardins makes a similar assessment: "L'intrigue sentimentale occult[e]nt les véritables enjeux historiques" (the sentimental plot line hides the real historical stakes). Desjardins, review of *Nouvelle-France*.

31 Weinmann, *Du Canada au Québec*.

32 Pettigrew, "Review of *La Corriveau*," 122.

33 Philippe Aubert de Gaspé, *père*, drew on the oral tradition for his account of "La Corriveau," and it has since been repeatedly exploited, becoming a *lieu de mémoire*. Aubert de Gaspé, *Les anciens Canadiens*, 38–47. Louis Fréchette published an English version in 1893. Fréchette, "La Corriveau." For a full account of

this multivalent figure's historical origins and cultural meaning, see Ferland and Corriveau, *La Corriveau*.

34 Billon, *Nouvelle-France*.

35 See Nester, *The French and Indian War*.

36 Voltaire, *Candide*, chap. 23. The iconic phrase was used as the title for the ONF documentary by Georges Dufaux and Jacques Godbout, *Pour quelques arpents de neige* (1962), about immigrants' first impressions of Canada, and in the title of Denis Héroux's Patriots Rebellion film, *Quelques arpents de neige* (1972).

37 Franklin was largely viewed by the British political elites in London as a "colonial upstart" and was outright avoided by Pitt. Skemp, *The Making of a Patriot*, 70.

38 His first visit occurred when he was only eighteen, lasting from 1724 to 1726; the mission of his second was to sway the Crown to assume control of Pennsylvania, thereby taking it out of the hands of its virtual owners, the Penn family. Morgan, *The Devious Dr. Franklin*.

39 Franklin actually did publish in the London press opinion pieces designed to influence the public in favour of Great Britain retaining territory gained in Canada through military victory that, it was feared, might be ceded back to France during treaty negotiations following the Seven Years' War. Morgan, *The Devious Dr. Franklin*, 47–8.

40 Franklin did publish several pamphlets expressing his outspoken opinions about the need for Britain to retain Canada and the need to assimilate French Canadians, whom he saw as a potential fifth column. Morgan, *The Devious Dr. Franklin*, 47–8.

41 Billon's characterization suggests that he read Christopher Hibbert's *Wolfe at Quebec*.

42 MacLeod, *Northern Armageddon*, 18.

43 Gray's famous "Elegy" is frequently cited as a landmark work of the waning gothic and developing Romantic aesthetics. The seemingly apocryphal anecdote about Wolfe reciting it before the Battle of Quebec is documented by several eyewitnesses. See Hibbert, *Wolfe at Quebec*, 130; MacLeod, *Northern Armageddon*, 19; Snow, *Death or Victory*, 330.

44 Indeed, the film is broadcast regularly in English on CBC and Anglo-Canadians have appropriated the French colonial era as an integral part of Canada's origin story.

45 Snow, *Death or Victory*, 173.

46 In his vivid account, *Northern Armageddon*, D. Peter MacLeod makes clear that local French Canadian militia participated actively and effectively in the battle.

47 This revisionist image reflects, however, previous literary works, including Anne Hébert's 1990 play *La cage*.

48 Fred Pellerin began performing as a storyteller and published his first book/CD in 2001, followed by six more volumes. In addition to the screenplays for *Babine* and *Ésimésac*, he also scripted the telefilm *De peigne et de misère* (2016), based on his stories, and Francis Leclerc's *Pieds nus dans l'aube* (2017), discussed in chapter 3.

49 "Comment transposer le merveilleux au grand écran?": Faradji, review of *Babine*.
50 Élène Dallaire found the film "délicieux," believing that "toutes les petites inventions « pellerinesques » … sont bien mises en scène dans des décors crédibles, respectueux du contexte fantastique": Dallaire, review of *Babine*. I agree more with Helen Faradji, who criticized its cartoonesque characters. See Faradji, review of *Babine*.
51 Pellerin, *Dans mon village*; *Il faut prendre*; *Comme une odeur*. The French titles offer nearly untranslatable wordplays. For example, *Dans mon village il y a belle Lurette* plays on the expression "il y a belle lurette," which means "a long time ago"; in the stories, however, Lurette becomes a beautiful female character.
52 Pellerin, *Il faut prendre*, 18.
53 Perrault, *Contes*.
54 The real-life French Canadian strongman is the subject of a biopic discussed in chapter 4.
55 Gibeault, "Le renouveau du conte."
56 Examples of Pellerin's blurring of past and present include references to Saint-Élie-de-Caxton as a "mini-cipalité" (*Dans mon village*, 12), the SPCA getting involved in a horse-shoeing incident gone wrong (*Dans mon village*, 32), and locals painting in blue the motto *Je me souviens* on their horses' behinds, a reference to the licence plates of today (*Dans mon village*, 73).
57 "Un conte donc, mais qui dépasse les limites de la féerie pour ambitionner un certain propos social": Protat, "Croire à la magie."
58 Protat.
59 Bachilega, *Fairy Tales Transformed?*, 28.
60 Forcier asserts, "On a voulu calquer le modèle américain, modèle impérialiste qui peut se suffire à lui-même en s'appuyant sur son immense marché et qui, de plus, occupe les écrans du monde entier. Ce modèle n'est pas adaptable au Canada." Qtd. in Gajan, "Entretien avec André Forcier," 51.
61 "Multiforme, irréductible, largement insaisissable": Barrette, "Délire forcé."
62 Sloan, "Parc Belmont," 50.
63 Chaput, "L'histoire réinventée"; Ranger, "Entre la réalité et l'imaginaire."
64 One example of the respect granted Forcier as a truly Québécois filmmaker appears in Marie-Claude Loiselle's – editor of *24 images* and a staunch defender of art film (as opposed to *cinéma grand public*) – monograph on his work, *La communauté indomptable d'André Forcier*.
65 Landy, *The Historical Film*, 43.
66 Not to be confused with Eric R. Scott's documentary of the same name about anti-Semitism in Duplessis-era Quebec, based on Esther Delisle's controversial 1992 historical study *Le Traître et le Juif. Lionel Groulx, Le Devoir, et le délire du nationalisme d'extrême droite dans la province de Québec, 1929–1939* (translated the following year as *The Traitor and the Jew: Anti-Semitism and the Delirium of Extremist Right-Wing Nationalism in French Canada from 1929–1939*.

67 Known as *la grève de l'amiante*, the four-month strike at the mines in Asbestos, Quebec, in 1949 is generally considered – much like the Rocket Riot – as a pivotal moment in French Canadians' developing demands for greater self-determination in Quebec. Pierre Elliott Trudeau edited a seminal publication on it in 1956. Trudeau, *La grève de l'amiante*.

68 Benoît Pilon's documentary *Nestor et les oubliés* (2006) deals with this topic, as does Claude Jutra's fiction feature *La Dame en couleurs* (1985).

69 "Une page occultée de l'histoire du Québec, celle des années 50. Une époque de grande noirceur bien sûr, mais aussi un temps où le militantisme commençait à ruer dans les brancards": Lussier, "*Je me souviens*."

70 Most likely born sometime in the 1960s, Asselin has apparently carefully curated this datum, which is not readily available online through the usual databases.

71 Jean, "Une âme à vendre."

72 "Dans le paysage bien sage du cinéma québécois, le travail d'Asselin fait figure de corps étranger tellement on ne peut le rattacher à aucun courant ni à aucune tradition": Jean, "Une âme à vendre." In a similar vein, senior statesman of Quebec's documentary tradition Jacques Godbout praised Asselin's work as "un accident, une aberration, un tour de force, et sa légitimité n'est ni industrielle, ni commerciale, ni politique. Les œuvres d'art ne se justifient pas, elles témoignent de notre humanité." Godbout, "Acheter, spéculer, vendre," 50.

73 Robert Daudelin proposes that Asselin may have been inspired by similar moves in the work of film greats Howard Hawks, Alfred Hitchcock, and Wes Anderson (among others), and relatively favourably judges his success in doing so, describing the film as "magnifiquement filmé et riche en mythologies multiples." Daudelin, "La passagère."

74 "Quelque part entre film populaire et expérimentation exigeante": Laporte-Rainville, "Potentialités."

75 See Kaku, *Parallel Worlds*, 158–9.

76 Daudelin, "La passagère"; Laporte-Rainville, "Potentialités."

77 The Internet Movie Database cites the Shanghai International Film Festival as its only venue for screening outside Canada.

78 Youth suicide, the exploitation of young women, urban and suburban alienation, are the subjects of multiple films by young directors, including, for example, *Le ring* (Anaïs Barbeau-Lavalette, 2007), *Derrière moi* (Rafaël Ouellet, 2008), *Tout est parfait* (Yves Christian Fournier, 2008), *Demain* (Maxime Giroux, 2009), *10 ½* (Grou 2010), *Jo pour Jonathan* (Maxime Giroux, 2010), *Laurentie* (Simon Lavoie et Mathieu Denis, 2011), and many others.

79 See, for example, Ferretti, "La 'Grande Noirceur'"; Turgeon, "'Toé, tais-toé!'"

80 "Signe de maturité, il se fait de plus en plus de films de genre au Québec": Bachand and Clément, "La rencontre des cultures," 252.

3. Adapting the *Grande Noirceur* to the Screen

1 Sprengler, *Screening Nostalgia*, 73.
2 "[Le scénario constitue] un lieu de traces et de mémoires qui, réfractant la littérature, réfléchit le cinéma, comme une matrice révélant les frontières entre la littérature et le cinéma": Larouche and Cardinal, "Le scénario," 21.
3 Anderson, *Imagined Communities*.
4 Higson, "Re-Presenting the National Past."
5 Pidduck, *Contemporary Costume Film*.
6 See, for example, Lafontaine, "Introduction," 24.
7 "Le rapport entre cinéma et littérature au Québec a toujours occupé une place considérable": Larouche, "Introduction," 9. Hu and Gagnon compile a repertoire of 315 literary adaptations for the period 1922–96 in "Adaptations filmiques au Québec." See also Cardinal, "La réception critique," 189.
8 See Gagnon, "Histoire de l'adaptation."
9 Loiselle, *Stage-Bound*, 9. Almost no adaptations were made in the 1960s. Gagnon, "Histoire de l'adaptation," 156.
10 A. Loiselle, "*Les Muses orphelines*," 98.
11 Pidduck, *Contemporary Costume Film*, 4.
12 Stam, "Introduction," 46; emphasis added.
13 Stam, "Beyond Fidelity," 55.
14 Pidduck, *Contemporary Costume Film*, 4.
15 Stam, "Introduction," 22.
16 Film studies' focus on the director as auteur frequently neglects the significance of the actor in film as art and industry. In his book *Stars*, Richard Dyer articulates this notion of the "star image" as a *constructed* image (97), a collage "made out of media texts that can be grouped together as *promotion, publicity, films* and *criticism and commentaries*" (60; original emphasis). He argues that this polysemic "*complex totality*" (63; original emphasis) influences viewers' reception of a film as spectators consciously or unconsciously reference the baggage of the star's image while watching a performance on-screen.
17 About the star system in Quebec, see Véronneau, "Genres and Variations," 103–5.
18 Czach, "The Quebec Heritage Film."
19 Czach, 48.
20 Czach, 47.
21 Pidduck, *Contemporary Costume Film*, 10.
22 Pidduck, 10–11.
23 Czach, "The Quebec Heritage Film," 47.
24 As previously mentioned, historians have now begun to question the use of this term, articulating how it developed as a historical myth and identifying how Quebec's modernization occurred in tandem with that of the rest of North

America. See, for example, Ferretti, "La 'Grande Noirceur'"; Turgeon, "'Toé, tais-toé!'"; Lamonde, *La modernité au Québec*, vols. 1 and 2.

25 See, for example, Bédard, "Ce passé qui ne passe pas," which also analyses *Séraphin*, *Aurore*, and *Le Survenant* along some of the same lines as Czach.

26 The popular television series *Les pays d'en haut / True North* (2016–22) contributes to this mythology.

27 See Servais-Maquoi, *Le roman de la terre au Québec* (1974) and B. Proulx, *Le roman du territoire* (1987). For a concise account of film adaptations of *Séraphin* and *Le Survenant*, see Cardinal, "Film Adaptation."

28 Mailhot, *La littérature québécoise*, 56–60.

29 Mailhot, 81–4.

30 Freitag, *The Farm Novel in North America*.

31 Czach, "The Quebec Heritage Film," 42, 48.

32 See Ransom, "Men in Pain."

33 See, for example, Elsaesser, "Tales of Sound and Fury."

34 Chartrand, *Chartrand cinéaste*, 281.

35 With 1.3 million entries, *Séraphin* beat the box-office record set by *Les Boys* (1999) and beat *C.R.A.Z.Y.* by half a million seats in Quebec; in comparison, its imitators' success was more modest, with *Aurore* at 706,000 and *Le Survenant* at about 400,000 tickets. Bédard, "Ce passé qui ne passe pas," 79.

36 Marie-Claude Loiselle decried its lack of naturalism and "minables" (pathetic) characters. M.-C. Loiselle, review of *Séraphin*. In contrast, Élie Castiel argued that it elevated its story to the level of tragedy. Castiel, "Le roman de la terre," 40–1.

37 Antonine Maillet (b. 1929) is a highly respected Acadian author; after Anne Hébert, she is one of the rare French Canadian authors to be recognized by the French literary establishment.

38 Grignon, *Un homme et son péché*.

39 On both film adaptations of Grignon's novel and that of *Le Survenant*, see Pascal, "Film Adaptation."

40 See Dumas, "Un western des pays d'en haut."

41 For an insightful discussion of this film, its relationship to the original novel and Gury's earlier adaptation, see Ravary-Pilon, *Femmes, nation et nature*, 37–51.

42 Czach, "The Quebec Heritage Film," 48–9.

43 "Notre passé ne devient ici qu'un pur prétexte pour faire de l'oppression, de la misère morale, un spectacle. Le spectacle d'un Québec dont nous nous sommes libérés, et le film est, à chaque plan, le témoignage, la preuve, l'affirmation arrogante et roublarde de cette libération. Binamé adopte cette hauteur confortable (et rassurante) pour nous faire contempler ce qui ne nous *regarde* plus, ne nous concerne plus": M.-C. Loiselle, review of *Séraphin*.

44 Weinmann, *Du Canada au Québec*, 291–5.

45 On Bigras's film, see É. Beaulieu, "Le murmure du hors-champ," 49–51; Tremblay-Daviault, "Avant la Révolution," 38–41; and Weinmann, *Cinéma de l'imaginaire*, 27–50.

46 "La première heroïne, encore négative certes, de ce Québec naissant": Weinmann, *Cinéma de l'imaginaire*, 29

47 Dionne, interview in the DVD of *Aurore*'s "Making of" segment.

48 Not to be confused with the composer of the same name, the subject of the biopic *L'enfant prodige*, discussed in chapter 4.

49 Mathieu, *Aurore*. Dionne visited Fortierville the site of Aurore's martyrdom and researched the events in the Archives nationales. Ranger, "Pour enfin briser," 40.

50 Ranger, "Pour enfin briser la loi du silence," 40.

51 "Même si *Aurore* se déroule de 1909 à 1920, je trouvais que le propos était malgré tout très contemporain": Ranger, "Pour enfin briser la loi du silence," 40, 41.

52 Colman, *Deleuze and Cinema*, 151.

53 Mathieu, *Aurore*, 9n1.

54 "Dans le cinéma de l'industrie, les Québécois de jadis … sont plutôt les témoins hagards qui servent à confirmer notre morale *à nous*": Galiero, review of *Aurore*.

55 Guèvremont marks a transition in Québécois literature, in that her novel questions the nostalgic vision of times past and the reinscription of traditional values found in previous *romans du terroir*, like that of her cousin, Claude-Henri Grignon. Instead, *Le Survenant*'s sympathetic portrayal of its title character critiques the small-minded rural community whose values he defies. Lepage, *Germaine Guèvremont*, 8.

56 Alain Chartrand was first considered as its potential director by producers Jacques Bonin and Claude Gagnon. Chartrand, *Chartrand, cineaste*, 102.

57 Critics like Simon Galiero preferred *Le Survenant* to *Séraphin* but also saw it as overproduced. See his review of *Le Survenant*. Pierre Ranger, typically more sympathetic to the *cinéma grand public*, describes it as "merveilleux" and "un film lumineux." Ranger, review of *Le Survenant*, 15.

58 For a rigorous discussion of the role of opening credit sequences in this and other literary adaptation films, see Pascal, "Prégénérique et générique."

59 The novel allows her to grow in attractiveness because of her own attraction to the Survenant. Guèvremont, *Le Survenant*, 120.

60 Guèvremont, 170–1.

61 "Le Survenant pour moi, c'est l'homme qui arrive et qui apporte la nouveauté, une nouvelle façon de penser, une ouverture d'esprit, un certain modernisme": Canuel qtd. in Ranger, "Érik Canuel," 237.

62 Czach, "The Quebec Heritage Film," 58.

63 "La plus belle et solide fiction que notre cinématographie a vue naître ces dernières années": M.-C. Loiselle, "Le chant de la terre."

64 For an insightful discussion of this film see Ravary-Pilon, *Femmes, nation et nature*, 112–25.

65 See Leach, "Double Vision."

66 This sequence also represents one of the significant changes that Leclerc makes to his father's book, often simplifications required to reduce the number of overall characters. Not only does the film attach to Fidor incidents that in the novel

involved Félix's farmer friend Ludger (e.g., the story of the wolf chewing off its paw to get free of a trap), but a different family also received the charitable delivery of firewood that opens the film.

67 The *collège classique* was the equivalent of secondary school, the only route to a university education in pre–Quiet Revolution Quebec. Typically open only to boys and often run by Jesuits, studies included a classic curriculum of Latin and the classics, French rhetoric and literature, and philosophy.

68 See Castiel, "Le souffle au coeur" and "Filmer l'émotion."

69 The film's dialogue follows almost word for word this monologue from Félix Leclerc's novel, but the episode occurs at the *end* of the book (as opposed to the *beginning* of the film). Leclerc, *Pieds nus*, 183–4.

70 "Conscient de s'attaquer à un monument": Pilote qtd. in M.-J. Roy, "Sébastien Pilote a trouvé."

71 M.-J. Roy, "Sébastien Pilote a trouvé."

72 "On ne lésinera sur aucun élément pour rendre plus vraie que vraie": M.-J. Roy, "Sébastien Pilote a trouvé."

73 "Ce bois-là, c'est chez nous. C'est le sable drainé par la rivière Péribonka depuis des milliers d'années. Saint-Ambroise, où je suis né, Sainte-Monique, Péribonka : c'est le même sol. Je le connais, tout comme je connais la végétation qui pousse dessus, intimement. J'ai passé mon enfance à l'explorer, cette forêt-là … C'est un projet qui me tient à cœur depuis longtemps, et c'est en continuité avec mes films précédents. C'est un roman qui m'obsède, que j'ai toujours aimé pour sa grande simplicité": Pilote qtd. in Carrier-Lafleur, "Les 'Maria Chapdelaine' de Sébastien Pilote."

74 Fradet, "Le néoterroir."

75 "Ma Maria Chapdelaine est une fille de son temps": Pilote qtd. in M.-J. Roy, "Sébastien Pilote a trouvé."

76 Hémon, *Maria Chapdelaine*, 198.

77 "De quelle histoire du Québec voudrons-nous traiter au travers de l'histoire du cinéma québécois?": Véronneau, "Quelles représentations?," 144.

78 See Charles, "'La maison où j'ai grandi;'" Clément "Voix de femmes, voies de femmes"; and Fradet, review of *Frisson des collines*.

79 Lussier, "*Je me souviens.*"

80 See White, "Recovering Quebec Culture," for a perceptive analysis of this significant period piece.

81 In 2010, both *La Presse* and *Le Devoir* published articles, triggered by public lectures, discussing the myths of the Quiet Revolution. Historians have also weighed in. See Dupuis, *Pour en finir avec le mythe de la Révolution tranquille*; Ferretti, "La 'Grande Noirceur'"; Meunier, "The French-Canadian Great Darkness."

82 The whimsical film *Henri Henri* (Martin Talbot, 2014), set in a nebulous time frame during the 1960s and 1970s also depicts the nuns who have cared for the title character, a quirky innocent somewhat like Fred Pellerin's Babine,

in a positive light and facing change as their orphanage is closed during the secularization of social services.

83 On Pilon's film, see Bertrand, "Présence autochtone"; Chaput, "Chaleur humaine"; de Blois, "Un tableau mémorial"; Wójcik, "La société québécoise."

84 Faradji, "*Le club Vinland.*"

85 See, among others, the work of Yvan Lamonde, *La modernité au Québec*, vols. 1 and 2.

86 "Une époque peuplée de fantasmes relevant de l'iconographie familière" … "toutes les religieuses enseignantes n'étaient pas de tyranniques devotes, tous les prêtres n'étaient pas des violeurs d'enfants, tous les parents n'étaient pas des bigots": Laurendeau, "Et la lumière fut."

87 Similar sequences involving classical music study in convent schools appear in *Louis Cyr* and *L'enfant prodige.*

88 Jean-François Hamel describes the main character of *Laurentie* as victim of an "aliénation à la fois physique et morale … marquée au sceau de cette même incertitude identitaire." Hamel, "Solitude amère." Kester Dyer's analysis of *Le torrent* mentions *Laurentie*, but also contrasts Lavoie's film with the work of Mi'kmaw filmmaker Jeff Barnaby.

89 Hamel, "Récit d'une dépossession"; Rancourt, "*Le torrent*"; Robin, "Dans la tourmente." For an academic analysis of *Le torrent*, see K. Dyer, "Landscape, Trauma, and Identity."

90 "Archétype du Canadien français": Bishop, "À la source," 131.

91 Although his literary output was cut short by his early death of a heart attack, Gaétan Soucy's (1958–2013) works have come to be considered postmodern classics of the Quebec canon.

92 On the novel's significance, see Paterson, "L'espace sexué," 297.

93 André Loiselle, who has worked extensively on Quebec horror film and literature, has a forthcoming study of *Le poil de la bête* and *Rouge sang*, two horror films that take place in historical settings, tentatively titled *Gothic Degeneration in 21st Century Quebec Cinema* with Anthem Press.

94 Lavoie departs from his source text with this explicit choice signalled by the vehicles and costumes of the villagers. Soucy's novel is fuzzy and takes place in "un temps anhistorique, mais nous pouvons supposer que l'histoire se déroule dans les années 1980," according to Magali Blanc in "Comment survivre," 86.

95 The visual nature of the film allows for a certain ambiguity, but because of both the casting of a young actress and many viewers' prior knowledge of a now classic literary work, the element of surprise involved in Soucy's revelation of the narrator's gender confusion, imposed by her father, is missing from the film.

96 Perrault, *Contes.*

97 Paul-Marie's attraction to the protagonist and his willingness to risk ostracism and help her is explained in the novel as deriving from his poetic sensibility; in Lavoie's

film, this remains unclear. The fact that he rides a motorcycle, however, is perhaps the novel's only clue to its time frame. See Soucy, *The Little Girl*.

98 Paterson, "L'espace sexué," 306–8.

99 Perhaps significantly, Soucy cites in epigraph Emmanuel Wittgenstein's comment on pain, whereas Lavoie's choice of epigraph (from Saint-Simon) refocuses on memory.

4. Creating New Sites of Memory

1 Custen, *Bio/Pics*, 4.

2 Bingham, *Whose Lives*, 10.

3 Nora, "Between Memory and History."

4 Melançon, *The Rocket*.

5 Fortin, "Biofictions au cinéma," 235.

6 Fortin, 236.

7 Czach, "The Quebec Heritage Film."

8 Fortin, "Biofictions au cinéma," 240–4.

9 See, for example, essays collected in N. Baillargeon and Boissinot, eds., *La vraie dureté du mental*; Bauer and Barreau, eds., *La religion du Canadien de Montréal*.

10 See, for example, Cermak, *The Cinema of Hockey*; Crosson, *Sport and Film*; Ransom, *Hockey P.Q.*

11 Ramond, "Maurice Richard."

12 On the film see Czach, "The Quebec Heritage Film," 53–5; Ransom, *Hockey P.Q.*, 28–39; Sanaker, *La rencontre des langues*, 77–80. For Richard as a precursor to the Quiet Revolution, see J. Harvey, "Whose Sweater Is This?," 38–9; S. Laberge, "L'affaire Richard/Campbell"; and A. Bélanger, "The Last Game."

13 See L.P. Leroux, "Reinventing Tradition"; Boudreault, "Quebec Circuses"; and Jacob "The Québécois Circus."

14 L.P. Leroux, "Reinventing Tradition," 6, 3.

15 L.P. Leroux, 20.

16 L.P. Leroux, "A Tale of Origins," 46.

17 D. Laurence Rogers asserts that the American legend is based on real-life logger Fabian Fournier (1845–75). Rogers, *Paul Bunyan*.

18 L.P. Leroux, "A Tale of Origins," 46.

19 Ohl, *Louis Cyr*.

20 Jorane Pelletier (b. 1975) turned her alternative rock cello stylings to scoring for film and television not long after her debut album in 1999. With twenty-two composer credits, her haunting works accompany auteur independent films like *La cicatrice* (2012), thrillers like *Détour* (2009), and big box-office productions like *Chasse-galerie* (2016).

21 See Vermette, *A Distinct Alien Race*, for a compelling account of the Franco-Americans of New England.

22 Although his name invokes Montreal's famous amusement venue of the era, the Parc Sohmer, the film's cheating Irishman appears to be entirely fictional. Sohmer Park was founded by French Canadian Ernest Lavigne.

23 Czach, "The Quebec Heritage Film," 57.

24 "Le conte de Cyr, un Québécois vrai": Delgado, "Le conte de Cyr."

25 "Quasi-oubli"; "devoir de mémoire"; "les espoirs d'une collectivité": Delgado, "Le conte de Cyr."

26 "Un cinéma divertissant, populaire, sans poids politique ou culturel": Godin, "French Canada's Got Talent."

27 Custen outlines the conventions of the classical biopic, arguing for the connection between the biopic and the general public's conception of history as collective memory: "The biographical film (the 'biopic') routinely integrates disparate historical episodes of selected individual lives into a nearly monochromatic 'Hollywood view of history.'" Custen, *Bio/Pics*, 3.

28 Godin, "French Canada's Got Talent."

29 "Personnage lié à une époque, à un Québec qui s'éveille": Houdassine, "Charles Binamé," 30.

30 Aspects of this analysis were first presented as "Portraits of the Artist as a Young (Mad)man: The Musical Biopic in Quebec," at the American Council for Quebec Studies Conference, Montreal, 16–18 October 2014.

31 As of this writing, two film projects relating her life story have been released or announced: *Aline* (2020), "une fiction librement inspirée de la vie de Céline Dion," starring and directed by French actress Valérie Lemercier. Originally announced for 2020, another project, *Céline avant Céline*, by Québécois director Marc-André Lavoie, is still listed as in pre-production. See Etan Vlessing, "Celine Dion Biopic 'Céline Before Celine' in the Works (Exclusive)," *Hollywood Reporter*, 22 February 2019, https://www.hollywoodreporter.com/news/general-news/celine-dion-biopic-celine-before-celine-works-1188313/.

32 That early *biopic québécois* covered the life of the nation's adolescent prodigy, symbolist poet Émile Nelligan (1879–1941), tragically interned in a mental institution before the age of twenty.

33 "Le biopic témoigne … de la culture d'un peuple permettant la réhabilitation de figures ambiguës ou ignorées par l'histoire officielle": C.-S. Roy, "Le biopic," 8.

34 "Le mythe de la célébrité, de cette volonté démesurée … qui ne peut finalement que s'avérer déstructeur": Charest-Sigouin, "Gloire et eau bénite," 28.

35 Dufour, *La Bolduc*.

36 See Charest, "Chansons de travail."

37 Dufour, *La Bolduc*, 79.

38 The film spares viewers the gory reality of a botched dental procedure by an inexperienced dentist who attempted to forcibly extract teeth rendered particularly recalcitrant because of their intertangled roots. Dufour, *La Bolduc*, 84.

39 Here and in other places, the film takes artistic liberty with the "facts" of La Bolduc's biography; she had been offered a recording contract prior to her husband's accident. The film also elides the fact that she – like so many other provincial girls – first arrived in Montreal to serve as a maid, a job opportunity arranged by her stepsister, who already worked for a prosperous doctor living on the famous Square St-Louis. Dufour, *La Bolduc*, 87, 26–46.

40 Pierre Lavoie documents her road tours across Quebec and in New England in *Mille après mille*, 68–111.

41 "Carrière avant-gardiste de la première auteure-compositeure-interprète du Québec": Dufour, *La Bolduc*, 161.

42 Dufour, 15.

43 This notion was explicated by Micheline Cambron in a course lecture I attended as a guest at Université de Montréal in September 2013. See also Bellemare, "Le réseau des 'lyriques'"; Bouliane, "Goodbye Broadway."

44 "La première star du Québec": Beaunoyer, *Fleur d'Alys*, 19. See also Castiel, "Entretien: Denise Filiatrault."

45 Dion, "*Alys en cinémascope.*"

46 Robi, *Un long cri dans la nuit*, 112

47 Barrette, "Made in Hollywood"; M.-C. Loiselle, "Editorial." Its average score for the five reviewers contributing to *Séquences*'s rubric "Mises aux points," a rubric rating all films released prior to the issue, is about 2 stars (2.1 to be exact), indicated as a "Bon" on their ratings chart, but films can be rated as highly as 5 stars. *Séquences* 236 (2005): 64.

48 Robi, *Un long cri dans la nuit*, 118.

49 For an account of this entertainment practice of combining a film showing with live entertainment, see Lacasse, *Le bonimenteur.*

50 Pierre Lavoie documents Robi's career in *Mille après mille*, 206–12.

51 Robi, *Ma carrière et ma vie*, 23; 118; Beaunoyer, *Fleur d'Alys*, 163–65.

52 Czach, "The Quebec Heritage Film," 53.

53 Laurendeau, "Jack Paradise."

54 "Réhabiliter l'oeuvre": Schlager, "L'enfant prodige."

55 Schlager, "L'enfant prodige"; D. Harvey, "Review."

56 Rudel-Tessier, *André Mathieu*. For a more recent, minutely researched biography published in 2010, see Nicholson, *André Mathieu.*

57 This incident appears apocryphal. Nicholson does not mention it; however, the two composers may have met at the French chateau of mutual patrons, the Montblancs, where both stayed as guests at various moments. Rudel-Tessier, *André Mathieu*, 122.

58 Nicholson, *André Mathieu*, 247, 282–3.

59 On the *chansonniers'* role in nationalist politics, see Aubé, *Chanson et politique*; Durand, "Les chroniqueurs artistiques"; B. Roy, *Pouvoir chanter.*

60 In addition to *Gerry,* Natalie Petrowski's other *long-métrage* scripts include *Maman Last Call* (2005), based on her own novel; she also scripted the spin-off television movie and series *Miss Météo* (2005 and 2008) starring Anne-Marie Cadieux.

61 "Une version québécoise de *The Doors* d'Oliver Stone": Robin, "*Gerry,*" 38.

62 M. Roy, *Gerry Boulet.*

63 Recent academic scholarship focuses on this topic. See Larose and Rondeau, *La contre-culture;* Warren and Fortin, *Pratiques et discours.*

64 C. Bouchard, "The Sociolinguistic History," 169–70.

65 See Léger, *La chanson québécoise en question.*

66 Directed by Claude Faraldo, *Tabarnac* (1974) pioneers as a fictionalized rockumentary; excerpts of the group's concert introductions in France can be heard on the live tracks of the album *Tabarnac.*

67 Delgado, "L'hommage à un poète." All three *Séquences* critics who rated the film gave it three stars in the rubric "Mises aux points," a surprisingly unanimous rating of "très bon." *Séquences* 260 (2009): 64.

68 "Une série de clips illustrant le travail d'un artiste": Delgado, "L'hommage à un poète."

69 At the time of the film's development, only personal memoirs, such as Jean Barbe's ambivalent *Autour de Dédé Fortin* (2001) and Raymond Paquin's hagiographic *Dédé* (2004), had been published. Since then, Philippe Meilleur published a complete (but non-scholarly) biography, *André Fortin : l'homme qui brillait comme une comète* (2013).

70 See Ransom, *Hockey, P.Q.,* 158–64.

71 "Avant d'être un mythe, Alys Robi avait été la cible de prédilection des potineurs, des calomniateurs et des marchands de ragots": Beaunoyer, *Fleur d'Alys,* 222.

72 "Les Québécois ont préféré depuis cinquante ans les victimes aux idoles dont ils ne pouvaient supporter le poids": Beaunoyer, *Fleur d'Alys,* 185.

73 See chapter 1, note 81.

74 It is worth recalling that "franco-nationalism" represents a broad position that merely favours the promotion and preservation of the French language and francophone culture in Quebec; one does not necessarily need to be separatist to be a nationalist in Quebec.

75 As demonstrated by Simon Rainville's recent publication, *Pour la suite du Québec* (2019), a certain sector of Quebec's intelligentsia, but also of the working class, continue to embrace the stance of victimhood and precarity. Chaniac, review of *Pour la suite du Québec.*

76 "La mise à profit rapide (et facile) d'icônes devenues les piliers spontantés d'un patrimoine immediate": C.-S. Roy, "Le biopic," 8. See also Barrette, "Made in Hollywood," 18.

77 "En s'assumant, les Québécois ont assumé leurs stars": Beaunoyer, *Fleur d'Alys,* 221.

78 In addition, Mario Azzopardi's English-language telefilm *Savage Messiah / Moïse* (2002) tells the story of French Canadian cult leader Roch Thériault (played by Luc Picard) in the late 1970s, and Marc Bisaillon's independent film *La lâcheté* (2007) was inspired by a real-life case of kidnapping and murder in the 1960s.

79 Caillard, "Erreur sur la personne."

80 "Ces antihéros nationaux que l'histoire semble oublier": Castiel, "The French Connection," 28.

81 "Place le Québec sur l'échiquier du monde. Le territoire national n'est plus isolé. Des choses se passent. Le Québec n'est plus une terre qui se reconnait uniquement par sa culture, sa langue, son patrimoine et sa politique, mais également par les pratiques douteuses de certains individus": Castiel, "The French Connection," 28.

82 See Butts, "Lucien Rivard"; Goldfarb, *Perfect Villains*, 140–2.

83 "Épisode peu connu du grand public de l'histoire socio-politique québécoise": Castiel, "The French Connection," 29.

84 "Charles Binamé a fait de Lucien Rivard un héros populaire": Castiel, 29.

85 "L'histoire est pour moi l'outil idéal pour extirper des profondeurs les souvenirs du passé": qtd. in Houdassine, "Charles Binamé," 30.

86 "Un documentaire véridique"; "un point de vue sur les relations malsaines entre la mafia et la politique": qtd. in Houdassine, 31.

87 Significant films in which Québécois protagonists leave the province include, among others, *Un crabe dans la tête* (André Turpin, 2001), *Turbulence des fluides* (Manon Briand, 2002), *2 Frogs dans l'Ouest* (Dany Papineau, 2010), *Inch'allah* (Anaïs Barbeau-Lavalette, 2011), *Ego Trip* (Benoît Pelletier, 2015).

88 Houdassine, "Charles Binamé," 30.

89 Nygaard, "Monica Proietti."

90 Germain, *Souvenirs de Monica*.

91 Ranger, "Intériorité," 43.

92 Ranger, 42.

93 Dupuis appears in a similar role in *Mesrine* as real-life criminal Jean-Paul Mercier.

94 An array of films deal with girls' and women's issues like domestic and sexual abuse, sexual exploitation, and so on; these include *Délivrez-moi* (Denis Chouinard, 2006), *Demain* (Maxime Giroux, 2009), *2 fois une femme* (François Delisle, 2010), *Décharge* (Benoît Pilon, 2011), to name just a few.

95 Isabelle Fortier (b. 1973 in Lac-Mégantic), a.k.a. Nelly Arcan, perpetuated her own myths; although 1973 is her actual birthdate, she lied about her age to her French publisher, and the biographical notices on many of her works still state that she was born in 1975. Émond's film addresses this incident in the segment with an adult character called Peggy (Catherine Brunet).

96 Smart, *Writing Herself Into Being*, 257.

97 Mercédès Baillargeon effectively discusses "le pari risqué qui confond personne réelle, écrivaine et personnalité publique, sur lequel repose son autofiction, [ce qui]

a amené les médias à la victimisation de Nelly Arcan, et à sa sacralisation comme 'écrivaine maudite.'" See "Pari manqué?," 144.

98 Smart, *Writing Herself Into Being*, 257.

99 Smart, 256–7

100 Smart, 259–60.

101 Smart reads Arcan's literary works specifically for their connection to the author's *québécitude*, including a heavily colonial dynamic. Paradoxically, whereas the prestige of her publication in France resulted in jealousy and resentment within Quebec's literary establishment, internally colonized with its own sense of inferiority, Arcan was mocked by a French television host for her "affreux accent québécois." Smart, *Writing Herself Into Being*, 295n29. Mercédès Baillargeon addresses this issue as well in "Pari manqué?," 164.

102 The notion of gender as a performance is most frequently traced back to the work of feminist theorist Judith Butler, especially in *Gender Trouble*. Mercédès Baillargeon links the construction of Nelly Arcan as a persona to Richard Dyer's theorization of the Hollywood star in *Stars*. M. Baillargeon, "Pari manqué?," 144, 162–3.

103 Arcan, "Peggy."

104 See, for example, the essays in Bourdeau, ed., *Horrible Mothers*.

105 For an analysis of *Putain's* "matriphobia" see Henry-Tierney, "The Whore and Her Mother." For discussions of this trope in film see Bourdeau, "Introduction: Failing Successfully" and "Politics and Motherhood"; Ransom, "Forgiving the Horrible Mother." In contrast, the suicidal protagonist of Arcan's *Paradis, clef en mains*, is smothered by an overly present mother.

106 Émond inexplicably changes the name of the protagonist of the young adult short story, "Peggy," with whom the first-person narrator eventually breaks off her friendship, largely out of jealousy. Émond then gives this name to an adult character (Catherine Brunet), who announces her pregnancy to the adult writer in a sequence I have not been able to find in Arcan's fiction, and which seems out of place in the film. Her selection of a pretty actress to depict the adolescent *Nelly* contradicts Arcan's oeuvre, in which she describes herself as an unattractive bookworm.

107 Émond's dialogue modifies a citation from Arcan, "Peggy."

108 Arcan, *Putain*, 38.

109 Arcan, 19. This "opening" line is preceded by a sort of preface in italics in the novel.

110 Smart, *Writing Herself Into Being*.

111 Hair and eye colour are consistently significant in Arcan's oeuvre; the personage of *Folle* has hair that is neither blonde nor brown, the sandy blonde referred to as *châtain* in French, also the hair colour of the older writer avatar in the film, *Nelly*, as opposed to the bleached blondes, Cynthia and the younger writer.

112 This line appears on page 7 of *Folle* and on page 5 of its English translation as *Hysteric*.

113 Smart, *Writing Herself Into Being*, 270.

114 Smart, 270.

115 Mercédès Baillargeon effectively analyses the ambivalence of Quebec's media institutions to Arcan, looking at the short story "La honte," in *Burqa de chair*. See M. Baillargeon, "Pari raté?," 169–78.

116 Nancy Huston's preface to the posthumous collection of short works, *Burqa de chair*, makes this eminently clear, as does the growing body of literary criticism dedicated to Arcan's oeuvre cited in Mercédès Baillargeon's study. See Huston, "Arcan, philosophe"; M. Baillargeon, "Pari manqué?"

117 "Symbole de notre succès littéraire": M. Baillargeon, "Pari manqué?," 141.

118 Fortin, "Biofictions au cinéma," 261–6.

119 Two more difficult-to-categorize period pieces bear mention here for their relationship to criminality or notorious individuals. Ken Scott's period comedy *Les doigts croches / Sticky Fingers* (2009) is set in a nostalgic 1960s and offers a redemption story for a group of criminals who embark on a pilgrimage to Santiago de Compostela. Daniel Roby's *Funkytown* (2011) memorializes the disco era with a fictionalization of real-life media personality Alain Montpetit, played by Patrick Huard.

120 F. Bouchard, "De poésie et d'esprit." In addition, filmmaker Rudy Barichello connects Quebec to world literature with *Meetings with a Young Poet* (2013), in his artsy depiction of interactions between Samuel Beckett (Stephen McHattie) and Montreal poet Paul Susser (Vincent Hoss-Desmarais).

121 "Si donc les biofictions cinématographiques produites au Québec sont, dans leur ensemble, des films à thèse, ces thèses portent non sur les personnes dont elles racontent la vie, mais sur le Québec dans son ensemble : l'histoire du Québec a été traversée de combats collectifs, au premier chef le nationalisme, mais aussi le féminisme, et plusieurs personnes dont on raconte la vie doivent se battre pour atteindre l'autonomie, jusqu'à devenir des victimes de cette lutte. L'histoire est marquée par des institutions politiques, juridiques, religieuses et culturelles dont il faut se déprendre, ce que n'ont pas toujours réussi les personnages des biofictions. Cette histoire se doit d'être transmise, ce qui s'effectue non seulement par les films, mais aussi à l'intérieur d'eux" : Fortin, "Biofictions au cinéma," 267.

5. "Enthralling Narrative[s] of Bittersweet Reminiscence"

1 A. Loiselle, *Cinema as History*, 169.

2 "Le récit autobiographique est la mise en forme de souvenirs": Chaput, "L'enfance de l'art," 40.

3 Sprengler, *Screening Nostalgia*.

4 Cook, *Screening the Past*, 3.

5 Robertson, "After Nostalgia?," 49, qtd. in Sprengler, *Screening Nostalgia*, 14.

6 Boym, *Future of Nostalgia*, xiv.

7 For a concise account of this period, see Zubrzycki, *Beheading the Saint*, 1–18.

8 For further treatment of several films discussed in this section, see Ransom, "Forgiving the Horrible Mother."

9 Chartier, "Le cinéma du pays de la neige devient pluriculturel," 145; Lever, "Cinéma québécois et mémoire," 87.

10 Robert Schwartzwald's *C.R.A.Z.Y.: A Queer Film Classic* (2016) is a rare monograph devoted to a single film from Quebec, and it documents the film's international appeal.

11 Schwartzwald, 42.

12 In addition to Schwartzwald, for critical readings of homophobia, masculinity, and sovereignty in Vallée's film, see also Blanchard, "L'aliénation tranquille" and "Le Québec libre"; Fisher, "Invisibilités"; and Powell, "*C.R.A.Z.Y.* Québec."

13 Schwartzwald, *C.R.A.Z.Y.*, 61.

14 Leach, "'It Takes Monsters,'" 51

15 Charles, "'La maison où j'ai grandi'"; Clément, "Voix de femmes, voies de femmes."

16 On Hébert's fiction, see den Toonder, "Voyages de l'imaginaire."

17 See, for example, Gilbert and Santoro, "Transforming Visions"; Pallister, "*L'angst.*"

18 As the film undermines the father's authority, depicting the Jewish immigrant from Europe as an ineffectual dreamer, and privileges the daughter's quest for independence, particularly via Hanna's sexual exploration, *Emporte-moi* prefigures another type of twenty-first-century film that looks frankly at young women's problematic position in a contemporary setting. Ironically, though, these films suggest that for many young women the promises offered by the Quiet Revolution and the subsequent women's movement were empty ones. Thus, the young female protagonists of *Délivrez-moi* (2006), *Demain* (2009), *Derrière-moi* (2009), *Décharge* (2011), and other films set in contemporary Quebec, find themselves in situations similar to that of Hanna in the 1960s, their actual freedom undermined by men's insistence on seeing them as sexual objects and the persistence of prostitution, abuse, and exploitation.

19 For a more detailed discussion of nostalgia in Quebec cinema, see Ransom, "Men in Pain." For a more theoretical engagement of nostalgia and film, from which I draw, see Sprengler, *Screening Nostalgia*, 11–14.

20 In addition to most of Xavier Dolan's oeuvre, turn-of-the millennium films *2 secondes* (Manon Briand, 1998), *Full Blast* (Rodrigue Jean, 1999), and *Les muses orphelines* (Robert Favreau, 2000) feature gay protagonists, as did Émile Gaudreault's Montreal-set English-language breakout comedy *Mambo Italiano* (2003). A growing body of films address the issues of gay identity in the twenty-first century, including *Ville-Marie* (Guy Édoin, 2015). Quebec's ongoing struggle with a latent homophobia appears both in comedies that mock gayness and in teen dramas centred on the stress of coming out (or not), some of which end in

suicide for the gay protagonist, including *Tout est parfait* (Yves-Christian Fournier, 2008), *1:54* (Yan England, 2016), and *La chute de Sparte* (Tristan Dubois, 2018).

21 B. Hébert, *C'est pas moi, je le jure* (1997) and *Alice court avec René* (2000). Falardeau states to an interviewer that he had wanted to make a film based on these works since their initial reading nearly a decade earlier, thus denying that *C.R.A.Z.Y.*'s success influenced him personally; he also notes that his film's release the same year as Pool's *Maman est chez le coiffeur* was coincidental. Defoy, "Entretien," 20.

22 Falardeau adresses the essential difference between the two films: "Dans le film de Léa, il est beaucoup question de la débrouillardise des enfants dans un univers où les parents sont absents alors que pour moi *C'est pas moi, je le jure!*, l'histoire tourne autour de la quête métaphysique d'un garçon extralucide de 10 ans nourrissant un mal-être face à cette situation." Qtd. in Defoy, "Entretien."

23 "Des films souvent déroutants où l'invraisemblable courtise le possible et dont l'écriture faussement désinvolte piège le spectateur": Daudelin, "Les grandes vacances."

24 The monologue is adapted from the prologue of Hébert's autofiction, *C'est pas moi*, 9.

25 "Ce cinéma *mainstream* qui est désormais une des composantes évidentes du cinéma québécois": Daudelin, "Les grandes vacances."

26 "On a tous des souvenirs assez précis de cette époque de notre vie. Ce peut être agréable, une fois adulte, de revisiter cette période": qtd. in Defoy, "Entretien," 18.

27 "C'est le moment où, dans cette société où tout bascule, les intellectuels qu'on dit de gauche sont issues de l'Action catholique et, comme le père de Léon, s'identifient à la revue *Cité libre* … À travers le personnage de Léon … c'est un portrait du Québec – d'un certain Québec en train de se réveiller": Daudelin, "Les grandes vacances."

28 The film's action takes place around the time of the "Querelle du joual," debates over which *type* of French should be spoken in Quebec: the Standard International French supported by educators, the church, and political and economic elites, or vernacular Québécois French, referred to in shorthand as *joual*, as argued leftists, intellectuals, and many film and musical artists. C. Bouchard, "The Sociolinguistic History," 169–71.

29 Marie-Claude Loiselle describes "la veine d'un certain jeune cinéma québécois, dynamique et tonitruant, dont la préoccupation première semble souvent de produire une impression forte chez le spectateur par la mise en valeur ostentatoire de l'image, du son, d'une musique qui se veut grisante et de pirouettes scénaristiques." M.-C. Loiselle, "Au-delà des apparences." Simon Beaulieu argues for Quebec film to deal with serious topics (read: politics and social issues as opposed to personal storoies) and accuses young filmmakers of exploiting the funding systems' preferences: "cette tendance qui se place quelque part entre l'ouverture à la relève et l'exploitation des rouages d'un establishment qui sait exactement où se trouve son profit." S. Beaulieu, review of *Ma voisine danse le ska*.

30 Mariloup Wolfe's much later film *Jouliks* (2019) also focalizes events in this era
through a child character, but with a very different tone. Adapted from Marie-
Christine Lê-Huu's 2005 stage play, it is more of a horror/thriller depicting an
uncanny child raised by nonconformist parents in the 1960s and 1970s.

31 Lepage-Boily, "Michel Monty Parle." This is Monty's only French-language feature
as a director; he also directed an English-language telefilm, *Burden of Evil* (2012).

32 Robitaille, *Histoires d'hiver.*

33 Institutional critics commented on the film's appeal to nostalgia as a *valeur sûre*
in Quebec box offices: "La nostalgie a toujours la cote au cinéma québécois":
Mandolini, "Chronique d'une attente," 34. See also Barrette, review of *Histoires
d'hiver.* Bouvier himself asserts that "*Histoires d'hiver*, c'est le souvenir, la mémoire,
la nostalgie, la mélancolie. Des thèmes récurrents dans le cinéma québécois." See
Castiel, "La mémoire indélébile," 15.

34 Robitaille, *Un été.*

35 Castiel, "La mémoire indélébile."

36 R. Proulx, "À la croisée des chemins," offers an incisive comparison of the film and
its source text.

37 See Lamonde, "Quebec's Americanicity."

38 This resulted in a problem for the film's theatrical release in the United States
due to a copyright dispute over its use of a Pink Floyd song. Schwartzwald,
C.R.A.Z.Y., 23.

39 Robinson had played for the Brooklyn Dodgers' minor league farm team, the
Montreal Royals, before breaking the colour barrier in the MLB in 1947.

40 Jane Moss, "Family Films," 113.

41 One of the external reviewers for this manuscript perceptively connects this catchy
title, which draws on fairy tale formulas, to a classic Québécois film that engages
masculinity in a very different manner, Michel Tremblay and André Brassard's *Il
était une fois dans l'Est* (1973), set in Montreal's Gay Village.

42 Ransom, *Hockey P.Q.*, 118–57.

43 Monk, *Weird Sex*, 278.

44 "Grossièrement commercial jusqu'au bout des ongles": Mandolini, "Qu'est-ce qui
nous fait courir?," 38. As a commercial film, *Il était une fois les Boys* acknowledges
its major sponsor, Harvey's, both at the film's beginning and with a sequence
in which the Boys eat at the iconic Canadian burger chain. Acknowledging its
commanditaires is not unique to this franchise, and commercial Quebec films (as do
Bollywood films, for example) go beyond the hidden product placement practices
of Hollywood.

45 "Alors que le premier film montrait la difficile affirmation de l'identité masculine,
Les Boys II traduit le malaise de l'homme québécois dans son rapport à l'*Autre*":
Mandolini, "Qu'est-ce qui nous fait courir?," 38.

46 "Un conte de fées pour adultes": Picard, "*Les Boys*," 17

47 "Un préjugé défavorable": Picard, 17.

48 "La cinésérie *Les Boys* a joué un rôle clé dans notre cinématographie"; "entre le grand écran et la salle": Picard, 17,

49 For a discussion of popular culture iterations of the "Fantôme du Forum," see Ransom, *Hockey P.Q.*, 43–6, 172–6.

50 Edensor, *National Identity*, 17.

51 For a complete account of this visit and its origins, see Lacasse, "*Chasse au Godard*," 33. See also Julie Perron's brief documentary *Mai en décembre (Godard en Abitibi)* (2000), available online at https://www.onf.ca/film/mai_en_decembre_godard _en_abitibi/.

52 Germain Lacasse reads him as an avatar of counterculture filmmaker and one-time member of Gerry Boulet's Offenbach, Pierre Harel (b. 1944); "*Chasse au Godard*," 35. Harel was a central figure in Quebec's counterculture, producing several experimental films, including *Bulldozer* (1974). Éric Morin's *We Are Gold* (2019) pays tribute to that iconic counterculture film.

53 The Collège d'éducation générale et profesionnel, or CÉGEP, was a product of the Quiet Revolution's education reforms, a publicly funded analogue to the junior or community college, it offers a two-year program prior to university studies.

54 Initiated by Anne-Claire Poirier, the ONF released a six-film, explicitly feminist series called *En tant que femmes* in 1972.

55 Examples that come to mind include *Jo pour Jonathan* (Maxime Giroux, 2010), *Décharge* (Benoît Pilon, 2011), *Laurentie* (Simon Lavoie and Mathieu Denis, 2011), and *La cicatrice* (Jimmy Larouche, 2012), among others.

56 Lacasse explains that communications between Pierre Harel and Godard over the value of film festivals resulted in an invitation to Godard by the producer Claude Nedjar to "tenter une expérience de télévision rebelle," so Godard invited Harel to join him in Abitibi using the new Sony Portapak devices. They interview student leaders and workers, and local television (Radio-Nord) broadcast the interviews. However, the anti-establishment assertions made enraged the company elites, and the local newspaper ridicules the experiment, ostensibly at their behest. Lacasse, "*Chasse au Godard*," 34.

57 Lacasse, 35.

58 Monia Chokri's *La femme de mon frère* (2019) exploits this social phenomenon tragi-comically.

59 "Le renouveau du cinéma québécois et sa reconnaissance internationale sont le fruit du travail de quelques cinéastes dans la trentaine et la quarantaine": Lafleur, "Bouches cousues."

60 For example, the *De père en flic* films (Émile Gaudreault, 2009 and 2017) do this in a comedic fashion.

61 As an American, I think of programs from my childhood like *The Red Skelton Show* or *The Carol Burnett Show*. For a history of variety reviews in Quebec, see Lacasse et al., *Le diable en ville*; Larrue, "Le théâtre au Québec."

62 See my analysis of Bélanger's first film: Ransom, "Deterritorialization."

63 Critic Yves Rousseau asserts the commonality between these two films: "les
deux films ont cependant en commun de se situer dans un milieu populaire et
de présenter une vision précise et juste du phénomène du travail." Rousseau, "Le
plein de sens."

64 Laurendeau, "Audacieusement drôle"; Rousseau, "Le plein de sens." Bélanger's
father owned a gas station in Limoilu, a working-class suburb of Quebec City.
Ranger, review of *Gaz Bar Blues*; Gingras, "L'esprit du lieu."

65 "C'est surtout le respect des valeurs traditionnelles qui ressort dans ce film, en
particulier celles de la famille … et du travail bien fait": Gingras, "L'esprit du lieu."

66 "Bélanger situe également son film dans l'Histoire": Rousseau, "Le plein de sens."

67 Laurendeau, "Audacieusement drôle"; Rousseau, "Le plein de sens"; and Tourigny,
review of *Gaz Bar Blues*, all mention one or more of these items.

68 "Le réalisateur s'interroge sur la perte de nos idéaux et sur les bienfaits – réels ou
imaginaires – du progrès et du changement qui nous touchent tous": Tourigny,
review of *Gaz Bar Blues*, 51.

69 "Un des réalisateurs québécois les plus importants de sa génération": Chaput,
"L'enfance de l'art," 41.

70 Houdassine, "Ricardo Trogi," 43.

71 Ur-texts from the 1990s codify two images of Italians: Jean-Claude Lauzon's *Léolo*,
and the cult Mafia-themed television series *Omertà, la loi du silence* (1996–8). Jean-
Philippe Duval's adaptation of Alexis Martin's play *Matroni et moi* (1999), a big-
screen reboot of *Omertá* (2011), and Daniel Grou's *Mafia Inc.* (2020) reprised these
images. Émile Gaudreault exploits the comedic potential of Italian stereotypes in
his breakout English-language, Montreal-set comedy *Mambo Italiano* (2003).

72 Already the object of an edited volume (Lafontaine, *ReFocus: The Films of Xavier
Dolan*), the fact that Dolan writes, directs, and even edits his films makes him a
true auteur, exercizing a "volonté de faire une oeuvre d'art totale." Protat, "Ecce
homo," 16.

73 See Fradet, "Aux profondeurs"; Lafontaine, "Introduction."

74 Mokkil, "Xavier Dolan in India."

75 *Laurence Anyways* is not the first Quebec film to address transgender issues;
the protagonist of Paule Baillargeon's *Le sexe des étoiles* (1993), an adaptation
of Monique Proulx's 1987 novel, underwent a female-to-male transition. See
Dickinson, *Screening Gender*, 126–8; M.-E. Lapointe and Gauvin, "Lectures
croisées."

76 Fradet, "Aux profondeurs." Zoé Protat views Dolan's use of music as far more
inventive, though, than that of Vallée. Protat, "Ecce homo," 17.

77 "Ces singularités ne sont pas des inepties; elles témoignent de la volonté du
cinéaste de travailler *à partir* de la surface pour captiver le regard et échafauder un
discours": Fradet, "Aux profondeurs."

78 Rees-Roberts, "Dolan's Pop Fashion," 218. Indeed Rees-Roberts points out
that Dolan admits to the French magazine *Les Inrockuptibles* that "he used mostly

fashion magazines to convey the mood of the decade rather than precise historical documentation from the era" (213).

79 Dolan's casting of Nathalie Baye, an eminent French leading actress, apparently addresses the potential continuity error in the fact that Laurence, ostensibly Québécois, speaks with a French accent.

80 A fictional location; Leach identifies it as a wordplay/opposite reference to England's "Isle of Wight." Leach, "In-Between," 102.

81 I admit struggling with pronouns throughout this section, but I ultimately decided to refer to Laurence with "he/him/his" in order to distinguish from Fred's pronouns "she/her/hers." At this moment of no return, it seems right to now refer to Laurence with "she/her/hers."

82 Cavell and Dickinson, "Sex and Canada," xv, qtd. in Leach, "In-Between," 92.

83 Leach, 92.

84 Leach, 99–101.

85 Lafontaine, "'I Am Looking,'" 191.

86 Lafontaine, 202.

87 Czach and Loiselle, "Introduction," 3.

Bibliography

Aldred, Lisa. "Plastic Shamans and Astroturf Sun Dances: New Age Commercialization of Native American Spirituality." *American Indian Quarterly* 24, no. 3 (2000): 329–52. https://doi.org/10.1353/aiq.2000.0001.

Anderson, Benedict. *Imagined Communities: Reflections on the Origin and Spread of Nationalism.* Rev. ed. Verso, 1991.

Angenot, Marc. *Les idéologies du ressentiment.* XYZ, 1997.

Araujo, Juliana, and Michel Marie, eds. *À grande allure : l'œuvre de Pierre Perrault.* Presses de la Sorbonne Nouvelle, 2015.

Arcan, Nelly. *Burqa de chair.* Seuil, 2011.

– *Folle.* Seuil, 2004.

– *Paradis, clef en mains.* Les 400 coups, 2009.

– "Peggy." In Premières amours. La Courte échelle, 2008.

– *Putain.* Seuil, 2001.

Attebery, Brian. *Strategies of Fantasy.* Indiana University Press, 1992.

Aubé, Jacques. *Chanson et politique au Québec (1960–1980).* Triptyque, 1990.

Aubert de Gaspé, Philippe (*père*). "La Corriveau." In *Les anciens Canadiens.* Fides, 1961. Originally published in 1864.

Aubrac, Lucie. *La Résistance expliquée à mes petits-enfants.* Seuil, 2000.

Bachand, Denis. "Du national au transnational : l'empreinte documentaire dans les films de Denis Villeneuve, Philippe Falardeau et Kim Nguyen." *Contemporary French Civilization* 44, nos. 2–3 (2019): 151–66. https://doi.org/10.3828/cfc.2019.9.

Bachand, Denis, and Annie Lise Clément. "La rencontre des cultures dans le cinéma québécois : violence et altérité." In *Le cinéma au Québec : tradition et modernité,* edited by Stéphane-Albert Boulais. Fides, 2006.

Bachilega, Cristina. *Fairy Tales Transformed? Twenty-First Century Adaptations and the Politics of Wonder.* Wayne State University Press, 2013.

Baillargeon, Denyse. *A Brief History of Women in Quebec.* Wilfrid Laurier University Press, 2014.

– *To Be Equals in Our Own Country: Women and the Vote in Quebec.* UBC Press, 2019.

Baillargeon, Mercédès. "Joy, Melancholy, and the Promise of Happiness in Xavier Dolan's *Mommy*." In *ReFocus: The Films of Xavier Dolan*, edited by Andrée Lafontaine. Edinburgh University Press, 2019. https://www.jstor.org/stable /10.3366/j.ctvrxk1cv.15.

– "Pari manqué? Nelly Arcan, les médias et le destin tragique d'une écrivaine." In *Le personnel est politique : médias, esthétique et politique de l'autofiction chez Christine Angot, Chloé Delaume et Nelly Arcan*. Purdue University Press, 2019. https://doi .org/10.2307/j.ctvhhhd91.

– "Romantic Disillusionment, (Dis)Identification, and the Sublimation of National Identity in Québec's 'New Wave': *Heartbeats* by Xavier Dolan and *Night #1* by Anne Émond." *Québec Studies* 57 (2014): 171–92. https://doi.org/10.3828/QS .2014.11.

Baillargeon, Mercédès, and Karine Bertrand, eds. "Rencontres interculturelles." Special issue, *Nouvelles vues : revue sur les pratiques, les théories et l'histoire du cinéma au Québec*, no. 22 (2023). https://doi.org/10.7202/1106684ar.

Baillargeon, Normand, and Christian Boissinot, eds. *La vraie dureté du mental : hockey et philosophie*. Presses de l'Université Laval, 2009.

Barbe, Jean. *Autour de Dédé Fortin*. Leméac, 2001.

Barrette, Pierre. "Délire forcé : *Les États-Unis d'Albert* d'André Forcier." *24 images*, no. 122 (2005): 57.

– "Le désert de l'âme : *Un 32 août sur Terre* de Denis Villeneuve." *24 images*, no. 95 (1998–9): 51.

– "L'Histoire comme engagement : *15 février 1839* de Pierre Falardeau." *24 images*, no. 105 (2000): 46–7.

– "Made in Hollywood." *24 images*, no. 128 (2006): 17–18.

– Review of *Histoires d'hiver*, directed by François Bouvier. *24 images*, no. 96 (1999): 59.

Bauer, Olivier, and Jean-Marc Barreau, eds. *La religion du Canadien de Montréal*. Fides, 2009.

Beaulieu, Étienne. "Le murmure du hors-champ. La voix et l'image dans trois films québécois." *Revue des sciences humaines*, no. 288 (October–December 2007): 45–55.

Beaulieu, Simon. Review of *Ma voisine danse le ska*, directed by Nathalie Saint-Pierre. *Séquences*, no. 229 (2004): 54.

Beaunoyer, Jean. *Fleur d'Alys*. Leméac, 1994.

Bédard, Éric. "Ce passé qui ne passe pas. La Grande Noirceur catholique dans les films *Séraphin. Un Homme et son péché, Le survenant* et *Aurore*." *Globe : revue internationale d'études québécoises* 10–11, nos. 1–2 (2007–8): 75–93. https://doi .org/10.7202/1000492ar.

Bélanger, Anouk. "The Last Game? Hockey and the Experience of Masculinity in Québec." In *Sport and Gender in Canada*, edited by Philip White and Kevin Young. Oxford University Press, 1999.

Bélanger, Nicole. *Salut, mon roi mongol.* Québec Loisirs, 1998.

Bellemare, Luc. "Les réseaux des « lyriques » et des « veillées » : une histoire de la chanson au Québec dans l'entre-deux-guerres par la radiodiffusion au poste CKAC de Montréal." PhD diss., Université Laval, 2012.

Bertrand, Karine. "Arnait Video Productions and the Fictional Work of the Inuit/Québécois Collective." In *Quebec Cinema in the 21st Century,* edited by Michael Gott and Thibaut Schilt. Liverpool University Press, 2024. https://doi.org/10.3828/liverpool/9781802074765.003.0003.

– "De Gilles Groulx à Jean-Marc Vallée : transnationalisme, américanité et territoire dans le cinéma québécois." *American Review of Canadian Studies* 42, no. 1 (2019): 70–84. https://doi.org/10.1080/02722011.2019.1579742.

– "Indigenous Women's Cinema in Quebec: The Works and Words of Mohawk Filmmaker Sonia Bonspille Boileau." In *Canadian Cinema in the New Millennium,* edited by Lee Carruthers and Charles Tepperman. McGill-Queen's University Press, 2023. https://doi.org/10.1515/9780228014928-007.

– "La présence autochtone et la figure du médiateur blanc dans le cinéma des Premières Nations." *Recherches amérindiennes du Québec* 14, no. 1 (2015): 51–8. https://doi.org/10.7202/1035164ar.

Billon, Pierre. *Nouvelle-France.* Leméac, 2004.

Bingham, Dennis. *Whose Lives Are They Anyway? The Biopic as Contemporary Film Genre.* Rutgers University Press, 2010.

Bishop, Neil. "À la source de la Révolution Tranquille : *Le Torrent* d'Anne Hébert." In *The Art and Genius of Anne Hébert: Essays on Her Works,* edited by Janis L. Pallister. Fairleigh Dickinson University Press, 2001.

Blais, Mélissa. *J'haïs les féministes : le 6 décembre 1989 et ses suites.* Remue-ménage, 2009.

Blais, Mélissa, Francis Dupuis-Déri, Lyne Kurtzman, and Dominique Payette, eds. *Retour sur un attentat antiféministe : École Polytechnique de Montréal, 6 décembre 1989.* Remue-ménage, 2010.

Blanc, Magali. "Comment survivre sans la figure paternelle?" *Voix Plurielles* 14, no. 1 (2017): 86–95. https://doi.org/10.26522/vp.v14i1.1548.

Blanchard, Maxime. "L'aliénation tranquille: *C.R.A.Z.Y* de Jean-Marc Vallée." *Contemporary French and Francophone Studies* 13, no. 1 (2009): 71–9. https://doi.org/10.1080/17409290802606846.

– "Le Québec libre : *C.R.A.Z.Y* de Jean-Marc Vallée." *French Forum* 34, no. 3 (2009): 101–19. https://doi.org/10.1353/frf.0.0092.

Bloemraad, Irene. "Who Claims Dual Citizenship? The Limits of Postnationalism, the Possibilities of Transnationalism, and the Presence of Traditional Citizenship." *International Migration Review* 37, no. 2 (2006): 389–426. https://doi.org/10.1111/j.1747-7379.2004.tb00203.x.

Bocage, Pierre. *Gilles Groulx, le cinéaste résistant.* Lux, 2013.

Bordwell, David. "The Art Cinema as a Mode of Film Practice." In *The European Cinema Reader,* edited by Catherine Fowler. Routledge, 2002.

Bouchard, Chantal. "The Sociolinguistic History of French in Quebec." *Quebec Questions: Quebec Studies for the Twenty-First Century*, edited by Stéphan Gervais, Christopher Kirkey, and Jarrett Rudy. 2nd ed. Oxford University Press, 2016.

Bouchard, Denis, Éric Cardinal, and Ghislain Picard. *De Kebec à Québec : cinq siècles d'échanges entre nous*. Les Intouchables, 2008.

Bouchard, Frédéric. "De poésie et d'esprit : *À tous ceux qui ne me lisent pas* de Yan Giroux." *Ciné-Bulles* 37, no. 1 (2019): 46.

Boudreault, Julie. "Are Quebec Circuses of Foreign Origin?" Translated by Tania Grant. In *Cirque Global: Quebec's Expanding Circus Boundaries*, edited by Louis Patrick Leroux and Charles R. Batson. McGill-Queen's University Press, 2016.

Bouliane, Sandria P. "'Good-Bye Broadway, Hello Montréal': Traduction, appropriation et création de chansons populaires canadiennes-françaises dans les années 1920." PhD diss., Université Laval, 2013.

Bourdeau, Loïc. "Introduction: Failing Successfully." In *Horrible Mothers: Representations Across Francophone North America*, edited by Loïc Bourdeau. University of Nebraska Press, 2019. https://doi.org/10.2307/j.ctvr0qt7n.

– "Politics and Motherhood in Xavier Dolan's *J'ai tué ma mère* and *Mommy*." In *Horrible Mothers: Representations Across Francophone North America*, edited by Loïc Bourdeau. University of Nebraska Press, 2019. https://doi.org/10.2307/j.ctvr0qt7n.

Boym, Svetlana. *The Future of Nostalgia*. Basic Books, 2001.

Bruce, Jean. "Querying/Queering the Nation." In *Gendering the Nation: Canadian Women's Cinema*, edited by Kay Armatage, Kass Banning, Brenda Longfellow, and Janine Marchessault. University of Toronto Press, 1999. https://doi.org/10.3138/9781442675223-020.

Burelle, Julie. *Encounters on Contested Lands: Indigenous Performances of Sovereignty and Nationhood in Quebec*. Northwestern University Press, 2019.

Butler, Judith. *Gender Trouble: Feminism and the Subversion of Identity*. Routledge, 1990.

Butts, Edward. "Lucien Rivard: The Great Escape." In *Wrong Side of the Law: True Stories of Crime*. Dundurn, 2013.

Caillard, Guilhem. "Erreur sur la personne : *Suspect numéro un*." *Séquences*, no. 324 (2020): 28.

Cairns, Lucille. "Mères manquantes and Queer Triangulations in *Emporte-moi* and *Lost and Delirious*." In *Cinematic Queerness: Gay and Lesbian Hypervisibility in Contemporary Francophone Feature Films*, edited by Florian Grandena and Cristina Johnston. Peter Lang, 2011.

Cambron, Micheline. "Cinéma, histoire et pédagogie : *15 février 1839*." *Spirale*, no. 180 (2001): 21–2.

Cameron, Emilie. *Far Off Metal River: Inuit Lands, Settler Stories, and the Making of the Modern Arctic*. UBC Press, 2015.

Cardinal, Serge. "La réception critique des adaptations filmiques." In *Cinéma et littérature au Québec : Rencontres médiatiques*, edited by Michel Larouche. XYZ, 2003.

Carle, Gilles. *La nature d'un cinéaste*. Liber, 1999.

Carrière, Louise, ed. *Femmes et cinéma québécois*. Boréal Express, 1983.

Carrier-Lafleur, Thomas. "Les 'Maria Chapdeleine' de Sébastien Pilote." *La Liberté*, no. 324 (Summer 2019): 73–5.

Carruthers, Lee, and Charles Tepperman, eds. *Canadian Cinema in the New Millennium*. McGill-Queen's University Press, 2023.

Castiel, Élie. "Entretien : Denise Filiatrault." *Séquences*, no. 220 (2002): 42–3.

– "Filmer l'émotion : Francis Leclerc." *Séquences*, no. 215 (2001): 41–2.

– "The French Connection: *Le piège américain* de Chalres Binamé." *Séquences*, no. 254 (2008): 28–9.

– "La mémoire indélébile : François Bouvier." *Séquences*, no. 201 (1999): 14–16.

– "Le roman de la terre : *Un homme et son péché* de Charles Binamé." *Séquences*, no. 222 (2002): 40–1.

– "Le souffle au cœur : *Une jeune fille* à la fenêtre de Francis Leclerc." *Séquences*, no. 215 (2001): 40–1.

Cavell, Richard, and Peter Dickinson. "Sex and Canada: A Theoretical Introduction." In *Sexing the Maple: A Canadian Sourcebook*, edited by Richard Cavell and Peter Dickinson. Broadview Press, 2006.

Celis, Leila, Dia Dabby, Dominique Leydet, and Vincent Romani, eds. *Modération ou extrémisme? Regards critiques sur la loi 21*. Presses de l'Université Laval, 2020.

Cermak, Iri. *The Cinema of Hockey*. McFarland, 2017.

Chaput, Luc. "Chaleur humaine : *Ce qu'il faut pour vivre* de Benoît Pilon." *Séquences*, no. 256 (2008): 33.

– "L'enfance de l'art." *Séquences*, no. 262 (2009): 40–1.

– "L'histoire réinventée : *Embrasse-moi comme tu m'aimes* de André Forcier." *Séquences*, no. 304 (2016): 4–5.

– Review of *Sans elle*, directed by Jean Beaudin. *Séquences*, no. 245 (2006): 57.

Charest, Marie-Josée. "Chansons de travail, chansons de chômage : une lecture du monde ouvrier pendant la crise à travers l'œuvre de La Bolduc." *Études littéraires* 40, no. 2 (2009): 57–68. https://doi.org/10.7202/037963ar.

Charest-Sigouin, Violaine. "Gloire et eau bénite : *Ma vie en cinémascope* de Denise Filiatrault." *Ciné-Bulles* 23, no. 1 (2005): 28–9.

Charles, Julia Morgan. "La maison où j'ai grandi: The Changing Landscape of Nostalgia in Quebec's Contemporary Coming of Age Films." Master's thesis, McGill University, 2009.

Chartier, Daniel. "Le cinéma du pays de la neige devient pluriculturel." *Études romanes* 59 (2009): 141–53. http://archipel.uqam.ca/id/eprint/6361.

Chartrand, Alain, with Diane Cailhier. *Chartrand, cinéaste*. Stanké, 2007.

Churchill, Ward. "Spiritual Hucksterism: The Rise of the Plastic Medicine Man." In *Shamanism: A Reader*, edited by Graham Harvey. Routledge, 2003.

Clandfield, David. "The Fatal Leap: Accessing the Films of Claude Jutra Through History and Symbol." In *Great Canadian Film Directors*, edited by George

Melnyk. University of Alberta Press, 2007. https://doi.org/10.1515 /9780888645289-003.

– *Pierre Perrault and the Poetic Documentary.* Indiana University Press, 2004.

Clément, Frédéric. "Voix de femmes, voies de femmes : la fin des années 60 dans le cinéma récent." *Perspectives étudiantes féministes : actes électroniques du colloque étudiant,* Université Laval, 12–13 March 2010. http://bv.cdeacf.ca/CF _PDF/151903.pdf.

Collard, Nathalie. "Un avant-goût des *Rois mongols.*" *La Presse,* 14 July 2017. https:// www.lapresse.ca/cinema/cinema-quebecois/201707/14/01-5116161-un-avant -gout-des-rois-mongols.php.

Colman, Felicity J. *Deleuze and Cinema: The Film Concepts.* Berg, 2011.

Cook, Pam. *Screening the Past: Memory and Nostalgia in Cinema.* Routledge, 2005.

Cornelius, Nathalie G. "Boxes and Bridges: Robert Lepage's *Le Confessionnal* and *La Face cachée de la lune.*" *French Review* 82, no. 1 (2008): 118–28. https://www.jstor .org/stable/25481479.

Cornellier, Bruno. *La "chose indienne" : cinéma et politiques de la représentation autochtone au Québec et au Canada.* Nota Bene, 2015.

Coulombe, Michel. "De quelques histoires inventées, ou le cinéma québécois des années 90." *Ciné-Bulles* 16, no. 2 (1997): 30–5.

– *Entretiens avec Gilles Carle : le chemin secret du cinéma.* Liber, 1995.

Coulombe, Michel, and Marcel Jean. *Dictionnaire du cinéma québécois. Nouvelle édition revue et augmentée.* Boréal, 1999.

Crosson, Seán. *Sport and Film.* Routledge, 2013.

Cuillerier, Martine. "Le cinéma historique québécois : le cas des Patriotes." Paper delivered at the Colloque Association des cycles supérieurs en sociologie, Université de Montréal, 25 March 2011. https://socio.umontreal.ca/public /FAS/sociologie/Documents/5-Departement/Colloques_et_actes_de_colloques /Actes_Colloque_2011.pdf.

Custen, George F. *Bio/Pics: How Hollywood Constructed Public History.* Rutgers University Press, 1992.

Czach, Liz. "The Quebec Heritage Film." In *Cinema of Pain: On Quebec's Nostalgic Screen,* edited by Liz Czach and André Loiselle. Wilfrid Laurier University Press, 2020. https://doi.org/10.51644/9781771124348.

Czach, Liz, and André Loiselle. "Introduction." In *Cinema of Pain: On Quebec's Nostalgic Screen,* edited by Liz Czach and André Loiselle. Wilfrid Laurier University Press, 2020. https://doi.org/10.51644/9781771124348.

Dallaire, Élène. Review of *Babine,* directed by Luc Picard. *Séquences,* no. 258 (2009): 49.

Daudelin, Robert. "Les grandes vacances de 1968 : *C'est pas moi, je le jure !* de Philippe Falardeau." *24 images,* no. 138 (2008): 61.

– "La passagère : *Le cyclotron* d'Olivier Asselin." *24 images,* no. 181 (2017): 27.

Davis, Natalie Zemon. "'Any Resemblance to Persons Living or Dead': Film and the Challenge of Authenticity." *Yale Review* 76, no. 4 (1987): 461–82. Reprinted in *The History on Film Reader*, edited by Marnie Hughes-Warrington. Routledge, 2009.

de Blois, Marco. "L'accueil médiatique de *15 février 1839* : Falardeau, mets-nous des nuances!" *24 images*, no. 106 (2001): 40–1.

– "L'Affaire Falardeau-Téléfilm : des Patriotes avec un *flag* sur le *hood* ?" *24 images*, no. 86 (1997): 2–3.

– "Leçon d'histoire : *Quand je serai parti … vous vivrez encore* de Michel Brault." *24 images*, no. 97 (1999): 54–5.

– "Un tableau memorial : *Ce qu'il faut pour vivre* de Benoît Pilon." *24 images*, no. 138 (2008): 59.

Deer, Jessica. "McGill Dumps Redmen Team Name After Calls from Indigenous Community." *CBC News*, 12 April 2019. https://www.cbc.ca/news/indigenous/mcgill-redmen-name-1.5095289.

Defoy, Stéphane. "Entretien : Philippe Falardeau." *Ciné-Bulles* 26, no. 4 (2008): 18–23.

Delgado, Jérôme. "L'hommage à un poète : *Dédé, à travers les brumes* de Jean-Philippe Duval." *Séquences*, no. 260 (2009): 42.

– "Le conte de Cyr, un Québécois vrai : *Louis Cyr, l'homme le plus fort du monde* de Daniel Roby." *Séquences*, no. 286 (2013): 53.

de Lorimier, Chevalier. "Political Testament." In *Les Patriotes*, edited by L.-O. David. Éditions Leméac, 1978.

Demers, Dominique. *Maïna*. Québec Amérique, 2006. Originally published in 1997. English translation by Leonard Sugden, Ekstasis Editions, 2000. All citations refer to the 2006 French edition.

den Toonder, Jeanette. "Voyages de l'imaginaire dans trois romans contemporains : l'écriture intimiste de Bruno Hébert, Gaétan Soucy et Marie Laberge." *Globe : revue internationale d'etudes québécoises* 3, no. 1 (2000): 65–81. https://doi.org/10.7202/1000566ar.

Desjardins, Denis. Review of *Nouvelle-France*, directed by Jean Beaudin. *Séquences*, no. 235 (2005): 56.

– "Voyage au pays des glaces : *Maïna* de Michel Poulette." *Séquences*, no. 290 (2014): 57.

Desmeules, Georges. "Un pur produit Falardeau : *15 février 1839*." *Québec français*, no. 122 (2001): 98–9.

Desroches, Vincent. "Suspicions and Castrations: Robert Morin's *Que Dieu bénisse l'Amérique*." *American Review of Canadian Studies* 43, no. 2 (2013): 231–40. https://doi.org/10.1080/02722011.2013.795029.

Detchberry, Damien. "*Sonatine*." Translated by Kathy Durnin. In *Cinema of Canada*, edited by Jerry White. Wallflower, 2006.

Dickinson, Peter. "Double Take: Adaptation, Remediation, and Doubleness in the Films of Robert Lepage." In *Great Canadian Directors*, edited by George Melnyk. University of Alberta Press, 2007. https://doi.org/10.1515/9780888645289-010.

– *Screening Gender, Framing Genre: Canadian Literature into Film*. University of Toronto Press, 2007. https://doi.org/10.3138/9781442679658.

Dion, Robert. "*Alys en cinémascope* – ou la vie est un songe." *Urgences* 26 (1989): 64–73.

Dubois, Sylvie. "De Roberto Rosselini à Gilles Carle : la réalité par la parole." *Nouvelles Vues* (2018): 1–19. https://nouvellesvues.org/de-roberto-rossellini -a-gilles-carle-la-realite-par-la-parole/.

Dubuc, Pierre. "Maison rose et carré rouge." *L'aut'journal*, 6 September 2013. https://www.lautjournal.info/20130906/maison-rose-et-carre-rouge.

Duchesne, André. "*La Maison du pêcheur* : combler un trou de mémoire collectif." *La Presse*, 2 December 2012.

Dufour, Christine. *La Bolduc : la turluteuse du people*. XYZ, 2001.

Dumais, Manon. "Il était une fois dans l'Est : Luc Picard signe une charmante adaptation du roman de Nicole Bélanger." *Le Devoir*, 23 September 2017. https://www.ledevoir.com/culture/cinema/508631/les-rois-mongols-il -etait-une-fois-dans-l-est

Dumas, Hugo. "Un western des pays d'en haut." *La Presse*, 2 May 2015. https://www.lapresse.ca/debats/chroniques/hugo-dumas/201504/29/01 -4865400-un-western-des-pays-den-haut.php.

Dunderjovic, Aleksandar. *The Cinema of Robert Lepage: The Poetics of Memory*. Wallflower, 2003.

Dupuis, Jean-Claude. *Pour en finir avec le mythe de la Révolution tranquille*. Fondation littéraire Fleur de lys, 2019.

Durand, Caroline. "Les chroniqueurs artistiques et la politisation de la chanson, 1960–1980." In *La chanson francophone engagée*, edited by Lise Bizzoni and Cécile Prévost-Thomas. Triptyque, 2008.

Dyer, Kester. "Landscape, Trauma, and Identity: Simon Lavoie's *Le Torrent*." In *Cinema of Pain: On Québec's Nostalgic Cinema*, edited by Liz Czach and André Loiselle. Wilfrid Laurier University Press, 2020. https://doi.org/10.51644 /9781771124348.

Dyer, Richard. *Stars*. New ed. British Film Institute, 1998.

Edensor, Tim. *National Identity, Popular Culture and Everyday Life*. Berg, 2002.

Elsaesser, Thomas. *European Cinema: Face to Face with Hollywood*. Amsterdam University Press, 2005.

– "Tales of Sound and Fury: Observations on the Family Melodrama." *Monogram* 4 (1972): 2–15. Reprinted in *Home Is Where the Heart Is: Studies in Melodrama and the Woman's Film*, edited by Christine Gledhill. British Film Institute, 1987.

Euvrard, Michel, and Pierre Véronneau. "Direct Cinema." In *Self Portrait: Essays on the Canadian and Quebec Cinemas*, edited by Piers Handling and Pierre Véronneau. Canadian Film Institute, 1980.

Falkowska, Janina, and Lenuta Giukin. "Introduction." In *Small Cinemas in Global Markets: Genres, Identities, Narratives*, edited by Lenuta Giukin, Janina Falkowska, and David Dresser. Lexington, 2015.

Faradji, Helen. "Le club Vinland : l'hommage aux enseignants de Benoît Pilon." *Radio-Canada*, 1 April 2021. https://ici.radio-canada.ca/tele/cinema/blogue /1781579/le-club-vinland-lhommage-aux-enseignants-de-benoit-pilon-cinema -quebecois-histoire-archeologie-viking-sebastien-ricard-remy-girard.

— Review of *Babine*, directed by Luc Picard. *24 images*, no. 140 (2008): 62.

Ferland, Catherine, and Dave Corriveau. *La Corriveau : de l'histoire à la légende*. Septentrion, 2014.

Ferretti, Lucia. "La « Grande Noirceur », *mère de la Révolution tranquille?*" In *La Révolution tranquille en héritage*, edited by Guy Berthiaume and Claude Corbo. Boréal, 2011.

Ferretti, Lucia, and François Rocher, eds. *Les enjeux d'un Québec laïque. La loi 21 en perspective*. Del Busso Éditeur, 2020.

Filteau, Gérard. *Histoire des Patriotes*. L'Aurore, 1980.

Fisher, Dominique. "Invisibilités et mises en scènes de l'homophobie : Variations françaises et québécoises, ou du *Placard à C.R.A.Z.Y.*" In *Cinematic Queerness: Gay and Lesbian Hypervisibility in Contemporary Francophone Feature Films*, edited by Florian Grandena and Cristina Johnston. Peter Lang, 2011.

Fortin, Andrée. "Biofictions au cinéma et mémoire collective." *Les Cahiers des Dix* 73 (2019): 235–70. https://doi.org/10.7202/1067999ar.

Fradet, Pierre-Alexandre. "Aux profondeurs de la surface : *Laurence Anyways* de Xavier Dolan." *Séquences*, no. 279 (2012): 48.

— "Le néoterroir au cinéma : entretien avec Rafaël Ouellet." *Spirale*, no. 250 (2014): 37–40.

— *Philosopher à travers le cinéma québécois : Xavier Dolan, Denis Côté, Stéphane Lafleur et autres cinéastes*. Hermann, 2018.

— Review of *À trois*, Marie s'en va, directed by Anne-Marie Ngô. *Séquences*, no. 274 (2011): 57.

— Review of *Frisson des collines*, directed by Richard Roy. *Séquences*, no. 273 (2011): 62.

Fréchette, Louis. "La Corriveau." *Arena* 48 (November 1893): 747.

Freitag, Florian. *The North American Farm Novel*. Camden House, 2013.

Gagnon, François. "Histoire de l'adaptation filmique." In *Cinéma et littérature au Québec : rencontres médiatiques*, edited by Michel Larouche. XYZ, 2003.

Gajan, Philippe. "Entretien avec André Forcier." *24 images*, no. 141 (2009): 48–51.

Gajan, Philippe, and Marie-Claude Loiselle. "Entretien : Pierre Falardeau." *24 images*, no. 118 (2004): 42–7.

Galiero, Simon. Review of *Aurore*, directed by Luc Dionne. *24 images*, no. 123 (2005): 67.

— Review of *Le Survenant*, directed by Érik Canuel. *24 images*, no. 122 (2005): 63–4.

Galt, Rosalind, and Karl Schoonover. "Introduction: The Impurity of Art Cinema." In *Global Art Cinema: New Theories and Histories*, edited by Rosalind Galt and Karl Schoonover. Oxford University Press, 2010.

Garel, Sylvain. "Le Front de libération du Québec dans la cinématographie québécoise." *Ciné-Bulles* 19, no. 1 (2000): 48–9.

Gauthier, Jennifer L. "Living In/Between: The Cinema of Léa Pool." In *Great Canadian Directors*, edited by George Melnyk. University of Alberta Press, 2007. https://doi.org/10.1515/9780888645289-012.

Gauthier, Maude. "Le film *Polytechnique* entre contre-mémoire féministe et héritage national." *Québec Studies* 55 (2013): 33–47. https://doi.org/10.3828/qs.55.1.33.

Gauthier, Philippe. "The Role of Orality in Robert Morin's *Le nèg* and *Quiconque meurt, meurt à douleur.*" *Québec Studies* 66 (2018): 27–48. https://doi.org/10.3828/qs.2018.15.

Gendron, Nicolas. "Prophètes d'ici." *Ciné-Bulles* 32, no. 3 (2014): 22–30.

Germain, Georges-Hébert. *Souvenirs de Monica.* Libre Expression, 1997.

Gervais, Marc. "*Jésus de Montréal*: The Vision of Denys Arcand." In *Through a Catholic Lens: Religious Perspectives of Nineteen Film Directors from Around the World*, edited by Peter Malone. Sheed and Ward, 2007.

Gervais, Stéphan, Christopher Kirkey, and Jarrett Rudy. "Quebec Models." In *Quebec Questions: Quebec Studies for the Twenty-First Century*, edited by Stéphan Gervais, Christopher Kirkey, and Jarrett Rudy. 2nd ed. Oxford University Press Canada, 2016.

Gibeault, Stéphan. "Le renouveau du conte : entre popularité et pop-oralité." *Spirale*, no. 192 (2003): 23–4.

Gibson, Margaret. "The Truth Machine: Polygraphs, Popular Culture and the Confessing Body." *Social Semiotics* 11, no. 1 (2001): 61–73. https://doi.org/10.1080/10350330124540.

Gilbert, Paula Ruth, and Miléna Santoro. "Transforming Visions: Pedagogical Approaches to Léa Pool's *Emporte-moi (Set Me Free)*." In "French/Francophone Culture and Literature Through Film," edited by Catherine R. Montfort and Michele Bissiere. Special issue, *Women in French Studies*, no. 2006 (2006): 139–55. https://doi.org/10.1353/wfs.2006.0040.

Gingras, Chantale. "L'esprit du lieu : *Gaz bar blues.*" *Québec français*, no. 132 (2004): 98–100.

Gittings, Christopher E. *Canadian National Cinema: Ideology, Difference and Representation.* Routledge, 2002.

Godbout, Jacques. "Acheter, spéculer, vendre : *Un capitalisme sentimental* d'Olivier Asselin." *Spirale*, no. 228 (2009): 49–50.

Goldfarb, Ronald. *Perfect Villains, Imperfect Heroes: Robert F. Kennedy's War Against Organized Crime.* Random House, 1995.

Gott, Michael, and Thibaut Schilt, eds. *Quebec Cinema in the 21st Century: Transcending the National.* Liverpool University Press, 2024. https://doi.org/10.3828/liverpool/9781802074765.001.0001.

Grandena, Florian. "Léa Pool: The Art of Elusiveness." In *The Gendered Screen: Canadian Women Filmmakers*, edited by Brenda Austin-Smith and George Melnyk. Wilfrid Laurier University Press, 2011.

Gravel, Jean-Philipp. "Métaphysique de la douleur : *Martyrs* de Pascal Laugier." *Ciné-Bulles* 27, no. 2 (2009): 32–5.

Green, Mary Jean. "Claude Jutra: A *Nouvelle vague* Filmmaker in Quebec." *Québec Studies* 13 (1991–2): 87–94. https://doi.org/10.3828/qs.13.1.87.

– "Léa Pool's *La femme de l'hôtel* and Women's Film in Québec." *Québec Studies* 9 (1989–90): 49–62. https://doi.org/10.3828/qs.9.1.49.

Greer, Allan. *The Patriots and the People: The Rebellion of 1837 in Rural Lower Canada*. University of Toronto Press, 1993. https://doi.org/10.3138/9781442657328.

Grenier, Pascal. Review of *Martyrs*, directed by Pascal Laugier. *Séquences*, no. 259 (2009): 54.

Grignon, Claude-Henri. *Un homme et son péché*. Stanké, 2002. Originally published in 1933.

Guèvremont, Germain. *Le Survenant*. Fides, 1984. Originally published in 1945.

Hamel, Jean-François. "Récit d'une dépossession : *Le Torrent* de Simon Lavoie." *Ciné-Bulles* 31, no. 1 (2013): 22–5.

– "Solitude amère : *Laurentie* de Mathieu Denis et Simon Lavoie." *Ciné-Bulles* 29, no. 4 (2011): 57.

Harcourt, Peter. "*Le Déclin de l'Empire américain / The Decline of the American Empire*." In *The Cinema of Canada*, edited by Jerry White. Wallflower, 2006.

Harvey, Dennis. "Toronto Film Review: François Girard's *Hochelaga, Land of Souls*." *Variety*, 10 September 2017. https://variety.com/2017/film/reviews/hochelaga -land-of-souls-review-1202553538/.

Harvey, Jean. "Whose Sweater Is This? The Changing Meanings of Hockey in Quebec." In *Artificial Ice: Hockey, Culture, and Commerce*, edited by David Whitson and Richard Gruneau. Broadview Press, 1990.

Hayward, Susan. *French National Cinema*. Routledge, 1993.

Hebding, Vanessa. "Interroger le réel : étude du *Chat dans le sac* de Gilles Groulx et de ses intertextes essayistiques." Master's thesis, Université Laval.

Hébert, Anne. *La cage, suivi de L'île de la Demoiselle*. Boréal; Seuil, 1990. English translation by Pamela Grant, Gregory J. Reid, and Sheila Fischman, in *Two Plays: The Cage and L'île de la Demoiselle*, Playwrights Canada Press, 2010. All citations refer to the 1990 French edition.

Hébert, Bruno. *Alice court avec René*. Boréal, 2000.

– *C'est pas moi, je le jure!* Boréal, 1997.

Hedetoft, Ulf, and Mette Hjort, eds. *The Postnational Self: Belonging and Identity*. University of Minnesota Press, 2002.

Hémon, Louis. *Maria Chapdelaine*. Boréal, 1995. Originally published in 1914.

Henry-Tierney, Pauline. "The Whore and Her Mother: Exploring Matrophobia in Nelly Arcan's *Putain*." In *Horrible Mothers: Representations across Francophone North*

America, edited by Loïc Bourdeau. University of Nebraska Press, 2019. https://doi
.org/10.2307/j.ctvr0qt7n.5.

"L'Histoire au grand écran." *Cap-aux-diamants,* no. 77 (Spring 2004): 64.

Hibbert, Christopher. *Wolfe at Quebec: The Man Who Won the French and Indian War.*
World Publishing Company, 1959.

Higson, Andrew. "Re-Presenting the National Past: Nostalgia and Pastiche in the
Heritage Film." In *British Cinema and Thatcherism,* edited by Lester D. Friedman.
UCL Press, 1993.

– "The Concept of National Cinema." *Screen* 30, no. 4 (1989): 36–47. Reprinted
in *The European Cinema Reader,* edited by Catherine Fowler. Routledge, 2002.
https://doi.org/10.1093/screen/30.4.36.

Hobsbawm, Eric, and Terence Ranger, eds. *The Invention of Tradition.* Cambridge
University Press, 1992.

Houdassine, Ismaël. "Charles Binamé." *Séquences,* no. 254 (2008): 30–1.

– "Ricardo Trogi: « Je veux exploiter la signature de ma voix en narration … »"
Séquences, no. 262 (2009): 42–3.

Hu, Xiangwen, and François Gagnon. *Adaptations filmiques au Québec: Répertoire
1922–1996.* Centre de recherche cinéma/réception, 1997.

Hughes-Warrington, Marnie. "History on Film: Theory, Production, Reception."
In *The History on Film Reader,* edited by Marnie Hughes-Warrington. Routledge,
2009.

Huston, Nancy. "Arcan, philosophe." In *Burqa de chair,* by Nelly Arcan. Seuil, 2011.

Jacob, Pascal. "The Québécois Circus in the Concert of Nations: Exchange
and Transversality." Translated by Tiffany Templeton. In *Cirque Global:
Quebec's Expanding Circus Boundaries,* edited by Louis Patrick Leroux and
Charles R. Batson. McGill-Queen's University Press, 2016. https://doi.
org/10.1515/9780773598706-005.

Jean, Marcel. "Une âme à vendre : *Un capitalisme sentimental* d'Olivier Asselin." *24
images,* no. 139 (2008): 62.

Kaku, Michio. *Parallel Worlds: A Journey Through Creation, Higher Dimensions, and the
Future of the Cosmos.* Anchor Books, 2006.

Kelly, Brendan. "He Shoots, He Scores!" *Variety,* 28 January 2002, 20.

Kirby, William. *Le chien d'or / The Golden Dog: A Legend of Quebec.* Critical ed.;
edited by Mary Jane Edwards. McGill-Queen's University Press, 2012.

Laberge, Suzanne. "L'affaire Richard/Campbell : le hockey comme vecteur de
l'affirmation francophone québécoise." In *Le Canadien de Montréal : une légende
repensée,* edited by Audrey Laurin-Lamothe and Nicolas Moreau. Presses de
l'Université Laval.

Laberge, Yves. "Rapports réels et imaginaires entre le Québec et les États-Unis dans
le cinéma documentaire : la notion d'identité dans le long métrage *Alias Will
James* de Jacques Godbout." *Études canadiennes / Canadian Studies* 36 (1994): 81–91.

Lacasse, Germain. *Le bonimenteur de vues animées.* Nota Bene, 2005.

– "*Chasse au Godard d'Abbitibbi* : chronotope d'une culture cinématographique régionale." *Synoptique* 3, no. 2 (2015): 29–48.

– "Quebec Cinema: Telling Pictures." In *Quebec Questions: Quebec Studies for the Twenty-First Century*, edited by Stéphan Gervais, Christopher Kirkey, and Jarrett Rudy. 2nd ed. Oxford University Press Canada, 2016.

Lacasse, Germain, Johanne Massé, and Bethsabée Poirier. *Le diable en ville : Alexandre Silvio et l'émergence de la modernité populaire au Québec.* Presses de l'Université de Montreal, 2012.

Lacoursière, Jacques, and Robin Philpot. *A People's History of Quebec.* Baraka, 2009.

Lafleur, Guillaume. "Bouches cousues : *Curling* de Denis Côté." *Spirale,* no. 236 (2011): 17.

Lafontaine, Andrée. "'I Am Looking for Someone Who Understands My Language and Speaks It': Dolan's Excessive Dialogues." In *ReFocus: The Films of Xavier Dolan*, edited by Andrée Lafontaine. Edinburgh University Press, 2019. https://www.jstor.org/stable/10.3366/j.ctvrxk1cv.16.

– "Introduction." In *ReFocus: The Films of Xavier Dolan*, edited by Andrée Lafontaine. Edinburgh University Press, 2019. https://www.jstor.org/stable/10.3366/j.ctvrxk1cv.7.

–, ed. *ReFocus: The Films of Xavier Dolan.* Edinburgh University Press, 2019.

Lamonde, Yvan. *La modernité au Québec.* Vol. 1, *La crise de l'homme et de l'esprit (1929–1939).* Fides, 2011.

– *La modernité au Québec.* Vol. 2, *La victoire différée du présent sur le passé (1939–1963).* Fides, 2016.

– "Quebec's Americanicity." In *Quebec Questions: Quebec Studies for the Twenty-First Century*, edited by Stéphan Gervais, Christopher Kirkey, and Jarrett Rudy. 2nd ed. Oxford University Press Canada, 2016.

Lamoureux, Diane. "The Paradoxes of Quebec Feminism." In *Quebec Questions: Quebec Studies for the Twenty-First Century*, edited by Stéphane Gervais, Christopher Kirkey, and Jarrett Rudy. 2nd ed. Oxford University Press Canada, 2016.

– "*Polytechnique* : Des réactions officielles entre commémoration et banalisation." In *Retour sur un attentat antiféministe : École Polytechnique de Montréal, 6 décembre 1989*, edited by Mélissa Blais, Francis Dupuis-Déry, Lynn Kurtzmann, and Dominique Payette. Remue-ménage, 2010.

Landy, Marcia. "The Historical Film: History and Memory in Media." In *The Historical Film: History and Memory in Media*, edited by Marcia Landy. Rutgers University Press, 2001. Reprinted in *The History on Film Reader*, edited by Marine Hughes-Warrington. Routledge, 2009.

Lapointe, Martine-Emmanuelle, and Lise Gauvin. "Lectures croisées d'un texte en plusieurs états. *Le sexe des étoiles* de Monique Proulx : roman, scénarios et film." In *Cinéma et littérature au Québec : rencontres médiatiques*, edited by Michel Larouche. XYZ, 2003.

Laporte-Rainville, Luc. "Potentialités : *Le cyclotron* d'Olivier Asselin." *Ciné-Bulles* 35, no. 1 (2017): 48.

Larose, Karim, and Frédéric Rondeau, eds. *La contre-culture au Québec*. Presses de l'Université de Montréal, 2016.

Larouche, Michel. "Introduction." In *Cinéma et littérature au Québec : Rencontres médiatiques*, edited by Michel Larouche. XYZ, 2003.

Larouche, Michel, and Serge Cardinal. "Le scénario : point de vue." In *Cinéma et littérature au Québec : rencontres médiatiques*, edited by Michel Larouche. XYZ, 2003.

Larrue, Jean-Marc. "Le théâtre au Québec entre 1930 et 1950 : les années charnières." *L'Annuaire théâtral : revue québécoise d'études théâtrales* 23 (1998): 19–37.

Laurendeau, Francine. "Audacieusement drôle et tendre : *Gaz Bar Blues* de Louis Bélanger." *Séquences*, no. 228 (2003): 47.

— "Et la lumière fut : *Pour l'amour de Dieu*." *Séquences*, no. 273 (2011): 52.

Lavoie, André. Review of *Maelström*, directed by Denis Villeneuve. *Ciné-Bulles* 19, no. 1 (2000): 61–2.

Lavoie, Pierre. *Mille après mille : célébrité et migration dans le Nord-Est américain*. Boréal, 2022.

Leach, Jim. *Claude Jutra: Filmmaker*. McGill-Queen's University Press, 1999.

— "Double Vision: *Mon oncle Antoine* and the Cinema of Fable." In *Canada's Best Features: Critical Essays on 15 Canadian Films*, edited by Eugene P. Walz. Rodopi, 2002.

— *Film in Canada*. Oxford University Press, 2006.

— "In-Between States: Sarah Polley's *Take This Waltz* and Xavier Dolan's *Laurence Anyways*." *Brno Studies in English* 39, no. 2 (2013): 91–106. https://doi.org/10.5817/BSE2013-2-6.

— "'It Takes Monsters to Do Things Like That': The Films of Jean-Claude Lauzon." In *Great Canadian Directors*, edited by George Melnyk. University of Alberta Press, 2007. https://doi.org/10.1515/9780888645289-004.

LeBlanc, Julie M.-A. "Elvis Gratton: Québec's Contemporary Folk Hero?" In *Folklore/Cinema: Popular Film as Vernacular Culture*, edited by Sharon R. Sherman and Mikel J. Koven. Utah State University Press, 2007.

Leclerc, Félix. *Pieds nus dans l'aube*. Fidès, 1982. Originally published 1946.

Léger, Robert. *La chanson québécoise en question*. Québec Amérique, 2003.

Lepage, Yvan G. *Germaine Guèvremont : la tentation autobiographique*. Presses de l'Université d'Ottawa, 1998.

Lepage-Boily, Elizabeth. "Michel Monty parle d'*Une vie qui commence*." Cinoche. com, 20 January 2011. https://www.cinoche.com/actualites/michel-monty-parle-d-une-vie-qui-commence.

Leroux, Darryl. *Distorted Descent: White Claims to Indigenous Identity*. University of Manitoba Press, 2019.

Leroux, Louis Patrick. "Reinventing Tradition, Building a Field: Quebec Circus and Its Scholarship." In *Cirque Global: Quebec's Expanding Circus Boundaries*, edited by Louis Patrick Leroux and Charles R. Batson. McGill-Queen's University Press, 2016. https://doi.org/10.1515/9780773598706-004.

– "A Tale of Origins: Deconstructing North American 'Cirque' Where Québécois and American Circus Cultures Meet." In *Cirque Global: Quebec's Expanding Circus Boundaries*, edited by Louis Patrick Leroux and Charles R. Batson. McGill-Queen's University Press, 2016. https://doi.org/10.1515/97807 73598706-006.

Létourneau, Jocelyn. *La condition québécoise : une histoire dépaysante*. Septentrion, 2020.

– *A History for the Future: Rewriting Memory and Identity in Quebec*. McGill-Queen's University Press, 2004.

– "Mythistoires de losers : introduction au roman historial des Québécois." *Histoire sociale / Social History* 39, no. 77 (2006): 157–80.

Lever, Yves. *Le cinéma de la Révolution tranquille : de* Panoramique *à* Valérie. Yves Lever, 1991.

– "Cinéma québécois et mémoire." In *Le cinéma au Québec : tradition et modernité*, edited by Stéphane-Albert Boulais. Fides, 2006.

– *Claude Jutra*. Boréal, 2016.

– *Histoire générale du cinéma au Québec*. Boréal, 1995. Originally published in 1988.

Levin, Colette G. "Le roman à l'écran : trois modèles d'adaptation dans le cinéma québécois." In *Le Québec aujourd'hui : identité, société et culture*, edited by Marie-Christine Weidmann. Les Presses de l'Université Laval, 2003.

Linteau, Paul-André, René Durocher, and Jean-Claude Robert. *Quebec: A History, 1867–1930*. Translated by Robert Chodos. James Lorimer, 1983.

Linteau, Paul-André, René Durocher, Jean-Claude Robert, and François Ricard. *Histoire du Québec Contemporain*. 2 vols. Boréal, 1989.

– *Quebec Since 1930*. Translated by Robert Chodos and Ellen Garmaise. James Lorimer, 1991.

Loiselle, André. *Cinema as History: Michel Brault and Modern Quebec*. Toronto International Film Festival Group, 2007.

– *Denys Arcand's* Le Déclin de l'empire américain *and* Les Invasions Barbares. University of Toronto Press, 2008. https://doi.org/10.3138/9781442687851.

– "Despair as Empowerment: Melodrama and Counter-Cinema in Anne Claire Poirier's *Mourir à tue-tête*." *Canadian Journal of Film Studies* 8, no. 2 (1999). 21–43. https://doi.org/10.3138/cjfs.8.2.21.

– "*La Forteresse / Whispering City*." In *The Cinema of Canada*, edited by Jerry White. Wallflower, 2006.

– "Michel Brault's *Les Ordres*: Documenting the Reality of Experience and the Fiction of History." In *Canada's Best Features: Critical Essays on 15 Canadian Films*, edited by Eugene P. Walz. Rodopi, 2002.

– "*Les Muses orphelines* du théâtre au cinéma : en conversation avec Robert Favreau." *L'annuaire théâtral*, no. 30 (Fall 2001): 97–106.

– *A Scream from Silence / Mourir à tue-tête*. Flicks Books, 2000.

– *Stage-Bound: Feature Film Adaptations of Canadian and Québécois Drama.* McGill-Queen's University Press, 2003.

– "Subtly Subversive or Simply Stupid: Notes on Popular Quebec Cinema." *Post Script* 15, no. 3 (1999): 75–84.

Loiselle, André, and Brian McIlroy, eds. *Auteur/Provocateur: The Films of Denys Arcand.* Greenwood, 1995.

Loiselle, Marie-Claude. "Au-delà des apparences : *Maelström* de Denis Villeneuve." *24 images*, no. 105 (2001): 49.

– "Le chant de là terre : *Mariages* de Catherine Martin." *24 images*, nos. 107–8 (2001): 88–9.

– *La communauté indomptable d'André Forcier.* Les Herbes rouges, 2017.

– Editorial. *24 images*, no. 121 (2005): 3.

– Review of *Séraphin : un homme et son péché*, directed by Charles Binamé. *24 images*, no. 114 (2003): 60.

– "Téléfilm Canada ou le règne de la bêtise." *24 images*, nos. 88–9 (1997): 3.

Loiselle, Marie-Claude. "Au-delà des apparences : *Maelström* de Denis Villeneuve." *24 images*, no. 105 (2001): 49.

– "Le chant de la terre : *Mariages* de Catherine Martin." *24 images*, nos. 107–8 (2001): 88–9.

– *La communauté indomptable d'André Forcier.* Les Herbes rouges, 2017.

– Editorial. *24 images*, no. 121 (2005): 3.

– Review of *Séraphin : un homme et son péché*, directed by Charles Binamé. *24 images*, no. 114 (2003): 60.

– "Téléfilm Canada ou le règne de la bêtise." 24 images, nos. 88–9 (1997): 3.

Longfellow, Brenda. "*The Red Violin*, Commodity Fetishism and Globalization." *Canadian Journal of Film Studies* 10, no. 2 (2001): 6–20. https://doi.org/10.3138/cjfs.10.2.6.

Lussier, Marc-André. "*Je me souviens*: l'urgence de raconter." *La Presse*, 3 October 2009.

MacKenzie, Scott. *Screening Québec: Québécois Moving Images, National Identity, and the Public Sphere.* Manchester University Press, 2004. https://doi.org/10.3138/cjfs.14.2.94.

MacLeod, D. Peter. *Northern Armageddon: The Battle of the Plains of Abraham and the Making of the American Revolution.* Alfred A. Knopf, 2016.

Mailhot, Laurent. *La littérature du Québec.* TYPO, 1997.

Mandolini, Carlo. "Chronique d'une attente : *Histoires d'hiver* de François Bouvier." *Séquences*, no. 201 (1999): 34–6.

– "Qu'est-ce qui nous fait courir? *Les Boys II* de Louis Saïa." *Séquences*, no. 201 (1999): 37–8.

Marie, Michel. "Le direct et la parole." *Écritures de Pierre Perrault.* Cinémathèque Québécoise, 1983.

Marsolais, Gilles. *L'aventure du cinéma direct revisitée.* Les 400 coups, 1997.

– *Cinéma québécois : de l'artisanat à l'industrie.* Triptyque, 2011.

Marsolais, Sophie. "Du livre au film, les plus récentes adaptations." *Lurelu* 37, no. 2 (2014): 9–10.

Martin-Jones, David. *Scotland: Global Cinema – Genres, Modes and Identities.* Edinburgh University Press, 2009.

Massicotte, Claudie. "Hantise et architecture cryptique : transmission du passé dans *Le Confessionnal* de Robert Lepage." *Canadian Journal of Film Studies* 21, no. 2 (2012): 93–114. https://doi.org/10.3138/cjfs.21.2.93.

Mathieu, André. *Aurore : la vraie histoire de l'enfant martyre.* Coup d'œil, 2016. Originally published 1990.

McGill University. "The McGill Redbirds: New Name for a New Era to Wear, and Cheer for with Pride." McGill Newsroom, 17 November 2020. https://www .mcgill.ca/newsroom/channels/news/mcgill-redbirds-new-name-new-era-wear -and-cheer-pride-326286.

Melançon, Benoît. *The Rocket: A Cultural History of Maurice Richard.* Translated by Fred A. Reed. Greystone, 2009.

Mellier, Denis. "Sur la dépouille des genres. Néohorreur dans le cinéma français (2003–2009)." *Cinémas* 20, nos. 2–3: 143–64. https://doi.org/10.7202/045148ar.

Meilleur, Philippe. *André Fortin : l'homme qui brillait comme une comète.* VLB Éditeur, 2013.

Melnyk, George. *Film and the City: The Urban Imaginary in Canadian Cinema.* Athabasca University Press, 2014.

–, ed. *Great Canadian Film Directors.* University of Alberta Press, 2007.

– *100 Years of Canadian Cinema.* University of Toronto Press, 2004.

– "Quebec's Next Generation: From Lauzon to Turpin." *CineAction* 61 (2003): 10–17.

Mercer, John, and Martin Shingler. *Melodrama: Genre, Style, Sensibility.* Wallflower, 2004.

Meunier, E.-Martin. "The French-Canadian Great Darkness (*Grande Noirceur*) in Québécois History and Memory: Revisiting the Dominant Interpretation." *Vingtième siècle : revue d'histoire* , no. 1 (2016): 43–59. https://doi.org/10.3917/ving.129.0043.

Michaud, Stéphane. "Historia 101." *Séquences*, no. 236 (2005): 16.

Moffat, Alain-Napoléon. "*À tout prendre* de Claude Jutra : le Docu-drame de la confession." *Québec Studies* 12 (1991): 147–54. https://doi.org/10.3828/qs.12.1.147.

Mokkil, Navaneetha. "Xavier Dolan in India: The Alchemy of Film Viewing." In *ReFocus: The Films of Xavier Dolan,* edited by Andrée Lafontaine. Edinburgh University Press, 2019.

Monk, Katherine. *Weird Sex and Snowshoes, and Other Canadian Film Phenomena.* Raincoast Books, 2001.

Morgan, David. *The Devious Dr. Franklin, Colonial Agent: Benjamin Franklin's Years in London.* Mercer University Press, 1996.

Morris, Peter. "Canadian Gothic and *Les bons débarras*: The Night Side of the Soul." In *Canada's Best Features: Critical Essays on 15 Canadian Films,* edited by Eugene P. Walz. Rodopi, 2002.

Moss, Jane. "Family Films: Québec Style." *American Review of Canadian Studies* 41, no. 2 (2011): 109–16. https://doi.org/10.1080/02722011.2011.568627.

Moyes, Craig. "*On est au coton / Cotton Mill, Treadmill*." In *Cinema of Canada*, edited by Jerry White. Wallflower, 2006.

Murphy, Graham J. "Cyberpunk's Masculinist Legacy: Puppetry, Labour, and *Ménage-à-Trois* in *Blade Runner 2049*." *Science Fiction Film and Television* 13, no. 1 (2020): 97–107. https://doi.org/10.3828/sfftv.2020.6.

Nadeau, Jean-Benoît, and Julie Barlow. *The Story of French*. St. Martin's Press, 2008.

Nester, William R. *The French and Indian War and the Conquest of New France.* University of Nebraska Press, 2014.

Nicholson, Georges. *André Mathieu*. Québec Amérique, 2010.

Nora, Pierre. "Between Memory and History: *Les Lieux de mémoire*." Translated by Marc Roudebush. *Representations* 26 (1989): 7–24. https://doi.org/10.2307/2928520.

— *Les Lieux de mémoire*. 3 vols. Gallimard, 1984–92.

Nygaard, Betty King. "Monica Proietti, a.k.a. 'Machine Gun Molly': Canada's Bonnie Parker." In *Hell Hath No Fury: Famous Women in Crime*. Borealis, 2001.

Ohl, Paul. *Louis Cyr*. Libre Expression, 2013.

Olibet, Ylenia. "Chloé Robichaud and Sophie Deraspe: Women Auteurs on the International Film Festival Circuit." In *Quebec Cinema in the 21st Century*, edited by Michael Gott and Thibaut Schilt. Liverpool University Press, 2024.

Pallister, Janis L. "L'angst de l'adolescente : *Emporte-moi* de Léa Pool." *Nouvelles Études Francophones* 22, no. 1 (2007): 89–108.

— *The Cinema of Quebec: Masters in Their Own House*. Fairleigh Dickinson University Press, 1995.

— "*Les Fous de Bassan*: The Film." In *The Art and Genius of Anne Hébert: Essays on Her Works*, edited by Janis L. Pallister. Fairleigh Dickinson University Press, 2001.

Papillon, Joëlle, and Tania Grégoire, eds. "La relève autochtone : voix contemporaines au Québec / Young Indigenous Authors from Québec." Special issue, *Québec Studies* 75, no. 1 (2023). https://doi.org/10.3828/qs.2023.3.

Paquette, Jean-Marcel. "Maria sous trois regards." *Revue d'histoire littéraire du Québec et du Canada Français* 11 (1986): 33–41.

Paquin, Raymond. *Dédé*. Quitte ou double, 2009.

Pascal, Marie. "Film Adaptation and the Emancipation of Quebec Country Novels: *The Woman and the Miser* and *The Outlander*." In *Rural Writing: Geographic Imaginary and Expression of a New Regionality*, edited by Mauricette Fournier. Cambridge Scholars, 2018.

— "Prégénériques et génériques dans les adaptations cinématographiques québécoises." *Journal of Canadian Film Studies* 26, no. 2 (2017): 93–116. https://doi.org/10.3138/cjfs.26.2.2017-0009.

Paterson, Janet M. "L'espace sexué de l'autre dans *La petite fille qui aimait trop les allumettes*." In *Sexuation, espace, écriture : la littérature québécoise en transformation*, edited by Louise Dupré, Jaap Lintvelt, and Janet M. Paterson. Nota Bene, 2002.

Pellerin, Fred. *Comme une odeur de muscles.* Sarrazine, 2019.

– *Dans mon village, il y a belle Lurette.* Planète rebelle, 2001.

– *Il faut prendre le taureau par les contes.* Planète rebelle, 2003.

Perrault, Charles. *Contes de ma mère l'oye.* J'ai lu, 2014. Originally published 1697.

Perreault, Mathieu. "Le portraitiste scrutant – Michel Brault tourne : *Quand je serai parti … vous vivrez encore.*" *Séquences,* no. 196 (1998): 20–1.

Pettigrew, Stephanie. Review of *La Corriveau,* directed by Catherine Ferland and Dave Corriveau. *Magic, Ritual, and Witchcraft* 10, no. 1 (2015): 122–4.

Picard, Yves. "*Les Boys :* autopsie d'une cinésérie « mythique »." *24 images,* no. 137 (2007): 17–19.

Pidduck, Julianne. *Contemporary Costume Film: Space, Place, and the Past.* British Film Institute, 2004.

Pike, David. *Canadian Cinema Since the 1980s: At the Heart of the World.* University of Toronto Press, 2012.

Poirier, Christian. "Le cinéma québécois et la question identitaire. La Confrontation entre les récits de l'empêchement et de l'enchantement." *Recherches sociographiques* 45, no. 1 (2004): 11–38. https://doi.org/10.7202/009233ar.

Powell, David A. "*C.R.A.Z.Y.* Québec: Vallée's Performance of Masculinity and Sovereignty." In *Cinematic Queerness: Gay and Lesbian Hypervisibility in Contemporary Francophone Feature Films,* edited by Florian Grandena and Cristina Johnston. Peter Lang, 2011.

Privet, Georges. "Pierre Falardeau : d'*Octobre* en septembre." *24 images,* no. 145 (2011): 6–9.

Protat, Zoë. "Croire à la magie : *Ésimésac* de Luc Picard." *Ciné-Bulles* , no. 1 (2013): 57.

– "Ecce homo : *Laurence Anyways* de Xavier Dolan." *Ciné-Bulles* 30, no. 3 (2012): 16–17.

Proulx, Bernard. *Le roman du territoire.* Presses de l'Université du Québec à Montréal, 1987.

Proulx, Robert. "À la croisée des chemins entre le récit et le film." *Sélection des Actes du XIe Colloque international d'études françaises de l'APFFUE.* Université de La Rioja, 2004.

"Quebecers Form a Nation Within Canada: PM." *CBC News,* 22 November 2006. https://www.cbc.ca/news/canada/quebecers-form-a-nation-within-canada-pm -1.624141.

"Quebec Film Awards Renamed Prix Iris After Claude Jutra Sex Scandal." *CBC News,* 14 October 2016. https://www.cbc.ca/news/canada/montreal/claude -jutra-rename-prix-iris-1.3804694.

Raboy, Marc. "Public Television, the National Question, and the Preservation of the Canadian State." In *Television in Transition: Papers from the First International Television Studies Conference, 1985,* edited by Philip Drummond. British Film Institute, 1986.

Raheja, Michelle H. *Reservation Reelism: Redfacing, Visual Sovereignty, and Representations of Native Americans on Film.* University of Nebraska Press, 2010.

Ramer, Jodi. "*Mourir à tue-tête / Scream from Silence*." In *Cinema of Canada*, edited by Jerry White. Wallflower, 2006.

Ramond, Charles-Henri. "De grandes espérances : *La Maison du pêcheur* d'Alain Chartrand." *Séquences*, no. 286 (2013): 54.

Rancourt, David. "*Le torrent* de Simon Lavoie : folie et acouphène." *Québec français*, no. 168 (2013): 97–9.

Ranger, Pierre. "Érik Canuel: "Adapter *Le Survenant*, c'est célébrer la différence." *Séquences*, no. 237 (2005): 34–5.

– "Entre la réalité et l'imaginaire : tournage – *Embrasse-moi comme tu m'aimes*." *Séquences*, no. 297 (2015): 35.

– "Intériorité d'une vie en accéléré : *Monica la Mitraille*." *Séquences*, no. 231 (2004): 42–3.

– "Pour enfin briser la loi du silence : Luc Dionne." *Séquences*, no. 238 (2005): 40–1.

– Review of *Gaz Bar Blues*, directed by Louis Bélanger (DVD). *Séquences*, no. 232 (2004): 22.

– Review of *Le Survenant*, directed by Érik Canuel. *Séquences*, no. 235 (2005): 14–15.

Ransom, Amy J. "Denis Villeneuve: Québécois and Citizen of the World." In *ReFocus: The Films of Denis Villeneuve*, edited by Marie Cardinal and Jeri English. Edinburgh University Press, 2022. https://doi.org/10.3366/edinbu rgh/9781474497381.003.0002.

– "Deterritorialization and the Crisis of Recognition in Turn of the Millennium Québec Film." In "Québec Cinema in the 21st Century," edited by Denis Bachand, Vincent Desroches, André Loiselle, and Miléna Santoro. Special issue, *American Review of Canadian Studies* 43, no. 2 (2013): 176–89. https://doi.org/10.10 80/02722011.2013.795032.

– "Forgiving the Horrible Mother: Children's Needs and Women's Desires in Twenty-First Century Québécois Film." In *Horrible Mothers: Representations Across Francophone North America*, edited by Loïc Bourdeau. University of Nebraska Press, 2019. https://doi.org/10.2307/j.ctvr0qt7n.12.

– *Hockey P.Q.: Canada's Game in Québec Popular Culture*. University of Toronto Press. 2014. https://doi.org/10.3138/9781442670013.

– "Lovecraft in Quebec: Transcultural Fertilization and Esther Rochon's Reevaluation of the Powers of Horror." *Journal of the Fantastic in the Arts* 26, no. 3 (2015): 452–70. https://www.jstor.org/stable/i26321167.

– "Men in Pain: Home, Nostalgia, and Masculinity in Twenty-First Century Québec Film." In *A Cinema of Pain: Essays on Quebec's Nostalgic Screen*, edited by Liz Czach and André Loiselle. Wilfrid Laurier University Press, 2018. https://doi .org/10.51644/9781771124348-007.

– "Québec History X: Re-Visioning the Past Through Rap." *American Review of Canadian Studies* 43, no. 1 (2013): 12–39. https://doi.org/10.1080/02722011.2013 .769018.

- "La représentation de la *Nouvelle-France* dans le film de Jean Beaudin et dans sa novélisation par Pierre Billon." In *La Nouvelle-France. Les Cahiers de la SIELEC 14, la Société Internationale d'étude des littératures de l'ère coloniale*, edited by Victor Bernovsky. Kailash, 2023.
- "Violence and Uncertainty on the French-Canadian Margins: The Films of Denis Côté." *Québec Studies* 65 (2018): 103–23. https://doi.org/10.3828/qs.2018.8.
- "What Is the Libano-Québécois? The 'entre-deux' in Quebec's Migrant Cinema." In "Rencontres interculturelles," edited by Mercédès Baillargeon and Karine Bertrand. Special issue, *Nouvelles vues : revue sur les pratiques, les théories et l'histoire du cinéma au Québec* 22 (2023). https://nouvellesvues.org/what-is-the-libano-quebecois-representing-the-migrant-subject-in-quebec-national-cinema/.

Ravary-Pilon, Julie. *Femmes, nation et nature dans le cinéma québécois*. Les Presses de l'Université de Montréal, 2018.

Ravary-Pilon, Julie, and Ersy Contogouris, eds. *Pour des histoires audiovisuelles des femmes au Québec. Confluences et divergences*. Les Presses de l'Université de Montréal, 2022.

Rees-Roberts, Nick. "Fade to Grey: Dolan's Pop Fashion and Surface Style." In *ReFocus: The Films of Xavier Dolan*, edited by Andrée Lafontaine. Edinburgh University Press, 2019. https://www.jstor.org/stable/10.3366/j.ctvrxk1cv.17.

Renan, Ernest. "What Is a Nation?" In *The Poetry of the Celtic Races, and Other Essays*. Walter Scott Publishing Co., 1896.

Renaud, André. "Jacques Godbout : romancier et cinéaste." *Revue d'histoire littéraire du Québec et du Canada Français* 11 (1986): 65–84.

Robi, Alys. *Ma carrière et ma vie*. Québécor, 1980.
- *Un long cri dans la nuit*. Édimag, 1990.

Robin, Patricia. "Dans la tourmente de l'être blessé : *Le Torrent* de Simon Lavoie." *Séquences*, no. 281 (2012): 58.
- "Gerry toujours vivant : sur les portées d'un rocker majeur." *Séquences*, no. 273 (2011): 38–9.

Robitaille, Marc. *Histoires d'hiver, avec des rues, des écoles et du hockey*. VLB, 1987.
- *Un été sans point ni coup sûr*. Les 400 coups, 2004.

Rogers, D. Laurence. *Paul Bunyan: How a Terrible Timber Feller Became a Legend*. Historical Press, 1993.

Rosadiuk, Adam. "*Thirty Two Short Films About Glenn Gould*." In *The Cinema of Canada*, edited by Jerry White. Wallflower, 2006.

Rosen, Philip. "History, Textuality, Nation: Kracauer, Burch and Some Problems in the Study of National Cinemas." In *Theorising National Cinema*, edited by Valentina Vitali and Paul Willemen. British Film Institute, 2006.

Rosenberg, Susan. "Neither Forgotten nor Fully Remembered: Tracing an Ambivalent Public Memory on the Tenth Anniversary of the Montreal

Massacre." In *Killing Women: The Visual Culture of Gender and Violence*, edited by Annette Burfoot and Susan Lord. Wilfrid Laurier University Press, 2006.

Rousseau, Yves. "Le plein de sens, avec du plomb : *Gaz bar blues* de Louis Bélanger." *24 images*, nos. 116–17 (2004): 23.

Roy, Bruno. *Pouvoir chanter. Essai d'analyse politique*. VLB, 1991.

Roy, Charles Stéphane. "Le biopic : la gloire après la gloire." *Séquences*, no. 250 (2007): 8–9.

Roy, Marie-Josée. "Sébastien Pilote a trouvé sa Maria Chapdelaine." *Journal de Montréal*, 17 February 2020. https://www.journaldemontreal.com/2020/02/17 /sebastien-pilote-a-trouve-sa-maria-chapdelaine.

Roy, Mario. *Gerry Boulet : avant de m'en aller*. Arts global, 2011. Originally published 1991.

Rudel-Tessier, J. *André Mathieu : un génie*. Héritage, 1976.

Sanaker, John Kristian. *La Rencontre des langues dans le cinéma francophone : Québec, Afrique subsaharienne, France-Maghreb*. Presses Universaires de Laval; L'Harmattan, 2011.

Santoro, Miléna. "Does It Matter Who Directs the Story? Comparing Québec's Immigrant Cinema and the Cinema of Immigration through Case Studies of Karaman and Deraspe, Villeneuve and Bensaddek." *Québec Studies* 76 (2023): 61–88. https://doi.org/10.3828/qs.2023.18.

– "Reel Visions: Snapshots from a Half Century of First Nations Cinema." In *Hemispheric Indigeneities: Native Identity and Agency in Mesoamerica, the Andes, and Canada*, edited by Miléna Santoro and Erick D. Langer. University of Nebraska Press, 2018. https://doi.org/10.2307/j.ctv7vcsx1.14.

– "The Rise of First Nations' Fiction Films: Shelley Niro, Jeff Barnaby, and Yves Sioui Durand." *American Review of Canadian Studies* 43, no. 2 (2013): 267–82. https://doi .org/10.1080/02722011.2013.795031.

Santoro, Miléna. "The Rise of First Nations' Fiction Films: Shelley Niro, Jeff Barnaby, and Yves Sioui Durand." *American Review of Canadian Studies* 43, no. 2 (2013): 267–82. https://doi.org/10.1080/02722011.2013.795031.

Scheppler, Gwen. "*Pour la suite du monde*." Translated by Christa Polley. In *The Cinema of Canada*, edited by Jerry White. Wallflower, 2006.

Schilt, Thibaut. "Denis Côté on the Road from Radisson to Lucarno." In *Quebec Cinema in the 21st Century*, edited by Michael Gott and Thibaut Schilt. Liverpool University Press, 2024. https://doi.org/10.2307/jj.6947052.12.

Schlager, Catherine. "Le génie de la musique : *L'enfant prodige* de Luc Dionne." *Séquences*, no. 267 (2010): 49.

Schwartzwald, Robert. *C.R.A.Z.Y.: A Queer Film Classic*. Arsenal Pulp Press, 2016.

Séguin, Denis. "The Battle for Hollywood North." *Canadian Business*, 15 September 2003, 54–62.

Servais-Maquoi, Mireille. *Le roman de la terre au Québec*. Presses de l'Université Laval, 1974.

Shek, Ben-Z. "Lemelin sur film : entre réalisme et mélodrame." *Revue d'histoire littéraire du Québec et du Canada Français* 11 (1986): 43–56.

Simons, Tony. "Denys Arcand: *Jésus de Montréal.*" In *Where Are the Voices Coming From? Canadian Culture and the Legacies of History*, edited by Coral Ann Howells. Rodopi, 2004. https://doi.org/10.1163/9789004487154_016.

— "Gilles Carle: *Maria Chapdelaine.*" In *Where Are the Voices Coming From? Canadian Culture and the Legacies of History*, edited by Coral Ann Howells. Rodopi, 2004. https://doi.org/10.1163/9789004487154_014.

— "Léa Pool: *Anne Trister.*" In *Where Are the Voices Coming From? Canadian Culture and the Legacies of History*, edited by Coral Ann Howells. Rodopi, 2004. https://doi.org/10.1163/9789004487154_022.

Sirois-Trahan, Jean-Pierre. "*Le cinéma à l'estomac*: Denis Côté and the New Wave of Quebec Cinema (2004–19)." In *Canadian Cinema in the New Millennium*, edited by Lee Carruthers and Charles Tepperman. McGill-Queen's University Press, 2023. https://doi.org/10.1515/9780228014928-008.

— "La mouvée et son dehors : renouveau du cinéma québécois." *Cahiers du cinéma*, no. 660 (October 2010): 76–8.

Skemp, Sheila. *The Making of a Patriot: Benjamin Franklin at the Cockpit.* Oxford University Press, 2012.

Skinner, David. "Television in Canada: Continuity or Change?" In *Television and Public Policy: Change and Continuity in an Era of Global Liberalization*, edited by David Ward. Lawrence Erlbaum, 2008.

Sloan, Johanne. "Parc Belmont Flashback: André Forcier's *La Comtesse de Baton Rouge.*" In *(Re)Discovering "America": Road Movies and Other Travel Narratives in North America*, edited by Graciela Martínez-Zalce and Wilfried Zaussert. Wissenschaftlicher Verlag, 2012.

Smart, Patricia. *Writing Herself into Being: Quebec Women's Autobiographical Writings from Marie de l'Incarnation to Nelly Arcan.* McGill-Queen's University Press, 2017.

Smith, Anthony. "Images of the Nation: Cinema, Art, and National Identity." In *The Cinema of Small Nations*, edited by Mette Hjort and Duncan Petrie. Indiana University Press, 2007.

Smith, Kristen. "(In)visible Borders in *Beans* by Tracey Deer." *Québec Studies* 75 (2023): 109–30. https://doi.org/10.3828/qs.2023.8.

Snow, Dan. *Death or Victory: The Battle of Quebec and the Birth of an Empire.* Penguin Canada, 2011.

Sorlin, Pierre. *The Film in History: Restaging the Past.* Blackwell, 1980.

Soucy, Gaétan. *The Little Girl Who Was Too Fond of Matches.* Translated by Sheila Fischman. Arcade, 2000.

Spencer, Philip, and Howard Wollman, eds. *Nations and Nationalism: A Reader.* Rutgers University Press, 2005.

Sprengler, Christine. *Screening Nostalgia: Populuxe Props and Technicolor Aesthetics in Contemporary American Film*. Berghahn Books, 2009.

Stam, Robert. "Beyond Fidelity: The Dialogics of Adaptation." In *Film Adaptation*, edited by James Naremore. Rutgers University Press, 2000.

– "Introduction: The Theory and Practice of Adaptation." In *Literature and Film: A Guide to the Theory and Practice of Film Adaptation*, edited by Robert Stam and Alessandra Raengo. Blackwell, 2005.

Stefanelli, Maria Anita. "Queering Spectatorship in Lea Pool's and Judith Thompson's *Lost and Delirious*." In *Modes and Facets of the American Scene: Studies in Honor of Cristina Giorcelli*, edited by Dominique Marçais. Italo-Latino-Americana Palma, 2014.

Stewart, Sara. "You'll Love the New *Blade Runner* – Unless You're a Woman." *New York Post*, 4 October 2017. https://nypost.com/2017/10/04/youll-love-the-new-blade-runnerunless-youre-a-woman/.

Sugars, Cynthia. *Canadian Gothic: Literature, History, and the Spectre of Self-Invention*. University of Wales Press, 2014.

Sugars, Cynthia, and Gerry Turcotte, eds. *Unsettled Remains: Canadian Literature and the Postcolonial Gothic*. Wilfrid Laurier University Press, 2009.

Sullivan, Rebecca. "Work It Girl! Sex, Labour, and Nationalism in *Valérie*." In *Working On Screen: Representations of the Working Class in Canadian Cinema*, edited by Malek Khouri and Darrell Varga. University of Toronto Press, 2006. https://doi.org/10.3138/9781442683686-006.

Testa, Bart. "The Decline of Frivolity and Denis Arcand's American Empire." In *Canada's Best Features: Critical Essays on 15 Canadian Films*, edited by Eugene P. Walz. Rodopi, 2002. https://doi.org/10.1163/9789401200141_012.

Toles, George. "Drowning in Love: Jean-Claude Lauzon's *Léolo*." In *Canada's Best Features: Critical Essays on 15 Canadian Films*, edited by Eugene P. Walz. Rodopi, 2002. https://doi.org/10.1163/9789401200141_016.

Tourigny, Manon. Review of *Gaz Bar Blues*, directed by Louis Bélanger. *Ciné-Bulles* 21, no. 4 (2003): 50–1.

Tremblay-Daviault, Christiane. "Avant la Révolution tranquille : une Terre-Mère en perdition." In *Femmes et cinéma québécois*, edited by Louise Carrière. Boréal Express, 1983.

Trudeau, Pierre Elliott, ed. *La grève de l'amiante*. Cité libre, 1956.

Tschofen, Monique. "*Le Confessionnal / The Confessional*: Robert Lepage, 1995." In *The Cinema of Canada*, edited by Jerry White. Wallflower, 2006.

Turgeon, Alexandre. "'Toé, tais-toé !' et la Grande Noirceur duplessiste. Genèse d'un mythhistoire." *Histoire sociale / Social History* 46, no. 92 (2013): 367–96.

Urquhart, Steven. "Displacement or the Deconstruction of Place in Three Recent Xavier Dolan Films." *Québec Studies* 65 (2018): 125–48. https://doi.org/10.3828/qs.2018.9.

Vaillancourt, Julie. "*La femme d'hôtel* et *Anne Trister* : silences éloquents, désirs saphiques et revendication d'un nouvel espace." In *Cinematic Queerness: Gay and*

Lesbian Hypervisibility in Contemporary Francophone Feature Films, edited by Florian Grandena and Cristina Johnston. Peter Lang, 2011.

— "Sorties du placard, à l'aube du nouveau millénaire : *Lost & Delirious* et *Mambo Italiano*." *Nouvelles Vues : revue sur les pratiques, les théorie et l'histoire du cinéma au Québec* 9 (2008). https://nouvellesvues.org/wp-content/uploads/2021/09/VaillancourtNVCQ9.pdf

Vallières, Pierre. *L'exécution de Pierre Laporte : les dessous de l'Opération Essai*. Québec Amérique, 1977.

Vermette, David. *A Distinct Alien Race: The Untold Story of the Franco-Americans*. Baraka Books, 2018.

Vernier, Richard. "*Le Matou*, Tiger in Disguise?" In *Essays on Quebec Cinema*, edited by Joseph I. Donohoe Jr. Michigan State University Press, 1991.

Véronneau, Pierre. "Denys Arcand: A Moralist in Search of His Audience." In *Great Canadian Directors*, edited by George Melnyk. University of Alberta Press, 2007. https://doi.org/10.1515/9780888645289-005.

— "*En pays neufs*." Translated by Lynn Penrod. In *The Cinema of Canada*, edited by Jerry White. Wallflower, 2006.

— "Genres and Variations: The Audiences of Quebec Cinema." In *Self Portraits: The Cinemas of Canada Since Telefilm*, edited by André Loiselle and Tom McSorley. Canadian Film Institute, 2006.

— *Histoire du cinéma au Québec*. 2 vols. Cinémathèque québécoise, 1979.

— "Quelles représentations de l'histoire du Québec construit le cinéma québécois?" *Bulletin d'histoire politique* 23, no. 3 (2015): 144–79.

Vizenor, Gerald. "Aesthetics of Survivance. Literary Theory and Practice." In *Survivance: Narratives of Native Presence*. University of Nebraska Press, 2008.

Voltaire, François-Marie Arouet de. *Candide*. Penguin, 2006. Originally published in 1759.

Walls, Matthew. *Caribou Inuit Traders of the Kivalliq Nunavut, Canada*. British Archaeological Reports, 2009.

Warren, Jean-Philippe, and Andrée Fortin, eds. *Pratiques et discours de la contre-culture au Québec*. Septentrion, 2015.

Weinmann, Heinz. *Cinéma de l'imaginaire au Québec, de la petite Aurore à Jésus de Montréal*. L'Héxagone, 1990.

— *Du Canada au Québec : généalogie d'une histoire*. L'Héxagone, 1987.

West, Alexandra. *Films of the New French Extremity: Visceral Horror and National Identity*. McFarland, 2016.

White, Jerry ed. *The Cinema of Canada*. Wallflower, 2006.

— "Pat Murphy's *Maeve* and Michel Brault's *Les Ordres*." *Canadian Journal of Irish Studies* 26–7, nos. 1–2 (2000–1): 89–103. https://doi.org/10.2307/25515352.

— "Pierre Falardeau and Michel Brault, the FLQ and the Patriotes: Hollywood vs. Modernism." *Québec Studies* 37 (2004): 45–61. https://doi.org/10.3828/qs.37.1.45.

– *The Radio Eye: Cinema in the North Atlantic, 1938–1988*. Wilfrid Laurier University Press, 2009.
– "Recovering Québec Culture: The Feature Films of Bernard Émond." *American Review of Canadian Studies* 43, no. 2 (2013): 204–17. https://doi.org/10.1080/02722011.2013.795024.
Wójcik, Katarzyna. "(Re)visions télévisuelles de la colonisation du Nord : série médiatique d'*Un homme et son péché* de Claude-Henri Grignon." *Romanica Silesiana* 2, no. 18 (2020): 86–97.
– "La société québécoise et les autochtones : la parole inuite dans le film de Benoît Pilon *Ce qu'il faut pour vivre*." *Transcanadia: Polish Journal of Canadian Studies* 8 (2016): 147–63.
Zéau, Caroline. *L'Office National du film et le cinéma canadien (1939–2003) : éloge de la frugalité*. Peter Lang, 2006.
Zubrzycki, Geneviève. *Beheading the Saint: Nationalism, Religion, and Secularism in Quebec*. University of Chicago Press, 2016.

Filmography: Films Since 1999 Set in the Historical or Imaginary Past

15 février, 1839, dir. Pierre Falardeau. ACPAV, 2001.

1981, dir. Ricardo Trogi. Go Films, 2009.

1987, dir. Ricardo Trogi. Go Films, 2014.

1991, dir. Ricardo Trogi. Go Films, 2018.

1995, dir. Ricardo Trogi. Go Films, 2024.

À tous ceux qui ne me lisent pas, dir. Yan Giroux. Seville, 2018.

affaire Dumont, L', dir. Daniel Grou (Podz). Go films, 2012.

arracheuse de temps, L', dir. Francis Leclerc. Attraction Images, 2021.

Aurore, dir. Luc Dionne. Cinémaginaire, 2005.

Babine, dir. Luc Picard. Cité-Amérique, 2008.

Belle Bête, La, dir. Karim Hussain. Equinoxe Productions, 2006.

Bolduc, La, dir. François Bouvier. Caramel Film, 2018.

C.R.A.Z.Y., dir. Jean-Marc Vallée. Attraction Images, 2005.

C'est pas moi, je le jure!, dir. Philippe Falardeau. Les Films Christal; Micro_scope, 2008.

Cabotins, dir. Alain Desrochers. Les Films Christal; Seville, 2010.

Ce qu'il faut pour vivre, dir. Benoît Pilon. ACPAV, 2008.

chasse au Godard d'Abbittibbi, La, Éric Morin. Parce Que Films, 2013.

Chasse-galerie, la légende, dir. Jean-Philippe Duval. Les Films Christal; Les Films du Boulevard, 2016.

Cité, La, dir. Kim Nguyen. Bohemian Films; Thalie, 2010.

Club Vinland, Le, dir. Benoît Pilon. Productions Avenida, 2020.

Confessions, dir. Luc Picard. Christal Films, 2021.

Corbo, dir. Mathieu Denis. Max Films, 2015.

Crépuscule pour un tueur, dir. Raymond St. Jean. Les Productions Megafun, 2023.

cyclotron, Le, dir. Olivier Asselin. Camera Oscura; Fun Films, 2018.

Dédé, à travers les brumes, dir. Jean-Philippe Duval. Max Films; Zone 3, 2008.

dernier tunnel, Le, dir. Érik Canuel. Bloom Films, 1998; Christal Films, 2004.

déserteur, Le, dir. Simon Lavoie. Films du boulevard, 2008.

doigts croches, Les, dir. Ken Scott. Caramel Films; Area 54 Films; Melenny Productions, 2009.

Embrasse-moi comme tu m'aimes, dir. André Forcier. Les Films du Paria, 2016.

Emporte-moi, dir. Léa Pool. Cité-Amérique, 1999.

enfant prodige, L', dir. Luc Dionne. Cinémaginaire, 2010.

Ésimésac, dir. Luc Picard. Cité Amérique; Seville; Entertainment One, 2012.

États-Unis d'Albert, Les, dir. André Forcier. Les Films du Paria, 2005.

femme qui boit, La, dir. Bernard Émond. Christal Films, 2001.

fleurs oubliées, Les, dir. André Forcier. Les Films du Paria, 2019.

Frisson des collines, dir. Richard Roy. Les Films Seville; Solo Films, 2011.

Funkytown, dir. Daniel Roby. Caramel Films, 2011.

Gaz Bar Blues, dir. Louis Bélanger. Coop Vidéo de Montréal; Productions 23, 2003.

Gerry, dir. Alain Desrochers. Christal Films, 2011.

Grande Noirceur, La, dir. Maxime Giroux. Metafilms, 2018.

Henri Henri, dir. Martin Talbot. Christal Films, 2014.

Histoire de famille, dir. Michel Poulette. Cité-Amérique, 2006.

Histoires d'hiver, dir. François Bouvier. Aska Film Productions, 1999.

Hochelaga, terre des âmes, dir. François Girard. Max Films, 2017.

Il était une fois les Boys, dir. Richard Goudreau. Caramel Film; Melenny Productions, 2013.

Jack Paradise (Les Nuits de Montréal), dir. Gilles Noël. Nanouk Films; Verseau International, 2004.

Je me souviens, dir. André Forcier. Les Films du Paria, 2009.

Jouliks, dir. Mariloup Wolfe. Films Vision 4; TVA Films, 2019.

jour avant le lendemain, Le, dir. Marie-Hélène Cousineau and Madeline Ivalu. Igloolik Isuma Productions, 2009.

Journals of Knud Rasmussen, dir. Zacharias Kunuk and Norman Cohn. Igloolik Isuma Productions, 2006.

lâcheté, La, dir. Marc Bisaillon. Camera Oscura, 2007.

Laurence Anyways, dir. Xavier Dolan. Lyla Films; MK2 Productions, 2012.

Louis Cyr, l'homme le plus fort du monde, dir. Daniel Roby. Christal Films, 2013.

Ma vie en cinémascope, dir. Denise Filiatrault. Cinémaginaire, 2004.

Maïna, dir. Michel Poulette. Union Pictures; Équinoxe; TVA Films, 2012.

Maison du pêcheur, La, dir. Alain Chartrand. Groupe PVP, 2013.

Maman est chez le coiffeur, dir. Léa Pool. ARTE; Équinoxe, 2008.

marais, Le, dir. Kim Nguyen. Film Tonic; Productions Thalie, 2002.

Maria Chapdelaine, dir. Sébastien Pilote. Item 7; Multipix Management, 2021.

Mariages, dir. Catherine Martin. Coop Vidéo de Montréal; Productions 23, 2001.

Maurice Richard, dir. Charles Binamé. Cinémaginaire; Alliance Atlantis Vivafilm, 2005.

Meetings with a Young Poet, dir. Rudy Barichello. Item 7, 2013.

Monica la Mitraille, dir. Luc Dionne. Cité-Amérique, 2004.

Most Wanted, dir. Daniel Roby. Caramel Film; Goldrush Entertainment, 2020.

Nelly, dir. Anne Émond. Cactus Films; Go Films, 2016.

Norbourg, dir. Maxime Giroux. Les Films du Boulevard, 2022.

Nouvelle-France, dir. Jean Beaudin. Lions Gate; Melenny Productions, 2004.

passion d'Augustine, La, dir. Léa Pool. Lyla Films, 2015.

petite fille qui aimait trop les allumettes, La, dir. Simon Lavoie. GPA Films, 2017.

Piché : entre ciel et terre, dir. Sylvain Archambault. MELS; TVA Films, 2010.

Pieds nus dans l'aube, dir. Francis Leclerc. Attraction Images, 2017.

piège américain, Le, dir. Charles Binamé. Aetios Productions, 2008.

poil de la bête, Le, dir. Philippe Gagnon. Film du Boulevard, 2010.

Polytechnique, dir. Denis Villeneve. Remstar, 2009.

Pour l'amour de Dieu, dir. Micheline Lanctôt. Lycaon Pictus; Sherpas Films, 2011.

Quand je serai parti… vous vivrez encore, dir. Michel Brault. Nanouk Films; Regine, 1999.

rois mongols, Les, dir. Luc Picard. Fullum Films Studios; Echo Media, 2017.

Rouge sang, dir. Martin Doepner. Ciné Télé Action, 2013.

Savage Messiah, dir. Mario Azzopardi. Astral Films; Bernard Zukerman Productions; Corus, 2002.

Séraphin : un homme et son péché, dir. Charles Binamé. Alliance Atlantis Vivafilm; Cité-Amérique, 2002.

Survenant, Le, dir. Érik Canuel. Les Films Vision 4, 2005.

Timekeeper, The, dir. Louis Bélanger. Coop Vidéo de Montréal; Perfect Cercle Productions, 2009.

torrent, Le, dir. Simon Lavoie. Lusio Films, 2012.

Truffe, dir. Kim Nguyen. Shen Studio, 2008.

Un capitalisme sentimental, dir. Olivier Asselin. K Films Amérique; Arrimage Production, 2008.

Un été sans point ni coup sûr, dir. Francis Leclerc. Palomar, 2008.

Une jeune fille à la fenêtre, dir. Francis Leclerc. Palomar, 2001.

Une vie qui commence, dir. Michel Monty. Cirrus Communications; Item 7, 2010.

Vivre à 100 milles à l'heure, dir. Louis Bélanger. Lyla Films, 2019.

War Witch, dir. Kim Nguyen. Item 7; Shen Studio, 2012.

Index